Betty Crocker's

NEW CHOICES
COOKBOOK

MACMILLAN • USA

MACMILLAN
A Simon & Schuster Macmillan Company
1633 Broadway
New York, NY 10019

Library of Congress Cataloging-in-Publication
Crocker, Betty.
[New choices]
Betty Crocker's new choices cookbook.
p.   cm.
Includes index.
ISBN 0-671-86767-9
1. Cookery.   I. Title.
TX714.C763   1993
641.5'63—dc20   92-41048
CIP

GENERAL MILLS, INC.

Betty Crocker Food and Publications Center
Director: Marcia Copeland
Editor: Karen Couné
Recipe Development: Mary Hallin Johnson, Hallie Harron
Food Stylists: Kate Courtney Condon, Cindy Lund, Carol Grones

Medical Department
Vice President and Director, Health and Human Services: James L. Craig, M.D.
Director, Employee Health Services: Sue H. Wester, M.D.

Nutrition Department
Nutritionists: Elyse A. Cohen, M.S., Nancy Holmes, R.D.

Photographic Services
Photographer: Carolyn Luxmoore

Designed by Levavi & Levavi Associates, Inc.

Manufactured in the United States of America

10 9 8 7 6 5 4 3

Preceding page: Club Luncheon (page 33)

Front cover: Asian Turkey (page 244) showing how to use chicken breast, Lemon-Chive Fettuccine
(page 126) and Luscious Frozen-Yogurt Pie (page 400)

Back cover: Cheesecake with Strawberry Topping (page 392)

Foreword

In planning our daily menu it can be worth-while to remind ourselves what the word *diet* really means. It may be surprising to learn that *diet* has ancient origins in Greek and Latin, meaning "a manner of living," that is to say, a way of life. If we are to remain healthy, we have to make a long-term commitment to taking care of ourselves, our families and friends, remembering that diet is one of the most important and effective ways to accomplish this goal.

Medical scientists are learning more and more about the vital role that food plays in promoting health and preventing disease. There is increasing evidence that proper attention to diet may help prevent many of the leading causes of disability and death, namely heart disease and stroke, high blood pressure, diabetes, osteoporosis and even some kinds of cancer.

Most physicians agree that in the United States today the most common form of malnutrition (i.e., bad nutrition) that we encounter is not starvation or undernutrition, but obesity—or what could be called "overnutrition." About 25 percent of adults in the United States are overweight. Up to 27 percent of children are overweight as well, and one-third already have an elevated serum cholesterol count. Obesity during childhood predisposes people to many chronic diseases in later life, and leads to early mortality.

With an abundance of food, the convenience of prepared foods and the enormous number and variety of stimuli in the environment, it is not surprising that many people eat more than they should. The nutrient that appears to contribute most significantly to weight gain is dietary fat, which provides more than twice the number of calories per gram than are contributed by protein and carbohydrate. For many people, an important step towards good health is to reduce total dietary fat.

These days we hear much talk about "junk foods" and the need to eliminate them from our diet, particularly from the diets of children. More and more, nutrition scientists are moving away from the idea of "junk foods" towards the concept of "junk diets." This means that what is most relevant is total dietary intake over an extended period of time, rather than the nature of a single food item. We shouldn't be too hard on ourselves if we have an occasional, indulgent high-fat snack or dessert; we just don't want to make a regular habit of it!

In thinking about maintaining weight and health, we should remember that how we burn off calories is equally important. Just as it is impossible to keep accurate records of a bank balance by looking only at the deposits, we must also look at our caloric "withdrawals." If we want to develop and maintain a certain body weight, reducing calorie intake must be accompanied by increasing energy expenditure. Some unlucky people actually gain weight when they go on a diet to lose weight. The reason for this is that while their calorie intake is being reduced, their physical activity is reduced even more, and they go into positive caloric balance. The trick is to cultivate and enjoy a lifetime habit of regular physical exercise.

As we get older, we find that food selection becomes more important to health. With age we become less efficient in chewing, absorbing, digesting and utilizing dietary nutrients and have more difficulty in excreting waste products. The composition of our bodies also changes with age. We develop relatively less muscle and more fat; this change influences our caloric requirements and older individuals generally need fewer calories in order to maintain a stable body weight. Calcium is important for adults of all ages, not just for children, to maintain bone mass. It is never too late to begin a nutrition-based prevention strategy. It is estimated that about 85 percent of older Americans may have one or more chronic diseases that could be positively influenced by nutritional intervention.

There is still a great deal that we do not know about food and health, such as which food items alone and in combinations with one another are best able to help us maintain vigor and energy, while preventing disability and death. Clearly, we need to obtain more knowledge about nutrition, and one way to do this is to provide more funds for nutrition research; from studies in human populations to basic research in test tubes and model systems. The establishment of twelve Clinical Nutrition Research Units and Obesity Research Centers at medical schools in the United States by the National Institutes of Health has done much already to stimulate new research in diet and nutrition. However, research in nutrition needs more financial support than it receives at present.

The study of food and nutrition is a serious science. Experts in the use of nutrition in patient care must gain recognition as official medical specialists having equal standing with cardiologists, endocrinologists and others. The academic societies in nutrition, most notably The American Society for Clinical Nutrition and the American Institute of Nutrition, are comprised of highly qualified scientists, teachers and health-care providers who are able to offer assistance on vital issues relating to nutrition and health care. To reduce the costs of health care, it is preferable to prevent disease, rather than treat it, and nutrition is a crucial element in any strategy of disease prevention.

We are all concerned with maintaining our own good health as long as possible and in preventing disability and death. For the nation as a whole, further studies in nutrition would translate into an enormous reduction of healthcare costs and in better health for Americans.

But most important of all, eating is fun; we eat to socialize and celebrate different occasions. Eating in a healthy fashion need not detract from the enjoyment of food, and should help us lead more vigorous and fulfilling lives. Using the right recipes to make nutritious choices helps us plan satisfying, healthful meals—and enjoy our food!

RICHARD S. RIVLIN, M.D.
Program Director
Clinical Nutrition Research Unit
GI-Nutrition Service
Memorial Sloan-Kettering Cancer Center
Professor of Medicine & Chief
Nutrition Division
New York Hospital-Cornell Medical School

Contents

Introduction

We all know that healthy eating is essential as well as rewarding. However, the thought of changing the eating habits of a lifetime can be overwhelming. That's why we created *Betty Crocker's New Choices Cookbook*; to take the confusion and difficulty out of building a healthy eating plan that a single person or an entire family can follow every day.

Do you think low-fat, low-sodium or low-calorie foods are bland or that meatless meals are boring? Do you believe healthy eating means no more desserts or tempting snacks? Well, you'll be pleasantly surprised to learn that healthy eating with Betty Crocker is both delicious and satisfying. All the tested recipes here were carefully developed to meet the latest nutritional guidelines. The results? Fabulous food that promotes good health without sacrificing great taste.

To bring you the best book possible, we worked in partnership with our nutrition and medical departments. So in addition to the more than 500 taste-tempting recipes here, you'll find all the information you need to make healthy meals. There are suggestions for recipe "makeovers," to help you change favorite recipes to fit your eating plan, guidelines for cooking to promote good health, useful menus and menu-planning tips and a complete, easy-to-understand discussion of nutrition. We have also included the new Food Guide Pyramid so you can learn the latest on how to eat in a healthy way.

Finally, chapter 10, "Eating for Good Health," explains how to control many common diseases with proper diet. While not meant as a substitute for medical advice, this chapter will help you target problem areas and plan ways to minimize medical problems now, and in the years to come.

Betty Crocker's New Choices Cookbook is a cookbook you can enjoy every day. This is not a "diet" book, rather it's a cookbook for a healthy lifestyle to support and encourage you in reaching your goal of healthy eating every day. With Betty Crocker, you'll find that eating right is also eating well!

THE BETTY CROCKER EDITORS

Eating Right

There's welcome news today for people interested in healthy eating. Food that's good for you can be enjoyable! What's more, by building nutrition basics into a plan for eating that is delicious and satisfying, you actually increase your chances to permanently improve your healthy eating habits. But you certainly don't have to be a nutrition expert to succeed. This chapter gives you all the information you need to make healthful eating a reality for you and your family.

CUTTING BACK ON DIETARY FAT AND CHOLESTEROL

It seems hard to find a current magazine that doesn't include an article about how to cut back on dietary fat. Why is this tasty nutrient getting so much attention? Part of the answer lies in the fact that fat tastes good. It provides flavor and contributes to how satisfied you feel after eating a meal. In short, fat's a nutrient that makes foods very appealing, so appealing that we tend to eat too many and too much of foods that contain a high percentage of fat.

Excess fat in the diet, however, has been implicated in the development of some of the major health problems afflicting Americans today, such as heart disease and certain types of cancer. High-fat diets also may contribute to the development of obesity. For healthy eating, we must take care not to overindulge where dietary fat is concerned.

ALL ABOUT FAT

With everything you've read or heard about fat, you may believe it's a good idea to try to eliminate it from your diet. But the truth is we actually need some fat. It is our only source of linoleic acid, a fatty acid essential for proper growth, healthy skin and the proper metabolism of cholesterol.

Also essential is the role fat plays in the transport, absorption and storage of fat-soluble vitamins (A, D, E, K). In addition, fat helps the body use carbohydrate and protein more efficiently. And finally, fat deposits—where much of the body's excess fat is stored—play an important role in insulating and cushioning the body and organs.

On the average, Americans eat about 38 percent of their daily calories in the form of fat. Health and nutrition experts recommend people over the age of twenty reduce fat to an average of 30 percent—less than one-third—of daily calories. In a typical 1800-calorie diet, it means a drop from 75 grams to 60 grams of fat a day.

RECOMMENDED DAILY NUTRIENT LEVELS		
Calories	Fat (g)	Saturated Fat (g)
1200	40	13
1500	50	17
1800	60	20
2100	70	23
2400	80	27
2700	90	30
3000	100	33

Although about one-third of all the fat Americans eat comes from meat, fish and poultry, fat from animal sources actually has decreased in the past 40 years. Fourteen percent of the fat we eat is made up of fats such as butter, margarine, mayonnaise, oils and sauces. Mixed dishes such as casseroles, pizza, and lasagna, as well as milk and milk products, each

SOURCES OF FAT

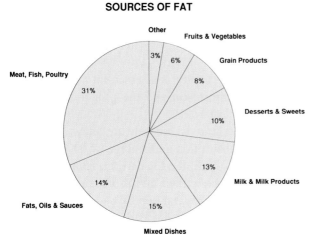

Other 3%
Fruits & Vegetables 6%
Grain Products 8%
Desserts & Sweets 10%
Milk & Milk Products 13%
Mixed Dishes 15%
Fats, Oils & Sauces 14%
Meat, Fish, Poultry 31%

Source: General Mills, Inc., Diet Study 1986–88

provides 13 percent of total dietary fat. The pie chart above presents a complete breakdown of dietary fat sources in the average American diet.

Along with limiting the total amount of fat we eat, we're also advised to cut back on how much saturated fat we eat. All dietary fat is made up of mixtures of three types of fatty acids: saturated, monounsaturated and polyunsaturated. Because saturated fat has been linked to high blood cholesterol levels, a major risk factor for coronary heart disease (CHD), it's recommended we reduce our intake of this type of fat to no more than 10 percent of daily calories. In a typical diet, about 13 percent of calories comes from saturated fat.

Animal foods such as meats, eggs and dairy products including cheese, butter and cream contain the greatest amounts of saturated fats. Tropical fats—coconut, palm and palm kernel oils—are unique because they are derived from plant sources, yet they too contain significant amounts of saturated fats.

Saturated fats have a greater effect on blood cholesterol levels than any other dietary factor. As long as total fat intake is still within the suggested range (not more than 30 percent), substituting polyunsaturated or monounsaturated fats such as olive, peanut, corn, soybean and safflower (canola) oils for saturated fats may help lower blood cholesterol.

Not all saturated fatty acids have the same cholesterol-raising potential. Research shows that stearic acid, a saturated fatty acid found in beef and chocolate, does not increase blood cholesterol levels. Palm oil, high in saturated fatty acids, seems to behave differently from other saturated fats, too. However, more research is needed to investigate the long-term effects of these fatty acids on blood cholesterol levels.

The level of saturation of any fat can be changed by hydrogenation. The hydrogenation process changes unsaturated fatty acids to a more saturated—and more stable—chemical structure. Highly unsaturated vegetable oils, for example, are not stable enough for use in packaged foods because they develop "off" flavors in short periods of time. To increase stability, these oils are "saturated" with hydrogen, thereby hydrogenating them and making them more shelf stable.

Typical hydrogenated fats include shortening, which is made by blending hydrogenated vegetable oils to provide desirable physical properties of taste and shelf stability for packaged foods. Vegetable oil margarine becomes solid and spreadable at room temperature as a result of the hydrogenation process.

WHAT ABOUT CHOLESTEROL?

In the effort to reduce dietary fat in order to lower blood cholesterol, it's easy to get confused. What about the cholesterol we eat? Where does that fit in?

The cholesterol in the foods we eat is dietary cholesterol. However, the cholesterol in our blood comes from two sources: the foods we eat and the body's own manufacturing process. Dietary cholesterol is found only in animal foods such as meat and milk. For most individuals, dietary cholesterol seems to have minimal influence on blood cholesterol because the body regulates the level.

You may have heard about two other types of cholesterol—"bad" cholesterol, or low-density lipoproteins (LDL), and "good" cholesterol, high-density lipoproteins (HDL). LDL and HDL together make up total blood cholesterol along with VLDL (very-low-density lipoproteins). Thought to be the culprit in heart disease, LDL contains most of the cholesterol found in the blood and is associated with making cholesterol available for cell structures, hormones and nerve coverings. LDL deposits cholesterol on artery walls as well. HDL seems to help remove cholesterol from body tissues and blood so it can be recycled and used again. Studies indicate that the more HDL in the blood, the lower the risk for heart disease.

The National Heart, Lung and Blood Institute's National Cholesterol Education Program (NCEP) initially classifies risk for heart disease based on total blood cholesterol levels as follows:

> Under 200 mg/dl*—Desirable
> 200–239 mg/dl—Borderline–High
> 240 mg/dl or over—High

NCEP recommends that individuals with cholesterol readings of 200 mg/dl and above have another test done to reconfirm the readings. Then, if levels remain borderline-high or above and the individual has two or more risk factors for coronary heart disease (CHD) or has been diagnosed with the disease, lipoprotein levels should be analyzed, particularly the amounts of LDL and HDL. NCEP classifications for LDL and HDL are listed below:

HDL Cholesterol

> Under 35 mg/dl—Low
> Under 130 mg/dl—Desirable

LDL Cholesterol

> Under 130 mg/dl—Desirable
> 130–159 mg/dl—Borderline-High
> 160 mg/dl or over—High

Major risk factors for CHD include heredity, cigarette smoking, high blood pressure, obesity, physical inactivity and diabetes mellitus. All individuals over the age of twenty with

* Milligrams of cholesterol per deciliter of blood.

desirable cholesterol levels should have them rechecked every five years.

Like fat, cholesterol is essential to life, so we don't want to eliminate it from our diets. Cholesterol is vital, and our bodies have a built-in safeguard to ensure we get the cholesterol we need. The body makes 800 to 1500 milligrams of cholesterol daily, which circulates through the bloodstream to meet various needs. Among its many important functions, cholesterol is involved in manufacturing certain hormones and is an essential part of the brain and nervous system.

Americans also tend to eat more dietary cholesterol than is recommended. Average intakes run more than 400 milligrams a day; health experts recommend no more than 300 milligrams. The most concentrated sources of dietary cholesterol are organ meats, such as liver, brain and kidney. Egg yolk contains a significant amount of dietary cholesterol too.

WHAT IS FIBER?

Although there is no universal agreement on a definition, fiber is usually described as those components of plant foods that are not broken down in the human digestive tract or absorbed into the blood stream. Fiber is a complex carbohydrate, one of the foods we are encouraged to eat more of as we eat less fat, sugar and cholesterol. Moreover, fiber contributes virtually no calories.

Fiber, part of the structural material in plants, is present in most foods containing complex carbohydrates, such as whole-grain cereals and breads and many vegetables and fruits. Fiber is not found in meat and dairy products.

FILLING UP WITH FIBER

You don't have to be a scientist to recognize that high-fiber foods go a long way toward helping you feel full and satisfied after a meal. Studies of fiber's effect on appetite control and obesity are now being conducted. Fiber-rich

High-Fiber Foods—Citrus fruits, apples, bananas, pineapple, carrots, potatoes, broccoli, cauliflower, lentils, dried beans, whole grains, corn on the cob, popcorn, whole-grain breads and whole-grain crackers.

foods take longer to digest and may help tame hunger between meals and even make you less hungry at the next one.

But there's much more to fiber than that. It appears that a high-fiber diet may have a positive effect on cancer of the colon and rectum, cardiovascular disease and diabetes, in addition to effecting intestinal regularity and diverticular disease.

Many of these beneficial effects are due to the water-holding capacity of one type of fiber called insoluble fiber, especially the insoluble fiber from wheat and corn bran. While this fiber does not dissolve in water, it does have the effect of drawing more water into the intestinal tract and keeping it there. More water means softer, bulkier and heavier stools, which move more quickly through the digestive tract and help prevent constipation.

SOLUBLE AND INSOLUBLE FIBER COMPARISONS

Food	Serving Size	Total Dietary Fiber (g)	Amount of Fiber (g) Soluble	Insoluble
Kidney beans	³/₄ cup	9.3	2.3	7.0
Oat bran	¹/₃ cup	4.0	2.0	2.0
Carrots	¹/₂ cup	3.2	1.5	1.7
Apple	1 small	2.8	1.0	1.8
Broccoli	¹/₂ cup	2.8	1.3	1.5
Oatmeal	³/₄ cup	2.5	1.2	1.3
Cheerios®	1¹/₄ cup	2.0	1.0	1.0
Orange	1 medium	1.9	1.1	0.8
Corn	¹/₂ cup	1.9	0.2	1.7
Cornflake cereal	1 cup	0.5	0.1	0.4

Furthermore, this water-holding capacity is thought to be one of the chemical properties that influences cancer risk. It may dilute the concentration of carcinogens in the stool and by moving the stool quickly through the intestines, help reduce the time the intestinal wall is exposed to carcinogens. Another property may be fiber's capacity to bind carcinogens, thus making them unable to influence the body.

Until recently, the other type of fiber—soluble fiber—was ignored largely because its role in the diet was unclear. But it has been shown to have important effects in digestive and absorptive processes and may help control blood sugar levels in people with diabetes mellitus. In addition, research confirms repeatedly that when soluble fiber is included in a low-fat diet, it may help lower blood cholesterol a small but significant amount. This effect seems to be more pronounced in individuals with high levels of blood cholesterol. Some of these benefits may result from the ability of soluble fibers to dissolve in aqueous or watery solutions, thereby forming gels that slow the digestion and absorption of some substances.

Despite these good health benefits, the daily dietary fiber intake of the average American has decreased since the turn of the century. While there is no established Recommended Dietary Allowance (RDA) for dietary fiber, nutrition experts currently suggest individuals should consume between 20 and 30 grams per day. Larger individuals should consume more fiber than smaller individuals.

It's estimated that we now eat 10 to 20 grams of dietary fiber per day. The goal recently established by the National Cancer Institute means, for most Americans, doubling their intake.

Many people are confused about the relationship of bran to dietary fiber. Bran is the coarse, outer layer of the whole-grain kernel and is the source of fiber in the kernel. In addition to fiber, bran contains some starch, protein, a very small amount of fat, and minerals such as iron and zinc. But all bran is not alike. Depending on the grain source of the bran, it will have different amounts of soluble and insoluble fiber (see table at left).

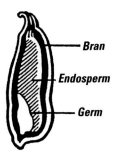

Oat Kernel

Bran

Endosperm

Germ

Whole-grain cereals are excellent sources of insoluble fiber; it's also found in dried beans and peas, vegetables and nuts. Soluble fiber is perhaps best known in the form of oat bran, but other good sources include whole-grain oats and barley, apples, oranges, dried beans and other legumes. A healthful intake of both insoluble and soluble fiber is recommended. To ensure that, eat a variety of whole grains, vegetables and fruits.

VITAL VITAMINS AND MINERALS

Vitamins and minerals are crucial to good health. Vitamins and minerals typically come from the foods we eat, and different foods provide different nutrients—one reason why our diets should be balanced and varied.

Vitamins help to control most body processes. They are important for vision and maintaining healthy tissues such as skin and hair. Vitamins aid our nerve activity and even help our ability to release energy from the foods we eat. They are organic compounds that contain carbon and are found in small amounts in many foods.

Vitamins are classified according to their ability to dissolve in water or fat. Water-soluble vitamins are not retained by the body and must be replenished daily. Fat-soluble vitamins are stored in the fatty tissue of the body and can build up with time. Water-soluble vitamins include thiamin (B_1), riboflavin (B_2), niacin (B_3), B_6, B_{12}, biotin, folic acid, pantothenic acid and vitamin C. Vitamins A, D, E and K are fat-soluble.

Minerals differ from vitamins because they are inorganic, meaning they do not contain the element carbon. Examples of key dietary minerals are calcium, iron, potassium, sodium, phosphorus, magnesium and zinc. Minerals are important for strong bones and teeth, for normal growth, for oxygen transfer in blood and in helping to maintain body water balance.

BONING UP ON CALCIUM

You may already know that healthy bones and teeth depend on getting enough calcium during the growing years. But even as adults, we need to make sure we meet our calcium needs. Calcium plays an important role in the normal functioning of muscles and nerves, blood clotting and various hormonal systems. Plus, current research points to calcium as vital to the prevention and treatment of diseases commonly seen as we grow older such as osteoporosis (weak, brittle bones) and possibly high blood pressure.

Dairy products such as milk and cheese contribute more than half of the calcium consumed in the United States. Other sources include leafy green vegetables such as broccoli, kale and collards, tortillas processed with lime, tofu made with calcium and calcium-fortified foods. The soft bones of fish such as sardines and canned salmon also contain significant amounts of calcium.

For women and men twenty-five years old and older, the RDA for calcium is 800 milligrams per day. The RDA is set at 1200 milligrams for girls and boys between the ages of eleven and twenty-four, and pregnant and nursing women. Recent surveys, however, indicate many Americans do not meet their need for calcium. This is especially worrisome for adolescent girls and adult women, who run the greatest risk of developing osteoporosis.

One reason for this calcium shortfall is the misconception that all dairy foods are high in fat and calories. As a result, many girls and women eliminate dairy foods from their diets to lose or maintain weight. But that isn't necessary to control calories. Many types of reduced-fat milk, cheeses and other dairy products are

High-Calcium Foods—Low-fat dairy products (including cheeses, milks, yogurts, frozen yogurt and ice milk), spinach, kale, collard greens, broccoli, dried beans and canned salmon and sardines (with bones).

now available. And they taste good, too, making it easier to meet calcium needs while controlling weight.

Other people cut back on dairy products because they suffer from lactose intolerance, which means they cannot digest lactose (milk sugar). They lack the intestinal enzyme lactase that breaks down lactose so it can be absorbed. As a result, when they drink milk or other dairy foods that contain a lot of lactose, they may become bloated and suffer from cramps and/or diarrhea. The people most often affected include those of African American, Hispanic, Asian, Native American and Mediterranean descent.

Some lactose-intolerant people, however, don't need to eliminate dairy foods from their diets. The symptoms appear to be dose-related, meaning that an individual may be able to tolerate small amounts of dairy foods without developing symptoms. Exactly how much a person can tolerate is quite individual. Some people can drink a whole cup of milk with a meal without experiencing symptoms, while others have problems after drinking very small amounts of milk.

If you suffer from lactose intolerance, you can find your individual tolerance for dairy foods by eating them in small portions, then gradually increasing the portion size until you begin to notice symptoms. Then, don't exceed that portion per serving. To meet your calcium needs, space several servings of dairy products throughout the day.

Symptoms may also be avoided by drinking milk with solid foods rather than drinking it by itself. In addition, lactose-reduced milks are now available in many supermarkets. Also, aged hard cheeses such as cheddar, Swiss and Parmesan do not cause symptoms for many people, because most of the lactose is removed during processing. Yogurt with active cultures is also well tolerated because the cultures contain enzymes that break down lactose.

CALCIUM-RICH FOOD

Food	Calcium (mg)
Beans, dried, cooked, 1 cup	90
Broccoli, cooked, ½ cup	90
Cheese	
American, pasteurized processed, 1 ounce	174
Cottage, 2% low-fat, ½ cup	77
Ricotta, part skim, ½ cup	337
Cheddar, 1 ounce	204
Mozzarella, part skim, 1 ounce	207
Swiss, 1 ounce	272
Collards, fresh, cooked, ½ cup	74
Ice cream, ½ cup	88
Ice milk, hardened, ½ cup	88
Ice milk, soft serve, ½ cup	137
Kale, frozen, cooked, ½ cup	90
Milk	
Buttermilk, 1 cup	285
Whole, 1 cup	291
1% low-fat, 1 cup	300
2% low-fat, 1 cup	297
Skim, 1 cup	302
Pudding, chocolate, ½ cup	133
Salmon, with bones, 3 ounces	167
Sardines, with bones, 3 ounces	371
Spinach, fresh, cooked, ½ cup	122
Tofu, 4 ounces	108
Yogurt	
Low-fat, flavored, 1 cup	389
Low-fat, fruit, 1 cup	345
Low-fat, plain, 1 cup	415

Source: The All-American Guide to Calcium-Rich Foods, National Dairy Council, Rosemont, IL, 1987.

BEING SENSIBLE ABOUT SODIUM

Attention on sodium in recent years is due to its link with high blood pressure in some people. While no single factor causes high blood pressure, experts generally agree that different factors play greater or lesser roles in different people. Some people, it seems, inherit a genetic tendency for high blood pressure that is sodium sensitive. Too much sodium in their diets causes their blood pressure to rise. On the other hand, some people can eat all the sodium they want and seem never to suffer negative effects.

The trouble is, there's no good way to test for sodium sensitivity prior to the actual onset of high blood pressure. The cause of high blood pressure is unknown in the majority of Americans. The word to the wise then, points to moderation in sodium consumption.

As with the other dietary substances we've discussed, sodium is essential. It is needed to regulate blood pressure and blood volume and also aids the proper functioning of nerves and muscles. The National Research Council, which sets the RDAs, has established a safe and adequate range of sodium intake for adults at 1,100 to 3,300 milligrams per day. Surveys indicate Americans are in no danger of suffering a shortage of sodium. Estimates of average sodium intake in America range up to 5,000 milligrams a day.

Sodium occurs naturally in a wide variety of foods such as dairy products, eggs, meat, poultry and vegetables. Sodium is added to other foods during processing in the form of ingredients used to enhance flavor or act as preservatives or emulsifiers. Salt is one such ingredient; it is 40 percent sodium and serves a variety of purposes in foods. Other sodium-rich ingredients feature the word sodium in their names: monosodium glutamate (a flavor enhancer), sodium benzoate (a preservative), sodium caseinate (a thickener and binder). These names are listed in the ingredient list of packaged foods that contain them. Other sources of sodium include condiments, seasonings and sauces such as soy, steak and barbecue sauces, catsup, relishes and bouillon cubes. Manufacturers today are introducing sodium-reduced versions of many of these items.

Food Guide Pyramid
A Guide to Daily Food Choices

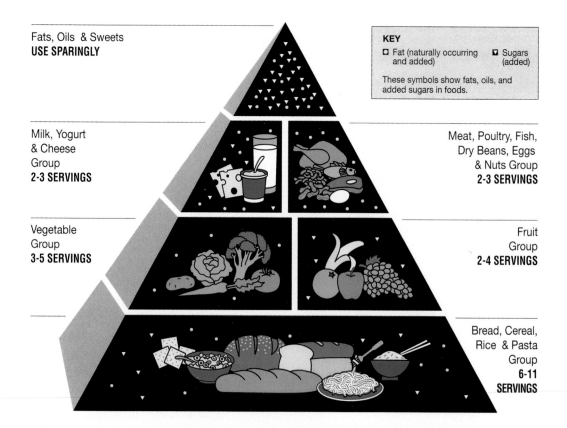

Fats, Oils & Sweets
USE SPARINGLY

KEY
☐ Fat (naturally occurring and added)   ▼ Sugars (added)

These symbols show fats, oils, and added sugars in foods.

Milk, Yogurt
& Cheese
Group
2-3 SERVINGS

Meat, Poultry, Fish,
Dry Beans, Eggs
& Nuts Group
2-3 SERVINGS

Vegetable
Group
3-5 SERVINGS

Fruit
Group
2-4 SERVINGS

Bread, Cereal,
Rice & Pasta
Group
**6-11
SERVINGS**

BUILDING A HEALTHFUL DIET

After reading the preceding pages, you may think our claim that you don't need to be a nutrition expert to eat healthfully isn't true! After all, how can you balance concerns about fat, cholesterol, fiber, calcium and sodium yet still have a food plan that includes foods you love and have eaten all your life?

It's actually fairly easy if you take it one step at a time. Approach it as though you're building a house (in a sense, you are—you're building your body for a long, healthy life). Start with a good, solid foundation. The foundation of a nutritious diet is a wide variety of foods. You need more than 40 different nutrients to maintain good health, and no single food supplies them all in the necessary amounts. And that's just as well because it would be boring to eat just one item day after day. Much of the pleasure of food comes from enjoying the flavors and textures of the wonderful assortment of items available to us today.

To best ensure you meet both your nutrient and pleasure requirements, select a wide variety of foods from the Food Pyramid Guide (left). Choose low-fat items most of the time but when you wish, you can occasionally enjoy higher-fat, higher-calorie items too.

Eat at least the minimum recommended number of servings from each food group daily. Whether you eat more depends on your individual needs. For example, if you exercise regularly, you may require more servings from each group in order to maintain your weight. If you're unsure of how to handle your new food plan, a registered dietitian can help decide what is best for you.

When planning meals, remember the special nutrient concerns discussed earlier. To control fat, saturated fat and cholesterol, select more plant foods, such as cereals, rice, pasta and beans. Use meat, poultry and fish as "flavor enhancers" rather than the main feature of meals. Use fats and oils sparingly in cooking.

To increase fiber, choose whole-grain cereals and breads, brown rice and dried peas or beans. Serve fruits and vegetables unpeeled. Meet your calcium needs with a wide variety of reduced-fat dairy products. And be wise about sodium by carefully managing the amount of high-sodium foods you eat and how much salt you add to foods during cooking or at the table. Learn to enjoy the natural flavors of foods; enhance flavors with spices and herbs and a small amount of salt only when necessary.

THE FRAMEWORK—A HEALTHY ATTITUDE

The framework for your healthy body is formed by your attitude about eating and exercise. How you approach making changes, your ideas about weight management and how you manage special eating occasions all combine to help you decide whether your initial changes become permanent. There is always room for adjustment.

Lasting changes are truly important. Fluctuation back and forth between old and new habits may not only prevent you from ever reaching your goals, but can even cause harm. For instance, constantly losing and regaining weight may end up adding to health problems rather than helping to alleviate them. As a result, experts today support an approach to improving eating and exercise habits that recognizes individual needs.

Gone are the days of preprinted diet and exercise plans. For long-term effectiveness, individual desires, obstacles and issues must be addressed. In short, the approach must be realistic, practical and tailored to each individual. Furthermore, experts advise a slow start to building new habits. If you're a couch potato who skips breakfast and lunch, then starts eating the moment you get home from work and doesn't stop until your head hits the pillow, you're not likely to succeed if you try to totally revamp your diet and begin training for marathons at the same time. A better way, and one that is more manageable, is to focus on two or three major eating or exercise habits. For example, you may decide to start eating breakfast and lunch and focus on reducing after-dinner snacking. And you might set a goal for three 20-minute walks a week. When you achieve those goals, you can address other areas you think need improvement. Nothing succeeds better than success, so set yourself up to win by defining small, achievable goals along the way to your overall goal.

Going slowly where weight is concerned is vital, too. The best approach to managing your weight is to eat moderately following the Food Guide Pyramid and to exercise regularly. Quick weight-loss schemes, particularly those that advise eliminating any food group, can jeopardize both your nutritional status and your chances for success at weight management.

An effective approach to weight management also considers "healthy" weights. Healthy weights depend on the individual, and for some people, that's far from the super-slim-fashion-model image popular today. Indeed, you may be healthy at a higher weight than your neighbor, even though you both are the same height. A realistic approach allows for a small amount of weight gain, maybe a few extra pounds, as we age.

Two simple measures of healthy weight include determining where excess fat is located (it's considered a greater health risk if fat is found primarily on the abdomen) and if you or your family has a history of health problems that may be aggravated by excess weight, such as diabetes or heart disease. Check to see if your weight falls within a healthy range as defined in the table on the left.

Being realistic during the food-filled holidays and other special celebrations is important as well. At those times, it seems that tasty, high-fat, high-calorie tidbits lurk in every corner, just waiting to sabotage our efforts. But there's really no need to throw in the towel at these times. You can have your cake and eat it, too. All it takes is a little planning.

It helps tremendously to remember that healthful eating depends on balance, variety and moderation. All foods can fit within a healthy diet; what's important is how often and how much you eat of certain foods. To successfully navigate special occasions anticipate meals high in fat or cholesterol. Offset them by eating low-fat, low-cholesterol foods the days before and after.

Remember, too, that one mistake does not destroy all your good efforts. If you overeat—for one meal, one day or even one week—you can still salvage your healthy eating efforts by returning to your plan. Compare this behavior with totally giving up because you've made a mistake, and you can see that over time you're

SUGGESTED HEALTHY WEIGHTS FOR ADULTS

| Height* | Weight (lbs)** | |
	Age 19 to 34 years	Age 35 years and over
5'0"	†97–128	108–138
5'1"	101–132	111–143
5'2"	104–137	115–148
5'3"	107–141	119–152
5'4"	111–146	122–157
5'5"	114–150	126–162
5'6"	118–155	130–167
5'7"	121–160	134–172
5'8"	125–164	138–178
5'9"	129–169	142–183
5'10"	132–174	146–188
5'11"	136–179	151–194
6'0"	140–184	155–199
6'1"	144–189	159–205
6'2"	148–195	164–210
6'3"	152–200	168–216
6'4"	156–205	173–222
6'5"	160–211	177–228
6'6"	164–216	182–234

* Without shoes.
** Without clothes.
† The higher weights in the ranges generally apply to men, who tend to have more muscle and bone; the lower weights more often apply to women; who have less muscle and bone.

Source: Nutrition and Your Health: Dietary Guidelines for Americans, Third Edition, 1990, U.S. Department of Agriculture, U.S. Department of Health and Human Services, Washington, D.C.

CALORIES BURNED IN VARIOUS PHYSICAL ACTIVITIES

Activity	Calories per Minute	Activity	Calories per Minute	Activity	Calories per Minute
Aerobics		road/field		**Shoveling (depends**	
low-intensity	3.0–4.0	(3.5 mph)	5.6–7.0	on weight of	
high-intensity	8.0–10.0	snow, soft-hard		load, rate of	
Archery	5.2	(2.5–3.5 mph)	10.0–20.0	work, height of lift)	5.4–10.5
Badminton		uphill		**Showering**	3.4
recreation	5.2	5–15 percent		**Singing in loud**	
competition	10.0	grade (3.5 mph)	8.0–15.6	voice	0.9
Baseball (except		**Hill climbing (100**		**Sitting quietly**	0.5
pitcher)	4.7	feet/hour)	8.2	**Skipping rope**	10.0–15.0
Basketball		**Hockey**	12.0–15.0	**Skiing (snow)**	
half court	6.0	**Horseback riding**		moderate to	
fastbreak	9.0	trot	5.0	steep	8.0–12.0
Bowling (while active)	7.0	walk	1.6	downhill racing	16.5
Calisthenics	6.0–8.0	**Horseshoes**	3.8	cross-country	
Canoeing		**Ironing clothes**	4.2	(3.8 mph)	11.0–20.0
(2.5–4.0 mph)	3.0–7.0	**Jogging alternated**		**Sleeping**	0.5–1.2
Carpentry	3.8	with walking, 5		**Snowshoeing**	
Cleaning windows	3.7	minutes each	10.0	(2.5 mph)	10.0
Clerical work	1.2–1.6	**Judo and karate**	13.0	**Soccer**	9.0
Cycling		**Knitting or**		**Standing, light**	
fast (12 mph)	8.0–10.0	crocheting	0.5–0.8	activity	2.6
slow (6 mph)	4.0–5.0	**Making beds**	3.4	**Standing, relaxed**	0.6
10-speed bicycle		**Meal preparation**	2.5	**Sweeping with:**	
5–15 mph	4.0–12.0	**Mopping floors**	4.9	broom	1.6
Dancing (moderate		**Mountain climbing**	10.0	vacuum cleaner	3.2
to vigorous)	4.2–7.7	**Piano playing**	1.6	**Swimming**	
Dishwashing	1.2	**Plastering walls**	4.1	pleasure	6.0
Dressing	3.4	**Pool or billiards**	1.8	backstroke,	
Driving car	2.8	**Racquetball**		breaststroke,	
Driving motorcycle	3.4	recreation	8.1	crawl (25–50	
Dusting	2.5	competition	11.5	yard/minute)	6.0–12.5
Eating	2.5	**Reclining**		butterfly (50	
Farming chores		(watching TV)	1.5	yard/minute)	14.0
haying	6.7	**Roller skating**		**Table tennis**	5.1
planting	4.7	(moderate to		**Talking**	1.0–1.2
Football (while		vigorous)	5.0–15.0	**Tennis**	
active)	13.3	**Rowing**		recreation	7.0
Gardening		pleasure	5.0	competition	11.0
digging	8.6	vigorous	15.0	**Tree felling (ax)**	8.4–12.7
weeding	5.6	**Running**		**Truck and auto**	
Golf		12-minute mile		repair	4.2
foursome	2.7	(5 mph)	9.0	**Typing (rapidly)**	1.2
twosome	3.0	8-minute mile		**Volleyball**	
Gymnastics		(7.5 mph)	11.0	recreation	3.5
balancing	2.5	6-minute mile		competition	8.0
abdominal	3.0	(10 mph)	20.0	**Walking**	
trunk bending	3.5	5-minute mile		3 mph	4.0–5.0
hopping	6.5	(12 mph)	25.0	4 mph	6.0–7.0
Handball	10.0	**Sawing**		downstairs	4.0
Hiking		chain saw	6.2	upstairs	8.0–10.0
downhill, 5–10		crosscut saw	7.5–10.5	**Washing and**	
percent grade		**Sewing (hand or**		dressing	2.6
(2.5 mph)	3.5–3.6	machine)	0.6	**Washing clothes**	3.1
downhill, 15–20		**Shining shoes**	3.2	**Water skiing**	8.0
percent grade				**Wrestling**	14.4
(2.5 mph)	3.7–4.3			**Writing**	0.5

GOOD EATING GUIDE

	Recommended Serving Size	Eat Any Time	Eat in Moderation	Eat Occasionally
Breads/Cereals (6 to 11 servings daily. Includes whole grain, enriched breads and cereals, pasta, rice and crackers.)	1 to 1½ ounces ready-to-eat cereal (varies if it contains fruits, nuts) ½ cup cooked cereal, pasta or rice 1 slice bread ½ hamburger or hot dog bun ½ English muffin or bagel 1 small roll or muffin ½ pita (6 inches in diameter) 3 to 4 small or 2 large crackers 2 breadsticks (4x½ inch) 1 tortilla (6 inches in diameter) 3 cups popcorn 2 medium cookies	Whole grain* or fortified breakfast cereal Whole grain* or enriched bread, rolls, bagels, English muffins, tortillas, low-fat crackers Brown or enriched white rice Whole grain or enriched pasta Plain popcorn, pretzels and low-fat cookies (such as fig bars) and cake (angel food)	Biscuits Bread stuffing Corn bread Muffins and other quick breads Pancakes, waffles Popcorn made with added fat Taco shells	High-fat crackers Croissants Doughnuts Sweet rolls Snack chips (potato chips, corn chips, etc.) Most cookies and cakes
Fruits/Vegetables (5 to 9 servings daily. Include at least one serving citrus or other choice high in vitamin C daily. Include orange or leafy, dark green vegetables 3 to 4 times a week.)	1 medium fruit such as apple, orange, banana ½ grapefruit ¾ cup juice 1 medium wedge melon ½ cup berries ¼ cup dried fruit ½ cup cooked or canned fruit or vegetable 1 medium potato 10 French-fried potatoes (2 to 3½ inches long) ½ cup raw chopped vegetables 1 cup leafy raw vegetable, such as spinach ⅛ medium avocado	All fresh, canned or frozen fruits and fruit juices All fresh, canned or frozen vegetables and vegetable juices Plain potato or potato with low-fat topping (such as yogurt)	Vegetables with added butter or margarine Potatoes topped with butter, sour cream or sauces	Fruit pies Deep-fried vegetables French-fried potatoes Vegetables in cream or cheese sauce

more likely to reach your goals. Use the Good Eating Guide above to help you select foods you enjoy that are also healthy. This keeps your eating plan pleasurable and varied.

Finally, any discussion of healthful habits must include a word about exercise. Physical inactivity places more Americans at risk for CHD—our number one killer today—than any other factor. Although a slightly greater risk for the disease comes from cigarette smoking, high blood cholesterol or high blood pressure, the number of Americans who are physically inactive actually exceeds the number who face these other risks. Yet we really don't give exer-

GOOD EATING GUIDE (continued)

	Recommended Serving Size	Eat Any Time	Eat in Moderation	Eat Occasionally
Meat/Protein (2 to 3 servings with a total of about 6 ounces daily. Includes meat, fish, poultry and eggs. Dried beans, peas and nuts are alternatives.)	2 ounces beef (maximum 3 ounces of beef daily) 2 ounces poultry or fish 4 ounces tofu **Count the following as 1 ounce of meat:** 1 egg (maximum 3 eggs weekly); 3 egg whites; 2 tablespoons peanut butter or whole nuts or seeds; ½ cup cooked beans, peas or lentils	**Beef:** Lean beef including round, sirloin, chuck and loin **Pork:** Lean cuts including ham and tenderloin **Veal:** All trimmed cuts except ground **Poultry:** All poultry without skin **Fish:** All fresh and frozen fin fish or shellfish **Other:** Egg whites, all beans, peas and lentils	**Beef:** Most cuts including all ground beef, short ribs, corned beef brisket **Pork:** Most cuts including chops, loin roast **Poultry:** All poultry with skin **Other:** Fat-free or low-fat luncheon meats,** peanut butter and other nuts or seeds **Eggs:** Limit to three eggs per week	**Beef:** USDA prime-grade cuts and heavily marbled cuts **Pork:** Spareribs, ground pork **Lamb:** Ground lamb **Fish:** Fried fish **Other:** Luncheon meats**, sausages**, frankfurters**, bacon**
Milk/Dairy (2 servings daily: 3 for pregnant or breast-feeding women, 4 for pregnant or breast-feeding teenagers. Includes milk, yogurt, cheese, cottage cheese and pudding.)	1 cup milk 1 cup yogurt 1½ ounces cheese 1 cup pudding 1½ cups ice cream, ice milk or frozen yogurt 2 cups cottage cheese	Skim milk 1% low-fat milk Low-fat buttermilk** Plain nonfat or low-fat yogurt Low-fat cheeses	2% low-fat milk Part-skim milk cheese** Ice milk	Whole milk, cream, half-and-half Whole milk yogurt All regular cheese** such as American, Cheddar, Brie, etc. Cream cheese and sour cream

* Good source of fiber.
** For those who need to limit sodium intake, these foods may be high in sodium (read nutrition labels for sodium content).

cise the attention it deserves when it comes to its ability to improve and protect our health.

The good news is that we're not necessarily talking about running marathons. Increasing evidence suggests that light to moderate physical activity can have significant health benefits, including a decreased risk of CHD. For inactive people, even relatively small increases in activity are associated with measurable health benefits. In addition, light to moderate physical activity is more readily adopted and maintained than vigorous physical activity.

As a result, experts today emphasize light to moderate physical activity as the goal for many Americans. Such activity requires sustained, rhythmic muscular movements and is performed at less than 60 percent of maximum heart rate for your age (subtract your age from 220 to get your maximum heart rate). Examples of such activity include walking, swimming, cycling, dancing, gardening, yardwork and even running after young children! (See chart on page 17.)

In short, today's advice for adopting healthy lifestyles is to be flexible. A flexible approach to healthy living forms a basic structure that can withstand the assaults of individual strengths and weaknesses. It allows us to live happily, and healthily every day.

Nutrition Glossary

Have you been confused by the terms used by nutrition and health experts? Consult this list for explanations of some key words.

Nutrients Substances necessary for life and to build, repair and maintain body cells. Nutrients include protein, carbohydrates, fat, water, vitamins and minerals.

Vitamins Essential substances, found in small amounts in many foods, necessary for controlling body processes. Vitamins, unlike minerals, are organic compounds containing carbon. Vitamins include vitamin A, B vitamins (such as thiamin, niacin, riboflavin) and vitamin C, among others.

Minerals Essential elements other than carbon, hydrogen, oxygen and nitrogen, nutritionally necessary in very small amounts. Minerals are inorganic elements, such as calcium and iron, and are found in our foods and water.

Protein Vital for life and provides energy and structural support of body cells and is also important for growth. Made from amino-acid building blocks that contain nitrogen.

Carbohydrate Key human energy source. All simple sugars and complex carbohydrates (starches) fit into this category.

Fat Provides energy—more than twice the amount supplied by an equal quantity of carbohydrate or protein. Also provides essential nutrients, insulation and protection of body organs.

Saturated fat Primarily found in animal foods, this type of fat is solid at room temperature. Diets high in saturated fats have been linked to higher blood cholesterol levels, however, not all saturated fats have the same blood cholesterol-raising potential.

Unsaturated fat Found most commonly in plant foods, this type of fat is usually liquid at room temperature. Unsaturated fats may be monounsaturated or polyunsaturated. A laboratory process called hydrogenation is used to alter the chemical structure of unsaturated fats, making them saturated and more shelf stable.

Cholesterol Essential fatlike substance found in animal foods that is needed by the body for hormones to function properly. Our bodies also make cholesterol.

LDL Low-density lipoprotein. Often tagged the "bad" cholesterol, low-density lipoprotein cholesterol travels through the bloodstream depositing cholesterol on artery walls, and making cholesterol available for cell structures, hormones and nerve coverings.

HDL High-density lipoprotein. This type of cholesterol helps to remove cholesterol from body tissues and blood and return it to the liver to be used again. This recycling process has earned it the reputation of "good" cholesterol.

Dietary fiber Often described as the components of plant foods that are not broken down or absorbed by the human digestive tract. Fiber is a complex carbohydrate based on its chemical structure.

Additive Substance added to food to perform certain functions, such as to add color or flavor, prevent spoilage, add nutritional value, or improve texture or consistency.

Food Guide Pyramid Newly developed nutrition educational guide from the U.S. Department of Health and Human Services to teach people about foods and the recommended number of servings from each food group in order to maintain a balanced and healthy diet. It replaces the former Four Basic Food Groups. See diagram on page 14.

% U.S. RDA Percentage of United States Recommended Daily Allowance was developed as a relative standard for nutrition labeling of protein, vitamins and minerals on foods and drugs. It is based on the needs of healthy people of various ages and is generally the highest recommended level of each nutrient for all age groups.

CHD Coronary Heart Disease. High blood cholesterol levels and build-up of fatlike plaques that limits the flow of blood to body tissues on the lining of artery walls that may cause tissue damage (heart attack, stroke in the brain) and death. Risk factors include family history of CHD, smoking, high blood pressure and lack of exercise. Dietary guidelines, exercise and/or drug treatment are usually warranted. Also called atherosclerosis.

Understanding Nutrition Information

Nutrition information per serving includes amounts of calories, protein, carbohydrate, fat, cholesterol, sodium and fiber. The percentage of U.S. RDA is indicated for protein, vitamin A, vitamin C, thiamin, riboflavin, niacin, calcium and iron. The U.S. RDAs are set by the Food and Drug Administration and are based on the average needs of most healthy adults.

◆ If a choice of ingredients is given (for example, 1 cup plain low-fat or nonfat yogurt), the first choice is the one used to calculate nutrition information.

◆ If a range of an ingredient amount is given (for example, "2 to 3 teaspoons low-fat milk"), the first amount (2 teaspoons) is the one used to calculate nutrition information.

◆ "If desired" ingredients such as "sprinkle with brown sugar if desired" and recipe variations are not included in nutrition information calculations.

◆ White rice is used to calculate nutrition information wherever cooked rice is listed in the ingredients, unless otherwise indicated.

◆ Cooked rice, pasta or vegetables are unsalted when called for as an ingredient.

◆ Two-percent milk is used to calculate the nutrition information wherever low-fat milk is listed in the ingredients. Skim milk will further reduce calories, fat and cholesterol.

◆ Canned chicken broth is used to calculate nutrition information wherever chicken broth is listed in the ingredients. Unsalted or lightly salted homemade chicken broth or canned low-sodium chicken broth will further reduce sodium.

◆ An asterisk (*) indicates U.S. RDA levels of less than 2 percent.

Nutrition Symbols

You may find it hard to believe that every one of the delicious recipes in this book meets at least one of the five nutritional criteria described at right; many meet several. It is unrealistic to expect each dish, or even each meal, to meet all nutritional needs or guidelines. The introduction you just read, Eating Right, gives you the information you need to use the nutrition analysis provided with each recipe to put together a healthy eating plan for yourself or your family.

 Low Calorie Recipes have 350 or fewer calories per serving, with the exception of desserts. Low-calorie dessert recipes have 250 or fewer calories per serving.

 Low Fat Recipes have 3 or fewer grams of fat per serving.

 Low Cholesterol Recipes have 20 or fewer milligrams of cholesterol per serving.

 Low Sodium Recipes have 140 or fewer milligrams of sodium per serving.

 High Fiber Recipes have 3 or more grams of fiber per serving.

1
Meal Planning and Menus

1

Meal Planning and Menus

When searching for delicious, satisfying meals, many of us become confused trying to reconcile our desire for good health with our love of food. It can be difficult to plan healthy meals, especially for family members who don't want to give up their favorite high-fat foods and who just aren't very interested in good nutrition. It may also seem impossible to eat healthy meals away from home. If these uncertainties sound familiar, you aren't alone. In this chapter, you'll find many "secrets" to help you plan healthy, good-tasting meals you and your family will enjoy—whether eating at home or dining out.

HEALTHY EATING AT HOME

Few people would disagree with the old saying that variety is the spice of life. And when it comes to planning meals, variety is what makes eating fun. Eating many different foods, with contrasting flavors and textures, helps to ensure we're getting the many nutrients that are vital to feeling and looking good while keeping boredom at bay.

The Food Guide Pyramid (page 14) illustrates a variety of different foods along with the amounts of each food you need to eat daily in order to maintain good health. To create meals that are appealing, both in taste and appearance, incorporate different foods from each group, and try unfamiliar foods. For instance, you could plan at least one meatless meal a

Preceding page: Cozy Winter Get-together (page 34)

week as a way to become more acquainted with the wonderful variety of delicious beans and grains—foods that are also important, low-fat sources of protein. And don't forget the many different forms of your favorite foods, such as canned, juiced, dried or frozen fruit. These can be a treat when fresh produce is out of season, or is very expensive. Whichever version you choose, it will contribute valuable—and delicious—nutrients to your diet.

Anything's Okay in Moderation

Nutrition experts today advise most of us to reduce the amounts of fat, saturated fat, cholesterol and sodium that we eat. They also recommend we boost our intake of fiber and that women and children eat more calcium and iron. While that's sound advice, it doesn't mean we must completely omit fat, cholesterol and sodium from our diets, nor should we go overboard on fiber, calcium and iron. And it doesn't mean we need to count every calorie, gram of fat or milligram of sodium we eat.

What this advice does encourage is *moderation* as an overall approach to healthier eating. That means all foods can be part of a healthy diet if we control *how much* of them we eat; reasonable-sized portions of all the foods we eat—whether high in fat and calories or not— is a key to healthy eating. When we plan our meals to feature foods high in fiber, calcium and iron, and enjoy small amounts of foods high in fat, cholesterol and/or sodium, healthy eating is simple and enjoyable. (See Good Eating Guide, page 18.)

The Cooking Connection

The way you cook can be just as important as what you choose to cook. Consider investing in nonstick cookware and use a nonstick cooking spray. Many cooking methods enable you to use significantly less fat and still prepare a tasty meal. A brief description of some of these cooking methods follows.

◆ **Grill** or **roast** meat on a rack. This allows the fat to drip off instead of pooling around the meat where it can be reabsorbed.

◆ **Microwave** foods. Minimal amounts of added fat or liquid are needed, thereby reducing calories from added fat and minimizing loss of water-soluble vitamins in cooking liquids.

◆ **Pan-broil** foods by starting with a cold, ungreased skillet in which meats are cooked slowly. Fat is poured off as it accumulates, before it can be reabsorbed.

◆ **Poach** foods by simmering them in a hot liquid just below the boiling point. No added fat is necessary.

◆ **Steam** foods in a steamer basket over boiling water. This allows foods such as vegetables to retain their water-soluble vitamins.

◆ **Stir-fry** foods in a small amount of oil. Cook small, uniform pieces of food over high heat, stirring constantly. A wok or large skillet is used to stir-fry.

Remember that important vitamins found in vegetables can be destroyed by overcooking or lost entirely by being cooked in too much water; aim for a crisp–tender mixture by cooking for only a short period of time, and cook in as little water as possible. To gain the benefit of vitamins that dissolve into cooking liquids, use the leftover liquid in creative ways; add it to soups, stews and sauces, or use it for basting meats. (See Steaming Fresh Vegetables and Microwaving Fresh Vegetables, pages 118 and 112.)

Poaching

To poach means to cook food in a hot liquid kept just below the boiling point. Liquids and seasonings are used to infuse a subtle flavor into the food. Water can certainly be used but other liquids like wine, broth and fruit juices will add more flavor. Eggs, fruits, chicken breasts and fish are some common foods that are often poached. Here are basic poaching directions for chicken breasts and fish fillets and steaks.

Poached chicken breasts Place 4 skinless, boneless chicken breast halves (about 1 pound), $1/4$ cup water, 1 tablespoon lemon juice and $1/4$ teaspoon salt in 10-inch nonstick skillet. Heat to boiling; reduce heat. Cover and simmer about 10 minutes or until juices run clear. Remove breasts from skillet with slotted spoon; drain. Serve immediately, or cover and refrigerate up to 2 days for cold dishes.

Stovetop poached fish fillets Place 1 pound firm, lean fish fillets (see chart on page 266), cut into 4 serving pieces, 2 cups water, $1/3$ cup low-fat milk, $1/4$ teaspoon salt and 1 lemon, thinly sliced, in 10-inch nonstick skillet. Heat to boiling; reduce heat. Simmer uncovered 8 to 10 minutes or until fish flakes easily with fork. Remove fillets from skillet with slotted spatula; drain. Serve immediately, or cover and refrigerate up to 2 days for cold dishes.

Oven-poached fish steaks Heat oven to 450°. Place 4 lean fish steaks (see chart on page 266), 1 inch thick (about $1 1/2$ pounds), in ungreased rectangular baking dish, $12 \times 7 1/2 \times 2$ inches. Sprinkle with $1/4$ teaspoon salt and $1/8$ teaspoon pepper. Place 1 sprig of dill weed and 1 slice of lemon on each steak. Pour $1/4$ cup dry white wine or water over fish. Bake uncovered 20 to 25 minutes or until fish flakes easily with fork. Remove steaks from dish with slotted spatula; drain. Serve immediately, or cover and refrigerate up to 2 days for cold dishes.

More Ways to Limit Fats

Use a nonstick cooking spray. Try cooking onions, garlic or chopped vegetables in water, broth, flavored vinegars or wine instead of using oil, butter or margarine to sauté. Baste meats with their own juices, broth or vegetable juices instead of oil, margarine or butter then, make a low-fat sauce or gravy by skimming the fat from the pan juices and reducing the juices by boiling in a skillet. You'll get delicious concentrated flavor. Choose herbs and spices, mustard, lemon juice or flavored vinegars instead of butter or oils to "spike" foods that need a splash of flavor.

Shaping up Your Favorite Recipes

Changing favorite recipes to fit your plan for healthy eating often boils down to a few simple steps, such as those listed below. By following these suggestions, you can cut fat, cholesterol and sodium and add significantly to the fiber, vitamin and mineral content of foods.

Don't try to make too many changes in your recipes at once. Pick one or two ingredients to focus on first, then make gradual changes until you achieve your desired results.

◆ Cut by one-fourth the amount of fat or oil called for in a recipe. If that yields good results, cut the fat by one-third the next time you prepare that recipe. Keep reducing the fat until you find the minimum that will still produce an appealing dish.

◆ Choose low-fat or nonfat versions of dairy products. Most dairy items offer reduced-fat options.

◆ Try substituting apple sauce for half or all of the fat in muffins, cookies and other baked goods.

◆ Sauté chopped vegetables in a small amount of water, chicken broth, apple juice, flavored vinegar or wine instead of butter, margarine or oil.

◆ Use reduced-fat mayonnaises and salad dressings as alternatives to regular products.

◆ Use egg whites, homemade egg substitute or purchased cholesterol-free egg product instead of whole eggs. (See recipe and guidelines on page 28 to learn how.)

◆ Add new and unusual greens and other vegetables or cooked beans to salads. These simple additions add fiber and increase vitamins and minerals.

◆ Limit portions of cooked meat to 2 to 3 ounces per serving by boosting the amounts of vegetables, pasta and beans in chile, soups, stews, stir-fries and casseroles.

◆ Substitute whole-wheat flour for up to one-half of all-purpose flour in recipes. Foods will be slightly heavier, darker and heartier.

◆ Decrease or eliminate salt from recipes except for yeast breads, which need salt to prevent excessive rising. Reduce added salt in recipes calling for ingredients that already contain salt, such as chicken broth, tomato sauce or soy sauce. Or choose low- or reduced-sodium versions of those ingredients.

◆ Do not add salt to the cooking water of rice, pasta or vegetables.

Recipe Makeover

Using the suggestions above, we made several changes to this Raisin-Spice Coffee Cake. As you can see, the sugar, margarine, salt and nuts were all decreased. Half of the all-purpose flour was replaced with whole-wheat flour, the whole egg was replaced with egg whites or cholesterol-free egg product and skim milk was used instead of whole milk. We've compared the amounts of calories, fat, cholesterol, sodium and fiber from the original recipe to those from the revised recipe in the chart on page 27. You will find our "healthier" version of Raisin-Spice Coffee Cake on page 88.

Raisin-Spice Coffee Cake

1 cup WHOLE-WHEAT FLOUR
1 ~~2~~ cup$ all-purpose flour
¾ ~~1~~ cup sugar
¼ ~~⅓~~ cup margarine or butter, softened
1 cup ~~whole~~ milk *SKIM*
3 teaspoons baking powder
1 teaspoon ground cinnamon
½ ~~1~~ teaspoon salt
¼ teaspoon ground allspice
¼ teaspoon ground nutmeg
~~1 egg~~ *2 EGG WHITES OR ¼ CUP CHOLESTEROL-FREE EGG PRODUCT*
½ cup raisins
Streusel

Heat oven to 350°. Spray square pan, 9×9×2 inches, with nonstick cooking spray. Beat all ingredients except raisins and Streusel on low speed 30 seconds. Beat on medium speed 2 minutes, scraping bowl occasionally. Stir in raisins. Spread batter in pan. Sprinkle with Streusel. Bake 40 to 45 minutes or until toothpick inserted in center comes out clean. Serve warm. *9 servings*

Streusel

2 tbsp ~~⅓ cup~~ firm margarine ~~or butter~~
¼ ~~⅓~~ cup all-purpose flour
2 tbsp ~~⅓ cup~~ packed brown sugar or granulated sugar
½ teaspoon ground cinnamon
¼ ~~⅓~~ cup chopped nuts

Cut margarine into flour, brown sugar and cinnamon with pastry blender or fork until crumbly. Stir in nuts.

RECIPE MAKEOVER COMPARISON

	Original	Revised
Calories	465	320
Fat	19 g	10 g
Cholesterol	30 mg	0 mg
Sodium	550 mg	370 mg
Fiber	2 g	3 g

Do You Need to Eliminate Eggs?

Eggs suffer from an undeservedly bad reputation. Although egg yolks are high in cholesterol, they're relatively low in fat. And egg whites are fat- and cholesterol-free!

Judicious use of egg yolks can result in cholesterol-trimmed versions of your favorite foods that taste very similar to the original. In dishes calling for several eggs, use only one or two whole eggs and substitute egg whites for the remaining whole eggs. Sometimes you can replace all of the yolks with egg whites. Many baked goods can be made without any yolks, but most custards need some yolk for satisfactory results. (See Egg White Substitutions for Whole Eggs, below.) Cholesterol-free or reduced-cholesterol egg substitutes are available commercially, or you can make your own (see page 28).

EGG WHITE SUBSTITUTIONS FOR WHOLE EGGS*

Use	For
2 egg whites	1 whole egg
3 egg whites	2 whole eggs
5 egg whites	3 whole eggs
6 egg whites	4 whole eggs
8 egg whites	5 whole eggs
9 egg whites	6 whole eggs
11 egg whites	7 whole eggs
12 egg whites	8 whole eggs

* Based on whole large eggs, about ¼ cup each.

Egg Substitute

Combine egg and food color well before adding oil. One large egg equals about ¼ cup. Substitute the ½-cup recipe below for 2 whole eggs or ½ cup cholesterol-free egg product. Cover and refrigerate no longer than 2 days.

For ½ cup

3 egg whites
3 drops yellow food color
1 teaspoon vegetable oil

For 1 cup

6 egg whites
6 drops yellow food color
2 teaspoons vegetable oil

Mix egg whites and food color in small bowl. Mix in oil. Cover and refrigerate up to 2 days. *2 to 4 servings*

Per Serving: Calories 45; Protein 3 g; Carbohydrate 1 g; Sodium 80 mg; Fat 2 g; Unsaturated 2 g; Saturated 0 g; Cholesterol 0 mg.

Please Your Palate with Produce

Each season of the year brings a delightful variety of produce guaranteed to please discriminating palates as well as supply nutrients vital to healthy diets. Experiment with the "exotic" fruits and vegetables such as golden raspberries, passion fruit, chayote squash and Jerusalem artichokes that flood today's supermarkets; many stores provide printed materials to help you prepare these new items. Visit local farmers' markets and "pick-your-own" gardens and orchards to purchase produce fresh off the tree or out of the field at the best prices of the season. For great flavor year 'round, you can freeze, can or dry some of your favorite fruits and vegetables.

Take Advantage of Whole Grains

Packed with complex carbohydrates, B vitamins and iron, low-fat grain foods form the foundation of a healthy diet. The Food Guide Pyramid (page 14) recommends 6 to 11 servings daily of these satisfying foods and specifies that several servings should be *whole grain*.

Whole grains add delicious flavor, hearty texture and important dietary fiber to foods. To meet your daily requirement, try whole-grain cereals for breakfast, snacks—even dinner! Serve whole-grain breads and rolls, brown rice and whole-wheat pasta often. Combine brown rice or whole-wheat pasta with beans or peas for a low-fat, complete-protein alternative to meats. Add flavor, pleasing texture and extra nutrition to biscuits, muffins, breads and coffee cakes by substituting whole-wheat flour for half of the whole flour. (See Know Your Grains on page 64 for information about individual grains.)

Plan for Snacks

Most people can benefit from a snack now and then to boost their energy and help them through the day. Plan ahead to keep your snacks healthy. For instant snacking, keep a large container of plain nonfat yogurt on hand. Eat it plain, stir in fresh fruit or blend in a favorite fruit juice for a refreshing shake. For fast, crunchy satisfaction, keep cut-up-vegetables such as carrots, peppers, celery, cucumber, jícama or broccoli ready in the refrigerator. If you choose to dunk your vegetables, stir together nonfat plain yogurt and dill weed for an easy and tasty low-fat dip.

Delicious, high in fiber, low in calories and economical, popcorn is one of the best all-around snacks. Use "light" varieties of microwave popcorn, buy a microwave popper and pop without oil, or rely on a hot-air popper to keep fat and calories low. Add flavor by sprinkling on favorite herbs and spices. Try munching on breakfast cereal for a quick pick-me-up; most varieties are low in fat and packed with vitamins and minerals. Pretzels also rate high as a low-fat healthy snack. If you're concerned about sodium intake, look for low-sodium pretzels.

The Wonders of Water

While it may seem a trivial tip to planning healthy meals, getting enough water is absolutely essential to a healthy diet. We need about 64 fluid ounces of water daily, but that doesn't mean we have to drink eight 8-ounce glasses every day. The fluid in fruits and vegetables, soups, sauces and so forth helps meet our requirements for water. It's a good idea, however, to drink several glasses of water or other fluid each day to ensure you get enough. Because they have a diuretic—ultimately dehydrating—effect, don't include any caffeinated or alcoholic beverages you drink as part of your water quota.

STOCKING UP

Grocery shopping can be a pleasant experience when you follow these tips for smooth sailing through the supermarket.

Before You Shop

◆   Plan meals and make a grocery list. Stick to your list.

◆   Don't shop when you're hungry. Eat something nutritious, such as a banana or slice of whole-grain bread before you go shopping. Extra items have a way of sneaking into your cart when you are feeling hungry.

◆   Leave the kids at home if possible. Satisfying their demands may distract you from carefully selecting food, and their desires can result in a cart full of foods that aren't on your list.

While You Shop

◆   Read food labels. Knowledge is power, so becoming familiar with what labels tell you increases your awareness. Be sure you understand the label terminology. For example, "reduced-fat" does not necessarily mean that a product is low in fat; it's just that the food has less fat than the original product. New food labeling regulations are designed to clear up confusion about different terms. See Learning the Nutrition Facts on page 30. For more information, you can call the National Center for Nutrition and Dietetics at 1-800-366-1655, or call or write individual food companies.

◆   Study the ingredient list as you read food package labels. Ingredients are always listed in descending quantity. If the ingredient list on a can of baked beans reads "beans, water, brown sugar and salt," you know the can contains more beans than water, more water than brown sugar and more sugar than salt.

◆   When buying meat, look for lean cuts such as rounds and tenderloins. Many cuts of meat are now labeled with percentages of fat to help you choose the fat content you want.

◆   Purchase turkeys that are not self-basting. Select ground turkey breast or ground turkey labeled *lean*; if not so labeled, it may not be low in fat.

◆   Buy water-packed canned fish products, such as water-packed tuna or salmon, instead of products packed in oil.

◆   Select skim, nonfat or low-fat dairy products such as milk, yogurt, cheese and sour cream. Many of the new products on the market taste as good—or better—than the original!

◆   Opt for low-fat or reduced-calorie salad dressings. If you're watching sodium consumption, be aware that many reduced-fat dressings have added extra salt to compensate for the flavor lost with the removal of fat. Read the label to check the sodium content.

◆ Choose whole-grain versions of breads, cereals, crackers, muffins, English muffins, rice and pasta.

◆ Select healthy options when a busy schedule demands "convenience" foods. Canned beans are ready-to-serve and offer the same fiber and low-fat protein as their dried counterparts. If you like, rinse them to remove much of the sodium added in the canning process. Try stir-frying thinly-sliced turkey cutlets with ready-cut vegetables to produce a great-tasting meal in minutes. Select tomato products without added salt, or choose reduced-salt versions. Look for canned fruits packed in juice, or rinse fruit packed in heavy syrups.

Learning the Nutrition Facts

Nutrition Facts is the revised nutrition label that food manufacturers are required by law to use in order to tell us the nutritional content of foods. The hope is that this improved label will be more meaningful to everyone and will enable us to make better food choices. This new label should start appearing on food packaging in 1994.

Nutrition Facts provides much of the same information as the former label with changes in lay-out and in the emphasis on certain nutrients we want to know more about, namely total fat, calories from fat, and total carbohydrate (fiber and sugar). Nutrition Facts is listed for a serving of the food by itself (as packaged), as in dry cereal, and also may be listed for the food plus an added ingredient, such as cereal plus skim milk, or as prepared, since so many foods require us to cook or add other ingredients before we eat them.

Information about specific nutrients is provided in grams or milligrams per serving as packaged; as prepared information may be footnoted only. Percent Daily Value, listed for each nutrient, is a new measure of how a food stacks up when compared to an average diet of 2,000 calories per day and may be listed for the product as packaged and as prepared. Percent

Daily Value replaces the former Percent U.S. RDA for vitamins A and C, calcium and iron. The calories per gram for fat, carbohydrate and protein listed at the bottom of the label enable the reader to calculate the number of calories that come from each component.

NUTRITION FACTS		
Serving Size 1 cup (35g)		
Servings Per Container 10		
Amount Per Serving	**Cereal**	**Cereal with ½ cup Skim Milk**
Calories	130	170
Calories from Fat	0	0
		% Daily Value**
Total Fat 0g*	0%	0%
Saturated Fat 0g	0%	0%
Cholesterol 0mg	0%	0%
Sodium 200mg	8%	11%
Total Carbohydrate 30g	10%	12%
Dietary Fiber 4g	16%	16%
Sugars 18g		
Protein 3g		
Vitamin A	25%	25%
Vitamin C	25%	25%
Calcium	0%	15%
Iron	10%	10%

* Amount in Cereal. One half cup skim milk contributes an additional 40 calories, 65 mg sodium, 6g total carbohydrate (6g sugars), and 4g protein.

** Percent Daily Values are based on a 2,000 calorie diet. Your daily values may be higher or lower depending on your calorie needs:

	Calories:	2,000	2,500
Total Fat	Less than	65g	80g
Sat Fat	Less than	20 g	25 g
Cholesterol	Less than	300mg	300mg
Sodium	Less than	2,400mg	2,400mg
Total Carbohydrate		300g	375g
Dietary Fiber		25g	30g

Calories per gram:
Fat 9 · Carbohydrate 4 · Protein 4

Healthy Staples to Keep on Hand

Keep a plentiful supply of healthy staples in the house to be certain you have what you need when preparing meals. The list that follows contains items you will use frequently and that you can stock up on easily.

Herbs and Spices Dried or fresh (chopped and frozen), these are essentials for any healthy-cooking kitchen. Herbs and spices enhance foods and boost flavor without adding extra fat or salt. Stock your cabinets with basil, bay leaves, dill weed, oregano, garlic, ginger, red pepper sauce, ground red pepper, salt, chile powder, curry powder, pepper, cinnamon, nutmeg and cloves. Items such as garlic and oregano can be purchased pre-chopped or minced but must be refrigerated after opening.

Baking and Cooking Essentials Cornstarch, baking powder, baking soda, flour, rolled oats, raisins, vegetable oil(s) vinegar(s) and reduced-sodium soy sauce should be mainstays in any kitchen.

Whole Grains, Dried Beans and Pasta These items can be kept as staples because they remain edible indefinitely. For optimum flavor, store tightly sealed in a cool, dry place and use within one year of purchase.

Perishables Foods that will not last for long periods of time, but that you will probably use quite frequently include nonfat or low-fat yogurt, other dairy products, lemons, carrots, celery, onions and potatoes.

HEALTHY EATING OUT OF THE HOUSE AND ON THE ROAD

We all enjoy, and probably need, a break from preparing meals. With virtually 30 percent of calories and 40 percent of every food dollar spent on foods eaten away from home, knowing how to make healthy choices when eating out is vital.

At the Restaurant

Don't just depend on ambience; select restaurants according to what they offer in terms of dining options.

◆ Call in advance to find out if healthy menu items are available. Low-fat choices are often noted on the menu.

◆ Ask about the size of the portions. Ask whether special requests, such as food preparation without extra fat, are honored.

Once you're seated at the table with menu in hand, follow these guidelines to ensure a healthy meal.

◆ Just as at home, choose lean meats, fish and poultry without skin, and ask that they be prepared with a minimum of added fat. Most chefs are more than willing to broil, grill, bake, steam and poach foods at your request.

◆ Restaurants often serve large portions of meat. Ask if half portions or appetizer sizes are available. If not, order the item and plan to take some home for another meal.

◆ Vegetables are naturally low in fat, but the way they're prepared can quickly change their calorie content. Request plain vegetables; you can add butter or margarine at the table, if you wish. Choose baked potatoes instead of French fried potatoes or chips.

◆ Salad dressings and sauces may be requested "on the side," so you can decide how much you'd like to use. Just remember that the small dishes in which side items are served often hold much more than the amount a chef would normally add to the food. Beware: In examining plates after a meal, chefs report many diners end up eating *more* of the dressing or sauce than they would have if it had been served on the food.

◆ Desserts can be sweet, satisfying and slimmed down as well. Choose fruit desserts (look in the appetizer section of the menu, too). Sorbet, sherbet or nonfat frozen yogurt are great choices with less fat and fewer calories than ice cream. If you decide to indulge, split a richer treat with a friend, or eat only a few bites.

◆ There's a world of healthy beverages in restaurants. Nonalcoholic "mocktails" are increasingly common, and many restaurants offer nonalcoholic wines and beers along with juice-based nonalcoholic specials. Try flavored mineral waters or herbal teas for a flavor punch. Tap water is free and a great thirst-quencher! Have it spritzed with your favorite citrus juice or served with a twist of lemon or lime.

◆ Remember, if a meal is not prepared as you requested, feel free to send it back and have it made correctly.

Full-service restaurants provide the greatest variety and flexibility for the health-conscious diner. Foods are usually prepared to order, so you can request specific preparation with ease. Such orders may take somewhat longer to prepare, leaving you tempted to nibble while waiting. Munch on a whole-grain roll, without butter or margarine, or choose a tossed salad, easy on the dressing, to tide you over.

Cafeterias and buffets provide a wide variety of foods but many items may not be prepared as you prefer. Limit fried foods or those with heavy sauces, gravies and dressings. Some establishments allow you to choose your own portion size, so you can more easily control the amount you eat.

Fast-food restaurants usually offer a limited menu with many high-fat items. Choose lighter fare, such as salads or grilled chicken sandwiches and low-fat milk or juice as a beverage.

If ordering fried chicken, remove the skin before eating. If you crave a burger, order a "junior" size without the cheese and extra sauce. Order a small serving of frozen yogurt if you need to satisfy your sweet tooth.

Salad bars provide lots of options—some offer as many as fifteen or more choices. Concentrate on the plain fresh fruits and vegetables. Though prepared creamy salads, such as coleslaw, pasta and potato salads, and other combinations of higher-fat foods are available, help yourself to only a bite. Marinated vegetable salads can be a better choice if you drain off the oily marinade. Go easy on the cheese, bacon bits, nuts, hard-cooked eggs and croutons. And of course, choose the lower-fat salad dressings, or use a sprinkle of vinegar with a dash of pepper.

Other Adventures in Eating

If you travel by air, call the airline at least 24 hours in advance of your flight to request a special meal. Most airlines graciously accommodate passengers with special needs such as low-calorie, vegetarian and kosher meals. If you travel by car or bus, pack your own meals and snacks. By carrying your own foods, you can ensure you have healthy, well-balanced meals to enjoy. You can snack as you go or eat a sit-down meal during a rest stop.

IN THE END

As you can see, it's easy to blend creative, delicious foods with a healthy outlook. Keep it fun by experimenting with different foods and new ideas. Relax and take time to enjoy your food. Bon appetit—and good health!

Menus

Whether putting together a meal for yourself, family or friends, it's easy to plan fun and flavorful menus. As you can see, healthy menus fit all ages and lifestyles, and we've given you some ideas to help you begin planning healthy menus. As you become familiar with the recipes gathered here, you'll become adept at combining them in creative and delicious ways to plan any occasion.

PATIO PICNIC

Zucchini-Cilantro Dip (page 52)
Baked Pita Chips (page 44)
Strawberry-Lime Slush (page 58)
Hamburgers Ranchero (page 173)
Creamy Country Potato Salad (page 145)
Carrot Salad (page 135)
Mixed Summer Fruit Freeze (page 391)
Lemony Cornmeal Cookies (page 414)

TEEN NIGHT

Spicy Popcorn (page 42)
Chicken Calzones (page 263)
Creamy Slaw (page 136)
Banana-Peach Shake (page 57)
Chocolate-glazed Brownies (page 409)

BRIGHT MORNING BRUNCH

Honey-glazed Ruby Grapefruit (page 371)
Crunchy Oven French Toast (page 78)
Turkey Breakfast Sausage (page 249)
Orange-Cantaloupe Drink (page 59)
Blueberry–Whole Wheat Coffee Cake
(page 87)

CLUB LUNCHEON

Chilled Minted Melon Soup (page 43)
Curried Turkey and Rice Salad (page 254)
Sizzling Tomatoes (page 126)
Double-Oat Scones (page 73)
Ginger-Mint Tea Punch (page 60)
Berries with Warm Custard Sauce (page 369)

Meatless Asian Dinner

MEATLESS ASIAN DINNER

Asian Eggplant Spread (page 53)
Whole-grain crackers
Oriental Stew (page 318)
Ginger-glazed Carrots (page 116)
Oriental Daikon Salad (page 138)
Sesame Breadsticks (page 94)
Pineapple Ice (page 389)

ELEGANT DINNER FOR FOUR

Easy Tuna Spread (page 56)
Peppery Wheat Crackers (page 43)
Broiled Caribbean Swordfish (page 283)
Red Pepper Bows with Peas (page 127)
Tossed Salad with Apple Cider Dressing
(page 139)
Whole Wheat Baguette (page 100)
Baked Maple Apples (page 381)

COZY WINTER GET-TOGETHER

Hot Tomato Sipper (page 59)
Chicken-stuffed Mushrooms (page 50)
Garbanzo-Rice Chile (page 204)
Wintery Root-Vegetable Salad (page 139)
Winter Hearth Bread (page 102)
Lemon-topped Gingerbread (page 406)

APPETIZER BUFFET

Fiesta Dip (page 53)
Baked Tortilla Chips (page 44)
Chilled Artichokes with Basil Sauce
(page 37)
Ricotta Crostini (page 45)
Maple-glazed Chicken Kabobs (page 52)
Baby Carrot–Tarragon Pickles (page 39)
Savory Mini Scones (page 46)

2

Beverages and Appetizers

2

Beverages and Appetizers

Appetizers can set the stage for a meal, or sometimes even be the meal itself. They also make great snacks. Elegantly served at a dinner party as a first course or casually displayed for guests to help themselves, appetizers don't have to be full of calories and fat to be satisfying.

Healthy eating doesn't mean you have to forego your favorite creamy dips. Make them using the array of nonfat or low-fat dairy products on the market today; there are also several brands of cholesterol-free or reduced-calorie mayonnaises and salad dressings available. We've made just those kinds of substitutions with many of the recipes here.

Keep a supply of low-fat Baked Pita Chips (page 44) or Baked Tortilla Chips (page 44) on hand for when the munchies strike—you'll be less likely to grab for a bag of fried chips. Dip pita chips and tortilla chips in salsa or combine them with the exotic flavors of Asian Eggplant Spread (page 53) or Mideastern Garbanzo Spread (page 55). Purchase crackers that are low in fat or make Peppery Wheat Crackers (page 43).

Beverages are an important part of healthy eating and are often overlooked. Instead of drinking a diet soda, drink a fruit or vegetable beverage that provides vitamins and minerals in addition to fluids.

Preceding page: Mediterranean Mixed-Herb Pizza Wedges (page 46), Zucchini-Cilantro Dip (page 52);
Above: Healthy Snack Ideas—Fresh fruits and vegetables, raisins, popcorn, low-fat and multi-grain
crackers, rice cakes, whole-grain muffins, bagels, pretzels, whole-grain and multi-grain cereals, low-fat
chips with salsa, low-fat cheeses, low-fat yogurts, peanut butter and fruit juices.

Chilled Artichokes with Basil Sauce

The basil sauce is also great as a dip served directly after it is made. As it chills the dip thickens. After you remove the leaves from the artichokes, don't throw the artichokes out. Remove the fuzzy "chokes" and toss the hearts and bottoms into a salad.

¾ cup plain nonfat yogurt

½ cup fresh basil leaves

3 tablespoons balsamic vinegar

½ package (8-ounce size) light cream cheese (Neufchâtel)

1 cup chopped red bell pepper (about 1 medium)

2 large globe artichokes, steamed and chilled

Place all ingredients except bell pepper and artichokes in blender or food processor. Cover and blend until smooth. Remove from blender; stir in bell pepper. Cover and refrigerate 2 hours.

Remove leaves from artichokes; arrange leaves on serving platter. Place 1 teaspoon sauce on each leaf, or place bowl of dip in center of leaves. *8 servings*

NUTRITION INFORMATION PER SERVING

1 serving		Percent of U.S. RDA	
Calories	85	Protein	6%
Protein, g	4	Vitamin A	12%
Carbohydrate, g	8	Vitamin C	48%
Fat, g	4	Thiamin	2%
Unsaturated	2	Riboflavin	6%
Saturated	2	Niacin	2%
Dietary Fiber, g	2	Calcium	10%
Cholesterol, mg	10	Iron	6%
Sodium, mg	110		
Potassium, mg	290		

Caponata

Caponata is a Sicilian dish featuring tomatoes and eggplant. It can be enjoyed as a side dish, as well as an appetizer, served with whole-grain crackers or crisp bread sticks.

½ cup chopped onion (about 1 medium)

2 cloves garlic, crushed

1 tablespoon olive oil

7 cups chopped peeled eggplant (about 1½ large)

¾ cup chopped tomato (about 1 medium)

2 tablespoons chopped fresh or 2 teaspoons dried basil leaves

2 tablespoons red wine vinegar

¼ teaspoon salt

¼ teaspoon pepper

Cook onion and garlic in oil in 10-inch nonstick skillet over medium heat about 3 minutes, stirring occasionally, until onion is tender. Stir in eggplant and tomato. Cook uncovered 8 to 10 minutes, stirring frequently, until eggplant is very tender. Stir in remaining ingredients. Cover and refrigerate about 2 hours or until cool. *9 servings (about ⅓ cup each)*

NUTRITION INFORMATION PER SERVING

1 serving		Percent of U.S. RDA	
Calories	45	Protein	*
Protein, g	1	Vitamin A	2%
Carbohydrate, g	6	Vitamin C	4%
Fat, g	2	Thiamin	4%
Unsaturated	2	Riboflavin	*
Saturated	0	Niacin	2%
Dietary Fiber, g	1	Calcium	*
Cholesterol, mg	0	Iron	2%
Sodium, mg	65		
Potassium, mg	210		

Red Onion Salsa, Baked Tortilla Chips (page 44), Baby Carrot–Tarragon Pickles, Pineapple Limeade (page 60)

Red Onion Salsa

1½ cups finely chopped red onion (about 2 medium)

¾ cup finely chopped tomato (about 1 medium)

¼ cup chopped green onions (2 to 3 medium)

¼ cup lemon juice

2 tablespoons chopped fresh cilantro leaves

2 tablespoons balsamic vinegar

1 tablespoon olive or vegetable oil

1 teaspoon reduced-sodium soy sauce

¼ teaspoon ground red pepper (cayenne)

4 cloves garlic, finely chopped

Mix all ingredients in glass or plastic bowl. Cover and refrigerate at least 2 hours. *About 2 cups salsa*

NUTRITION INFORMATION PER SERVING			
1 tablespoon		**Percent of U.S. RDA**	
Calories	10	Protein	*
Protein, g	0	Vitamin A	*
Carbohydrate, g	1	Vitamin C	4%
Fat, g	1	Thiamin	*
Unsaturated	1	Riboflavin	*
Saturated	0	Niacin	*
Dietary Fiber, g	0	Calcium	*
Cholesterol, mg	0	Iron	*
Sodium, mg	10		
Potassium, mg	30		

Baby Carrot–Tarragon Pickles

1 package (16 ounces) baby-cut carrots
½ cup tarragon vinegar
1 tablespoon chopped fresh or 1 teaspoon
   dried tarragon leaves
1 tablespoon olive or vegetable oil
¼ teaspoon pepper

Heat 2 quarts water to boiling. Add carrots; cook 3 minutes. Meanwhile, mix remaining ingredients in large glass or plastic bowl. Drain carrots; immediately stir into mixture in bowl. Cover and refrigerate 24 hours, stirring once. *14 servings (¼ cup each)*

NUTRITION INFORMATION PER SERVING

1 serving		Percent of U.S. RDA	
Calories	25	Protein	*
Protein, g	0	Vitamin A	50%
Carbohydrate, g	4	Vitamin C	2%
Fat, g	1	Thiamin	2%
Unsaturated	1	Riboflavin	*
Saturated	0	Niacin	2%
Dietary Fiber, g	1	Calcium	*
Cholesterol, mg	0	Iron	*
Sodium, mg	10		
Potassium, mg	115		

Tarragon-stuffed Eggs

½ cup Egg Substitute (page 28) or
   cholesterol-free egg product
¼ cup finely chopped watercress or fresh
   spinach

2 tablespoons cholesterol-free
   reduced-calorie mayonnaise or salad
   dressing
2 teaspoons chopped shallot
½ teaspoon chopped fresh or ¼ teaspoon
   dried tarragon leaves
½ teaspoon white wine vinegar
⅛ teaspoon salt
Dash of pepper
4 hard-cooked eggs

Spray 8-inch nonstick skillet with nonstick cooking spray. Heat over medium-high heat. Pour Egg Substitute into skillet. As mixture begins to set at bottom and side, gently lift cooked portions with spatula so that thin, un-cooked portion can flow to bottom. Avoid con-stant stirring. Cook 1 to 2 minutes or until thickened throughout but still moist; cool.

Mash cooked Egg Substitute with fork. Stir in remaining ingredients except hard-cooked eggs. Cut eggs lengthwise into halves; discard yolks. Fill whites with Egg Substitute mixture, mounding lightly. Place on serving plate. Cover and refrigerate up to 24 hours. Garnish with thinly sliced ripe olives if desired. *4 servings*

NUTRITION INFORMATION PER SERVING

1 serving		Percent of U.S. RDA	
Calories	50	Protein	14%
Protein, g	6	Vitamin A	2%
Carbohydrate, g	2	Vitamin C	*
Fat, g	2	Thiamin	2%
Unsaturated	2	Riboflavin	16%
Saturated	0	Niacin	*
Dietary Fiber, g	0	Calcium	2%
Cholesterol, mg	0	Iron	2%
Sodium, mg	220		
Potassium, mg	95		

Red Pepper and Salmon Fingers

This salmon is also nice served with radishes and small Roma or cherry tomatoes.

Red Pepper Dipping Sauce (right)
1½ pounds fresh skin-on salmon fillet, cut into 1-inch strips
2 cups apple juice
1 medium red bell pepper, cut into 12 strips

Prepare Red Pepper Dipping Sauce. Heat salmon and apple juice to boiling in 12-inch skillet; reduce heat to medium-low. Cover and cook 2 minutes; remove from heat. Let stand covered 5 minutes. Uncover and let stand until cool enough to handle. Carefully remove skin from salmon without breaking salmon strips. Cover and refrigerate about 2 hours or until chilled. Serve salmon and bell pepper strips with dipping sauce. *12 servings*

Red Pepper Dipping Sauce

1 medium red bell pepper, roasted (page 41)
¾ cup nonfat cottage cheese
2 tablespoons lime juice
2 tablespoons chopped fresh chives

Cut bell pepper into pieces. Place all ingredients except chives in blender or food processor. Cover and blend about 30 seconds or until smooth; remove from blender. Stir in chives. Cover and refrigerate until serving time.

NUTRITION INFORMATION PER SERVING

1 serving		Percent of U.S. RDA	
Calories	115	Protein	22%
Protein, g	14	Vitamin A	8%
Carbohydrate, g	6	Vitamin C	42%
Fat, g	4	Thiamin	6%
Unsaturated	3	Riboflavin	6%
Saturated	1	Niacin	18%
Dietary Fiber, g	0	Calcium	2%
Cholesterol, mg	20	Iron	4%
Sodium, mg	85		
Potassium, mg	320		

Red Pepper and Salmon Fingers, Double-Bean Terrine

Double-Bean Terrine

Serve this terrine in slices, each one topped with a dab of Sun-dried Tomato Dip (page 54), if you like. The slices may be cut in half and served on crackers or cocktail bread too.

2 cups cooked 1-inch pieces green beans
(about 11 ounces) or 1 package (9
ounces) frozen cut green beans, cooked
and drained

½ cup chopped green onions (about 5
medium)

1 tablespoon chopped fresh or 1 teaspoon
dried dill weed

1 tablespoon chopped fresh or 1 teaspoon
dried basil leaves

¼ teaspoon salt

¾ cup chicken broth

1¼ cups cholesterol-free egg product

2 cloves garlic, finely chopped

½ teaspoon ground sage leaves

1 teaspoon fresh or ½ teaspoon dried
rosemary leaves, crushed

¼ teaspoon pepper

1 can (about 15 ounces) white beans
(cannellini, great northern or navy),
rinsed and drained

2 medium red Roasted Bell Peppers (right)
or canned peppers, drained

1 cup nonfat ricotta cheese

⅛ teaspoon ground red pepper (cayenne)

Heat oven to 350°. Spray loaf pan, 9×5×3 inches, with nonstick cooking spray. Cook green beans, green onions, dill weed, basil, salt and ¼ cup of the broth in 12-inch skillet over medium heat about 3 minutes or until liquid has evaporated. Place green bean mixture and ½ cup of the egg product in blender or food processor. Cover and blend about 30 seconds or until smooth. Pour into pan.

Cook half of the garlic, the sage, rosemary, pepper, white beans and ¼ cup of the broth in same skillet 3 to 5 minutes or until liquid has evaporated. Place white bean mixture and ½ cup of the egg product in blender. Cover and blend about 30 seconds or until smooth. Spoon over green bean mixture.

Cut bell peppers into pieces. Place remaining garlic, broth and egg product and remaining ingredients in blender. Cover and blend about 30 seconds or until smooth. Pour over white bean mixture. Bake uncovered about 1¼ hours or until toothpick inserted in center comes out clean. Cool 15 minutes. Cover and refrigerate 4 hours; unmold. Cut into thin slices. *16 servings*

Roasted Bell Peppers

Set oven control to broil. Cut slit in each pepper. Broil peppers with tops about 5 inches from heat 12 to 15 minutes, turning occasionally, until skin is blistered and evenly browned (not burned). Place peppers in plastic bag and close tightly; let stand 20 minutes. Remove skin, stems, seeds and membranes from peppers.

NUTRITION INFORMATION PER SERVING			
1 serving		Percent of U.S. RDA	
Calories	75	Protein	10%
Protein, g	7	Vitamin A	8%
Carbohydrate, g	10	Vitamin C	16%
Fat, g	1	Thiamin	4%
Unsaturated	0	Riboflavin	8%
Saturated	1	Niacin	2%
Dietary Fiber, g	2	Calcium	8%
Cholesterol, mg	5	Iron	10%
Sodium, mg	200		
Potassium, mg	260		

Spicy Popcorn, Fresh Fruit Frappé (page 57)

Spicy Popcorn

1 tablespoon water
4 teaspoons margarine
1 teaspoon ground cinnamon
1 teaspoon ground turmeric
½ teaspoon salt
¼ teaspoon white pepper
⅛ teaspoon ground red pepper (cayenne)
10 cups unsalted hot air–popped popcorn

Cook all ingredients except popcorn in 6-inch nonstick skillet 3 minutes or until margarine is melted and mixture is bubbly. Pour over popcorn; toss. Serve immediately. *10 cups*

NUTRITION INFORMATION PER SERVING			
1 cup		Percent of U.S. RDA	
Calories	45	Protein	2%
Protein, g	1	Vitamin A	2%
Carbohydrate, g	6	Vitamin C	*
Fat, g	2	Thiamin	2%
Unsaturated	2	Riboflavin	*
Saturated	0	Niacin	*
Dietary Fiber, g	1	Calcium	*
Cholesterol, mg	0	Iron	2%
Sodium, mg	125		
Potassium, mg	25		

Chilled Minted Melon Soup

½ cup water

3 tablespoons honey

1 tablespoon coarsely chopped or ¼
   teaspoon dried mint leaves

½ medium honeydew melon (about
   5-pound size), peeled and cut into 1-inch
   pieces

2 tablespoons lime juice

½ cup low-fat milk

Heat water, honey and mint to boiling; remove
from heat. Let stand 5 minutes.

Pour honey mixture into blender or food processor; add melon and lime juice. Cover and
blend until smooth. Pour into medium glass or
plastic bowl or pitcher; stir in milk. Cover and
refrigerate about 3 hours or until chilled. Stir
before serving. Garnish with additional mint
leaves if desired. *6 servings*

NUTRITION INFORMATION PER SERVING

I serving		Percent of U.S. RDA	
Calories	95	Protein	2%
Protein, g	I	Vitamin A	2%
Carbohydrate, g	20	Vitamin C	46%
Fat, g	I	Thiamin	6%
Unsaturated	I	Riboflavin	2%
Saturated	0	Niacin	4%
Dietary Fiber, g	I	Calcium	2%
Cholesterol, mg	2	Iron	*
Sodium, mg	20		
Potassium, mg	330		

Peppery Wheat Crackers

¾ cup all-purpose flour

¾ cup whole wheat flour

1½ teaspoons sugar

½ teaspoon baking soda

½ teaspoon salt

½ cup nonfat buttermilk

2 tablespoons vegetable oil

2 tablespoons margarine, melted

Coarsely ground black pepper

Chopped fresh or dried dill weed

Heat oven to 350°. Mix flours, sugar, baking
soda and salt. Stir in buttermilk and oil. Shape
dough into 6 balls. Roll each ball into 9-inch
square on lightly floured cloth-covered surface.
Cut into 2¼-inch squares; brush lightly with
margarine. Place squares on ungreased cookie
sheet. Sprinkle with pepper and dill weed. Bake
8 to 10 minutes or until crisp and golden brown.
12 servings (4 crackers each).

NUTRITION INFORMATION PER SERVING

I serving		Percent of U.S. RDA	
Calories	90	Protein	2%
Protein, g	2	Vitamin A	2%
Carbohydrate, g	12	Vitamin C	*
Fat, g	4	Thiamin	6%
Unsaturated	3	Riboflavin	4%
Saturated	I	Niacin	4%
Dietary Fiber, g	I	Calcium	2%
Cholesterol, mg	0	Iron	4%
Sodium, mg	160		
Potassium, mg	55		

Baked Pita Chips

4 whole wheat pita breads (6 inches in diameter)

Heat oven to 400°. Cut around outside edges of pita breads to separate layers. Cut each layer into 8 wedges. Place in single layer on 2 ungreased cookie sheets. Bake about 9 minutes or until crisp and light brown; cool. *8 servings (8 chips each)*

NUTRITION INFORMATION PER SERVING

I serving		Percent of U.S. RDA	
Calories	115	Protein	6%
Protein, g	4	Vitamin A	*
Carbohydrate, g	23	Vitamin C	*
Fat, g	1	Thiamin	12%
Unsaturated	1	Riboflavin	4%
Saturated	0	Niacin	8%
Dietary Fiber, g	3	Calcium	2%
Cholesterol, mg	0	Iron	6%
Sodium, mg	240		
Potassium, mg	50		

Southwestern Popcorn Snack

6 cups unsalted hot air–popped popcorn
2 cups whole grain toasted oat cereal
2 tablespoons margarine
½ teaspoon chile powder
¼ teaspoon ground cumin
¼ teaspoon garlic powder
2 tablespoons grated Parmesan cheese

Mix popcorn and cereal in large bowl. Heat margarine, chile powder, cumin and garlic

powder until margarine is melted. Drizzle over popcorn mixture; toss. Immediately sprinkle with cheese; toss. Serve warm. *8 cups*

NUTRITION INFORMATION PER SERVING

I cup		Percent of U.S. RDA	
Calories	80	Protein	2%
Protein, g	2	Vitamin A	12%
Carbohydrate, g	9	Vitamin C	2%
Fat, g	4	Thiamin	6%
Unsaturated	3	Riboflavin	6%
Saturated	1	Niacin	6%
Dietary Fiber, g	1	Calcium	2%
Cholesterol, mg	0	Iron	10%
Sodium, mg	120		
Potassium, mg	40		

Baked Tortilla Chips

1 package (6 ounces) stone-ground corn tortillas

Heat oven to 450°. Spray 2 cookie sheets with nonstick cooking spray. Cut each tortilla into 8 wedges. Place in single layer on cookie sheets. Bake about 6 minutes or until crisp but not brown; cool. *8 servings (9 chips each)*

NUTRITION INFORMATION PER SERVING

I serving		Percent of U.S. RDA	
Calories	50	Protein	2%
Protein, g	1	Vitamin A	*
Carbohydrate, g	9	Vitamin C	*
Fat, g	1	Thiamin	2%
Unsaturated	1	Riboflavin	*
Saturated	0	Niacin	*
Dietary Fiber, g	1	Calcium	4%
Cholesterol, mg	0	Iron	2%
Sodium, mg	40		
Potassium, mg	35		

Ricotta Crostini (right), *Savory Mini Scones* (left) *(page 46), Hot Tomato Sipper (page 59)*

Ricotta Crostini

Ricotta Filling (below)
3 slices turkey bacon, cooked and chopped
24 slices day-old French bread, ¼ inch
  thick
¼ cup grated Parmesan cheese

Set oven control to broil. Mix Ricotta Filling and bacon. Spread about 1 tablespoon ricotta mixture on each bread slice. Sprinkle ½ teaspoon cheese on each. Broil with tops about 6 inches from heat about 3 minutes or until bubbly. Serve hot. *8 servings (3 slices each)*

Ricotta Filling

1 cup dry bread crumbs
1 cup nonfat ricotta cheese
2 egg whites or ¼ cup cholesterol-free egg
  product

3 tablespoons chopped fresh or 1
  tablespoon dried basil leaves
½ teaspoon salt
¼ teaspoon pepper
1 clove garlic, finely chopped

Mix all ingredients.

NUTRITION INFORMATION PER SERVING			
1 serving		**Percent of U.S. RDA**	
Calories	240	Protein	18%
Protein, g	12	Vitamin A	4%
Carbohydrate, g	37	Vitamin C	*
Fat, g	5	Thiamin	6%
Unsaturated	2	Riboflavin	10%
Saturated	3	Niacin	14%
Dietary Fiber, g	2	Calcium	18%
Cholesterol, mg	15	Iron	12%
Sodium, mg	660		
Potassium, mg	140		

Savory Mini Scones

2½ cups all-purpose flour

½ cup shredded reduced-fat Cheddar cheese

¼ cup chopped green onions (2 to 3 medium)

3 tablespoons chopped fresh cilantro leaves

2 teaspoons baking powder

¾ teaspoon baking soda

½ teaspoon salt

¼ teaspoon ground red pepper (cayenne)

¼ cup (½ stick) margarine

½ cup apple juice

⅓ cup plain nonfat yogurt

2 egg whites

2 tablespoons plain nonfat yogurt

Heat oven to 400°. Spray 2 cookie sheets with nonstick cooking spray. Mix flour, cheese, onions, cilantro, baking powder, baking soda, salt and red pepper in large bowl. Cut in margarine with pastry blender until mixture resembles fine crumbs. Mix apple juice, ⅓ cup yogurt and the egg whites; stir into flour mixture until dough leaves side of bowl.

Turn dough onto lightly floured surface; gently roll in flour to coat. Knead about 1 minute or until smooth. Divide dough in half. Pat each half directly on cookie sheet into 9-inch circle. Cut each circle into 12 wedges with floured knife, but do not separate. Brush 1 tablespoon yogurt over each circle. Bake 15 to 17 minutes or until golden brown. Remove from cookie sheets to wire rack. Serve warm. *12 servings (2 scones each)*

NUTRITION INFORMATION PER SERVING			
1 serving		**Percent of U.S. RDA**	
Calories	155	Protein	8%
Protein, g	5	Vitamin A	6%
Carbohydrate, g	22	Vitamin C	*
Fat, g	5	Thiamin	14%
Unsaturated	4	Riboflavin	12%
Saturated	1	Niacin	8%
Dietary Fiber, g	1	Calcium	10%
Cholesterol, mg	2	Iron	8%
Sodium, mg	290		
Potassium, mg	90		

Mediterranean Mixed-Herb Pizza Wedges

Herbed Pizza Crust (page 108)

Mixed-Herb Pesto Sauce (right)

½ cup crumbled feta cheese (about 4 ounces)

12 cherry tomatoes, cut into halves

½ cup finely chopped red onion (about ½ medium)

¼ cup finely chopped ripe olives

Prepare Herbed Pizza Crust—except do not roll into circle. Prepare Mixed-Herb Pesto Sauce. Heat oven to 425°. Spray 2 cookie sheets with nonstick cooking spray. Divide dough into 4 pieces. Roll each piece into 7-inch circle on lightly floured surface. Place on cookie sheets.

Spread 2 tablespoons pesto sauce over each circle. Divide cheese, tomatoes, onion and olives evenly among pizzas. Cut each pizza into 6 wedges. Bake 10 to 12 minutes or until dough is golden brown. Serve warm. *12 servings (2 wedges each)*

Mixed-Herb Pesto Sauce

½ cup packed fresh basil leaves
½ cup packed fresh mint leaves
½ cup chopped green onions (about 5 medium)
¼ cup nonfat cottage cheese
1 tablespoon olive or vegetable oil
1 tablespoon lemon juice
2 cloves garlic, finely chopped

Place all ingredients in blender or food processor. Cover and blend until smooth.

SPINACH-PESTO PIZZA WEDGES: Substitute ½ cup packed fresh spinach for the mint leaves.

Bell Pepper Nachos

½ green bell pepper, seeded and cut into 6 strips
½ red bell pepper, seeded and cut into 6 strips
½ yellow bell pepper, seeded and cut into 6 strips
¾ cup shredded reduced-fat Monterey Jack cheese
2 tablespoons chopped ripe olives
¼ teaspoon crushed red pepper

Cut bell pepper strips crosswise into halves. Arrange close together in ungreased broiler-proof pie pan, 9×1¼ inches, or round pan, 9×1½ inches. Sprinkle with cheese, olives and red pepper.

Set oven control to broil. Broil peppers with tops 3 to 4 inches from heat about 3 minutes or until cheese is melted. *6 servings (6 nachos each)*

NUTRITION INFORMATION PER SERVING			
1 serving		Percent of U.S. RDA	
Calories	175	Protein	8%
Protein, g	6	Vitamin A	4%
Carbohydrate, g	26	Vitamin C	8%
Fat, g	5	Thiamin	16%
Unsaturated	3	Riboflavin	14%
Saturated	2	Niacin	12%
Dietary Fiber, g	3	Calcium	8%
Cholesterol, mg	5	Iron	14%
Sodium, mg	180		
Potassium, mg	260		

NUTRITION INFORMATION PER SERVING			
1 serving		Percent of U.S. RDA	
Calories	50	Protein	6%
Protein, g	4	Vitamin A	10%
Carbohydrate, g	2	Vitamin C	24%
Fat, g	3	Thiamin	*
Unsaturated	1	Riboflavin	2%
Saturated	2	Niacin	*
Dietary Fiber, g	0	Calcium	10%
Cholesterol, mg	10	Iron	*
Sodium, mg	100		
Potassium, mg	50		

Creamy Onion Tartlets

To make quick work of chopping the onions use your food processor. The filling can be made up to 3 days in advance and stored, covered, in the refrigerator. Take care with the tartlets, as they are fragile; fill them just before baking.

Phyllo Tartlets (page 403)
8 cups chopped onions (about 4 pounds)
1 cup beef broth
¼ teaspoon pepper
2 slices turkey bacon, cooked and chopped
6 tablespoons grated Parmesan cheese

Prepare Phyllo Tartlets. Cook remaining ingredients except cheese in 10-inch nonstick skillet over medium heat 20 minutes; reduce heat to medium-low. Cook uncovered 50 minutes, stirring occasionally, until all liquid is absorbed and onions are consistency of marmalade.

Heat oven to 400°. Fill each tartlet with 2 teaspoons onion mixture. Place on ungreased cookie sheet. Sprinkle each tartlet with ½ teaspoon cheese. Bake 6 to 8 minutes or until cheese is light brown. Serve hot. *12 servings (3 tartlets each)*

NUTRITION INFORMATION PER SERVING			
1 serving		**Percent of U.S. RDA**	
Calories	90	Protein	4%
Protein, g	3	Vitamin A	2%
Carbohydrate, g	13	Vitamin C	6%
Fat, g	3	Thiamin	4%
Unsaturated	2	Riboflavin	2%
Saturated	1	Niacin	2%
Dietary Fiber, g	2	Calcium	6%
Cholesterol, mg	2	Iron	2%
Sodium, mg	140		
Potassium, mg	200		

Hot and Peppery Cocktail Shrimp

1½ pounds peeled and deveined raw medium shrimp (about 65)
¼ cup chopped green onions (2 to 3 medium)
¼ cup lime juice
1 tablespoon reduced-sodium soy sauce
2 teaspoons grated lime peel
¼ teaspoon pepper
⅛ teaspoon crushed red pepper
2 cloves garlic, finely chopped
2 teaspoons sesame oil

Mix all ingredients except oil in large glass or plastic bowl. Cover and refrigerate 4 hours.

Heat oven to 400°. Spray rectangular pan, 13×9×2 inches, with nonstick cooking spray. Arrange shrimp in single layer in pan. Bake 10 to 12 minutes or until shrimp are pink. Drizzle with oil. Serve hot with toothpicks. *12 servings (about 5 shrimp each)*

NUTRITION INFORMATION PER SERVING			
1 serving		**Percent of U.S. RDA**	
Calories	50	Protein	14%
Protein, g	9	Vitamin A	2%
Carbohydrate, g	1	Vitamin C	2%
Fat, g	1	Thiamin	*
Unsaturated	1	Riboflavin	*
Saturated	0	Niacin	6%
Dietary Fiber, g	0	Calcium	2%
Cholesterol, mg	80	Iron	8%
Sodium, mg	140		
Potassium, mg	90		

Hot and Peppery Cocktail Shrimp, Creamy Onion Tartlets

Smoked Fish Frittata

½ cup chopped red onion (about ½ medium)

¼ cup chicken broth

1 tablespoon chopped fresh or 1 teaspoon dried tarragon leaves

¼ teaspoon pepper

2 egg whites

1 container (8 ounces) cholesterol-free egg product

⅓ cup shredded smoked whitefish (about 2 ounces)

¼ cup shredded reduced-fat Monterey Jack cheese

Spray 12-inch ovenproof skillet with nonstick cooking spray. Cook onion, broth, tarragon and pepper in skillet over medium heat about 3 minutes or until broth has evaporated. Mix egg whites and egg product; pour into skillet. Cook, stirring occasionally, until eggs are firm around edges.

Set oven control to broil. Sprinkle fish and cheese over frittata. Broil 3 inches from heat 1 to 2 minutes or until brown. Cool slightly. Carefully slide frittata onto plate. Cool 10 minutes. Cut into wedges. *8 servings*

NUTRITION INFORMATION PER SERVING

1 serving		Percent of U.S. RDA	
Calories	45	Protein	10%
Protein, g	7	Vitamin A	2%
Carbohydrate, g	2	Vitamin C	*
Fat, g	1	Thiamin	2%
Unsaturated	0	Riboflavin	10%
Saturated	1	Niacin	2%
Dietary Fiber, g	0	Calcium	4%
Cholesterol, mg	5	Iron	4%
Sodium, mg	120		
Potassium, mg	120		

Chicken-stuffed Mushrooms

¼ cup chopped onion (about 1 small)

2 tablespoons chopped fresh cilantro leaves

3 tablespoons cholesterol-free egg product or egg white

1 tablespoon Dijon mustard

1½ teaspoons finely chopped gingerroot

2 teaspoons reduced-sodium soy sauce

1 clove garlic, finely chopped

½ pound ground chicken

12 large mushrooms, stems removed

Heat oven to 450°. Spray cookie sheet with nonstick cooking spray. Mix all ingredients except mushrooms. Fill mushroom caps with chicken mixture. Place mushrooms, filled sides up, on cookie sheet. Bake 7 to 10 minutes or until tops are light brown and chicken mixture is done. Serve hot. *12 mushrooms*

NUTRITION INFORMATION PER SERVING

1 mushroom		Percent of U.S. RDA	
Calories	35	Protein	8%
Protein, g	5	Vitamin A	*
Carbohydrate, g	2	Vitamin C	*
Fat, g	1	Thiamin	2%
Unsaturated	1	Riboflavin	8%
Saturated	0	Niacin	10%
Dietary Fiber, g	0	Calcium	*
Cholesterol, mg	10	Iron	4%
Sodium, mg	70		
Potassium, mg	140		

Chicken Pot Stickers

1½ pounds ground chicken

½ cup finely chopped red bell pepper (about 1 small)

½ cup shredded green cabbage

⅓ cup chopped green onions (about 3 medium)

2 teaspoons chopped gingerroot

1 teaspoon sesame oil

¼ teaspoon white pepper

1 egg white

1 package (10 ounces) round wonton skins

2 cups chicken broth

4 teaspoons reduced-sodium soy sauce

Mix all ingredients except wonton skins, broth and soy sauce. Brush each wonton skin with water. Place 1 scant tablespoon chicken mixture on center of skin. Pinch 5 pleats on edge of one half of circle. Fold circle in half over chicken mixture, pressing pleated edge to unpleated edge. Repeat with remaining skins and chicken mixture.

Spray 12-inch skillet with nonstick cooking spray. Heat over medium heat. Cook 12 pot stickers at a time in skillet 3 minutes or until light brown; turn. Stir in ½ cup of the broth and 1 teaspoon of the soy sauce. Cover and cook 5 minutes. Uncover and cook 1 minute longer or until liquid has evaporated. Repeat with remaining pot stickers, broth and soy sauce. *16 servings (3 pot stickers each)*

NUTRITION INFORMATION PER SERVING

1 serving		Percent of U.S. RDA	
Calories	125	Protein	16%
Protein, g	11	Vitamin A	2%
Carbohydrate, g	11	Vitamin C	6%
Fat, g	4	Thiamin	6%
Unsaturated	3	Riboflavin	6%
Saturated	1	Niacin	16%
Dietary Fiber, g	0	Calcium	2%
Cholesterol, mg	25	Iron	6%
Sodium, mg	240		
Potassium, mg	150		

Chicken Pot Stickers

Maple-glazed Chicken Kabobs

3 tablespoons reduced-calorie maple-flavored syrup

2 tablespoons lemon juice

1 tablespoon margarine, melted

1½ teaspoons chopped fresh or ½ teaspoon ground sage leaves

1 teaspoon grated lemon peel

¼ teaspoon pepper

1 yellow squash, cut lengthwise into halves, then cut crosswise into 16 pieces

1 bell pepper, cut into 16 pieces

8 ounces skinless boneless chicken breast, cut into 24 pieces

Mix all ingredients. Cover and refrigerate 4 hours.

Set oven control to broil. Thread chicken, squash and bell pepper alternately on each of eight 8-inch skewers. If using bamboo skewers, soak skewers in water at least 30 minutes before using to prevent burning. Broil 4 inches from heat 2 to 3 minutes; turn. Broil 2 to 3 minutes longer or until chicken is white. *8 kabobs*

NUTRITION INFORMATION PER SERVING

1 kabob		Percent of U.S. RDA	
Calories	60	Protein	14%
Protein, g	6	Vitamin A	2%
Carbohydrate, g	4	Vitamin C	8%
Fat, g	2	Thiamin	2%
Unsaturated	1	Riboflavin	2%
Saturated	1	Niacin	10%
Dietary Fiber, g	0	Calcium	*
Cholesterol, mg	15	Iron	2%
Sodium, mg	45		
Potassium, mg	140		

Zucchini-Cilantro Dip

Zucchini, nonfat cottage cheese and cilantro combine for a fresh-tasting dip that's equally delicious with vegetables and low-fat chips. Try vegetables such as jícama sticks, celery sticks, zucchini sticks and pea pods.

1½ cups shredded zucchini (about 2 small)

1 cup nonfat cottage cheese

¼ cup chopped green onions (2 to 3 medium)

2 tablespoons chopped fresh cilantro leaves

2 tablespoons lemon juice

¼ teaspoon pepper

1 clove garlic, finely chopped

Place ¾ cup of the zucchini and the remaining ingredients in blender or food processor. Cover and blend until smooth. Remove from blender; stir in remaining zucchini. Cover and refrigerate 4 hours. *About 2 cups dip*

NUTRITION INFORMATION PER SERVING

1 tablespoon		Percent of U.S. RDA	
Calories	10	Protein	2%
Protein, g	1	Vitamin A	*
Carbohydrate, g	1	Vitamin C	2%
Fat, g	0	Thiamin	*
Unsaturated	0	Riboflavin	*
Saturated	0	Niacin	*
Dietary Fiber, g	0	Calcium	*
Cholesterol, mg	0	Iron	*
Sodium, mg	30		
Potassium, mg	25		

Asian Eggplant Spread

An incredible fat-free spread that is still satisfying and tempting. If you'd like a smoother consistency for a dip, process spread in a food processor until smooth. This is a wonderful companion to Baked Pita Chips (page 44).

1 eggplant (about 1 pound)
⅓ cup finely chopped red onion (about ½ small)
⅓ cup chicken broth
2 tablespoons chopped fresh cilantro leaves
2 tablespoons frozen (thawed) apple juice concentrate
1 teaspoon finely chopped gingerroot
2 teaspoons reduced-sodium soy sauce
2 teaspoons cider vinegar
⅛ teaspoon crushed red pepper
1 clove garlic, finely chopped

Heat oven to 400°. Place eggplant on ungreased cookie sheet; pierce with fork. Bake about 40 minutes or until tender. Let stand until cool enough to handle. Cut eggplant into halves. Scrape out pulp; chop coarsely. Cook eggplant and remaining ingredients in 8-inch nonstick skillet over medium heat 5 minutes, stirring constantly, until liquid has evaporated. Cover and refrigerate 4 hours. *About 1½ cups spread*

NUTRITION INFORMATION PER SERVING

1 tablespoon		Percent of U.S. RDA	
Calories	10	Protein	*
Protein, g	0	Vitamin A	*
Carbohydrate, g	2	Vitamin C	*
Fat, g	0	Thiamin	*
Unsaturated	0	Riboflavin	*
Saturated	0	Niacin	*
Dietary Fiber, g	0	Calcium	*
Cholesterol, mg	0	Iron	*
Sodium, mg	30		
Potassium, mg	75		

Fiesta Dip

Great with chips or vegetables, this south-of-the-border-based sauce thickens as it chills. To use as a sauce for nachos, pour warm dip over a platter of Baked Tortilla Chips (page 44).

1 cup chopped tomato (about 1 large)
⅓ cup chopped red onion (about ½ small)
¼ cup white wine or apple juice
⅛ teaspoon crushed red pepper
½ package (8-ounce size) light cream cheese (Neufchâtel), cubed
4 ounces reduced-fat Muenster cheese, cubed
2 tablespoons chopped fresh cilantro leaves

Cook all ingredients except cilantro in 1-quart saucepan over medium-low heat 10 minutes, stirring occasionally, until cheese is melted and mixture is creamy. Stir in cilantro. Serve warm or cold. *About 2 cups dip*

NUTRITION INFORMATION PER SERVING

1 tablespoon		Percent of U.S. RDA	
Calories	15	Protein	2%
Protein, g	1	Vitamin A	2%
Carbohydrate, g	1	Vitamin C	*
Fat, g	1	Thiamin	*
Unsaturated	0	Riboflavin	*
Saturated	1	Niacin	*
Dietary Fiber, g	0	Calcium	2%
Cholesterol, mg	5	Iron	*
Sodium, mg	35		
Potassium, mg	25		

Cucumber-Dill Mousse

1 envelope unflavored gelatin
¼ cup white wine or apple juice
2½ cups finely chopped seeded peeled
   cucumbers (about 2½ medium)
½ cup nonfat buttermilk
½ cup chicken broth
¼ cup lime juice
⅓ cup chopped green onions (about 3
   medium)
¼ cup cholesterol-free reduced-calorie
   mayonnaise or salad dressing
1 tablespoon chopped fresh or 1 teaspoon
   dried dill weed
¼ teaspoon white pepper

Spray 4-cup mold or bowl with nonstick cooking spray. Sprinkle gelatin on wine in 1-quart saucepan to soften. Heat over medium heat about 2 minutes, stirring constantly, until gelatin is dissolved. Place 2 cups of the cucumbers and the remaining ingredients in blender or food processor. Cover and blend until smooth. Add gelatin mixture; blend 5 seconds.

Pour into mold. Stir in remaining cucumber. Cover and refrigerate about 4 hours or until firm; unmold. *About 3½ cups mousse*

NUTRITION INFORMATION PER SERVING

1 tablespoon		Percent of U.S. RDA	
Calories	10	Protein	*
Protein, g	0	Vitamin A	*
Carbohydrate, g	1	Vitamin C	*
Fat, g	1	Thiamin	*
Unsaturated	1	Riboflavin	*
Saturated	0	Niacin	*
Dietary Fiber, g	0	Calcium	*
Cholesterol, mg	0	Iron	*
Sodium, mg	15		
Potassium, mg	15		

Sun-dried Tomato Dip

8 sun-dried tomato halves (not oil-packed)
¼ cup chopped fresh parsley
1 tablespoon chopped fresh or 1 teaspoon
   freeze-dried chives
1 tablespoon olive or vegetable oil
2 teaspoons lemon juice
1 teaspoon red wine vinegar
½ teaspoon salt
½ teaspoon pepper
1 clove garlic, finely chopped
¾ cup plain nonfat yogurt
¾ cup low-fat sour cream

Heat tomato halves in 1 inch water to boiling; reduce heat to medium. Simmer uncovered about 5 minutes or until water has evaporated. Place tomatoes and remaining ingredients except yogurt and sour cream in blender or food processor. Cover and blend until smooth. Pour tomato mixture into medium glass or plastic bowl. Stir in yogurt and sour cream. Cover and refrigerate about 2 hours or until chilled. *About 2¼ cups dip*

NUTRITION INFORMATION PER SERVING

1 tablespoon		Percent of U.S. RDA	
Calories	15	Protein	*
Protein, g	0	Vitamin A	*
Carbohydrate, g	1	Vitamin C	*
Fat, g	1	Thiamin	*
Unsaturated	1	Riboflavin	2%
Saturated	0	Niacin	*
Dietary Fiber, g	0	Calcium	2%
Cholesterol, mg	2	Iron	*
Sodium, mg	40		
Potassium, mg	35		

Cucumber-Dill Mousse, Sun-dried Tomato Dip

Mideastern Garbanzo Spread

2 cups cooked or 1 can (16 ounces) drained
reduced-sodium garbanzo beans

⅓ cup orange juice

2 tablespoons lemon juice

1 tablespoon sesame tahini paste, if desired

2 teaspoons balsamic vinegar

½ teaspoon salt

½ teaspoon ground cumin

¼ teaspoon ground coriander

¼ teaspoon paprika

2 cloves garlic, finely chopped

¼ cup chopped green onions (2 to 3 medium)

Place all ingredients except onions in blender or food processor. Cover and blend until smooth. Remove from blender; stir in onions. Cover and refrigerate at least 2 hours. *About 2 cups spread*

NUTRITION INFORMATION PER SERVING			
1 tablespoon		**Percent of U.S. RDA**	
Calories	15	Protein	*
Protein, g	1	Vitamin A	*
Carbohydrate, g	3	Vitamin C	2%
Fat, g	0	Thiamin	*
Unsaturated	0	Riboflavin	*
Saturated	0	Niacin	*
Dietary Fiber, g	1	Calcium	*
Cholesterol, mg	0	Iron	2%
Sodium, mg	35		
Potassium, mg	40		

Easy Tuna Spread

1 cup nonfat ricotta cheese
2 tablespoons chopped fresh or 2 teaspoons
   dried basil leaves
2 tablespoons lemon juice
2 tablespoons low-fat sour cream
1 can (9¼ ounces) white tuna in water,
   drained

Place all ingredients in blender or food processor. Cover and blend until smooth. Line 2-cup metal bowl or mold with plastic wrap. Place mixture in bowl. Cover and refrigerate 2 hours. Carefully unmold onto serving plate. *About 2 cups spread*

CHICKEN-TARRAGON SPREAD: Substitute 2 cans (5 ounces each) white chicken in water, drained, for the tuna and 2 tablespoons chopped fresh or 2 teaspoons dried tarragon for the basil.

NUTRITION INFORMATION PER SERVING

1 tablespoon		Percent of U.S. RDA	
Calories	25	Protein	8%
Protein, g	3	Vitamin A	*
Carbohydrate, g	1	Vitamin C	*
Fat, g	1	Thiamin	*
Unsaturated	0	Riboflavin	2%
Saturated	1	Niacin	4%
Dietary Fiber, g	0	Calcium	2%
Cholesterol, mg	5	Iron	2%
Sodium, mg	40		
Potassium, mg	40		

Easy Tuna Spread, Peppery Wheat Crackers (page 43), Vegetable Medley Drink (page 59)

Fresh Fruit Frappé

1 cup cut-up cantaloupe or honeydew
  melon
1 cup cut-up pineapple
1 cup cut-up mango
1 cup strawberry halves (about half a pint)
1 cup orange juice
2 tablespoons sugar
Crushed ice

Mix all ingredients except ice. Fill blender half full of mixture; add crushed ice to fill to top. Cover and blend on high speed until uniform consistency. Repeat with remaining mixture. Serve immediately. Garnish with fruit if desired. *4 servings*

NUTRITION INFORMATION PER SERVING

1 serving		Percent of U.S. RDA	
Calories	135	Protein	2%
Protein, g	1	Vitamin A	28%
Carbohydrate, g	31	Vitamin C	100%
Fat, g	1	Thiamin	8%
Unsaturated	1	Riboflavin	4%
Saturated	0	Niacin	4%
Dietary Fiber, g	3	Calcium	2%
Cholesterol, mg	0	Iron	2%
Sodium, mg	5		
Potassium, mg	410		

Banana-Peach Shake

You can mash and freeze overripe bananas to have on hand to make this refreshing shake. The ingredients can be doubled easily to make 6 servings.

1 cup mashed ripe bananas (about 2 large),
  frozen
1 cup peach nectar
½ cup low-fat milk

Place all ingredients in blender. Cover and blend about 30 seconds or until smooth. Serve immediately over ice cubes. *3 servings*

BANANA-APRICOT SHAKE: Substitute 1 cup apricot nectar for the peach nectar. Add ¼ teaspoon vanilla to mixture in blender.

NUTRITION INFORMATION PER SERVING

1 serving		Percent of U.S. RDA	
Calories	135	Protein	4%
Protein, g	2	Vitamin A	4%
Carbohydrate, g	30	Vitamin C	18%
Fat, g	1	Thiamin	2%
Unsaturated	0	Riboflavin	8%
Saturated	1	Niacin	2%
Dietary Fiber, g	2	Calcium	6%
Cholesterol, mg	3	Iron	2%
Sodium, mg	25		
Potassium, mg	390		

Orange-Cantaloupe Drink (left), *Peachy Raspberry Sodas* (center) (*page 60*), *Strawberry-Lime Slush* (right)

Strawberry-Lime Slush

2 pints fresh or 4 cups (thawed) frozen
  strawberries
1½ cups crushed ice
¼ cup powdered sugar
2 tablespoons lime juice

Reserve 4 strawberries for garnish if desired. Place crushed ice and 1 pint of the strawberries in blender or food processor. Cover and blend until mixture is almost smooth. Pour into 1-quart (or larger) pitcher. Place remaining strawberries, the powdered sugar and lime juice in blender or food processor. Cover and blend until almost smooth.

Add mixture to pitcher; stir. Serve in 4 tall glasses. Garnish sides of glasses with reserved strawberries. Serve immediately. *4 servings*

NUTRITION INFORMATION PER SERVING			
I serving		**Percent of U.S. RDA**	
Calories	90	Protein	*
Protein, g	I	Vitamin A	*
Carbohydrate, g	19	Vitamin C	100%
Fat, g	I	Thiamin	2%
Unsaturated	I	Riboflavin	6%
Saturated	0	Niacin	2%
Dietary Fiber, g	2	Calcium	2%
Cholesterol, mg	0	Iron	2%
Sodium, mg	5		
Potassium, mg	260		

Orange-Cantaloupe Drink

1 large orange, peeled and seeded
½ small cantaloupe, peeled and seeded
¼ large lemon, peeled and seeded
Ice cubes or crushed ice

Extract juice from orange (½ cup), cantaloupe (½ cup) and lemon (1 tablespoon), using juice extractor. Pour fruit juices over ice. Stir before serving. *1 serving*

NUTRITION INFORMATION PER SERVING			
I serving		Percent of U.S. RDA	
Calories	205	Protein	6%
Protein, g	4	Vitamin A	76%
Carbohydrate, g	45	Vitamin C	100%
Fat, g	1	Thiamin	18%
Unsaturated	1	Riboflavin	8%
Saturated	0	Niacin	10%
Dietary Fiber, g	6	Calcium	10%
Cholesterol, mg	0	Iron	4%
Sodium, mg	25		
Potassium, mg	1170		

Vegetable Medley Drink

2 large carrots
2 large tomatoes
1 medium stalk celery
1 green onion
½ medium cucumber
½ medium red or green bell pepper
¼ large lemon, peeled and seeded
½ teaspoon chopped fresh basil leaves
⅛ teaspoon salt
3 drops red pepper sauce

Extract juice from vegetables and lemon, using juice extractor. Stir basil, salt and pepper sauce into juice. For best flavor, refrigerate about 30 minutes. Stir before serving. *2 servings*

NUTRITION INFORMATION PER SERVING			
I serving		Percent of U.S. RDA	
Calories	120	Protein	4%
Protein, g	3	Vitamin A	100%
Carbohydrate, g	25	Vitamin C	100%
Fat, g	1	Thiamin	18%
Unsaturated	1	Riboflavin	10%
Saturated	0	Niacin	12%
Dietary Fiber, g	6	Calcium	6%
Cholesterol, mg	0	Iron	10%
Sodium, mg	210		
Potassium, mg	970		

Hot Tomato Sipper

2 cans (10½ ounces each) condensed beef
   broth (about 2½ cups)
1 cup tomato juice
1 cup water
2 teaspoons prepared horseradish
1 teaspoon fresh or ½ teaspoon dried dill
   weed

Heat all ingredients to simmering. *6 servings*

NUTRITION INFORMATION PER SERVING			
I serving		Percent of U.S. RDA	
Calories	35	Protein	8%
Protein, g	5	Vitamin A	2%
Carbohydrate, g	4	Vitamin C	14%
Fat, g	0	Thiamin	2%
Unsaturated	0	Riboflavin	2%
Saturated	0	Niacin	4%
Dietary Fiber, g	1	Calcium	*
Cholesterol, mg	0	Iron	4%
Sodium, mg	720		
Potassium, mg	240		

3

Breads

Who doesn't love to smell bread, muffins or biscuits baking? Whether wrapped around a stick and cooked over an open fire, baked on a rock, in a clay oven or in a skillet, breads are an important part of every cuisine. And today it's no different, in fact, over the past few years, the bakery areas in supermarkets have expanded tremendously with a seemingly endless variety of bread shapes and textures. To appreciate the role of bread, see the Food Guide Pyramid on page 14. It is recommended that we eat 6 to 11 servings per day from the Bread, Cereal, Rice & Pasta Group, and nutrition experts suggest we consume 20 to 35 grams of fiber per day and bread is an excellent source.

The recipes that follow are anything but basic white breads. From muffins to waffles, scones to loaves, sweet breads to savory, they are packed with grains, fruits, vegetables and other delicious, nutritious ingredients. Triple Wheat–Honey Muffins (page 68) combines wheat flakes, whole-wheat flour and wheat bran for a high-fiber muffin that is a great start to the day as is the Bran Breakfast Loaf (page 83). Double-Oat Scones (page 73) made with rolled oats and oat bran are perfect for brunch. Barley-Corn Bread (page 81) is a twist on an old favorite that will add interest when you serve chile.

Whether you prefer to make quick breads (leavened with baking powder or baking soda) or are looking for yeast bread recipes, you will find many appealing choices here. On the sweeter side, there are Cranberry-Orange Muffins (page 63), Raisin-Spice Coffee Cake (page 88) and Holiday Dried-Fruit Loaf (page 105), to name a few. Individual breads such as Whole Wheat Popovers (page 71), Two-Onion Bagels (page 92) and Carrot-Dill Rolls (page 94) are always fun. There are also plenty of squares, rounds and loaves to be cut into slices or wedges. And, of course, you will find the basic, cozy breakfast breads such as pancakes and French toast.

The gluten in all-purpose white wheat flour is needed to give structure to most breads, but some whole-wheat flour or other grains can easily be mixed in for variety in flavor and texture. Your favorite bread recipes can easily be altered to suit your nutritional interests. To learn about adjusting a recipe to a more healthy version, see Shaping Up Your Favorite Recipes on page 26. For more information on grains, see page 64.

Preceding page: Corn and Zucchini Muffins (page 69), High-Fiber Honey–Whole Wheat Loaf (page 97)

Whole Wheat–Blueberry Muffins

¼ cup packed brown sugar
½ teaspoon ground cinnamon
¾ cup skim milk
¼ cup vegetable oil
¼ cup honey
2 egg whites or ¼ cup cholesterol-free
    egg product
1 cup all-purpose flour
1 cup whole wheat flour
3 teaspoons baking powder
½ teaspoon salt
1 cup fresh or frozen (thawed and well
    drained) blueberries

Heat oven to 400°. Spray bottoms only of 12 medium muffin cups, 2½×1¼ inches, with nonstick cooking spray, or line with paper baking cups. Mix brown sugar and cinnamon; reserve. Beat milk, oil, honey and egg whites in large bowl. Stir in flours, baking powder and salt just until flours are moistened (batter will be lumpy). Fold in blueberries. Divide batter evenly among muffin cups (cups will be full). Sprinkle with brown sugar mixture. Bake about 20 minutes or until golden brown. Immediately remove from pan. *12 muffins*

NUTRITION INFORMATION PER SERVING			
1 muffin		**Percent of U.S. RDA**	
Calories	170	Protein	6%
Protein, g	3	Vitamin A	*
Carbohydrate, g	28	Vitamin C	*
Fat, g	5	Thiamin	8%
Unsaturated	4	Riboflavin	8%
Saturated	1	Niacin	6%
Dietary Fiber, g	2	Calcium	8%
Cholesterol, mg	0	Iron	6%
Sodium, mg	200		
Potassium, mg	120		

Cranberry-Orange Muffins

1 cup skim milk
¼ cup vegetable oil
1 tablespoon grated orange peel
2 egg whites or ¼ cup cholesterol-free egg
    product
1 cup all-purpose flour
1 cup whole wheat flour
⅓ cup sugar
3 teaspoons baking powder
½ teaspoon salt
¾ cup fresh or frozen cranberries, chopped

Heat oven to 400°. Spray bottoms only of 12 medium muffin cups, 2½×1¼ inches, with nonstick cooking spray, or line with paper baking cups. Beat milk, oil, orange peel and egg whites in large bowl. Stir in remaining ingredients except cranberries just until flour is moistened (batter will be lumpy). Fold in cranberries. Divide batter evenly among muffin cups (cups will be full). Sprinkle with sugar if desired. Bake 20 to 25 minutes or until golden brown. Immediately remove from pan. *12 muffins*

NUTRITION INFORMATION PER SERVING			
1 muffin		**Percent of U.S. RDA**	
Calories	150	Protein	6%
Protein, g	3	Vitamin A	*
Carbohydrate, g	23	Vitamin C	*
Fat, g	5	Thiamin	8%
Unsaturated	4	Riboflavin	6%
Saturated	1	Niacin	6%
Dietary Fiber, g	2	Calcium	8%
Cholesterol, mg	0	Iron	4%
Sodium, mg	200		
Potassium, mg	100		

Know Your Grains

There are many grains available to us today in a variety of forms, from whole kernels to finely ground flours. Grains add color, texture and flavor to foods while providing benefits such as fiber. When they are combined with low-fat dairy products or beans, peas or lentils, they provide high-quality protein.

Grains vary in cooking time and water absorption, so follow package directions when making a recipe. (Ask for cooking directions if you buy your grains in bulk.) Rinse grains in water before cooking, be sure to use an extra-fine mesh strainer for small grains such as quinoa and teff. Grains lose moisture with age, so you may find that you need more or less water than the recipe calls for. If all the water is absorbed but the grain isn't quite tender, add a little more liquid and cook longer. If it is tender but all the liquid hasn't been absorbed, just drain. Cooked grains can be covered and refrigerated for up to a week. Use any leftover cooked grains in place of some of the meat in a casserole, mixed with cooked vegetables for a side dish or tossed into a salad.

Amaranth is a drought-resistant grain that was a food of the Aztec Indians in Mexico. It is a golden, poppy-seed-sized grain with an occasional dark seed. It provides iron, phosphorus, magnesium, potassium and complex carbohydrates. Amaranth is a good nutritional accompaniment to wheat, corn or legumes.

Barley was one of the first grains ever cultivated. Pearl barley is the most commonly available and has the hull, most of the bran and some of the germ removed to shorten cooking time. It contains vitamins B_3, B_1 and potassium. One cup of cooked barley provides the same amount of protein as a glass of milk.

Buckwheat kernels (groats) are hulled seeds of the buckwheat plant. Technically a fruit, it is used as a grain. Roasted groats are often called *kasha*. Buckwheat contains phosphorus, iron, potassium, vitamin E and B vitamins. It has a pungent flavor that can be overpowering. Buckwheat flour is usually mixed with all-purpose flour for pastas, pancakes, muffins and quick breads.

Corn is sometimes forgotten as a grain because we usually eat it as a vegetable. Whole kernel corn adds a naturally sweet flavor and a crunchy texture to breads, main dishes and side dishes. Paired with legumes or small amounts of animal protein from dairy products or eggs, corn provides a complete source of protein.

Cornmeal is available in degerminated and whole-grain forms. As *degerminated* indicates, the germ and bran have been removed. This type is widely available at grocery stores. Stone-ground whole-grain cornmeal may be a little harder to come by. It contains the germ and the bran which gives it more flavor, texture and fiber. Look for whole-grain cornmeal at health food stores or a local mill.

Flaxseed is a small, brown, teardrop-shaped seed used in small amounts as roughage in cereals and bread products.

Millet is a small yellow seed that resembles whole mustard seed. It can be added to baked goods or side dishes such as pilaf, and has a chewy texture and flavor similar to brown rice. Millet provides B vitamins, phosphorus, iron, manganese and copper.

Oats that we eat for breakfast as oatmeal are steamed and flattened groats (hulled oat kernels). They are available as either regular (old-fashioned), quick-cooking or instant. Regular and quick-cooking oats are often used interchangeably. If a recipe specifies just one, however, do not substitute the other—they have different absorption properties. Oats contribute fiber, vitamin B_1, phosphorus and magnesium to the diet.

Oat Bran is the broken husks of the oat kernels and is more easily digested than wheat bran. It can be used as hot cereal or as a baking and cooking ingredient and is a good source of soluble fiber.

Quinoa (keen-wa) was once the staple of the Inca Indians in Peru. It is a small grain with a soft crunch and can be used in any recipe calling for rice. Be sure to rinse well before using to remove the bitter-tasting, naturally occurring saponin (nature's insect repellent) that forms on the outside of the kernel. Quinoa provides B vitamins, calcium, iron, phosphorus and, unlike other grains, is a complete protein.

Brown Rice is unpolished, meaning the outer hull has been removed but the germ and bran layers have not been "polished" off. This gives it a nutlike flavor and chewier texture than white rice. It is also a good source of fiber and vitamin B_1.

Wild Rice is actually an aquatic grass native to North America. It is more expensive than other rices because of its limited supply. Stretch it by mixing with other rices or grains. Purchase less expensive packages of broken kernels, when you find them, and use in soups and quick breads. Wild rice contains fiber, B vitamins, iron, phosphorus, magnesium, calcium and zinc.

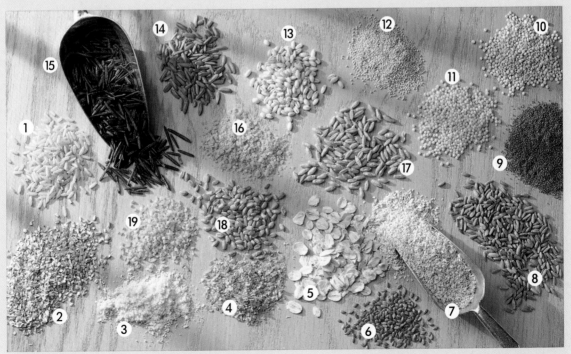

1) brown rice; 2) kasha; 3) whole-grain cornmeal; 4) wheat bran; 5) rolled oats; 6) flaxseed; 7) oatbran; 8) rye; 9) teff; 10) quinoa; 11) millet; 12) amaranth; 13) pearled barley; 14) basmati hybrid rice; 15) wild rice; 16) toasted wheat germ; 17) triticale; 18) wheat berries; 19) bulgur

Rye is a dark, earthy-flavored grain from which pumpernickel is made. Rye groats can be eaten as a cereal or used whole or cracked as a baking and cooking ingredient in casseroles, pilafs and breads. Rye is nutritionally similar to wheat.

Rye Flour is usually labeled "light" or "dark." The light flour has been sifted and has had most of the bran removed. Dark flour is sometimes referred to as pumpernickel flour. Although it is a very flavorful bread flour, it doesn't have much gluten and should be blended with wheat flour for baking.

Teff is a reddish brown seed that is the smallest of all grains. The consistency of cooked teff is similar to that of stiff cornmeal mush. It contains complex carbohydrates, iron and fiber.

Triticale is a hybrid of wheat and rye that contains more protein than either of its parents. Triticale berries resemble wheat berries except that the triticale berries are larger.

Wheat Berries are hulled whole-grain wheat kernels that still have the bran and germ. Cooked wheat berries can be used like rice in salads and side dishes. Wheat provides B vitamins, vitamin E and complex carbohydrates. Combining wheat with legumes or dairy products provides a complete protein.

Wheat Bran is the tough outer layer of the wheat berry. It is available unprocessed in its raw form or toasted, which makes it easier to chew. Wheat bran is a rich source of insoluble fiber.

Wheat Bulgur is whole wheat that's been cooked, dried and then broken into coarse fragments. It's different from cracked wheat because it is precooked. Bulgur supplies phosphorus and potassium and also contains some iron and B_1 and B_2 vitamins.

Cracked Wheat is whole wheat kernels that have been dried and then cracked by coarse milling. Like bulgur, its precooked cousin, cracked wheat contains phosphorus, potassium, iron, vitamins B_1 and B_2.

Wheat Flakes are wheat berries that have been rolled flat. They can be used in baking and cooking just like rolled oats.

Wheat Flour is available in several different forms. *Quick-mixing flour* is instantized all-purpose flour, which means it disperses instantly in cold liquids, resulting in smooth gravies, sauces and batters. *Cake flour* is milled from soft wheat, which has a weaker gluten structure, creating tender cakes with greater volume. *All-purpose flour* is either milled from hard winter wheat or a blend of hard and soft winter wheats to provide a flour that produces acceptable results in a wide range of baked products. *Bread flour* is milled from hard winter wheat, hard spring wheat or a combination of the two and provides the gluten structure needed in yeast breads. Quick-mixing, cake, all-purpose and bread flours don't contain the bran or the germ of wheat. *Whole wheat flour* is ground from the whole wheat kernel, usually from hard spring wheat, and contains the nutrients of whole wheat berries.

Wheat Germ is the flaked embryo of the berry. Because it's high in oil, it is usually toasted, to extend its shelf life. It has a nutty flavor and can be sprinkled over cereal or used in baked goods. It is a good source of vitamins B_1, B_3, B_2, potassium and zinc.

Cranberry-Orange Muffins (page 63), Oat-Peach Muffins

Oat-Peach Muffins

1 cup quick-cooking oats

1 cup nonfat buttermilk

¼ cup packed brown sugar

¼ cup vegetable oil

2 tablespoons light molasses

1 teaspoon vanilla

2 egg whites or ¼ cup cholesterol-free
   egg product

1¼ cups all-purpose flour

1½ teaspoons ground cinnamon

1 teaspoon baking soda

1 teaspoon baking powder

½ teaspoon salt

1 cup chopped fresh, frozen (thawed) or
   canned (well drained) peaches

Heat oven to 400°. Spray bottoms only of 12
medium muffin cups, 2½×1¼ inches, with
nonstick cooking spray, or line with paper baking cups. Mix oats and buttermilk in large bowl. Beat in brown sugar, oil, molasses, vanilla and egg whites. Stir in remaining ingredients except peaches just until flour is moistened (batter will be lumpy). Fold in peaches. Divide batter evenly among muffin cups (cups will be full). Sprinkle with sugar if desired. Bake about 20 minutes or until golden brown. Immediately remove from pan. *12 muffins*

NUTRITION INFORMATION PER SERVING			
1 muffin		**Percent of U.S. RDA**	
Calories	155	Protein	6%
Protein, g	4	Vitamin A	*
Carbohydrate, g	24	Vitamin C	*
Fat, g	5	Thiamin	10%
Unsaturated	4	Riboflavin	8%
Saturated	1	Niacin	4%
Dietary Fiber, g	1	Calcium	6%
Cholesterol, mg	0	Iron	8%
Sodium, mg	220		
Potassium, mg	160		

Triple Wheat–Honey Muffins

Three forms of wheat are combined in these tasty, nutritious muffins. Wheat flakes are wheat kernels, or berries, that have been rolled, just as rolled oats are. Whole wheat flour is made by grinding the entire wheat kernel, with nothing added or subtracted. And wheat bran is the hard outer layer of the kernel, a byproduct in milling all-purpose flour.

¼ cup uncooked wheat flakes (rolled wheat)*

¾ cup water

1¼ cups nonfat buttermilk

⅓ cup honey

¼ cup vegetable oil

1 teaspoon vanilla

2 egg whites or ¼ cup cholesterol-free egg product

1¼ cups whole wheat flour

1 cup wheat bran

1 teaspoon baking powder

½ teaspoon baking soda

½ teaspoon salt

Heat wheat flakes and water to boiling in 1-quart saucepan; reduce heat. Cover and simmer about 30 minutes or until liquid is absorbed. Cool 10 minutes.

Heat oven to 400°. Spray bottoms only of 12 medium muffin cups, 2½×1¼ inches, with nonstick cooking spray, or line with paper baking cups. Beat buttermilk, honey, oil, vanilla and egg whites in large bowl. Stir in flour, wheat bran, baking powder, baking soda and salt just until flour is moistened. Fold in cooked wheat flakes. Divide batter evenly among muffin cups (cups will be very full). Bake 22 to 24 minutes or until golden brown. Immediately remove from pan. *12 muffins*

* ¾ cup cooked brown rice can be substituted for the wheat flakes and water.

TRIPLE WHEAT–MOLASSES MUFFINS: Substitute ⅓ cup molasses for the honey. Stir ½ teaspoon ground ginger and ½ teaspoon ground cinnamon into flour mixture.

NUTRITION INFORMATION PER SERVING			
1 muffin		**Percent of U.S. RDA**	
Calories	155	Protein	6%
Protein, g	4	Vitamin A	*
Carbohydrate, g	23	Vitamin C	*
Fat, g	5	Thiamin	6%
Unsaturated	4	Riboflavin	8%
Saturated	1	Niacin	8%
Dietary Fiber, g	3	Calcium	6%
Cholesterol, mg	0	Iron	6%
Sodium, mg	190		
Potassium, mg	170		

Honey-Bran Muffins

1/4 cup wheat bran

3 tablespoons boiling water

1/4 cup skim milk

2 tablespoons packed brown sugar

2 tablespoons vegetable oil

2 tablespoons honey

2 egg whites or 1/4 cup cholesterol-free egg product

2/3 cup all-purpose flour

1 1/2 teaspoons baking powder

Dash of salt

Heat oven to 400°. Spray bottoms only of 6 medium muffin cups, 2 1/2 × 1 1/4 inches, with nonstick cooking spray, or line with paper baking cups. Mix wheat bran and boiling water; reserve. Beat milk, brown sugar, oil, honey and egg whites in medium bowl. Stir in bran mixture and remaining ingredients just until flour is moistened (batter will be lumpy). Divide batter evenly among muffin cups (cups will be about 3/4 full). Sprinkle with sugar if desired. Bake 20 to 25 minutes or until golden brown. Immediately remove from pan. *6 muffins*

NUTRITION INFORMATION PER SERVING			
1 muffin		**Percent of U.S. RDA**	
Calories	150	Protein	4%
Protein, g	3	Vitamin A	*
Carbohydrate, g	23	Vitamin C	*
Fat, g	5	Thiamin	8%
Unsaturated	4	Riboflavin	8%
Saturated	1	Niacin	6%
Dietary Fiber, g	1	Calcium	8%
Cholesterol, mg	0	Iron	6%
Sodium, mg	210		
Potassium, mg	100		

Corn and Zucchini Muffins

These vegetable-studded muffins are good with soups and stews, as well as meatless bean dishes like Kidney Bean and Macaroni Supper (page 325).

1 1/4 cups low-fat milk

2 tablespoons vegetable oil

2 egg whites or 1 egg

1 cup all-purpose flour

1 cup whole wheat flour

3 teaspoons baking powder

1/2 teaspoon salt

1/2 cup shredded zucchini (about 1/2 medium)

1/2 cup cooked whole kernel corn

Heat oven to 400°. Spray bottoms only of 12 medium muffin cups, 2 1/2 × 1 1/4 inches, with nonstick cooking spray, or line with paper baking cups. Beat milk, oil and egg in medium bowl. Stir in flours, baking powder and salt. Fold in zucchini and corn. Divide batter evenly among muffin cups (cups will be very full). Bake 22 to 24 minutes or until golden brown. Immediately remove from pan. *12 muffins*

NUTRITION INFORMATION PER SERVING			
1 muffin		**Percent of U.S. RDA**	
Calories	115	Protein	6%
Protein, g	4	Vitamin A	2%
Carbohydrate, g	18	Vitamin C	*
Fat, g	3	Thiamin	10%
Unsaturated	2	Riboflavin	8%
Saturated	1	Niacin	6%
Dietary Fiber, g	2	Calcium	10%
Cholesterol, mg	2	Iron	4%
Sodium, mg	230		
Potassium, mg	130		

Quinoa-Corn Muffins

Quinoa (pronounced KEEN-wa) is a tiny round grain that was once a staple in the diet of the Incas in Peru. The grain is naturally coated with a bitter substance that acts as an insect repellent, so wash the quinoa thoroughly in a strainer or bowl, and drain well before using.

1½ cups stone-ground or degerminated cornmeal
¾ cup cooked quinoa or brown rice
½ cup all-purpose flour
1½ cups nonfat buttermilk
2 tablespoons flaxseed, if desired
2 tablespoons vegetable oil
1 teaspoon baking powder
½ teaspoon salt
½ teaspoon baking soda
3 egg whites or ½ cup cholesterol-free egg product

Heat oven to 450°. Spray bottoms only of 12 medium muffin cups, 2½×1¼ inches, with nonstick cooking spray, or line with paper baking cups. Mix all ingredients; beat vigorously 30 seconds. Divide batter evenly among muffin cups. Bake 20 to 25 minutes or until golden brown. Serve warm. *12 muffins*

NUTRITION INFORMATION PER SERVING

1 muffin		Percent of U.S. RDA	
Calories	130	Protein	6%
Protein, g	4	Vitamin A	*
Carbohydrate, g	22	Vitamin C	*
Fat, g	3	Thiamin	12%
Unsaturated	2	Riboflavin	10%
Saturated	1	Niacin	6%
Dietary Fiber, g	1	Calcium	6%
Cholesterol, mg	0	Iron	6%
Sodium, mg	200		
Potassium, mg	100		

Wild Rice Muffins

1 cup low-fat milk
¼ cup vegetable oil
1 teaspoon maple flavoring
2 egg whites or ¼ cup cholesterol-free egg product
1½ cups cooked wild rice (about ½ cup uncooked)
2 cups whole wheat flour
¼ cup packed brown sugar
3 teaspoons baking powder
½ teaspoon salt
¼ teaspoon ground cinnamon
¼ cup chopped nuts

Heat oven to 400°. Spray bottoms only of 12 medium muffin cups, 2½×1¼ inches, with nonstick cooking spray, or line with paper baking cups. Beat milk, oil, maple flavoring and egg whites in medium bowl. Stir in wild rice. Stir in flour, brown sugar, baking powder, salt and cinnamon all at once just until flour is moistened (batter will be lumpy). Fold in nuts. Divide batter evenly among muffin cups.

Bake 18 to 20 minutes or until golden brown. Immediately remove from pan. *12 muffins*

NUTRITION INFORMATION PER SERVING

1 muffin		Percent of U.S. RDA	
Calories	185	Protein	8%
Protein, g	5	Vitamin A	*
Carbohydrate, g	25	Vitamin C	*
Fat, g	7	Thiamin	8%
Unsaturated	6	Riboflavin	6%
Saturated	1	Niacin	8%
Dietary Fiber, g	3	Calcium	10%
Cholesterol, mg	0	Iron	6%
Sodium, mg	270		
Potassium, mg	170		

Whole Wheat Popovers

To achieve the proper airy texture, whole eggs need to be used here. However, you can forgo butter and spread the popover with all-fruit jam and still remain within your own healthy eating guidelines.

¾ **cup all-purpose flour**
¼ **cup whole wheat flour**
1 **cup low-fat milk**
¼ **teaspoon salt**
2 **eggs**

Heat oven to 450°. Spray six 6-ounce custard cups or 6-cup popover pan with nonstick cooking spray. Mix all ingredients with hand beater just until smooth (do not overbeat). Fill cups about ½ full. Bake 20 minutes. Reduce oven temperature to 350°. Bake 20 minutes longer. Immediately remove from cups. Serve hot.
6 popovers

NUTRITION INFORMATION PER SERVING

1 popover		Percent of U.S. RDA	
Calories	120	Protein	8%
Protein, g	5	Vitamin A	4%
Carbohydrate, g	18	Vitamin C	*
Fat, g	3	Thiamin	10%
Unsaturated	2	Riboflavin	14%
Saturated	1	Niacin	6%
Dietary Fiber, g	1	Calcium	6%
Cholesterol, mg	75	Iron	6%
Sodium, mg	130		
Potassium, mg	120		

Whole Wheat Biscuits

¼ **cup shortening**
1 **cup all-purpose flour**
1 **cup whole wheat flour**
¼ **cup wheat germ**
3 **teaspoons baking powder**
½ **teaspoon salt**
About ¾ **cup low-fat milk**

Heat oven to 450°. Cut shortening into flours, wheat germ, baking powder and salt with pastry blender in medium bowl until mixture resembles fine crumbs. Stir in just enough milk so dough leaves side of bowl and forms a ball.

Turn dough onto lightly floured surface; gently roll in flour to coat. Knead lightly 10 times. Roll or pat ½ inch thick. Cut with floured 2½-inch biscuit cutter. Place about 1 inch apart on ungreased cookie sheet. Bake 10 to 12 minutes or until golden brown. Immediately remove from cookie sheet. Serve warm. *About 12 biscuits*

NUTRITION INFORMATION PER SERVING

1 biscuit		Percent of U.S. RDA	
Calories	125	Protein	6%
Protein, g	3	Vitamin A	*
Carbohydrate, g	17	Vitamin C	*
Fat, g	5	Thiamin	10%
Unsaturated	4	Riboflavin	6%
Saturated	1	Niacin	6%
Dietary Fiber, g	2	Calcium	8%
Cholesterol, mg	0	Iron	6%
Sodium, mg	190		
Potassium, mg	100		

Double-Oat Scones, Easy Cheese Crescents

Easy Cheese Crescents

1 cup shredded reduced-fat Cheddar cheese
(4 ounces)
½ cup nonfat ricotta cheese
¼ cup cholesterol-free egg product or 2 egg
whites
⅓ cup nonfat buttermilk
¼ cup low-fat sour cream
2 cups all-purpose flour
3 teaspoons baking powder
¼ teaspoon salt

Heat oven to 425°. Spray cookie sheet with nonstick cooking spray. Mix cheeses, egg product, buttermilk and sour cream in large bowl. Stir in flour, baking powder and salt until dough leaves sides of bowl.

Divide dough into halves. Turn each half onto lightly floured surface; gently roll in flour to coat and shape into ball. Pat or roll each ball into 9-inch circle. Cut each circle into 6 wedges. Roll up wedges, starting at wide end. Place rolls, with points underneath, on cookie sheet; curve slightly. Bake 15 to 20 minutes or until golden brown. Remove from cookie sheet. Cool on wire rack. *12 crescents*

NUTRITION INFORMATION PER SERVING			
1 crescent		Percent of U.S. RDA	
Calories	125	Protein	10%
Protein, g	7	Vitamin A	4%
Carbohydrate, g	18	Vitamin C	*
Fat, g	3	Thiamin	12%
Unsaturated	1	Riboflavin	10%
Saturated	2	Niacin	6%
Dietary Fiber, g	1	Calcium	18%
Cholesterol, mg	10	Iron	6%
Sodium, mg	220		
Potassium, mg	70		

Double-Oat Scones

3 tablespoons firm margarine
1 cup all-purpose flour
¼ cup packed brown sugar
1½ teaspoons baking powder
¼ teaspoon baking soda
¼ teaspoon salt
½ cup regular or quick-cooking oats
½ cup oat bran
½ cup dried cranberries or raisins
2 egg whites
About ½ cup nonfat buttermilk

Heat oven to 400°. Spray cookie sheet lightly with nonstick cooking spray. Cut margarine into flour, brown sugar, baking powder, baking soda and salt with pastry blender in large bowl until mixture resembles fine crumbs. Stir in oats, oat bran and cranberries. Stir in egg whites and just enough buttermilk so dough leaves side of bowl and forms a ball.

Turn dough onto lightly floured surface; gently roll in flour to coat. Knead lightly 10 times. Pat dough into 8-inch circle on cookie sheet. Cut into 8 wedges with floured knife, but do not separate. Bake 16 to 18 minutes or until golden brown. Remove from cookie sheet; separate wedges. Serve warm. *8 scones*

NUTRITION INFORMATION PER SERVING

1 scone		Percent of U.S. RDA	
Calories	175	Protein	8%
Protein, g	5	Vitamin A	6%
Carbohydrate, g	28	Vitamin C	*
Fat, g	5	Thiamin	16%
Unsaturated	4	Riboflavin	10%
Saturated	1	Niacin	4%
Dietary Fiber, g	2	Calcium	8%
Cholesterol, mg	0	Iron	8%
Sodium, mg	250		
Potassium, mg	140		

Poppy Seed Drop Scones

1 cup all-purpose flour
1 cup whole wheat flour
½ cup regular or quick-cooking oats
½ cup currants or raisins
1 tablespoon poppy seed
1½ teaspoons baking powder
½ teaspoon baking soda
½ teaspoon salt
1 tablespoon margarine
1 cup nonfat buttermilk
1 egg

Heat oven to 375°. Spray cookie sheet with nonstick cooking spray. Mix all ingredients except margarine, buttermilk and egg in large bowl. Cut in margarine with fork. Mix buttermilk and egg; stir into flour mixture. Drop dough by ¼ cupfuls onto cookie sheet. Bake about 20 minutes or until golden brown. Remove from cookie sheet. Serve warm. *12 scones*

NUTRITION INFORMATION PER SERVING

1 scone		Percent of U.S. RDA	
Calories	130	Protein	6%
Protein, g	4	Vitamin A	2%
Carbohydrate, g	24	Vitamin C	*
Fat, g	2	Thiamin	10%
Unsaturated	1	Riboflavin	8%
Saturated	1	Niacin	6%
Dietary Fiber, g	2	Calcium	6%
Cholesterol, mg	20	Iron	6%
Sodium, mg	210		
Potassium, mg	160		

Buckwheat Pancakes

2 egg whites or ¼ cup cholesterol-free egg
　product
½ cup buckwheat flour
½ cup whole wheat flour
1 cup skim milk
1 tablespoon sugar
2 tablespoons vegetable oil
3 teaspoons baking powder
½ teaspoon salt
¼ cup wheat germ or wheat bran

Beat egg whites with hand beater in medium bowl until foamy. Beat in remaining ingredients except wheat germ just until smooth. Spray griddle or 10-inch skillet with nonstick cooking spray. Heat griddle over medium heat or to 375°. (To test griddle, sprinkle with a few drops water. If bubbles skitter around, heat is just right.) For each pancake, pour about 3 tablespoons batter onto hot griddle. Cook pancakes until puffed and dry around edges. Sprinkle each pancake with about 1 teaspoon wheat germ. Turn and cook other sides until golden brown. *10 pancakes*

NUTRITION INFORMATION PER SERVING

1 pancake		Percent of U.S. RDA	
Calories	95	Protein	6%
Protein, g	4	Vitamin A	*
Carbohydrate, g	13	Vitamin C	*
Fat, g	3	Thiamin	6%
Unsaturated	2	Riboflavin	6%
Saturated	1	Niacin	4%
Dietary Fiber, g	1	Calcium	10%
Cholesterol, mg	0	Iron	4%
Sodium, mg	250		
Potassium, mg	120		

Oatmeal Pancakes

2 egg whites or ¼ cup cholesterol-free egg
　product
½ cup quick-cooking oats
¼ cup all-purpose flour
¼ cup whole wheat flour
¾ cup nonfat buttermilk
¼ cup skim milk
1 tablespoon sugar
2 tablespoons vegetable oil
1 teaspoon baking powder
½ teaspoon baking soda
½ teaspoon salt

Beat egg whites with hand beater in medium bowl until foamy. Beat in remaining ingredients until smooth. (For thinner pancakes, stir in additional 2 to 4 tablespoons milk.) Spray griddle or 10-inch skillet with nonstick cooking spray. Heat griddle over medium heat or to 375°. (To test griddle, sprinkle with a few drops water. If bubbles skitter around, heat is just right.) For each pancake, pour about 3 tablespoons batter onto hot griddle. Cook until puffed and dry around edges. Turn and cook other sides until golden brown. *12 pancakes*

NUTRITION INFORMATION PER SERVING

1 pancake		Percent of U.S. RDA	
Calories	65	Protein	4%
Protein, g	2	Vitamin A	*
Carbohydrate, g	8	Vitamin C	*
Fat, g	3	Thiamin	4%
Unsaturated	2	Riboflavin	4%
Saturated	1	Niacin	2%
Dietary Fiber, g	1	Calcium	4%
Cholesterol, mg	0	Iron	2%
Sodium, mg	180		
Potassium, mg	65		

Fruit Flapjacks

Try spreading flapjacks with all-fruit jam.

⅔ cup all-purpose flour

⅓ cup whole wheat flour

2 teaspoons baking powder

1 teaspoon baking soda

1 teaspoon ground cinnamon

1 container (6 ounces) unsweetened
  applesauce (¾ cup)

½ cup chopped fresh or drained canned
  crushed pineapple

½ cup plain nonfat yogurt

¼ cup low-fat milk

1 egg

1 egg white

Spray griddle or 10-inch skillet with nonstick cooking spray. Heat griddle over medium heat or to 375°. (To test griddle, sprinkle with a few drops water. If bubbles skitter around, heat is just right.) Mix flours, baking powder, baking soda and cinnamon in large bowl. Mix remaining ingredients; stir into flour mixture. For each flapjack, pour scant ¼ cup batter onto hot griddle. Cook about 2 minutes or until puffed and dry around edges. Turn and cook until golden brown. *12 flapjacks*

Ricotta-Banana Crepes

1¼ cups water

1 cup nonfat ricotta cheese

1 cup all-purpose flour

½ cup Egg Substitute (page 28)

½ cup chopped banana (about 1 medium)

2 tablespoons frozen (thawed) apple juice
  concentrate

½ teaspoon salt

½ teaspoon ground cinnamon

½ teaspoon vanilla

Place all ingredients in blender or food processor. Cover and blend until smooth. Spray 6-inch nonstick skillet with nonstick cooking spray. Heat over medium heat just until drop of water skitters when sprinkled in skillet. For each crepe, pour 2 tablespoons batter into skillet. *Immediately* rotate skillet until thin film covers bottom. Cook about 2 minutes or until light brown. Run wide spatula around edge to loosen; turn and cook about 30 seconds or until light brown. Stack crepes, placing waxed paper between each; keep covered.

Fill immediately with desired filling or cool completely. When cool, crepes may be wrapped in aluminum foil and refrigerated up to 4 days. Reheat crepes wrapped in foil in 350° oven 10 minutes. *24 crepes*

NUTRITION INFORMATION PER SERVING

1 flapjack		Percent of U.S. RDA	
Calories	70	Protein	4%
Protein, g	3	Vitamin A	*
Carbohydrate, g	12	Vitamin C	*
Fat, g	1	Thiamin	6%
Unsaturated	1	Riboflavin	6%
Saturated	0	Niacin	2%
Dietary Fiber, g	1	Calcium	8%
Cholesterol, mg	20	Iron	4%
Sodium, mg	150		
Potassium, mg	90		

NUTRITION INFORMATION PER SERVING

1 crepe		Percent of U.S. RDA	
Calories	40	Protein	2%
Protein, g	2	Vitamin A	*
Carbohydrate, g	6	Vitamin C	*
Fat, g	1	Thiamin	2%
Unsaturated	0	Riboflavin	4%
Saturated	1	Niacin	2%
Dietary Fiber, g	0	Calcium	2%
Cholesterol, mg	5	Iron	2%
Sodium, mg	65		
Potassium, mg	45		

Buckwheat-Orange Waffles

Top these refreshing waffles with fresh orange segments or orange low-fat yogurt.

1 cup buckwheat flour
2 teaspoons grated orange peel
1 cup orange juice (about 2 medium
  oranges)
¾ cup all-purpose flour
½ cup plain nonfat yogurt
½ cup low-fat milk
2 teaspoons baking powder
1 teaspoon baking soda
¼ teaspoon ground cloves
1 egg

Heat nonstick waffle iron; spray with nonstick cooking spray. Place all ingredients in blender or food processor. Cover and blend until smooth. For each waffle, pour ½ cup batter onto center of hot waffle iron. Bake about 5 minutes or until steaming stops. Carefully remove waffle. *Six 6-inch waffles*

NUTRITION INFORMATION PER SERVING			
1 waffle		Percent of U.S. RDA	
Calories	185	Protein	10%
Protein, g	7	Vitamin A	2%
Carbohydrate, g	35	Vitamin C	14%
Fat, g	2	Thiamin	14%
Unsaturated	1	Riboflavin	14%
Saturated	1	Niacin	10%
Dietary Fiber, g	2	Calcium	16%
Cholesterol, mg	35	Iron	8%
Sodium, mg	300		
Potassium, mg	260		

Whole Wheat Waffles

3 egg whites or ½ cup cholesterol-free egg
  product
2 cups whole wheat flour
¼ cup (½ stick) margarine, melted, or
  vegetable oil
1¾ cups milk
1 tablespoon sugar
3 teaspoons baking powder
½ teaspoon salt
6 tablespoons wheat germ

Heat nonstick waffle iron; spray with nonstick cooking spray. Beat egg whites with hand beater in medium bowl until foamy. Beat in remaining ingredients except wheat germ just until smooth. For each waffle, pour about ⅓ of batter onto center of hot waffle iron; sprinkle with 2 tablespoons wheat germ. Bake about 5 minutes or until steaming stops. Carefully remove waffle. *Twelve 4-inch waffle squares*

NUTRITION INFORMATION PER SERVING			
1 waffle		Percent of U.S. RDA	
Calories	145	Protein	8%
Protein, g	6	Vitamin A	6%
Carbohydrate, g	19	Vitamin C	*
Fat, g	5	Thiamin	10%
Unsaturated	4	Riboflavin	10%
Saturated	1	Niacin	8%
Dietary Fiber, g	3	Calcium	10%
Cholesterol, mg	5	Iron	6%
Sodium, mg	260		
Potassium, mg	180		

Buckwheat-Orange Waffles, Crunchy Oven French Toast (page 78), Oatmeal Pancakes (page 74)

Crunchy Oven French Toast

2 tablespoons margarine
3 tablespoons wheat germ
½ cup orange juice
2 tablespoons honey
6 egg whites or 1 cup cholesterol-free egg product
12 slices French bread, each 1 inch thick
2 tablespoons wheat germ

Heat oven to 450°. Heat margarine in jelly roll pan, 15½×10½×1 inch, in oven until melted; spread evenly in pan. Sprinkle 3 tablespoons wheat germ evenly over margarine. Beat orange juice, honey and egg whites with hand beater until foamy. Dip bread into egg mixture; place in pan. Drizzle any remaining egg mixture over bread. Sprinkle 2 tablespoons wheat germ evenly over bread. Bake about 10 minutes or until bottoms are golden brown. Turn and bake 6 to 8 minutes longer or until bottoms are golden brown. *12 slices*

NUTRITION INFORMATION PER SERVING

1 slice		Percent of U.S. RDA	
Calories	150	Protein	8%
Protein, g	6	Vitamin A	2%
Carbohydrate, g	25	Vitamin C	2%
Fat, g	3	Thiamin	6%
Unsaturated	2	Riboflavin	6%
Saturated	1	Niacin	8%
Dietary Fiber, g	1	Calcium	2%
Cholesterol, mg	0	Iron	6%
Sodium, mg	250		
Potassium, mg	100		

Amaranth–Brown Rice Bread

Try this bread toasted and spread with a light cream cheese, such as Neufchâtel, for a wonderful breakfast. It's also a great addition to a corn or wheat dish such as Sweet and Sour Vegetable Stew (page 333) as it's high in the amino acid lysine, which together with the wheat or corn provides complete protein.

¼ cup uncooked brown rice
1¼ cups water
½ cup uncooked amaranth
½ cup packed brown sugar
1 cup low-fat milk
¼ cup vegetable oil
¼ cup honey
3 egg whites or ½ cup cholesterol-free egg product
1½ cups whole wheat flour
1 cup all-purpose flour
3 teaspoons baking powder
½ teaspoon salt

Rinse rice; drain. Heat rice and water to boiling in heavy 1½-quart saucepan; reduce heat. Cover and simmer 30 minutes. Stir in amaranth. Cover and simmer about 20 minutes longer or until water is absorbed. After 10 minutes, check to see that mixture is not sticking to the pan. Stir in 1 to 2 tablespoons water if mixture is sticking. Cool 10 minutes.

Heat oven to 350°. Spray 2 loaf pans, 8½×4½×2½ inches, or 1 loaf pan, 9×5×3 inches, with nonstick cooking spray. Mix rice mixture, brown sugar, milk, oil, honey and egg whites in large bowl. Stir in remaining ingredients. Pour into pans.

Bake 45 to 55 minutes or until toothpick inserted in center comes out clean. Cool 5 minutes. Loosen sides of loaves from pans; remove from pans. Cool completely on wire rack before slicing. *2 loaves (12 slices each) or 1 loaf (24 slices)*

BROWN RICE BREAD: Omit amaranth. Increase uncooked brown rice to ¾ cup and water to 1¾ cups. Heat rice and water to boiling as directed above and simmer 40 to 50 minutes or until rice is tender. Do not use 9×5×3-inch loaf pan.

NUTRITION INFORMATION PER SERVING

I slice		Percent of U.S. RDA	
Calories	125	Protein	4%
Protein, g	3	Vitamin A	*
Carbohydrate, g	21	Vitamin C	*
Fat, g	3	Thiamin	6%
Unsaturated	2	Riboflavin	4%
Saturated	1	Niacin	4%
Dietary Fiber, g	1	Calcium	6%
Cholesterol, mg	0	Iron	6%
Sodium, mg	105		
Potassium, mg	90		

Apple-Spice Bread

The cozy combination of apples and spices is a welcoming way to start the day, and is also nice for afternoon tea. You can vary the flavor by your choice of apple. Try Red Delicious for a sweeter bread, Granny Smith for a tarter bread.

1 cup shredded apple (about 1 medium)
¼ cup low-fat sour cream
2 egg whites or ¼ cup cholesterol-free egg product
1½ cups all-purpose flour
2 tablespoons packed brown sugar
2 teaspoons baking powder
½ teaspoon baking soda
½ teaspoon salt
½ teaspoon ground cinnamon
¼ teaspoon ground nutmeg
¼ teaspoon ground cardamom

Heat oven to 350°. Spray loaf pan, 8½×4½×2½ or 7½×3¾×2½ inches, with nonstick cooking spray; dust with flour. Mix apple, sour cream and egg whites in large bowl. Stir in remaining flour and ingredients. Spread in pan. Bake 35 to 40 minutes or until golden brown. Cool in pan 5 minutes; remove from pan. Cool completely on wire rack before slicing. *1 loaf (20 slices)*

NUTRITION INFORMATION PER SERVING

I slice		Percent of U.S. RDA	
Calories	45	Protein	2%
Protein, g	1	Vitamin A	*
Carbohydrate, g	10	Vitamin C	*
Fat, g	0	Thiamin	4%
Unsaturated	0	Riboflavin	4%
Saturated	0	Niacin	2%
Dietary Fiber, g	0	Calcium	2%
Cholesterol, mg	0	Iron	2%
Sodium, mg	120		
Potassium, mg	35		

Apple-Raisin Soda Bread

3 cups all-purpose flour
1/2 cup wheat germ
1/2 cup raisins
1 teaspoon baking powder
1/2 teaspoon baking soda
1/2 teaspoon salt
1 cup nonfat buttermilk
1/2 cup shredded apple (about 1/2 medium)
1 tablespoon margarine, melted
3 egg whites or 1/2 cup cholesterol-free egg
  product
1/4 cup frozen (thawed) apple juice
  concentrate

Heat oven to 350°. Spray round pan, 9×1½ inches, or square pan, 8×8×2 inches, with nonstick cooking spray; sprinkle with 2 teaspoons of the flour. Mix remaining flour, the wheat germ, raisins, baking powder, baking soda and salt in large bowl. Stir in buttermilk, apple, margarine, egg whites and 3 tablespoons of the apple juice concentrate. Spread in pan. Bake 35 to 40 minutes or until golden brown. Brush with remaining apple juice concentrate. Serve warm. *12 servings*

NUTRITION INFORMATION PER SERVING

1 serving		Percent of U.S. RDA	
Calories	185	Protein	10%
Protein, g	6	Vitamin A	*
Carbohydrate, g	36	Vitamin C	*
Fat, g	2	Thiamin	22%
Unsaturated	1	Riboflavin	16%
Saturated	1	Niacin	10%
Dietary Fiber, g	2	Calcium	4%
Cholesterol, mg	0	Iron	12%
Sodium, mg	240		
Potassium, mg	200		

Baked Brown Bread

3/4 cup plain nonfat yogurt
1/4 cup low-fat sour cream
1 cup unsweetened grape juice
1/4 cup reduced-calorie maple-flavored
  syrup
1 cup stone-ground or degerminated
  cornmeal
1 cup all-purpose flour
1 cup rye flour
2 teaspoons grated orange peel
1 teaspoon baking powder
1 teaspoon baking soda
1 teaspoon ground cinnamon
1/2 teaspoon salt

Heat oven to 350°. Spray loaf pan, 9×5×3 or 8½×4½×2½ inches, with nonstick cooking spray. Mix yogurt, sour cream, grape juice and maple syrup in large bowl. Stir in remaining ingredients except apple juice concentrate. Spread in pan. Bake 35 to 40 minutes or until toothpick inserted in center comes out clean. Remove from pan. Brush with apple juice concentrate. Cool completely on wire rack before slicing. *1 loaf (24 slices)*

NUTRITION INFORMATION PER SERVING

1 slice		Percent of U.S. RDA	
Calories	70	Protein	2%
Protein, g	2	Vitamin A	*
Carbohydrate, g	16	Vitamin C	2%
Fat, g	0	Thiamin	6%
Unsaturated	0	Riboflavin	4%
Saturated	0	Niacin	4%
Dietary Fiber, g	1	Calcium	4%
Cholesterol, mg	0	Iron	4%
Sodium, mg	100		
Potassium, mg	65		

Barley-Corn Bread

This is a good dinner bread, a hearty accompaniment to soups and stews.

1 cup cooked pearl barley
1 cup stone-ground or degerminated
   cornmeal
1 cup all-purpose flour
½ cup whole kernel corn
1 tablespoon baking powder
½ teaspoon baking soda
½ teaspoon salt
¼ teaspoon white pepper
½ cup plain nonfat yogurt
1 cup nonfat buttermilk
1 tablespoon frozen (thawed) apple juice
   concentrate
2 egg whites or ¼ cup cholesterol-free egg
   product

Heat oven to 350°. Spray round pan, 9×1½ inches, or square pan, 8×8×2 inches, with nonstick cooking spray. Mix barley, cornmeal, flour, corn, baking powder, baking soda, salt and pepper in large bowl. Stir in remaining ingredients. Spread in pan. Bake 35 to 40 minutes or until golden brown. Serve warm. *12 servings*

NUTRITION INFORMATION PER SERVING

1 serving		Percent of U.S. RDA	
Calories	120	Protein	6%
Protein, g	4	Vitamin A	*
Carbohydrate, g	24	Vitamin C	*
Fat, g	1	Thiamin	12%
Unsaturated	1	Riboflavin	10%
Saturated	0	Niacin	10%
Dietary Fiber, g	2	Calcium	10%
Cholesterol, mg	0	Iron	6%
Sodium, mg	290		
Potassium, mg	130		

Corn Bread

Instead of serving whole pieces, try splitting pieces of cornbread and spread lightly with margarine. Broil for a few minutes until light brown.

1½ cups stone-ground or degerminated
   cornmeal
½ cup all-purpose flour
¼ cup shortening
1½ cups nonfat buttermilk
2 teaspoons baking powder
1 teaspoon sugar
½ teaspoon salt
½ teaspoon baking soda
3 egg whites or ½ cup cholesterol-free egg
   product

Heat oven to 450°. Spray round pan, 9×1½ inches, or square pan, 8×8×2 inches, with nonstick cooking spray. Mix all ingredients; beat vigorously 30 seconds. Pour into pan. Bake 20 to 25 minutes or until golden brown. Serve warm. *8 servings*

CHILE-CORN BREAD: Stir in 1 can (4 ounces) chopped green chiles, well drained, and ½ teaspoon chile powder.

NUTRITION INFORMATION PER SERVING

1 serving		Percent of U.S. RDA	
Calories	205	Protein	8%
Protein, g	6	Vitamin A	*
Carbohydrate, g	29	Vitamin C	*
Fat, g	7	Thiamin	16%
Unsaturated	5	Riboflavin	16%
Saturated	2	Niacin	8%
Dietary Fiber, g	2	Calcium	12%
Cholesterol, mg	2	Iron	8%
Sodium, mg	350		
Potassium, mg	140		

Cheese and Currant Wedges

1½ cups all-purpose flour

½ cup currants or raisins

1 teaspoon baking powder

½ teaspoon salt

¼ teaspoon baking soda

1 cup shredded reduced-fat mozzarella
    cheese

¾ cup nonfat buttermilk

2 tablespoons olive or vegetable oil

1 egg

Heat oven to 375°. Spray round pan, 9×1½ inches, with nonstick cooking spray. Mix flour, currants, baking powder, salt and baking soda in large bowl. Stir in remaining ingredients. Spread in pan. Bake 30 to 35 minutes or until golden brown. Cool 10 minutes before cutting. Serve warm. *12 wedges*

NUTRITION INFORMATION PER SERVING

1 wedge		Percent of U.S. RDA	
Calories	135	Protein	8%
Protein, g	5	Vitamin A	2%
Carbohydrate, g	18	Vitamin C	*
Fat, g	5	Thiamin	8%
Unsaturated	3	Riboflavin	10%
Saturated	2	Niacin	4%
Dietary Fiber, g	1	Calcium	10%
Cholesterol, mg	25	Iron	4%
Sodium, mg	210		
Potassium, mg	105		

Cheese and Currant Wedges

Bran Breakfast Loaf

1 cup oat bran
²/₃ cup golden raisins
¹/₂ cup chopped dried figs
¹/₃ cup nonfat dry milk (dry)
¹/₂ cup molasses
³/₄ cup boiling water
1 tablespoon margarine
2 egg whites or ¹/₄ cup cholesterol-free egg
  substitute
¹/₂ cup all-purpose flour
¹/₂ cup whole wheat flour
1 teaspoon ground cinnamon
¹/₂ teaspoon baking soda
¹/₂ teaspoon ground ginger
¹/₄ teaspoon salt

Heat oven to 350°. Spray loaf pan, 9×5×3 or 8¹/₂×4¹/₂×2¹/₂ inches, with nonstick cooking spray. Mix oat bran, raisins, figs, dry milk, molasses, water, margarine and egg whites in large bowl. Stir in remaining ingredients. Spread in pan. Bake 30 to 40 minutes or until toothpick inserted in center comes out clean. Cool 5 minutes. Loosen sides of loaf from pan; remove from pan. Cool completely on wire rack before slicing. *1 loaf (24 slices)*

NUTRITION INFORMATION PER SERVING

1 slice		Percent of U.S. RDA	
Calories	85	Protein	2%
Protein, g	2	Vitamin A	*
Carbohydrate, g	17	Vitamin C	*
Fat, g	1	Thiamin	6%
Unsaturated	1	Riboflavin	4%
Saturated	0	Niacin	2%
Dietary Fiber, g	1	Calcium	4%
Cholesterol, mg	0	Iron	6%
Sodium, mg	60		
Potassium, mg	190		

Molasses Crunch Bread

1¹/₂ cups all-purpose flour
1 cup rye flour
¹/₄ cup sunflower nuts
2 teaspoons baking soda
¹/₂ teaspoon baking powder
¹/₂ teaspoon salt
1 cup nonfat ricotta cheese
¹/₂ cup low-fat sour cream
³/₄ cup apple juice
2 tablespoons molasses

Heat oven to 350°. Spray round pan, 9×1¹/₂ inches, or square pan, 8×8×2 inches, with nonstick cooking spray. Mix flours, sunflower nuts, baking soda, baking powder and salt in large bowl. Mix remaining ingredients; stir into flour mixture. Spread in pan. Bake 25 to 30 minutes or until golden brown. Serve warm. *12 servings*

NUTRITION INFORMATION PER SERVING

1 serving		Percent of U.S. RDA	
Calories	160	Protein	8%
Protein, g	6	Vitamin A	4%
Carbohydrate, g	25	Vitamin C	*
Fat, g	4	Thiamin	16%
Unsaturated	2	Riboflavin	8%
Saturated	2	Niacin	6%
Dietary Fiber, g	2	Calcium	10%
Cholesterol, mg	10	Iron	8%
Sodium, mg	280		
Potassium, mg	170		

Potato-Caraway Loaf

1 package regular active dry yeast

$\frac{1}{2}$ cup warm water (105° to 115°)

1 cup mashed cooked potato (about 1
 medium)

1 cup plain nonfat yogurt

2 egg whites or $\frac{1}{4}$ cup cholesterol-free egg
 product

1 teaspoon caraway seed

$\frac{1}{4}$ teaspoon salt

3 to $3\frac{1}{2}$ cups all-purpose flour

Stone-ground or degerminated cornmeal

Dissolve yeast in warm water in large bowl. Stir in remaining ingredients except flour and cornmeal. Stir in enough flour, 1 cup at a time, to make dough easy to handle.

Turn dough onto lightly floured surface; gently roll in flour to coat. Knead 10 to 12 minutes or until smooth and elastic. Spray large bowl with nonstick cooking spray. Place dough in bowl, and turn greased side up. Cover and let rise in

warm place 1 to $1\frac{1}{2}$ hours or until double. (Dough is ready if indentation remains when touched.)

Spray 2 loaf pans, 9×5×3 or $8\frac{1}{2}$×$4\frac{1}{2}$×$2\frac{1}{2}$ inches, with nonstick cooking spray; sprinkle lightly with cornmeal. Punch down dough, and divide in half. Place in pans; pat and smooth with floured hands. Cover and let rise in warm place about 30 minutes or until double.

Heat oven to 375°. Bake about 35 minutes or until golden brown and loaves sound hollow when tapped. Remove from pans. Cool on wire rack. *2 loaves (16 slices each)*

NUTRITION INFORMATION PER SERVING

I slice		Percent of U.S. RDA	
Calories	50	Protein	2%
Protein, g	2	Vitamin A	*
Carbohydrate, g	II	Vitamin C	*
Fat, g	0	Thiamin	6%
Unsaturated	0	Riboflavin	6%
Saturated	0	Niacin	4%
Dietary Fiber, g	I	Calcium	2%
Cholesterol, mg	0	Iron	2%
Sodium, mg	45		
Potassium, mg	55		

Zucchini-Rice Bread

1½ cups all-purpose flour
1 cup cooked rice
1 tablespoon baking powder
¼ teaspoon salt
1½ cups shredded zucchini (about 1½ medium)
½ cup golden raisins
2 tablespoons nonfat dry milk (dry)
3 tablespoons frozen (thawed) apple juice concentrate
1 teaspoon grated lemon peel
3 egg whites or ½ cup cholesterol-free egg product

Heat oven to 350°. Spray round pan, 9×1½ inches, or square pan, 8×8×2 inches, with nonstick cooking spray; dust with flour. Mix flour, rice, baking powder and salt in large bowl. Stir in remaining ingredients. Spread in pan.

Bake about 30 minutes or until golden brown and toothpick inserted in center comes out clean. Cool 10 minutes. *12 servings*

NUTRITION INFORMATION PER SERVING			
1 serving		Percent of U.S. RDA	
Calories	110	Protein	6%
Protein, g	3	Vitamin A	2%
Carbohydrate, g	25	Vitamin C	2%
Fat, g	0	Thiamin	12%
Unsaturated	0	Riboflavin	8%
Saturated	0	Niacin	6%
Dietary Fiber, g	1	Calcium	8%
Cholesterol, mg	0	Iron	6%
Sodium, mg	230		
Potassium, mg	200		

Opposite page: Molasses Crunch Bread (page 83); Above: Zucchini-Rice Bread (right), Tomato-Herb Loaf (left) (page 102)

Savory Curry Loaf

1½ cups all-purpose flour
½ cup whole wheat flour
1½ teaspoons curry powder
1 teaspoon baking powder
1 teaspoon baking soda
½ teaspoon salt
1 cup shredded pear (about 1 medium)
1 cup plain nonfat yogurt
3 tablespoons frozen (thawed) apple juice
   concentrate
1 egg
2 egg whites

Heat oven to 350°. Spray loaf pan, 9×5×3 or 8½×4½×2½ inches, with nonstick cooking spray. Mix flours, curry powder, baking powder, baking soda and salt in large bowl. Mix in remaining ingredients. Spread in pan. Bake 40 to 45 minutes or until toothpick inserted in center comes out clean. Cool in pan 5 minutes; remove from pan. Cool completely on wire rack before slicing. *1 loaf (24 slices)*

NUTRITION INFORMATION PER SERVING

1 slice		Percent of U.S. RDA	
Calories	50	Protein	4%
Protein, g	2	Vitamin A	*
Carbohydrate, g	11	Vitamin C	*
Fat, g	0	Thiamin	4%
Unsaturated	0	Riboflavin	6%
Saturated	0	Niacin	2%
Dietary Fiber, g	1	Calcium	4%
Cholesterol, mg	10	Iron	2%
Sodium, mg	110		
Potassium, mg	70		

Apple-Oat Coffee Cake

Oat Streusel (below)
1 cup all-purpose flour
1 cup whole wheat flour
¾ cup sugar
¼ cup (½ stick) margarine, softened
1 cup low-fat milk
3 teaspoons baking powder
1 teaspoon ground cinnamon
½ teaspoon salt
¼ teaspoon ground nutmeg
¼ teaspoon ground allspice
2 egg whites or ¼ cup cholesterol-free egg
   product
2 cups chopped peeled apples (about 2
   medium)

Heat oven to 350°. Grease square pan, 9×9×2 inches. Prepare Oat Streusel; reserve. Beat remaining ingredients except apples in large bowl on low speed 30 seconds, scraping bowl frequently. Beat on medium speed 2 minutes, scraping bowl occasionally. Stir in apples. Spread half of the batter in pan; sprinkle with half of the streusel. Top with remaining batter; sprinkle with remaining streusel. Bake 40 to 45 minutes or until toothpick inserted in center comes out clean. Serve warm. *9 servings*

Oat Streusel

3 tablespoons firm margarine
1 cup quick-cooking oats
¼ cup chopped nuts
¼ cup all-purpose flour
¼ cup packed brown sugar

Cut margarine into remaining ingredients with pastry blender or fork until crumbly.

NUTRITION INFORMATION PER SERVING

1 serving		Percent of U.S. RDA	
Calories	375	Protein	10%
Protein, g	7	Vitamin A	14%
Carbohydrate, g	57	Vitamin C	*
Fat, g	13	Thiamin	20%
Unsaturated	10	Riboflavin	12%
Saturated	3	Niacin	10%
Dietary Fiber, g	4	Calcium	14%
Cholesterol, mg	2	Iron	12%
Sodium, mg	380		
Potassium, mg	230		

Blueberry–Whole Wheat Coffee Cake

1 cup all-purpose flour
1 cup whole wheat flour
1 cup sugar
⅓ cup margarine, softened
1 cup low-fat milk
3 teaspoons baking powder
½ teaspoon salt
2 egg whites or ¼ cup cholesterol-free egg product
2 cups fresh or frozen (thawed and well drained) blueberries
Glaze (right)

Heat oven to 350°. Spray rectangular pan, 13×9×2 inches, with nonstick cooking spray. Beat all ingredients except blueberries and Glaze in large bowl on low speed 30 seconds. Beat on medium speed 2 minutes, scraping bowl occasionally. Spread half of batter in pan; sprinkle with half of the blueberries. Top with remaining batter; sprinkle with remaining blueberries. Bake about 35 minutes or until toothpick inserted in center comes out clean. Cool 20 minutes. Drizzle warm coffee cake with Glaze. Serve warm. *12 servings*

Glaze

1 cup powdered sugar
1 teaspoon grated lemon peel
1 to 2 tablespoons lemon juice

Mix all ingredients until drizzling consistency.

BLUEBERRY-ORANGE–WHOLE WHEAT COFFEE CAKE: Stir 1 teaspoon ground cinnamon into the flour mixture. Substitute 1 teaspoon grated orange peel for the lemon peel and 1 to 2 tablespoons orange juice for the lemon juice in the glaze.

NUTRITION INFORMATION PER SERVING

1 serving		Percent of U.S. RDA	
Calories	260	Protein	6%
Protein, g	4	Vitamin A	8%
Carbohydrate, g	47	Vitamin C	2%
Fat, g	6	Thiamin	10%
Unsaturated	5	Riboflavin	8%
Saturated	1	Niacin	6%
Dietary Fiber, g	2	Calcium	8%
Cholesterol, mg	2	Iron	4%
Sodium, mg	260		
Potassium, mg	120		

Carrot Coffee Cake

1 cup all-purpose flour
1 cup whole wheat flour
1 cup plain nonfat yogurt
²/₃ cup sugar
¹/₃ cup margarine, softened
1 teaspoon baking powder
1 teaspoon baking soda
¹/₄ teaspoon ground ginger
3 egg whites or ¹/₂ cup cholesterol-free egg
    product
1 cup shredded carrot (about 1 large)
¹/₂ cup raisins or chopped dates
3 tablespoons sugar
1 tablespoon grated orange peel

Heat oven to 350°. Spray square pan, 9×9×2 inches, with nonstick cooking spray. Beat flours, yogurt, ²/₃ cup sugar, the margarine, baking powder, baking soda, ginger and egg whites in large bowl on low speed 30 seconds, scraping bowl frequently. Beat on medium speed 2 minutes, scraping bowl occasionally. Stir in carrot and raisins. Spread batter in pan. Mix 3 tablespoons sugar and the orange peel; sprinkle over batter. Bake 35 to 40 minutes or until toothpick inserted in center comes out clean. Serve warm. *9 servings*

NUTRITION INFORMATION PER SERVING			
I serving		Percent of U.S. RDA	
Calories	285	Protein	10%
Protein, g	6	Vitamin A	28%
Carbohydrate, g	49	Vitamin C	2%
Fat, g	7	Thiamin	14%
Unsaturated	6	Riboflavin	14%
Saturated	1	Niacin	10%
Dietary Fiber, g	3	Calcium	10%
Cholesterol, mg	0	Iron	8%
Sodium, mg	260		
Potassium, mg	270		

Raisin-Spice Coffee Cake

1 cup all-purpose flour
1 cup whole wheat flour
1 cup sugar
¹/₄ cup (¹/₂ stick) margarine, softened
1 cup low-fat milk
3 teaspoons baking powder
1 teaspoon ground cinnamon
¹/₂ teaspoon salt
¹/₄ teaspoon ground allspice
¹/₄ teaspoon ground nutmeg
2 egg whites or ¹/₄ cup cholesterol-free egg
    product
¹/₂ cup raisins
Streusel (below)

Heat oven to 350°. Spray square pan, 9×9×2 inches, with nonstick cooking spray. Beat all ingredients except raisins and Streusel on low speed 30 seconds. Beat on medium speed 2 minutes, scraping bowl occasionally. Stir in raisins. Spread batter in pan. Sprinkle with Streusel. Bake 40 to 45 minutes or until toothpick inserted in center comes out clean. Serve warm. *9 servings*

Streusel

2 tablespoons firm margarine
¹/₄ cup all-purpose flour
2 tablespoons packed brown sugar or
    granulated sugar
¹/₂ teaspoon ground cinnamon
¹/₄ cup chopped nuts

Cut margarine into flour, brown sugar and cinnamon with pastry blender or fork until crumbly. Stir in nuts.

NUTRITION INFORMATION PER SERVING			
I serving		**Percent of U.S. RDA**	
Calories	350	Protein	8%
Protein, g	6	Vitamin A	12%
Carbohydrate, g	57	Vitamin C	*
Fat, g	11	Thiamin	16%
Unsaturated	9	Riboflavin	12%
Saturated	2	Niacin	10%
Dietary Fiber, g	3	Calcium	12%
Cholesterol, mg	2	Iron	10%
Sodium, mg	360		
Potassium, mg	230		

Glazed Date Rolls

Out of dates? Try filling these morsels with a rounded teaspoonful of raisins or chopped mixed dried fruits.

1/4 **cup shortening**
1 **cup all-purpose flour**
1 **cup whole wheat flour**
2 **tablespoons sugar**
3 **teaspoons baking powder**
1/2 **teaspoon salt**
3/4 **cup plain nonfat yogurt**
1 **tablespoon low-fat milk**
12 **pitted whole dates**
Glaze (right)

Heat oven to 425°. Grease round pan, 8×1½ inches, or square pan, 8×8×2 inches. Cut shortening into flours, sugar, baking powder and salt in medium bowl with pastry blender until mixture resembles fine crumbs. Stir in yogurt and milk until dough forms a ball. Turn dough onto lightly floured surface; gently roll in flour to coat. Knead lightly 20 to 25 times. Divide dough into 12 pieces; keep dough covered while making rolls.

For each roll, pat 1 piece dough into 3-inch circle on floured surface. Place 1 date in center of circle. Bring edges of dough up over date; pinch and seal well to form a ball. Repeat with remaining dough pieces and dates. Place 8 or 9 balls, seam sides down, around edge of pan; place remaining balls in center. Bake 17 to 19 minutes or until golden brown. Remove from pan; place on wire rack. Cool 10 minutes. Drizzle with Glaze. Serve warm or let stand until cool. *12 rolls*

Glaze

1/3 cup powdered sugar
1½ teaspoons low-fat milk
1/8 teaspoon vanilla

Mix all ingredients until smooth.

NUTRITION INFORMATION PER SERVING			
I roll		**Percent of U.S. RDA**	
Calories	170	Protein	4%
Protein, g	3	Vitamin A	*
Carbohydrate, g	28	Vitamin C	*
Fat, g	5	Thiamin	8%
Unsaturated	4	Riboflavin	6%
Saturated	1	Niacin	6%
Dietary Fiber, g	2	Calcium	10%
Cholesterol, mg	0	Iron	4%
Sodium, mg	200		
Potassium, mg	150		

Buttermilk-Raisin Breakfast Buns

Instead of the usual sugar glaze, we've used strawberry spreadable fruit to top these buns with luscious flavor. You can also try apricot, raspberry, or your favorite flavor of spreadable fruit.

2 teaspoons margarine

3 to 3½ cups all-purpose flour

1 tablespoon baking powder

½ teaspoon salt

1 cup nonfat buttermilk

3 egg whites or ½ cup cholesterol-free egg product

1½ cups golden raisins

1 container (6 ounces) unsweetened applesauce (¾ cup)

2 teaspoons ground cinnamon

2 tablespoons strawberry spreadable fruit, melted

Heat oven to 400°. Spray rectangular pan, 13×9×2 inches, with nonstick cooking spray. Cut margarine into flour, baking powder and salt in large bowl with pastry blender until mixture resembles fine crumbs. Mix in buttermilk and egg whites.

Turn dough onto lightly floured surface; gently knead in enough flour to make dough easy to handle. (Dough will be soft.) Roll dough into 8-inch square. Mix raisins, applesauce and cinnamon; spread over dough. Roll up dough; pinch edge of dough into roll to seal. Cut roll into 8 slices. Place 1 inch apart in pan. Bake 20 to 25 minutes or until light brown. Brush with spreadable fruit. Remove from pan. Cool on wire rack. *8 buns*

BUTTERMILK-MIXED FRUIT BREAKFAST BUNS: Substitute 1½ cups diced dried fruit and raisin mixture for the raisins. Decrease cinnamon to 1 teaspoon. Stir 1 teaspoon ground ginger into the applesauce mixture.

NUTRITION INFORMATION PER SERVING			
1 bun		**Percent of U.S. RDA**	
Calories	320	Protein	12%
Protein, g	8	Vitamin A	2%
Carbohydrate, g	67	Vitamin C	2%
Fat, g	2	Thiamin	26%
Unsaturated	1	Riboflavin	22%
Saturated	1	Niacin	16%
Dietary Fiber, g	3	Calcium	14%
Cholesterol, mg	0	Iron	18%
Sodium, mg	350		
Potassium, mg	380		

From top: Glazed Date Rolls (page 89), Apple-Oat Coffee Cake (page 86), Buttermilk-Raisin Breakfast Buns

Tropical Banana Tea Wedges

These tea wedges, similar to scones, are lovely with a cup of tea. Drop a piece of crystallized ginger in your tea for extra flavor and interest.

1 cup all-purpose flour
1 cup whole wheat flour
1 cup chopped dried apricots
¹/₂ cup oat bran
¹/₄ cup packed brown sugar
2 teaspoons baking powder
1 teaspoon ground cinnamon
¹/₂ teaspoon ground cloves
¹/₂ teaspoon baking soda
¹/₄ teaspoon salt
3 tablespoons margarine
³/₄ cup mashed ripe banana
¹/₄ cup vanilla nonfat yogurt
2 egg whites or ¹/₄ cup cholesterol-free egg
    product

Heat oven to 375°. Spray cookie sheet with nonstick cooking spray. Mix flours, apricots, oat bran, brown sugar, baking powder, cinnamon, cloves, baking soda and salt in large bowl. Cut in margarine with pastry blender until mixture resembles fine crumbs. Mix remaining ingredients until smooth; stir into flour mixture until dough leaves side of bowl.

Turn dough onto lightly floured surface; gently roll in flour to coat. Knead lightly 10 times. Pat into 12-inch circle on cookie sheet. Cut into 16 wedges with floured knife, but do not separate. Bake about 30 minutes or until light brown. Remove from cookie sheet; separate wedges. Serve warm. *16 wedges*

NUTRITION INFORMATION PER SERVING			
1 wedge		Percent of U.S. RDA	
Calories	145	Protein	4%
Protein, g	3	Vitamin A	8%
Carbohydrate, g	26	Vitamin C	*
Fat, g	3	Thiamin	10%
Unsaturated	2	Riboflavin	8%
Saturated	1	Niacin	6%
Dietary Fiber, g	2	Calcium	4%
Cholesterol, mg	0	Iron	8%
Sodium, mg	140		
Potassium, mg	220		

Two-Onion Bagels

Authentic bagels are actually boiled for several minutes before baking. Our method is quicker, and produces a bread that is truly worthy of the name "bagel." Use a large slotted spoon to dip and remove the bagels from the water.

2 packages regular active dry yeast
1¹/₄ cups warm water (105° to 115°)
¹/₄ cup finely chopped onion (about 1 small)
¹/₄ cup finely chopped shallots (about 2
    large)
1 teaspoon salt
¹/₈ teaspoon pepper
3¹/₂ to 4 cups all-purpose flour
Stone-ground or degerminated cornmeal
Hot water

Dissolve yeast in warm water in large bowl. Stir in onion, shallots, salt, pepper and enough flour, 1 cup at a time, to make dough easy to handle.

Turn dough onto lightly floured surface; gently roll in flour to coat. Knead about 10 minutes or until dough is smooth and elastic. Spray large bowl with nonstick cooking spray. Place dough in bowl, and turn greased side up. Cover and let rise in warm place about 30 minutes or until almost double. (Dough is ready if indentation remains when touched.)

Spray cookie sheet with nonstick cooking spray; sprinkle with cornmeal. Punch down dough. Divide into 12 pieces; shape into balls with floured hands. Poke a hole into center of each ball and enlarge hole with thumb to 1½ inches. Place on cookie sheet. Cover and let rise in warm place 15 minutes.

Heat oven to 400°. Carefully lift each bagel off cookie sheet and dip into hot water. Place back on cookie sheet; reshape hole if necessary. Bake 25 to 30 minutes or until golden brown. Remove from cookie sheet. Cool on wire rack.
12 bagels

NUTRITION INFORMATION PER SERVING			
1 bagel		**Percent of U.S. RDA**	
Calories	130	Protein	6%
Protein, g	4	Vitamin A	*
Carbohydrate, g	29	Vitamin C	*
Fat, g	0	Thiamin	20%
Unsaturated	0	Riboflavin	14%
Saturated	0	Niacin	12%
Dietary Fiber, g	2	Calcium	*
Cholesterol, mg	0	Iron	10%
Sodium, mg	180		
Potassium, mg	80		

Two-Onion Bagels

Sesame Breadsticks

¾ cup warm water (105° to 115°)
2 teaspoons sesame seed, toasted
1 teaspoon regular active dry yeast
½ teaspoon salt
1 teaspoon honey
1½ teaspoons vegetable oil
1½ to 2 cups all-purpose flour

Spray rectangular pan, 13×9×2 inches, with nonstick cooking spray. Mix all ingredients except flour in large bowl until yeast is dissolved. Stir in enough flour, 1 cup at a time, to make dough easy to handle.

Turn dough onto lightly floured surface; gently roll in flour to coat. Knead about 5 minutes or until smooth and elastic. Place dough in pan; let rest 10 minutes. Spread dough to edges of pan. Cover and let rise in warm place 35 to 45 minutes or until double. (Dough is ready if indentation remains when touched.)

Heat oven to 400°. Spray cookie sheet with nonstick cooking spray. Turn dough onto floured surface. Fold lengthwise in half. Cut crosswise into 20 strips. Unfold and roll each strip to 12 inches in length. Place on cookie sheet. Bake about 20 minutes or until golden brown. *20 breadsticks*

NUTRITION INFORMATION PER SERVING			
1 breadstick		Percent of U.S. RDA	
Calories	45	Protein	2%
Protein, g	1	Vitamin A	*
Carbohydrate, g	8	Vitamin C	*
Fat, g	1	Thiamin	6%
Unsaturated	1	Riboflavin	4%
Saturated	0	Niacin	2%
Dietary Fiber, g	0	Calcium	*
Cholesterol, mg	0	Iron	2%
Sodium, mg	55		
Potassium, mg	20		

Carrot-Dill Rolls

1 package regular or quick-acting* active dry yeast
½ cup warm water (105° to 115°)
1 cup mashed cooked carrots (about 2 medium)
¼ cup low-fat sour cream
½ cup nonfat buttermilk
¼ cup frozen (thawed) apple juice concentrate
1 teaspoon dried dill weed
½ teaspoon salt
4 to 4½ cups all-purpose flour
Stone-ground or degerminated cornmeal

Dissolve yeast in warm water in large bowl. Stir in remaining ingredients except flour and cornmeal. Stir in enough flour, 1 cup at a time, to make dough easy to handle.

Turn dough onto lightly floured surface; gently roll in flour to coat. Knead about 10 minutes or until smooth and elastic. Spray bowl with nonstick cooking spray. Place dough in bowl, and turn greased side up. Cover and let rise about 1 hour or until double. (Dough is ready if indentation remains when touched.)

Spray cookie sheet with nonstick cooking spray; sprinkle with cornmeal. Punch down dough, and divide into halves. Divide each half into 6 pieces; shape into balls with floured hands. Place 2 inches apart on cookie sheet. Cover and let rise in warm place 30 minutes or until double.

Heat oven to 375°. Brush rolls with water. Bake about 35 minutes or until golden brown. *12 rolls*

* If using quick-acting yeast, let dough rest 10 minutes after kneading, and omit first rising time.

NUTRITION INFORMATION PER SERVING			
1 roll		**Percent of U.S. RDA**	
Calories	180	Protein	8%
Protein, g	5	Vitamin A	48%
Carbohydrate, g	38	Vitamin C	*
Fat, g	1	Thiamin	24%
Unsaturated	1	Riboflavin	16%
Saturated	0	Niacin	14%
Dietary Fiber, g	2	Calcium	2%
Cholesterol, mg	0	Iron	12%
Sodium, mg	150		
Potassium, mg	150		

Oat Bran Bread

4¹/₂ to 5 cups all-purpose flour

1 cup uncooked oat bran hot cereal

1 cup quick-cooking oats

¹/₃ cup molasses

3 tablespoons shortening

1 teaspoon salt

**2 packages regular or quick-acting* active
dry yeast**

2 cups very warm water (120° to 130°)

1 egg white, slightly beaten

1 tablespoon cold water

Quick-cooking oats

Mix 2 cups of the flour, the cereal, 1 cup oats, the molasses, shortening, salt and yeast in large bowl. Add warm water. Beat on low speed 1 minute, scraping bowl frequently. Beat on medium speed 1 minute, scraping bowl frequently. Stir in enough remaining flour, 1 cup at a time, to make dough easy to handle.

Turn dough onto lightly floured surface; gently roll in flour to coat. Knead about 10 minutes or until smooth and elastic. Spray large bowl with nonstick cooking spray. Place dough in bowl, and turn greased side up.

Cover and let rise in warm place about 1¹/₄ hours or until double. (Dough is ready if indentation remains when touched.)

Spray 2 loaf pans, 9×5×3 or 8¹/₂×4¹/₂×2¹/₂ inches, with nonstick cooking spray. Punch down dough, and divide into halves. Roll each half into rectangle, 18×9 inches, on lightly floured surface. (If dough shrinks, gently stretch into rectangle.) Roll up tightly, beginning at 9-inch side. Press with thumbs to seal after each turn. Pinch edge of dough firmly into roll to seal. Press each end with side of hand to seal. Fold ends under loaf. Place seam side down in pan. Cover and let rise in warm place about 1 hour or until double.

Move oven rack to lowest position. Heat oven to 375°. Mix egg white and 1 tablespoon cold water; brush over loaves. Sprinkle with oats. Bake 35 to 40 minutes or until loaves are deep golden brown and sound hollow when tapped. Remove from pans. Cool on wire rack. *2 loaves (16 slices each)*

* If using quick-acting yeast, let dough rest 10 minutes after kneading, and omit first rising time.

NUTRITION INFORMATION PER SERVING			
1 slice		**Percent of U.S. RDA**	
Calories	115	Protein	4%
Protein, g	3	Vitamin A	*
Carbohydrate, g	21	Vitamin C	*
Fat, g	2	Thiamin	14%
Unsaturated	2	Riboflavin	8%
Saturated	0	Niacin	6%
Dietary Fiber, g	1	Calcium	2%
Cholesterol, mg	0	Iron	8%
Sodium, mg	70		
Potassium, mg	95		

Bulgur Bread (left), *Pumpkin-Rye Bread* (right) (*page 99*)

Bulgur Bread

This hearty bread, made with a double dose of wheat, can be served in wedges or slices.

**1 package regular or quick-acting* active
  dry yeast**
1¼ cups warm water (105° to 115°)
1½ cups cooked bulgur
1 cup whole wheat flour
1 cup nonfat dry milk (dry)
2 teaspoons grated lemon peel
½ teaspoon salt
2½ to 2¾ cups all-purpose flour
1 tablespoon nonfat buttermilk
1 teaspoon uncooked bulgur

Dissolve yeast in warm water in large bowl. Mix in remaining ingredients except all-purpose flour, buttermilk and uncooked bulgur.

Stir in enough all-purpose flour, 1 cup at a time, to make dough easy to handle.

Turn dough onto lightly floured surface; gently roll in flour to coat. Knead about 10 minutes or until smooth and elastic. Spray large bowl with nonstick cooking spray. Place dough in bowl, and turn greased side up. Cover and let rise in warm place about 1½ hours or until double. (Dough is ready if indentation remains when touched.)

Spray round pan, 9×1½ or 8×1½ inches, with nonstick cooking spray. Punch down dough. Shape into round, slightly flattened loaf. Place in pan. Cover and let rise in warm place 30 to 40 minutes or until double.

Heat oven to 375°. Brush dough with buttermilk, and sprinkle with uncooked bulgur. Bake about 35 minutes or until golden brown and loaf sounds hollow when tapped. Remove from pan. Cool on wire rack. *1 loaf* (*16 wedges*)

* If using quick-acting yeast, let dough rest 10 minutes after kneading, and omit first rising time.

NUTRITION INFORMATION PER SERVING			
I wedge		Percent of U.S. RDA	
Calories	120	Protein	8%
Protein, g	5	Vitamin A	2%
Carbohydrate, g	25	Vitamin C	*
Fat, g	0	Thiamin	14%
Unsaturated	0	Riboflavin	12%
Saturated	0	Niacin	10%
Dietary Fiber, g	2	Calcium	6%
Cholesterol, mg	0	Iron	8%
Sodium, mg	170		
Potassium, mg	150		

High-Fiber Honey–Whole Wheat Loaf

2½ to 2¾ cups all-purpose flour
½ teaspoon salt
1 package regular or quick-acting* active
  dry yeast
1½ cups very warm water (120° to 130°)
¼ cup honey
1 tablespoon olive or vegetable oil
1 cup whole wheat flour
1 cup high-fiber bran cereal

Mix 1¾ cups of the all-purpose flour, the salt and yeast in large bowl. Add warm water, honey and oil. Beat on low speed 1 minute, scraping bowl frequently. Beat on medium speed 1 minute, scraping bowl frequently. Stir in whole wheat flour and cereal. Stir in enough remaining all-purpose flour, ¼ cup at a time, to make dough easy to handle.

Turn dough onto lightly floured surface; gently roll in flour to coat. Knead about 10 minutes or until smooth and elastic. Spray large bowl with nonstick cooking spray. Place dough in bowl, and turn greased side up. Cover and let rise in warm place about 1¼ hours or until double. (Dough is ready if indentation remains when touched.)

Spray cookie sheet with nonstick cooking spray. Punch down dough. Shape into round loaf. Place on cookie sheet. Cover and let rise in warm place about 40 minutes or until double.

Heat oven to 350°. Bake 30 to 35 minutes or until golden brown and loaf sounds hollow when tapped. Remove from cookie sheet. Cool on wire rack. *1 loaf (16 slices)*

* If using quick-acting yeast, let dough rest 10 minutes after kneading, and omit first rising time.

NUTRITION INFORMATION PER SERVING			
I slice		Percent of U.S. RDA	
Calories	135	Protein	4%
Protein, g	3	Vitamin A	4%
Carbohydrate, g	28	Vitamin C	*
Fat, g	1	Thiamin	16%
Unsaturated	1	Riboflavin	10%
Saturated	0	Niacin	12%
Dietary Fiber, g	3	Calcium	*
Cholesterol, mg	0	Iron	10%
Sodium, mg	85		
Potassium, mg	95		

Millet-Wheat Casserole Bread

Casserole breads are the easiest yeast breads— no kneading needed! Millet, considered the most digestible of all grains, adds a chewy texture to the bread. The flavor is similar to that of brown rice, and millet's high-quality protein (see page 64) makes it an excellent addition to any meatless meal.

1½ cups water

½ cup uncooked millet

¼ cup honey

¼ cup (½ stick) margarine

1 cup all-purpose flour

½ cup nonfat dry milk (dry)

½ cup wheat germ

1 teaspoon salt

1 package regular or quick-acting* active
   dry yeast

1½ cups whole wheat flour

½ cup sunflower nuts

Heat water and millet to boiling in 1-quart saucepan; reduce heat. Cover and simmer 10 minutes. Stir in honey and margarine; cool to very warm (120° to 130°).

Mix all-purpose flour, dry milk, wheat germ, salt and yeast in large bowl. Add millet mixture. Beat on low speed until flour is moistened. Beat on medium speed 2 minutes, scraping bowl occasionally. Stir in whole wheat flour and sunflower nuts. Scrape batter from side of bowl. Cover and let rise in warm place about 45 minutes or until double. (Dough is ready if indentation remains when touched.)

Spray 2-quart casserole with nonstick cooking spray. Stir down batter by beating 25 strokes. Spread in casserole. Cover and let rise in warm place about 30 minutes or until double.

Heat oven to 375°. Bake 40 to 45 minutes or until golden brown and loaf sounds hollow when tapped. *1 loaf (16 slices)*

* Do not omit first rising time if using quick-acting yeast.

NUTRITION INFORMATION PER SERVING			
1 serving		**Percent of U.S. RDA**	
Calories	175	Protein	8%
Protein, g	5	Vitamin A	4%
Carbohydrate, g	25	Vitamin C	*
Fat, g	6	Thiamin	20%
Unsaturated	5	Riboflavin	10%
Saturated	1	Niacin	10%
Dietary Fiber, g	3	Calcium	4%
Cholesterol, mg	0	Iron	8%
Sodium, mg	180		
Potassium, mg	180		

Oatmeal Bread

With its tender crumb, this is an ideal sandwich bread.

1 package regular active dry yeast

½ cup warm water (105° to 115°)

1½ cups cooked oatmeal

½ cup low-fat milk

½ teaspoon salt

1 container (6 ounces) unsweetened
   applesauce (¾ cup)

5 to 5½ cups all-purpose flour

2 tablespoons regular or quick-cooking oats

1 tablespoon nonfat buttermilk

Dissolve yeast in warm water in large bowl. Stir in oatmeal, milk, salt and applesauce. Stir in enough flour, 1 cup at a time, to make dough easy to handle.

Turn dough onto lightly floured surface; gently roll in flour to coat. Knead about 10 minutes, adding enough flour to keep dough from sticking, until smooth and elastic. Spray large bowl with nonstick cooking spray. Place dough in greased bowl, and turn greased side up. Cover and let rise in warm place about 1 hour or until double. (Dough is ready if indentation remains when touched.)

Heat oven to 375°. Spray cookie sheet with nonstick cooking spray; sprinkle with 1 tablespoon of the oats. Punch down dough. Turn onto lightly floured surface; gently roll in flour to coat. Knead 10 times. Divide dough into halves. Shape each half into round loaf. Place loaves on opposite corners of cookie sheet. Cover and let rise in warm place about 30 minutes or until double. Brush loaves with buttermilk. Sprinkle with remaining oats. Bake 40 to 45 minutes or until golden brown. Remove from cookie sheet. Cool on wire rack. *2 loaves (12 wedges each)*

NUTRITION INFORMATION PER SERVING

1 wedge		Percent of U.S. RDA	
Calories	115	Protein	4%
Protein, g	3	Vitamin A	*
Carbohydrate, g	23	Vitamin C	*
Fat, g	1	Thiamin	14%
Unsaturated	1	Riboflavin	8%
Saturated	0	Niacin	8%
Dietary Fiber, g	1	Calcium	*
Cholesterol, mg	0	Iron	8%
Sodium, mg	70		
Potassium, mg	55		

Pumpkin-Rye Bread

1 package regular active dry yeast
¼ cup warm water (105° to 115°)
½ cup warm apple juice (105° to 115°)
½ teaspoon salt
½ teaspoon ground nutmeg
½ teaspoon ground ginger
1 can (15 ounces) pumpkin
1 cup rye flour
3½ to 3¾ cups all-purpose flour

Dissolve yeast in warm water in large bowl. Stir in remaining ingredients except flours. Stir in rye flour. Stir in enough all-purpose flour, 1 cup at a time, to make dough easy to handle.

Turn dough onto lightly floured surface; gently roll in flour to coat. Knead about 10 minutes or until smooth and elastic. (Dough will be soft.) Spray large bowl with nonstick cooking spray. Place dough in bowl, and turn greased side up. Cover and let rise in warm place about 1¼ hours or until double. (Dough is ready if indentation remains when touched.)

Spray 2 loaf pans, 9×5×3 or 8½×4½×2½ inches, with nonstick cooking spray. Punch down dough. Turn dough onto lightly floured surface; gently roll in flour to coat. Knead 2 minutes. Divide dough in half, and place in pans. Cover and let rise in warm place about 30 minutes or until almost double.

Heat oven to 375°. Bake about 40 minutes or until golden brown and loaves sound hollow when tapped. Remove from pans. Cool on wire rack. *2 loaves (16 slices each)*

NUTRITION INFORMATION PER SERVING

1 slice		Percent of U.S. RDA	
Calories	70	Protein	2%
Protein, g	2	Vitamin A	28%
Carbohydrate, g	15	Vitamin C	*
Fat, g	0	Thiamin	8%
Unsaturated	0	Riboflavin	6%
Saturated	0	Niacin	4%
Dietary Fiber, g	1	Calcium	*
Cholesterol, mg	0	Iron	4%
Sodium, mg	55		
Potassium, mg	65		

Tex-Mex Pan Bread

You'll find the batter looks curdled after adding the lime juice, but after stirring in the flour, it will be just right. This bread is excellent with grilled summer foods or served with South-western Stir-fried Shrimp (page 295).

1 package regular active dry yeast
¼ cup very warm water (105° to 115°)
1 cup very warm low-fat milk (105° to 115°)
¼ cup lime juice
1 teaspoon chile powder
2 teaspoons vegetable oil
½ teaspoon salt
½ teaspoon ground cumin
½ cup semolina flour
2½ to 2¾ cups all-purpose flour

Dissolve yeast in warm water in large bowl. Stir in remaining ingredients except flours. (Mixture may appear curdled.) Stir in semolina flour. Stir in enough all-purpose flour, 1 cup at a time, to make dough easy to handle.

Turn dough onto lightly floured surface; gently roll in flour to coat. Knead 5 to 7 minutes or until smooth and elastic. Spray medium bowl with nonstick cooking spray. Place dough in bowl, and turn greased side up. Cover and let rise in warm place about 1 hour or until double. (Dough is ready if indentation remains when touched.)

Spray round pan, 9×1½ inches, or square pan, 8×8×2 inches, with nonstick cooking spray. Punch down dough. Turn onto lightly floured surface; gently roll in flour to coat. Knead 1 minute. Place in pan. Cover and let rise in warm place about 40 minutes or until double.

Heat oven to 350°. Bake 35 to 40 minutes or until golden brown and loaf sounds hollow when tapped. *12 servings*

NUTRITION INFORMATION PER SERVING			
I serving		**Percent of U.S. RDA**	
Calories	140	Protein	6%
Protein, g	4	Vitamin A	2%
Carbohydrate, g	26	Vitamin C	*
Fat, g	2	Thiamin	18%
Unsaturated	2	Riboflavin	12%
Saturated	0	Niacin	10%
Dietary Fiber, g	I	Calcium	2%
Cholesterol, mg	0	Iron	8%
Sodium, mg	100		
Potassium, mg	90		

Whole Wheat Baguette

½ cup water
¼ cup frozen (thawed) apple juice
   concentrate
1 package regular active dry yeast
¾ cup nonfat dry milk (dry)
½ cup whole wheat flour
½ teaspoon salt
2 egg whites or ¼ cup cholesterol-free egg
   product
1½ to 1¾ cups all-purpose flour
Stone-ground or degerminated cornmeal

Heat water and apple juice concentrate to 105° to 115°. Dissolve yeast in warm apple juice mixture in large bowl. Stir in remaining ingredients except all-purpose flour and cornmeal. Stir in enough all-purpose flour, 1 cup at a time, to make dough easy to handle.

Turn dough onto lightly floured surface; gently roll in flour to coat. Knead about 5 minutes or until smooth and elastic. Spray large bowl with nonstick cooking spray. Place dough in bowl, and turn greased side up. Cover and let rise in warm place about 1½ hours or until double. (Dough is ready if indentation remains when touched.)

Whole Wheat Baguette, Ratatouille Soup (page 133)

Spray cookie sheet with nonstick cooking spray; sprinkle lightly with cornmeal. Punch down dough, and divide into halves. Roll each half into rectangle, 13×6 inches. Roll up rectangle, beginning at 13-inch side. Pinch edge of dough into roll to seal, and taper ends. Place on cookie sheet. Make ¼-inch-deep slashes across loaves at 2-inch intervals. Cover and let rise in warm place about 30 minutes or until almost double.

Heat oven to 400°. Bake 20 to 25 minutes or until golden brown. Remove from cookie sheet. Cool on wire rack. *2 loaves (12 slices each)*

NUTRITION INFORMATION PER SERVING			
1 slice		**Percent of U.S. RDA**	
Calories	60	Protein	4%
Protein, g	3	Vitamin A	2%
Carbohydrate, g	12	Vitamin C	*
Fat, g	0	Thiamin	6%
Unsaturated	0	Riboflavin	8%
Saturated	0	Niacin	4%
Dietary Fiber, g	1	Calcium	4%
Cholesterol, mg	0	Iron	2%
Sodium, mg	70		
Potassium, mg	110		

Tomato-Herb Loaf

1 package regular active dry yeast

¹⁄₄ cup warm water (105° to 115°)

1¹⁄₂ cups plain nonfat yogurt

¹⁄₂ cup warm tomato juice (105° to 115°)

3 tablespoons chopped fresh or 1
    tablespoon dried basil leaves

2 tablespoons frozen (thawed) apple juice
    concentrate

1 tablespoon tomato paste

¹⁄₂ teaspoon salt

2 egg whites

1 egg

5 to 5¹⁄₂ cups all-purpose flour

Dissolve yeast in warm water in large bowl. Stir in remaining ingredients except flour. Stir in enough flour, 1 cup at a time, to make dough easy to handle.

Turn dough onto lightly floured surface; gently roll in flour to coat. Knead about 10 minutes or until smooth and elastic. Spray large bowl with nonstick cooking spray. Place dough in bowl, and turn greased side up. Cover and let rise in warm place about 1¹⁄₂ hours or until double. (Dough is ready if indentation remains when touched.)

Spray 2 loaf pans, 9×5×3 or 8¹⁄₂×4¹⁄₂×2¹⁄₂ inches, with nonstick cooking spray. Punch down dough, and divide into halves. Place in pans; pat and smooth with floured hands. Cover and let rise in warm place 45 to 60 minutes or until double.

Heat oven to 350°. Bake about 40 minutes or until golden brown and loaves sound hollow when tapped. Remove from pans. Cool completely on wire rack before slicing. *2 loaves (16 slices each)*

NUTRITION INFORMATION PER SERVING			
1 slice		**Percent of U.S. RDA**	
Calories	80	Protein	4%
Protein, g	3	Vitamin A	*
Carbohydrate, g	17	Vitamin C	*
Fat, g	0	Thiamin	10%
Unsaturated	0	Riboflavin	8%
Saturated	0	Niacin	6%
Dietary Fiber, g	1	Calcium	2%
Cholesterol, mg	5	Iron	6%
Sodium, mg	65		
Potassium, mg	80		

Winter Hearth Bread

This hearty bread recalls the days of hearth-baked loaves. Serve in wedges with soups and stews, or slice and substitute for the corn bread in Hot Open-faced Creole Sandwiches (page 310).

5 to 6 cups bread flour or all-purpose flour

3 tablespoons olive or vegetable oil

1 tablespoon crumbled dried sage leaves

1 teaspoon salt

¹⁄₄ teaspoon pepper

1 package regular or quick-acting* active
    dry yeast

1³⁄₄ cups water

¹⁄₂ cup dry white wine or apple juice

¹⁄₂ cup whole wheat flour

¹⁄₂ cup stone-ground or degerminated
    cornmeal

Stone-ground or degerminated cornmeal

Bread flour or all-purpose flour

Mix 3 cups of the bread flour, the oil, sage, salt, pepper and yeast in large bowl. Heat water and wine in 1¹⁄₂-quart saucepan to 120° to 130°; add

Winter Hearth Bread, Harvest Chicken Stew (page 260)

to flour mixture. Beat on low speed 1 minute, scraping bowl frequently. Beat on medium speed 1 minute, scraping bowl frequently. Stir in whole wheat flour and ½ cup cornmeal. Stir in enough remaining bread flour to make dough easy to handle.

Turn dough onto lightly floured surface; gently roll in flour to coat. Knead about 10 minutes or until smooth and elastic. Spray large bowl with nonstick cooking spray. Place dough in bowl, and turn greased side up. Cover and let rise in warm place about 1 hour or until double. (Dough is ready if indentation remains when touched.)

Spray cookie sheet with nonstick cooking spray; sprinkle lightly with cornmeal. Punch down dough, and divide in half. Shape each half into round loaf. Place loaves on opposite corners of cookie sheet. Sprinkle lightly with bread flour. Cover and let rise in warm place about 40 minutes or until almost double.

Heat oven to 400°. Bake 30 to 35 minutes or until loaves sound hollow when tapped. Remove from cookie sheet. Cool on wire rack. *2 loaves (12 slices each)*

* If using quick-acting yeast, let dough rest 10 minutes after kneading, and omit first rising time.

NUTRITION INFORMATION PER SERVING			
1 wedge		**Percent of U.S. RDA**	
Calories	145	Protein	6%
Protein, g	4	Vitamin A	*
Carbohydrate, g	28	Vitamin C	*
Fat, g	2	Thiamin	18%
Unsaturated	2	Riboflavin	10%
Saturated	0	Niacin	10%
Dietary Fiber, g	2	Calcium	*
Cholesterol, mg	0	Iron	10%
Sodium, mg	90		
Potassium, mg	60		

Sweet Orange Bread

1 package regular or quick-acting* active
   dry yeast

¼ cup warm water (105° to 115°)

1 tablespoon grated orange peel

½ cup orange juice

2 tablespoons frozen (thawed) apple juice
   concentrate

1 tablespoon plain nonfat yogurt

1 teaspoon vanilla

½ teaspoon salt

½ cup whole wheat flour

1½ to 1¾ cups all-purpose flour

1 tablespoon frozen (thawed) orange juice
   concentrate, if desired

Dissolve yeast in warm water in large bowl. Stir
in remaining ingredients except flours and orange juice concentrate. Stir in whole wheat
flour and enough all-purpose flour to make
dough easy to handle.

Turn dough onto lightly floured surface; gently
roll in flour to coat. Knead about 10 minutes or
until smooth and elastic. Spray bowl with nonstick cooking spray. Place dough in bowl, and
turn greased side up. Cover and let rise in warm
place about 1¼ hours or until double. (Dough is
ready if indentation remains when touched.)

Spray loaf pan, 9×5×3 or 8½×4½×2½
inches, with nonstick cooking spray. Punch
down dough. Knead 1 minute on lightly floured
surface. Place in pan; pat and smooth with
floured hands. Cover and let rise in warm place
30 to 40 minutes or until almost double.

Heat oven to 375°. Brush dough with orange
juice concentrate. Bake about 30 minutes or
until golden brown. Remove from pan. Cool
completely on rack. *1 loaf (16 slices)*

* If using quick-acting yeast, let dough rest 10 minutes
after kneading, and omit first rising time.

SWEET CRANBERRY-ORANGE BREAD: Substitute 2
tablespoons frozen (thawed) cranberry juice
cocktail concentrate for the apple concentrate.
Stir in ½ cup dried cranberries with the remaining ingredients.

NUTRITION INFORMATION PER SERVING			
1 slice		Percent of U.S. RDA	
Calories	65	Protein	2%
Protein, g	2	Vitamin A	*
Carbohydrate, g	14	Vitamin C	6%
Fat, g	0	Thiamin	8%
Unsaturated	0	Riboflavin	6%
Saturated	0	Niacin	6%
Dietary Fiber, g	1	Calcium	*
Cholesterol, mg	0	Iron	4%
Sodium, mg	70		
Potassium, mg	65		

Holiday Dried-Fruit Loaf

Try serving this festive bread on Christmas morning. It freezes well, so make it any time during the holidays, then use when you'd like. And, if you are lucky enough to have leftover bread, it makes superb French toast.

½ cup golden raisins

½ cup chopped dried apples

2 tablespoons orange-flavored liqueur or orange juice

5½ to 6 cups all-purpose flour

1 teaspoon salt

½ teaspoon ground cardamom

1 package regular or quick-acting* active dry yeast

½ cup cranberry juice cocktail

1 can (12 ounces) evaporated skimmed milk

1 tablespoon margarine, softened

2 teaspoons grated orange peel

3 egg whites or ½ cup cholesterol-free egg product

1 tablespoon sugar

½ teaspoon ground cinnamon

Mix raisins, apples and liqueur; reserve. Mix 2 cups of the flour, the salt, cardamom and yeast in large bowl. Mix cranberry juice cocktail and milk in 1½-quart saucepan (mixture may appear slightly curdled). Heat, stirring constantly, to 120° to 130°. Add cranberry juice mixture, margarine and orange peel to flour mixture. Beat on low speed 1 minute, scraping bowl frequently. Beat on medium speed 1 minute, scraping bowl frequently. Stir in egg whites and raisin mixture. Stir in enough remaining flour, 1 cup at a time, to make dough easy to handle.

Turn dough onto lightly floured surface; gently roll in flour to coat. Knead about 10 minutes or until smooth and elastic. Spray large bowl with nonstick cooking spray. Place dough in bowl, and turn greased side up. Cover and let rise in warm place about 1 hour or until double. (Dough is ready if indentation remains when touched.)

Spray cookie sheet with nonstick cooking spray. Punch down dough, and divide into halves. Shape each half into round, slightly flattened loaf. Place loaves on opposite corners of cookie sheet. Cover and let rise in warm place about 30 minutes or until double.

Heat oven to 350°. Mix sugar and cinnamon. Brush loaves with water; sprinkle with sugar mixture. Bake 40 to 45 minutes or until golden brown and loaves sound hollow when tapped. Remove from cookie sheet. Cool on wire rack. *2 loaves (16 slices each)*

* If using quick-acting yeast, let dough rest 10 minutes after kneading, and omit first rising time.

NUTRITION INFORMATION PER SERVING			
1 slice		Percent of U.S. RDA	
Calories	110	Protein	4%
Protein, g	3	Vitamin A	2%
Carbohydrate, g	22	Vitamin C	*
Fat, g	1	Thiamin	12%
Unsaturated	1	Riboflavin	10%
Saturated	0	Niacin	6%
Dietary Fiber, g	1	Calcium	4%
Cholesterol, mg	0	Iron	6%
Sodium, mg	90		
Potassium, mg	95		

Savory Focaccia

Focaccia is a flat Italian bread that can be served with a meal, eaten as a snack or used as a pizza crust.

4¹/₂ to 5 cups all-purpose flour
³/₄ cup chopped onions (about 1¹/₂ medium)
1 tablespoon olive or vegetable oil
1 teaspoon dried rosemary leaves, crushed
¹/₂ teaspoon salt
¹/₂ teaspoon white pepper
1 package regular or quick-acting* active
  dry yeast
2 cups very warm water (120° to 130°)
Stone-ground or degerminated cornmeal
Olive or vegetable oil
2 teaspoons dried rosemary leaves, crushed

Mix 2 cups of the flour, the onions, 1 tablespoon oil, 1 teaspoon rosemary, the salt, pepper and yeast in large bowl. Add warm water. Beat on low speed 1 minute, scraping bowl frequently. Beat on medium speed 1 minute, scraping bowl frequently. Stir in enough remaining flour, 1 cup at a time, to make dough easy to handle.

Turn dough onto lightly floured surface; gently roll in flour to coat. Knead about 10 minutes or until smooth and elastic. Spray large bowl with nonstick cooking spray. Place dough in bowl, and turn greased side up. Cover and let rise in warm place about 1¹/₂ hours or until double. (Dough is ready if indentation remains when touched.)

Spray jelly roll pan, 15¹/₂×10¹/₂×1 inch, with nonstick cooking spray; sprinkle lightly with cornmeal. Punch down dough. Press in pan. Cover and let rise in warm place about 30 minutes or until almost double.

Heat oven to 400°. Press dough to edges of pan. Brush lightly with oil; sprinkle with 2 teaspoons rosemary. Bake 30 to 35 minutes or until golden brown. Remove from pan. Cool on wire rack. *16 servings*

* If using quick-acting yeast, let dough rest 10 minutes after kneading, and omit first rising time.

NUTRITION INFORMATION PER SERVING

1 serving		Percent of U.S. RDA	
Calories	135	Protein	6%
Protein, g	4	Vitamin A	*
Carbohydrate, g	28	Vitamin C	*
Fat, g	1	Thiamin	18%
Unsaturated	1	Riboflavin	12%
Saturated	0	Niacin	10%
Dietary Fiber, g	2	Calcium	*
Cholesterol, mg	0	Iron	10%
Sodium, mg	70		
Potassium, mg	60		

Savory Focaccia, Herbed Pizza Crust (page 108), Sesame Breadsticks (page 94)

Herbed Pizza Crust

This oil-free crust is long on taste, thanks to tomato juice and herbs. Try it in your favorite pizza recipe, or in Shrimp and Artichoke Pizza (page 294).

1 package regular active dry yeast
½ cup warm water (105° to 115°)
½ cup whole wheat flour
½ cup tomato juice
2 tablespoons chopped fresh or
   1 tablespoon freeze-dried chives
1 tablespoon chopped fresh or 1 teaspoon
   dried rosemary leaves, crushed
1 teaspoon olive or vegetable oil
¼ teaspoon white pepper
1½ to 1¾ cups all-purpose flour

Dissolve yeast in warm water in medium bowl. Stir in remaining ingredients except all-purpose flour. Stir in enough all-purpose flour, ½ cup at a time, to make dough easy to handle.

Turn dough onto lightly floured surface; gently roll in flour to coat. Knead about 5 minutes or until smooth and elastic. Spray medium bowl with nonstick cooking spray. Place dough in bowl, and turn greased side up. Cover and let rise in warm place 45 to 60 minutes or until double. (Dough is ready if indentation remains when touched.)

Punch down dough. Roll into 10- to 12-inch circle on lightly floured surface. Top and bake as directed in your favorite pizza recipe.
10- to 12-inch pizza crust (6 slices)

CRACKED PEPPER PIZZA CRUST: Substitute 2 tablespoons chopped fresh parsley for the chives and 1 teaspoon coarsely-ground black pepper for the white pepper.

SOUTHWESTERN PIZZA CRUST: Omit rosemary. Stir in ¼ teaspoon ground cumin and ½ teaspoon chile powder with the remaining ingredients.

NUTRITION INFORMATION PER SERVING			
1 slice		**Percent of U.S. RDA**	
Calories	140	Protein	6%
Protein, g	4	Vitamin A	*
Carbohydrate, g	29	Vitamin C	2%
Fat, g	1	Thiamin	18%
Unsaturated	1	Riboflavin	12%
Saturated	0	Niacin	14%
Dietary Fiber, g	3	Calcium	*
Cholesterol, mg	0	Iron	10%
Sodium, mg	75		
Potassium, mg	140		

4
Vegetables and Salads

4

Vegetables and Salads

Vegetables have become even more popular recently due to the increased variety found in supermarkets, the resurgence of farmers' markets, the almost year-round availability of vegetables that once were seasonal, and the recognition of their importance to a healthy diet. Besides fresh vegetables, frozen and canned vegetables are available, and they can be used in a variety of ways. Vegetables such as broccoli, beans, carrots and bell peppers should be cooked until crisp–tender, so check them for doneness at the minimum cooking time, cooking longer if necessary. Cooking vegetables just until done not only keeps the color of the vegetable bright but also retains more vitamins and minerals than cooking for a longer period.

The recipes that follow take advantage of vegetables' naturally low-fat, low-calorie and cholesterol-free makeup.

The salads range from creamy Celeriac Salad (page 136) to tangy Sweet and Sour Cabbage Salad (page 137). And you'll discover delicious recipes for legumes and grains. Creamy soups and salad dressings take advantage of low-fat dairy products to produce recipes that are low in fat and calories, but rich in flavor. Although the salad dressings are called for in specific recipes throughout the chapter, feel free to use them on your favorite salad, or on your own new salad ideas. They can also be used as dips for vegetables or fruits, and as sandwich spreads.

Preceding page: Spring Vegetable Risotto (page 129), Artichoke-Asparagus Salad (page 141); Above: 1) Romaine lettuce; 2) curly endive; 3) white and green kale; 4) red Swiss chard; 5) Belgian endive; 6) radicchio; 7) red Boston lettuce; 8) Boston lettuce; 9) purple kale; 10) escarole; 11) red leaf lettuce; 12) arugula

Steamed Asparagus with Tarragon Mayonnaise

Steamed Asparagus with Tarragon Mayonnaise

Adding tarragon to creamy Tofu Mayonnaise (page 153) brings a delicately herbed flavor to tender asparagus. The mayonnaise is especially nice on young, spring asparagus.

Tofu Mayonnaise (page 153)
1 tablespoon chopped fresh or 1 teaspoon dried tarragon leaves
1 pound asparagus

Prepare Tofu Mayonnaise; stir in tarragon. Place steamer basket in ½ inch water in sauce-pan (water should not touch bottom of basket). Place asparagus in basket. Cover tightly and heat to boiling; reduce heat. Steam 6 to 8 minutes or until crisp-tender. Serve with Tofu Mayonnaise. *6 servings*

NUTRITION INFORMATION PER SERVING			
1 serving		**Percent of U.S. RDA**	
Calories	70	Protein	6%
Protein, g	4	Vitamin A	4%
Carbohydrate, g	4	Vitamin C	8%
Fat, g	4	Thiamin	4%
Unsaturated	3	Riboflavin	4%
Saturated	1	Niacin	2%
Dietary Fiber, g	1	Calcium	6%
Cholesterol, mg	0	Iron	14%
Sodium, mg	210		
Potassium, mg	160		

Microwaving Fresh Vegetables

The microwave not only saves time, it also allows foods to retain their valuable water-soluble nutrients because less water is needed for cooking. Because no added fat from margarine, butter or oil is needed during cooking, vegetables remain deliciously nutritious.

For whole vegetables, wash and pierce with a fork in several places to allow steam to escape. For vegetable pieces, wash, trim and peel as necessary; cut into pieces of the same size for even cooking.

Place vegetables (except whole potatoes and unhusked corn) with larger, denser parts toward the outside edge of microwavable dish; add a small amount of water. Cover tightly with lid or vented plastic wrap and microwave on high until crisp-tender or tender, rotating dish or stirring, turning over or rearranging food as directed in chart. Let stand covered.

For whole potatoes or unhusked corn, place uncovered (potatoes in a circle) on paper towel in microwave. After microwaving, let stand uncovered.

Follow the chart below for vegetable and water amounts and microwaving and stand times. All amounts are for 4 servings.

VEGETABLE	AMOUNT	WATER	MICROWAVING TIME (HIGH)	STAND TIME
Asparagus				
spears	1½ pounds	¼ cup	6 to 9 minutes, rotating dish ½ turn after 3 minutes	1 minute
1-inch pieces	1½ pounds	¼ cup	6 to 9 minutes, stirring after 3 minutes	1 minute
Beans—Green, Wax				
1-inch pieces	1 pound	½ cup	9 to 14 minutes, stirring every 5 minutes	5 minutes
Broccoli				
spears	1½ pounds	1 cup	9 to 12 minutes, rotating dish ½ turn every 4 minutes	5 minutes
1-inch pieces	1½ pounds	1 cup	9 to 12 minutes, stirring every 4 minutes	5 minutes
Brussels Sprouts	1 pound	¼ cup	8 to 13 minutes, stirring after 5 minutes	5 minutes
Cabbage—Green, Red and Savoy				
wedges	1 pound	½ cup	10 to 14 minutes, rotating dish ½ turn after 5 minutes	5 minutes
shredded	1 pound	¼ cup	8 to 10 minutes, stirring after 4 minutes	5 minutes

(continued)

VEGETABLE	AMOUNT	WATER	MICROWAVING TIME (HIGH)	STAND TIME
Carrots ¼-inch slices	1 pound	¼ cup	6 to 8 minutes, stirring after 4 minutes	1 minute
Cauliflower whole	2 pounds	¼ cup	12 to 14 minutes, rotating dish ½ turn after 6 minutes	1 minute
flowerets	2 pounds	¼ cup	12 to 14 minutes, stirring after 6 minutes	1 minute
Corn husked	4 ears	¼ cup	9 to 14 minutes, rearranging after 5 minutes	5 minutes
unhusked	4 ears	–	9 to 14 minutes, rearranging after 5 minutes	5 minutes
Peas, Green	2 pounds	¼ cup	9 to 11 minutes, stirring after 5 minutes	1 minute
Potatoes, White whole (4)	2 pounds	–	12 to 18 minutes, turning over after 6 minutes	5 minutes
pieces	2 pounds	½ cup	10 to 16 minutes, stirring after 7 minutes	1 minute
Potatoes, Sweet or Yams	1½ pounds	–	8 to 15 minutes, turning over after 4 minutes	5 minutes

Squash—Summer:
  Crookneck,
  Pattypan,
  Straightneck or
  Zucchini
  slices or cubes
	1½ pounds	¼ cup	8 to 10 minutes, stirring after 4 minutes	1 minute

Squash—Winter:
  Acorn, Buttercup,
  Butternut or
  Spaghetti
  whole or pieces
	2 pounds	–	4 to 6 minutes or until rind is easy to cut through; cut in half. Microwave 5 to 8 minutes longer	1 minute

White Beans with Sage

This is also delicious as a cold salad, served in lettuce cups or over shredded lettuce. Simply cover the bean mixture and refrigerate until chilled.

1 cup dried or 2 cans (15 ounces each) drained great northern beans
1 cup chopped tomato (about 1 large)
½ cup chopped onion (about 1 medium)
½ cup chopped yellow bell pepper (about 1 small)
2 tablespoons grated lemon peel
1 teaspoon dried sage leaves
1 teaspoon olive or vegetable oil
½ teaspoon salt
¼ teaspoon pepper
1 clove garlic, finely chopped (about ½ teaspoon)

Cook dried beans as directed on package—except omit salt; drain. (Do not cook canned beans.) Cook remaining ingredients in 2-quart saucepan over medium heat 5 minutes, stirring occasionally, until onion is tender. Stir in beans. Cook 5 minutes, stirring occasionally, until heated through. *6 servings*

NUTRITION INFORMATION PER SERVING			
1 serving		Percent of U.S. RDA	
Calories	130	Protein	12%
Protein, g	8	Vitamin A	6%
Carbohydrate, g	22	Vitamin C	20%
Fat, g	1	Thiamin	8%
Unsaturated	1	Riboflavin	2%
Saturated	0	Niacin	2%
Dietary Fiber, g	5	Calcium	8%
Cholesterol, mg	0	Iron	16%
Sodium, mg	190		
Potassium, mg	530		

Bok Choy with Cilantro Soy Sauce

1 cup tomato juice
2 cloves garlic, finely chopped (about 1 teaspoon)
1 teaspoon finely chopped gingerroot
4 cups chopped bok choy (about ⅓ medium head)
1 cup chopped mushrooms (about 4 ounces)
½ cup chopped yellow bell pepper (about 1 small)
¼ cup chopped green onions (2 to 3 medium)
2 tablespoons chopped fresh cilantro leaves
2 tablespoons lime juice
1 teaspoon reduced-sodium soy sauce

Mix ½ cup of the tomato juice, the garlic and gingerroot in 10-inch skillet. Cook over medium heat 2 minutes. Stir in remaining tomato juice, the bok choy, mushrooms, bell pepper and onions. Cook 3 minutes, stirring occasionally, until bok choy leaves are wilted. Stir in remaining ingredients. *6 servings*

NUTRITION INFORMATION PER SERVING			
1 serving		Percent of U.S. RDA	
Calories	25	Protein	2%
Protein, g	1	Vitamin A	22%
Carbohydrate, g	5	Vitamin C	40%
Fat, g	0	Thiamin	4%
Unsaturated	0	Riboflavin	6%
Saturated	0	Niacin	6%
Dietary Fiber, g	2	Calcium	6%
Cholesterol, mg	0	Iron	6%
Sodium, mg	215		
Potassium, mg	300		

Stir-fried Broccoli and Carrots

2 teaspoons finely chopped gingerroot

1 clove garlic, finely chopped (about ½ teaspoon)

1½ cups small broccoli flowerets

1 cup thinly sliced carrots (about 2 medium)

1 small onion, sliced and separated into rings

¾ cup chicken broth

¼ teaspoon salt

1 tablespoon cornstarch

1 tablespoon cold water

1 can (8 ounces) sliced water chestnuts, drained

1 cup sliced mushrooms (about 3 ounces)

2 tablespoons oyster sauce

Spray wok or 12-inch skillet with nonstick cooking spray; heat until hot. Add gingerroot and garlic; stir-fry about 1 minute or until light brown. Add broccoli, carrots and onion; stir-fry 1 minute. Stir in broth and salt; cover and cook about 3 minutes or until carrots are crisp-tender. Mix cornstarch and cold water; stir into vegetable mixture. Cook and stir about 10 seconds or until thickened. Add water chestnuts, mushrooms and oyster sauce; cook and stir 30 seconds. *4 servings*

NUTRITION INFORMATION PER SERVING

1 serving		Percent of U.S. RDA	
Calories	95	Protein	6%
Protein, g	3	Vitamin A	50%
Carbohydrate, g	18	Vitamin C	32%
Fat, g	1	Thiamin	6%
Unsaturated	1	Riboflavin	10%
Saturated	0	Niacin	10%
Dietary Fiber, g	4	Calcium	4%
Cholesterol, mg	0	Iron	6%
Sodium, mg	560		
Potassium, mg	440		

Stir-fried Broccoli and Carrots

Brussels Sprouts with Basil

¾ cup finely chopped onions (about 1½
  medium)
½ cup finely chopped red bell pepper
  (about 1 small)
¾ cup chicken broth
2½ cups cooked fresh or 1 package (16
  ounces) frozen cooked Brussels sprouts
  (about 1 pound)
¼ cup chopped fresh basil leaves
2 tablespoons lemon juice
1 teaspoon grated lemon peel
¼ teaspoon salt
¼ teaspoon pepper

Spray 10-inch skillet with nonstick cooking
spray. Cook onions, bell pepper and broth in
skillet over medium heat about 3 minutes, stirring occasionally, until onion is tender. Stir in
remaining ingredients. Cook about 3 minutes,
stirring occasionally, until Brussels sprouts are
heated through. *6 servings*

NUTRITION INFORMATION PER SERVING

1 serving		Percent of U.S. RDA	
Calories	60	Protein	6%
Protein, g	3	Vitamin A	10%
Carbohydrate, g	10	Vitamin C	40%
Fat, g	1	Thiamin	6%
Unsaturated	1	Riboflavin	6%
Saturated	0	Niacin	4%
Dietary Fiber, g	4	Calcium	8%
Cholesterol, mg	0	Iron	10%
Sodium, mg	200		
Potassium, mg	390		

Ginger-glazed Carrots

3 cups ¼-inch slices carrots (about 6
  medium)
½ cup water
½ cup dry white wine or apple juice
2 teaspoons margarine
1 teaspoon ground ginger
1 tablespoon lemon juice
2 teaspoons packed brown sugar

Cook all ingredients except lemon juice and
brown sugar in 10-inch skillet over medium
heat 12 to 15 minutes, stirring occasionally,
until liquid has evaporated. Reduce heat to
medium-low. Stir in lemon juice and brown
sugar. Cook 5 minutes, stirring occasionally,
until carrots are glazed. *6 servings*

NUTRITION INFORMATION PER SERVING

1 serving		Percent of U.S. RDA	
Calories	50	Protein	*
Protein, g	1	Vitamin A	86%
Carbohydrate, g	8	Vitamin C	4%
Fat, g	1	Thiamin	4%
Unsaturated	1	Riboflavin	2%
Saturated	0	Niacin	2%
Dietary Fiber, g	2	Calcium	2%
Cholesterol, mg	0	Iron	2%
Sodium, mg	35		
Potassium, mg	210		

Baked Cauliflower and Mushrooms

Baked Cauliflower and Mushrooms

3 cups cauliflowerets (about 1 pound)
1 cup chopped mushrooms (about 4 ounces)
½ cup chopped red onion (about ½ medium)
1 tablespoon olive or vegetable oil
2 teaspoons lemon juice
2 teaspoons cider vinegar
½ teaspoon salt
¼ teaspoon pepper
2 cloves garlic, finely chopped (about 1 teaspoon)
⅓ cup chopped green onions (about 5 medium)

Heat oven to 350°. Spray 9-inch square baking dish, with nonstick cooking spray. Mix all ingredients except green onions. Spread evenly in baking dish. Bake uncovered 40 to 45 minutes, stirring occasionally, until vegetables are tender and golden brown. Sprinkle with green onions. *6 servings*

NUTRITION INFORMATION PER SERVING			
1 serving		**Percent of U.S. RDA**	
Calories	40	Protein	2%
Protein, g	1	Vitamin A	*
Carbohydrate, g	5	Vitamin C	32%
Fat, g	2	Thiamin	4%
Unsaturated	2	Riboflavin	4%
Saturated	0	Niacin	4%
Dietary Fiber, g	1	Calcium	2%
Cholesterol, mg	0	Iron	2%
Sodium, mg	190		
Potassium, mg	270		

Steaming Fresh Vegetables

Steaming not only retains the flavor, shape and texture of vegetables, it's a healthy way of cooking. No added fat is necessary, and water-soluble vitamins aren't lost in cooking water. A large saucepan with a tight-fitting lid and a steamer basket or rack is all that you need to steam vegetables. Electric food steamers are also available; if you use one, we recommend that you follow the manufacturer's directions.

Wash, trim and peel vegetables as necessary. Leave vegetables whole or cut into pieces of the same size for even cooking. Place steamer basket in $1/2$ inch water in saucepan (water should not touch bottom of basket). Place vegetables in basket. Cover tightly and heat to boiling; reduce heat. Cook until vegetables are desired doneness. For longer-cooking vegetables, add more hot water, if necessary to prevent water from boiling away. Follow the chart on the right for amounts of vegetables, steaming time and doneness test. All amounts are for 4 servings.

New and unusual vegetables: 1) fennel; 2) celeriac; 3 & 4) sweet dumpling squash; 5) broccoli flower; 6) turban squash; 7) spaghetti squash; 8) delicata squash; 9) English (burpless) cucumber; 10) red sweet potato; 11) blue potatoes; 12) fava beans

VEGETABLE	AMOUNT	STEAMING TIME (MINUTES)	DONENESS TEST
Asparagus			
spears	1½ pounds	6 to 8	Crisp-tender
Beans—Green, Wax	1 pound		
whole		10 to 12	Crisp-tender
1-inch pieces		10 to 12	Crisp-tender
Broccoli	1½ pounds		
spears		10 to 11	Stems are tender
1-inch pieces		10 to 11	Stems are tender
Brussels Sprouts	1 pound	20 to 25	Tender
Cabbage—Green, Red, Savoy	1 small head		
wedges		18 to 24	Crisp-tender
shredded		5 to 7	Crisp-tender
Carrots			
¼-inch slices	6 to 7 medium	9 to 11	Tender
Cauliflower	1 medium head		
whole		18 to 22	Tender
flowerets		6 to 8	Tender
Celery			
1-inch pieces	1 medium bunch	18 to 20	Crisp-tender
Corn	4 ears	6 to 9	Tender
Pea Pods, Chinese	1 pound	5 to 7	Crisp-tender
Peas, Green			
shelled	2 pounds	10 to 12	Tender
Peppers, Bell			
whole	2 medium	8 to 10	Tender
Potatoes, New	10 to 12 whole	18 to 22	Tender
Squash—Summer: Chayote, Crookneck, Pattypan, Straightneck or Zucchini	1½ pounds		
small halves or ½-inch slices or cubes		5 to 7	Tender
Squash—Winter: Acorn, Buttercup, Butternut or Spaghetti	2 pounds		
1-inch slices		12 to 15	Tender
1-inch cubes		7 to 10	Tender

Italian Potatoes

Baking potatoes are best in this dish, as they retain their shape and don't become mushy. Use your food processor to chop the carrot, onions and garlic all at the same time—a time saver. These potatoes also keep nicely when placed over low heat for up to 20 minutes.

2 cups 1-inch cubes unpeeled baking potatoes (about 3 medium)
¾ cup finely chopped onions (about 1½ medium)
½ cup finely chopped carrot (about 1 medium)
½ cup chicken broth
2 tablespoons tomato paste
¼ teaspoon salt
¼ teaspoon pepper
2 cloves garlic, finely chopped (about 1 teaspoon)
2 tablespoons chopped fresh parsley

Cook all ingredients except parsley in 2-quart saucepan over medium-low heat 25 to 30 minutes, stirring occasionally, until potatoes are tender. Stir in parsley. *6 servings*

NUTRITION INFORMATION PER SERVING

1 serving		Percent of U.S. RDA	
Calories	90	Protein	4%
Protein, g	2	Vitamin A	16%
Carbohydrate, g	20	Vitamin C	12%
Fat, g	0	Thiamin	6%
Unsaturated	0	Riboflavin	2%
Saturated	0	Niacin	8%
Dietary Fiber, g	2	Calcium	2%
Cholesterol, mg	0	Iron	6%
Sodium, mg	210		
Potassium, mg	400		

Roasted Garlic Mashed Potatoes

These mashed potatoes prove that butter and sour cream aren't necessary for a satisfying dish. The sweet roasted garlic, olive oil and rosemary will please all mashed potato lovers!

6 medium potatoes (about 2 pounds)
6 unpeeled garlic cloves
2 tablespoons olive oil
1 teaspoon fresh chopped or ¼ teaspoon dried rosemary leaves
½ teaspoon salt
⅓ to ½ cup low-fat milk

Heat oven to 375°. Scrub potatoes; pierce with fork to allow steam to escape. Wrap garlic cloves in aluminum foil. Bake potatoes and garlic 1 hour or until potatoes are soft.

Heat oil and rosemary over medium heat 2 to 3 minutes or until rosemary is fragrant.

Open garlic packet to cool. Cut potatoes into halves; carefully spoon potatoes into large bowl. Save skins for another use or discard. Slip skins off cloves of garlic and place garlic in bowl; add oil mixture and salt. Mash until fluffy, adding milk until desired consistency. *6 servings*

NUTRITION INFORMATION PER SERVING

1 serving		Percent of U.S. RDA	
Calories	140	Protein	4%
Protein, g	2	Vitamin A	*
Carbohydrate, g	22	Vitamin C	10%
Fat, g	5	Thiamin	8%
Unsaturated	4	Riboflavin	2%
Saturated	1	Niacin	6%
Dietary Fiber, g	1	Calcium	2%
Cholesterol, mg	0	Iron	2%
Sodium, mg	190		
Potassium, mg	400		

Rosemary-baked Red Potatoes, Wilted Spinach with Fragrant Mushrooms (page 122), Broiled Sage Chicken (page 225)

Rosemary-baked Red Potatoes

2¼ pounds new potatoes

¼ cup finely chopped shallots (about 2 large)

2 tablespoons chopped fresh or 2 teaspoons crushed dried rosemary leaves

2 tablespoons olive or vegetable oil

Heat oven to 350°. Spray rectangular pan, 13×9×2 inches, with nonstick cooking spray. Place potatoes in pan. Sprinkle with shallots and rosemary. Drizzle with oil; stir to coat. Bake uncovered about 1¼ hours, stirring occasionally, until potato skins are crisp and potatoes are tender. *6 servings*

BASIL-BAKED RED POTATOES: Substitute ¼ cup chopped green onions for the shallots and 2 tablespoons chopped fresh or 2 teaspoons dried basil leaves for the rosemary.

NUTRITION INFORMATION PER SERVING			
1 serving		**Percent of U.S. RDA**	
Calories	235	Protein	6%
Protein, g	4	Vitamin A	*
Carbohydrate, g	43	Vitamin C	18%
Fat, g	5	Thiamin	12%
Unsaturated	4	Riboflavin	2%
Saturated	1	Niacin	14%
Dietary Fiber, g	3	Calcium	2%
Cholesterol, mg	0	Iron	12%
Sodium, mg	15		
Potassium, mg	710		

Sweet Potato and Squash Pancakes

1 teaspoon vegetable oil

2 cups shredded unpeeled sweet potato (about 1 large)

1 cup shredded unpeeled yellow squash (about 1 medium)

¼ cup shredded onion (about ½ small)

¼ cup cholesterol-free egg product or 2 egg whites

2 tablespoons chopped fresh or 1 tablespoon freeze-dried chives

1 tablespoon all-purpose flour

2 tablespoons lemon juice

½ teaspoon salt

¼ teaspoon pepper

Heat oven to 200°. Spray griddle or 10-inch skillet with nonstick cooking spray; add oil. Heat griddle over medium heat or to 375°. Mix remaining ingredients. For each pancake, spoon scant ⅓ cup batter onto hot griddle; flatten slightly. Cook about 5 minutes on each side or until dark brown. Place cooked pancakes on ungreased cookie sheet, and keep warm in oven while cooking remaining pancakes. *6 servings*

NUTRITION INFORMATION PER SERVING

1 serving		Percent of U.S. RDA	
Calories	55	Protein	2%
Protein, g	2	Vitamin A	66%
Carbohydrate, g	10	Vitamin C	10%
Fat, g	1	Thiamin	4%
Unsaturated	1	Riboflavin	6%
Saturated	0	Niacin	2%
Dietary Fiber, g	1	Calcium	2%
Cholesterol, mg	0	Iron	2%
Sodium, mg	200		
Potassium, mg	260		

Wilted Spinach with Fragrant Mushrooms

¼ cup chopped onion (about 1 small)

2 cloves garlic, finely chopped

¾ cup chicken broth

3½ cups sliced mushrooms (about 10 ounces)

¼ cup dry white wine or apple juice

1 tablespoon tomato paste

5 cups chopped spinach (about 6 ounces)

¼ cup chopped green onions (2 to 3 medium)

¼ cup chopped fresh parsley or 1 tablespoon dried parsley flakes

2 tablespoons lemon juice

¼ teaspoon salt

¼ teaspoon pepper

Spray 10-inch nonstick skillet with nonstick cooking spray. Cook onion, garlic and broth in skillet over medium-high heat 3 minutes, stirring occasionally, until liquid has evaporated. Stir in mushrooms, wine and tomato paste. Cook over medium-high heat 3 minutes, stirring occasionally. Stir in spinach, green onions and parsley. Cook 2 to 3 minutes, stirring occasionally, until spinach is wilted. Stir in remaining ingredients. *6 servings*

NUTRITION INFORMATION PER SERVING

1 serving		Percent of U.S. RDA	
Calories	45	Protein	4%
Protein, g	3	Vitamin A	40%
Carbohydrate, g	6	Vitamin C	18%
Fat, g	1	Thiamin	6%
Unsaturated	1	Riboflavin	18%
Saturated	0	Niacin	12%
Dietary Fiber, g	2	Calcium	6%
Cholesterol, mg	0	Iron	12%
Sodium, mg	250		
Potassium, mg	520		

Crumb-topped Butternut Squash

1½ pounds butternut squash, peeled and
    cut into ½-inch cubes (about 3½ cups)
2 tablespoons all-purpose flour
2 tablespoons lemon juice
1 teaspoon ground cinnamon
¼ teaspoon salt
⅓ cup dry bread crumbs
2 tablespoons chicken broth

Heat oven to 350°. Spray square pan, 8×8×2
inches, with nonstick cooking spray. Mix all
ingredients except bread crumbs and broth;
spread in pan. Bake uncovered 50 minutes or
until squash is tender. Mix bread crumbs and
broth; sprinkle over squash. Set oven control to
broil. Broil squash about 4 inches from heat 3
minutes or until bread crumbs are brown.
6 servings

NUTRITION INFORMATION PER SERVING			
1 serving		**Percent of U.S. RDA**	
Calories	75	Protein	2%
Protein, g	2	Vitamin A	28%
Carbohydrate, g	14	Vitamin C	6%
Fat, g	1	Thiamin	6%
Unsaturated	1	Riboflavin	2%
Saturated	0	Niacin	4%
Dietary Fiber, g	3	Calcium	2%
Cholesterol, mg	0	Iron	4%
Sodium, mg	150		
Potassium, mg	160		

Crumb-topped Butternut Squash, Rosemary-Mustard Chicken (page 235)

Chayote Squash with Mint

1 medium chayote (about ½ pound)
1 tablespoon olive or vegetable oil
1 tablespoon chopped fresh or 1 teaspoon
    dried mint leaves
¼ teaspoon salt
¼ cup apple juice
1 tablespoon lemon juice
1 cup cherry tomato halves

Peel chayote. Cut lengthwise into halves; re-move seed. Cut crosswise into thin slices. Heat oil in 10-inch skillet over medium heat. Stir in chayote, mint and salt. Cook 5 minutes, stirring occasionally. Stir in apple juice and lemon juice; reduce heat. Cover and simmer 8 to 10 minutes or until chayote is crisp-tender. Stir in tomatoes. Cover and simmer 30 seconds.
4 servings

NUTRITION INFORMATION PER SERVING

1 serving		Percent of U.S. RDA	
Calories	65	Protein	2%
Protein, g	1	Vitamin A	4%
Carbohydrate, g	6	Vitamin C	24%
Fat, g	4	Thiamin	4%
Unsaturated	3	Riboflavin	2%
Saturated	1	Niacin	2%
Dietary Fiber, g	1	Calcium	*
Cholesterol, mg	0	Iron	2%
Sodium, mg	140		
Potassium, mg	260		

Cajun Zucchini

1 cup chicken broth
2 teaspoons cornstarch
3 cups ¼-inch slices zucchini (about 2
    medium)
2 teaspoons paprika
1½ teaspoons chopped fresh or ½ teaspoon
    dried thyme leaves
1½ teaspoons chopped fresh or ½ teaspoon
    dried oregano leaves
⅛ teaspoon ground red pepper (cayenne)

Mix ¼ cup of the broth and the cornstarch in small bowl; reserve. Cook remaining broth and remaining ingredients in 10-inch skillet over medium heat 7 to 10 minutes, stirring occa-sionally, until zucchini is tender. Stir in corn-starch mixture. Cook and stir about 1 minute or until thickened. *6 servings*

NUTRITION INFORMATION PER SERVING

1 serving		Percent of U.S. RDA	
Calories	20	Protein	2%
Protein, g	1	Vitamin A	6%
Carbohydrate, g	4	Vitamin C	4%
Fat, g	0	Thiamin	2%
Unsaturated	0	Riboflavin	2%
Saturated	0	Niacin	4%
Dietary Fiber, g	1	Calcium	2%
Cholesterol, mg	0	Iron	6%
Sodium, mg	130		
Potassium, mg	220		

Mixed Fruit and Yam Gratin

Mixed Fruit and Yam Gratin

A hearty fall side dish, especially nice with pork, this recipe can also be served at brunch, topped with nonfat plain or vanilla yogurt. If you like, you can also bake these flavorful yams in an oval gratin dish.

2 medium yams (about ¾ pound)
1 cup chopped pineapple
1 cup sliced banana (about 1 medium)
¾ cup chopped apple (about 1 medium)
¼ cup raisins
⅓ cup dry white wine or apple juice
1 tablespoon packed brown sugar
1 teaspoon grated lemon peel
1 teaspoon ground cinnamon
½ teaspoon ground ginger
¼ teaspoon ground nutmeg

Heat oven to 350°. Spray rectangular dish, 10×6×1½ inches, with nonstick cooking spray. Peel and cut yams into ¼-inch slices. Layer half of the yams in dish. Mix pineapple, banana, apple and raisins. Spread half the fruit mixture over yams. Repeat with remaining yams and fruit mixture. Mix remaining ingredients; pour evenly over yams and fruit mixture. Cover and bake 50 to 60 minutes or until yams are tender. *6 servings*

NUTRITION INFORMATION PER SERVING

1 serving		Percent of U.S. RDA	
Calories	120	Protein	2%
Protein, g	1	Vitamin A	82%
Carbohydrate, g	29	Vitamin C	14%
Fat, g	0	Thiamin	4%
Unsaturated	0	Riboflavin	6%
Saturated	0	Niacin	2%
Dietary Fiber, g	2	Calcium	2%
Cholesterol, mg	0	Iron	4%
Sodium, mg	10		
Potassium, mg	400		

Sizzling Tomatoes

Try these tomatoes as an accompaniment to grilled foods or meatless dishes.

3 medium tomatoes, cut into halves and seeded
¼ cup dry bread crumbs
2 tablespoons chopped fresh parsley or 1 tablespoon dried parsley flakes
1½ teaspoons chopped fresh or ½ teaspoon dried basil leaves
½ teaspoon salt
¼ teaspoon pepper
2 cloves garlic, finely chopped
2 sun-dried tomatoes (not oil-packed), finely chopped
1 teaspoon olive or vegetable oil

Heat oven to 350°. Spray 10-inch nonstick skillet and square pan, 8×8×2 inches, with nonstick cooking spray. Place tomatoes, cut sides down, in skillet. Cook over high heat 2 minutes or until cooked sides are brown. Place tomatoes, cooked sides up, in pan. Mix remaining ingredients except oil. Top tomatoes with crumb mixture. Bake about 25 minutes or until crumb mixture is golden brown. Drizzle with oil. *6 servings*

NUTRITION INFORMATION PER SERVING

1 serving		Percent of U.S. RDA	
Calories	40	Protein	2%
Protein, g	1	Vitamin A	6%
Carbohydrate, g	7	Vitamin C	14%
Fat, g	1	Thiamin	4%
Unsaturated	1	Riboflavin	2%
Saturated	0	Niacin	4%
Dietary Fiber, g	1	Calcium	2%
Cholesterol, mg	0	Iron	4%
Sodium, mg	220		
Potassium, mg	200		

Lemon-Chive Fettuccine

As a side dish to poultry or fish, these lemon-kissed noodles are a welcome break from potatoes and rice.

6 ounces uncooked fettuccine
⅓ cup low-fat sour cream
3 tablespoons chopped fresh or 1 tablespoon freeze-dried chives
1 tablespoon grated lemon peel
2 tablespoons lemon juice
1 teaspoon margarine, softened
½ teaspoon salt
¼ teaspoon white pepper

Cook fettuccine as directed on package—except omit salt; drain. Mix remaining ingredients; toss with fettuccine. *6 servings*

NUTRITION INFORMATION PER SERVING

1 serving		Percent of U.S. RDA	
Calories	125	Protein	6%
Protein, g	4	Vitamin A	4%
Carbohydrate, g	21	Vitamin C	4%
Fat, g	3	Thiamin	10%
Unsaturated	2	Riboflavin	4%
Saturated	1	Niacin	6%
Dietary Fiber, g	30	Calcium	2%
Cholesterol, mg	1	Iron	6%
Sodium, mg	210		
Potassium, mg	65		

Red Pepper Bows with Peas

Red Pepper Sauce (below)

6 ounces uncooked farfalle (bow-tie–shape) pasta (about 2 cups)

1 cup cooked green peas

2 tablespoons chopped fresh parsley

Prepare Red Pepper Sauce. Cook pasta as directed on package—except omit salt; drain. Mix pasta, sauce, peas and parsley. *6 servings*

Red Pepper Sauce

2 cups chopped red bell pepper

½ cup chicken broth

1 tablespoon chopped fresh or 1 teaspoon dried oregano leaves

¼ teaspoon salt

¼ teaspoon pepper

1 tablespoon tomato paste

1 tablespoon balsamic vinegar

1 teaspoon honey

Cover and cook bell pepper, broth, oregano, salt and pepper in 2-quart saucepan over medium-low heat 20 minutes, stirring occasionally, until bell pepper is tender. Stir in remaining ingredients; remove from heat. Place mixture in blender. Cover and puree.

Polenta Sauté

4 cups water

1 cup cooked fresh, frozen (thawed) or drained canned whole kernel corn (about 2 medium ears)

½ teaspoon salt

1 teaspoon margarine

¼ teaspoon pepper

1 cup stone-ground or degerminated cornmeal

Spray rectangular baking dish, 10×6×1½ inches, with nonstick cooking spray. Heat all ingredients except cornmeal to boiling in 2-quart saucepan. Gradually add cornmeal, stirring constantly. Cook over medium-low heat 8 to 12 minutes, stirring occasionally, until mixture pulls away from side of saucepan. Pour into baking dish. Cool 15 minutes. Cover and refrigerate about 1 hour or until firm.

Heat oven to 250°. Spray 10-inch skillet with nonstick cooking spray. Cut polenta into six 3-inch squares; cut each square diagonally into 2 triangles. Heat skillet over medium heat. Cook 6 triangles at a time in skillet about 5 minutes on each side or until light brown. Place on ungreased cookie sheet, and keep warm in oven while cooking the remaining triangles. *6 servings*

NUTRITION INFORMATION PER SERVING

1 serving		Percent of U.S. RDA	
Calories	155	Protein	8%
Protein, g	6	Vitamin A	22%
Carbohydrate, g	30	Vitamin C	56%
Fat, g	1	Thiamin	16%
Unsaturated	1	Riboflavin	8%
Saturated	0	Niacin	10%
Dietary Fiber, g	3	Calcium	2%
Cholesterol, mg	0	Iron	10%
Sodium, mg	200		
Potassium, mg	190		

NUTRITION INFORMATION PER SERVING

1 serving		Percent of U.S. RDA	
Calories	110	Protein	4%
Protein, g	2	Vitamin A	2%
Carbohydrate, g	23	Vitamin C	*
Fat, g	1	Thiamin	12%
Unsaturated	1	Riboflavin	6%
Saturated	0	Niacin	6%
Dietary Fiber, g	2	Calcium	*
Cholesterol, mg	0	Iron	6%
Sodium, mg	185		
Potassium, mg	75		

Toasted Barley with Mixed Vegetables

Toasting the barley in the skillet brings out its nutty flavor, and it combines nicely with the onion, mushroom and green pepper for a different texture, as well as added nutrition.

½ cup uncooked pearl barley

½ cup chopped red onion (about ½ medium)

¼ cup sliced mushrooms

¼ cup sliced carrot

¼ cup chopped green bell pepper

1 tablespoon chopped fresh or 2 teaspoons dried dill weed

¼ teaspoon salt

¼ teaspoon pepper

1 can (14½ ounces) chicken broth

¼ cup chopped green onions (2 to 3 medium)

Spray 10-inch nonstick skillet with nonstick cooking spray. Cook barley in skillet over medium heat 8 minutes, stirring constantly, until light brown. Stir in remaining ingredients except green onions. Heat to boiling; reduce heat. Cover and simmer about 50 minutes or until vegetables are tender. Sprinkle with green onions. *6 servings*

NUTRITION INFORMATION PER SERVING

1 serving		Percent of U.S. RDA	
Calories	85	Protein	4%
Protein, g	3	Vitamin A	8%
Carbohydrate, g	16	Vitamin C	4%
Fat, g	1	Thiamin	2%
Unsaturated	1	Riboflavin	4%
Saturated	0	Niacin	10%
Dietary Fiber, g	3	Calcium	2%
Cholesterol, mg	0	Iron	4%
Sodium, mg	310		
Potassium, mg	180		

Above: Toasted Barley with Mixed Vegetables

Spring Vegetable Risotto

Risotto is a creamy Italian rice dish made by slowly adding broth to rice until it is rehydrated. Arborio is the preferred rice, though the more common long grain rice also works well.

³/₄ cup uncooked Arborio rice

2¹/₄ cups chicken broth

¹/₂ cup chopped red onion (about ¹/₂ medium)

1 cup ¹/₂-inch pieces asparagus (about 10 medium spears)

¹/₂ cup chopped zucchini (about 1 medium)

¹/₄ teaspoon pepper

3 tablespoons chopped fresh parsley

Spray 2-quart saucepan with nonstick cooking spray. Cook rice in saucepan without liquid over medium-high heat 5 minutes, stirring occasionally, until rice begins to brown. Stir in ³/₄ cup of the broth and the onion; reduce heat to medium. Cook, stirring occasionally. As liquid is absorbed, stir in remaining broth, ³/₄ cup at a time. Cook 15 minutes, stirring occasionally. Stir in asparagus, zucchini and pepper. Cook 5 to 6 minutes, stirring occasionally, until all liquid is absorbed and rice is tender. Stir in parsley. *6 servings*

NUTRITION INFORMATION PER SERVING

1 serving		Percent of U.S. RDA	
Calories	115	Protein	6%
Protein, g	5	Vitamin A	4%
Carbohydrate, g	22	Vitamin C	8%
Fat, g	1	Thiamin	8%
Unsaturated	1	Riboflavin	4%
Saturated	0	Niacin	12%
Dietary Fiber, g	2	Calcium	2%
Cholesterol, mg	0	Iron	8%
Sodium, mg	290		
Potassium, mg	240		

Rice Stir-fry

¹/₃ cup uncooked regular long grain rice

¹/₃ cup uncooked wild rice

³/₄ cup thinly sliced red onion

2 cloves garlic, finely chopped

³/₄ cup chicken broth

¹/₂ cup chopped yellow bell pepper

¹/₄ cup raisins

¹/₄ cup chopped dried apricots

¹/₄ teaspoon salt

¹/₄ teaspoon pepper

¹/₄ cup chopped fresh parsley

2 tablespoons red wine vinegar

1 teaspoon olive or vegetable oil

Prepare regular rice as directed on package—except omit salt. Prepare wild rice as directed on package—except omit salt. Cook onion, garlic and broth in 10-inch skillet over medium-high heat 5 to 6 minutes, stirring occasionally, until liquid has almost evaporated. Stir in regular rice, wild rice, bell pepper, raisins, apricots, salt and pepper. Cook over medium heat 2 minutes, stirring constantly, until heated through. Stir in parsley, vinegar and oil. *6 servings*

NUTRITION INFORMATION PER SERVING

1 serving		Percent of U.S. RDA	
Calories	130	Protein	6%
Protein, g	3	Vitamin A	10%
Carbohydrate, g	27	Vitamin C	16%
Fat, g	1	Thiamin	6%
Unsaturated	1	Riboflavin	4%
Saturated	0	Niacin	8%
Dietary Fiber, g	2	Calcium	2%
Cholesterol, mg	0	Iron	6%
Sodium, mg	190		
Potassium, mg	270		

Wild Rice and Dill Pancakes

In a hurry? Chop the green onions, shallots, carrot and celery together in your food processor. These hearty pancakes go well with poultry and pork, and they also make a terrific appetizer when served with a dollop of applesauce or low-fat sour cream.

2 cups cooked wild rice

²/₃ cup all-purpose flour

¹/₂ cup nonfat buttermilk

2 egg whites or ¹/₄ cup cholesterol-free egg product

¹/₂ cup finely chopped green onions (about 5 medium)

¹/₃ cup finely chopped shallots (about 2 large)

¹/₃ cup chopped carrot (about 1 small)

¹/₃ cup chopped celery (about 1 medium stalk)

¹/₃ cup chopped mushrooms (about 2 ounces)

¹/₄ cup chicken broth

2 tablespoons chopped fresh or 2 teaspoons dried dill weed

Mix wild rice, flour, buttermilk and egg whites in large bowl. Cook remaining ingredients in 10-inch skillet over medium heat 5 minutes, stirring frequently, until liquid has evaporated. Cool slightly; stir into wild rice mixture.

Heat oven to 200°. Spray griddle or cleaned 10-inch skillet with nonstick cooking spray. Heat griddle over medium heat or to 375°. For each pancake, spoon ¹/₄ cup batter onto hot griddle; flatten slightly. Cook about 3 minutes on each side or until golden brown. Place cooked pancakes on ungreased cookie sheet, and keep warm in oven while cooking remaining pancakes. *6 servings*

BROWN RICE AND SAGE PANCAKES: Substitute 2 cups cooked brown rice for the wild rice and 1 tablespoon chopped fresh or 1 teaspoon dried sage leaves for the dill.

NUTRITION INFORMATION PER SERVING			
1 serving		**Percent of U.S. RDA**	
Calories	135	Protein	10%
Protein, g	6	Vitamin A	10%
Carbohydrate, g	26	Vitamin C	4%
Fat, g	1	Thiamin	10%
Unsaturated	1	Riboflavin	14%
Saturated	0	Niacin	10%
Dietary Fiber, g	2	Calcium	4%
Cholesterol, mg	0	Iron	8%
Sodium, mg	85		
Potassium, mg	240		

Asparagus Soup

1 pound asparagus
2 cups water
1 tablespoon margarine
2 tablespoons all-purpose flour
1 cup water
1 teaspoon chicken bouillon granules
1 teaspoon curry powder
½ teaspoon salt
⅛ teaspoon pepper
1 cup low-fat milk
1 teaspoon grated lemon peel

Cut tips from asparagus stalks; reserve. Cut stalks into 2-inch pieces. Heat 2 cups water and the asparagus stalks to boiling; reduce heat. Cover and simmer about 10 minutes or until tender; do not drain. Pour asparagus with water into blender. cover and blend until smooth.

Heat margarine in 3-quart saucepan until melted. Stir in flour. Cook, stirring constantly, until mixture is smooth and bubbly; remove from heat. Stir in 1 cup water. Heat to boiling, stirring constantly. Boil and stir 1 minute. Stir in asparagus mixture, bouillon granules, curry powder, salt, pepper and asparagus tips. Heat to boiling; reduce heat. Simmer uncovered 10 minutes. Stir in milk; heat just until hot. Sprinkle with lemon peel. *4 servings*

NUTRITION INFORMATION PER SERVING

1 serving		Percent of U.S. RDA	
Calories	90	Protein	6%
Protein, g	4	Vitamin A	12%
Carbohydrate, g	9	Vitamin C	12%
Fat, g	4	Thiamin	6%
Unsaturated	3	Riboflavin	10%
Saturated	1	Niacin	4%
Dietary Fiber, g	1	Calcium	8%
Cholesterol, mg	5	Iron	4%
Sodium, mg	650		
Potassium, mg	240		

Creamy Cauliflower Soup

2 cans (14½ ounces each) chicken broth
1 medium head cauliflower separated into
   flowerets (about 6 cups)
¾ cup chopped celery (about 1 large stalk)
½ cup chopped onion (about 1 medium)
1 tablespoon lemon juice
2 tablespoons margarine
¼ cup all-purpose flour
1½ cups low-fat milk
⅛ teaspoon pepper
Dash of ground nutmeg

Heat 1 can broth to boiling in 3-quart saucepan. Stir in cauliflower, celery, onion and lemon juice. Heat to boiling; reduce heat to medium. Cover and cook 15 to 20 minutes or until tender; do not drain. Carefully pour about half of the cauliflower mixture in blender. Cover and blend until of uniform consistency. Repeat with remaining cauliflower mixture; reserve.

Melt margarine in 3-quart saucepan over low heat. Stir in flour. Cook stirring constantly, until flour is absorbed; remove from heat. Stir in milk and remaining 1 can broth with wire whisk. Heat to boiling, stirring constantly. Boil and stir 1 minute. Stir in reserved cauliflower mixture, pepper and nutmeg; heat until hot. *8 servings*

NUTRITION INFORMATION PER SERVING

1 serving		Percent of U.S. RDA	
Calories	85	Protein	6%
Protein, g	4	Vitamin A	6%
Carbohydrate, g	11	Vitamin C	44%
Fat, g	3	Thiamin	8%
Unsaturated	2	Riboflavin	8%
Saturated	1	Niacin	6%
Dietary Fiber, g	2	Calcium	8%
Cholesterol, mg	0	Iron	4%
Sodium, mg	240		
Potassium, mg	430		

Creamy Potato-Rutabaga Soup, Crab Pitas (page 312)

Creamy Potato-Rutabaga Soup

¼ cup chopped onion (about 1 small)

1 tablespoon margarine

3 cups water

1½ teaspoons chopped fresh or ½ teaspoon dried tarragon leaves

½ teaspoon salt

¼ teaspoon white pepper

1 medium rutabaga (about 1½ pounds), peeled and cut into ½-inch cubes

4 medium baking potatoes (about 1½ pounds), peeled and cut into ½-inch cubes

1 cup low-fat milk

Cook onion in margarine in Dutch oven over low heat, stirring frequently, until tender. Stir in remaining ingredients except potatoes and milk. Heat to boiling; reduce heat to low. Cover and cook 15 minutes; add potatoes. Cover and cook 15 to 20 minutes longer or until potatoes and rutabaga are very tender.

Carefully pour about half of the potato mixture into blender. Cover and blend until of uniform consistency. Pour into remaining mixture in Dutch oven; stir in milk. Heat over medium heat, stirring constantly, until hot. Garnish with fresh tarragon leaves if desired. *6 servings*

NUTRITION INFORMATION PER SERVING

1 serving		Percent of U.S. RDA	
Calories	120	Protein	4%
Protein, g	3	Vitamin A	4%
Carbohydrate, g	20	Vitamin C	14%
Fat, g	3	Thiamin	8%
Unsaturated	2	Riboflavin	6%
Saturated	1	Niacin	6%
Dietary Fiber, g	2	Calcium	8%
Cholesterol, mg	5	Iron	2%
Sodium, mg	230		
Potassium, mg	460		

Ratatouille Soup

1 tablespoon olive or vegetable oil

¼ cup chopped onion (about 1 small)

1 clove garlic, crushed

2¼ cups coarsely chopped tomatoes (about 3 medium)

2 cups ½-inch slices zucchini (about 1 medium)

½ cup chopped green bell pepper (about 1 small)

¼ teaspoon salt

¼ teaspoon pepper

1 small eggplant (about 1 pound), cut into ½-inch cubes

1 can (10½ ounces) condensed chicken broth

1 broth can water

Heat oil in Dutch oven over medium-high heat. Cook onion and garlic in oil about 3 minutes, stirring occasionally, until onion is tender. Stir in remaining ingredients. Heat to boiling; reduce heat. Cover and simmer about 10 minutes or until vegetables are crisp-tender. *6 servings*

NUTRITION INFORMATION PER SERVING

1 serving		Percent of U.S. RDA	
Calories	80	Protein	4%
Protein, g	3	Vitamin A	6%
Carbohydrate, g	10	Vitamin C	20%
Fat, g	3	Thiamin	8%
Unsaturated	3	Riboflavin	4%
Saturated	0	Niacin	8%
Dietary Fiber, g	3	Calcium	2%
Cholesterol, mg	0	Iron	4%
Sodium, mg	260		
Potassium, mg	480		

Orange and Radish Salad

1½ cups chopped orange sections (about 3 medium oranges)

1 cup sliced radishes (about 12 medium)

1 cup thinly sliced red onion (about 1 medium)

2 tablespoons chopped fresh or 2 teaspoons dried mint leaves

1 tablespoon grated orange peel

1 tablespoon lemon juice

1 teaspoon vegetable oil

½ teaspoon salt

½ teaspoon ground cinnamon

Mix all ingredients in glass or plastic bowl. Cover and refrigerate about 2 hours or until chilled. *6 servings*

NUTRITION INFORMATION PER SERVING

1 serving		Percent of U.S. RDA	
Calories	45	Protein	*
Protein, g	1	Vitamin A	*
Carbohydrate, g	8	Vitamin C	52%
Fat, g	1	Thiamin	2%
Unsaturated	1	Riboflavin	2%
Saturated	0	Niacin	*
Dietary Fiber, g	2	Calcium	2%
Cholesterol, mg	0	Iron	*
Sodium, mg	180		
Potassium, mg	160		

Crunchy Jícama and Melon Salad, Orange and Radish Salad (page 133)

Crunchy Jícama and Melon Salad

1½ cups julienne strips jícama (about ½ medium)

1½ cups ½-inch cubes cantaloupe (about ½ medium)

2 tablespoons lime juice

2 tablespoons chopped fresh or 1 tablespoon dried mint leaves

1 teaspoon grated lime peel

1 teaspoon honey

¼ teaspoon salt

Mix all ingredients in glass or plastic bowl. Cover and refrigerate about 2 hours or until chilled. *6 servings*

CRUNCHY JÍCAMA AND APPLE SALAD: Substitute 2 red eating apples for the cantaloupe, 2 tablespoons lemon juice for the lime juice and 1 teaspoon grated lemon peel for the lime peel. Sprinkle with chopped pecans if desired.

NUTRITION INFORMATION PER SERVING

1 serving		Percent of U.S. RDA	
Calories	35	Protein	*
Protein, g	1	Vitamin A	10%
Carbohydrate, g	8	Vitamin C	42%
Fat, g	0	Thiamin	2%
Unsaturated	0	Riboflavin	*
Saturated	0	Niacin	2%
Dietary Fiber, g	1	Calcium	*
Cholesterol, mg	0	Iron	2%
Sodium, mg	95		
Potassium, mg	190		

Apple Kabob Salad

Poppy Seed Dressing (page 152)

1 medium green bell pepper, cut into twelve 1½-inch squares

1 cooking apple, cut into 12 wedges

12 one-inch cubes pineapple (about 1 cup)

6 cauliflowerets (about 1 cup)

6 radishes

Prepare Poppy Seed Dressing. Thread remaining ingredients alternately onto each of six 10-inch skewers. Serve with dressing. *6 servings*

PEAR KABOB SALAD: Substitute 1 medium red bell pepper for the green pepper and 1 bosc pear for the apple.

NUTRITION INFORMATION PER SERVING			
I serving		**Percent of U.S. RDA**	
Calories	60	Protein	2%
Protein, g	I	Vitamin A	2%
Carbohydrate, g	10	Vitamin C	48%
Fat, g	2	Thiamin	4%
Unsaturated	I	Riboflavin	2%
Saturated	I	Niacin	2%
Dietary Fiber, g	I	Calcium	2%
Cholesterol, mg	0	Iron	2%
Sodium, mg	115		
Potassium, mg	170		

Carrot Salad

This Southwest-inspired salad is definitely not your everyday carrot-raisin salad! The salad can easily be made a day ahead, as its flavors blend nicely while refrigerating.

2½ cups shredded carrots (about 4 medium)

¾ cup finely chopped pineapple

⅓ cup plain nonfat yogurt

2 tablespoons chopped fresh mint leaves

2 tablespoons lemon juice

1 teaspoon honey

½ teaspoon ground cinnamon

¼ teaspoon ground cumin

3 cups bite-size pieces leaf lettuce (about ½ large head)

Mix all ingredients except lettuce in glass or plastic bowl. Cover and refrigerate about 2 hours or until chilled. Serve on lettuce. *6 servings*

NUTRITION INFORMATION PER SERVING			
I serving		**Percent of U.S. RDA**	
Calories	50	Protein	36%
Protein, g	2	Vitamin A	78%
Carbohydrate, g	10	Vitamin C	26%
Fat, g	0	Thiamin	6%
Unsaturated	0	Riboflavin	6%
Saturated	0	Niacin	2%
Dietary Fiber, g	2	Calcium	4%
Cholesterol, mg	0	Iron	4%
Sodium, mg	30		
Potassium, mg	290		

Oriental Daikon Salad

Oriental Daikon Salad

Daikon radishes are long and mild, and are also called Japanese or Oriental radishes. Daikon is often pickled or shredded and used as a garnish. Here it's sliced and combined with mushrooms and green onions in a tangy marinade.

2 tablespoons white wine vinegar

1 tablespoon vegetable oil

1 tablespoon reduced-sodium soy sauce

1 teaspoon grated gingerroot

½ teaspoon sesame oil

¼ teaspoon salt

2 cups diagonally sliced daikon radishes (about 3 medium)

1 cup sliced mushrooms (about 3 ounces)

¼ cup sliced green onions (2 to 3 medium)

6 Bibb lettuce leaves

1 tablespoon sesame seed, toasted

Shake vinegar, vegetable oil, soy sauce, gingerroot, sesame oil and salt in tightly covered container. Pour over daikon, mushrooms and onions; toss until evenly coated. Cover and refrigerate about 2 hours or until chilled. Serve on lettuce leaves. Sprinkle with sesame seed.
6 servings

NUTRITION INFORMATION PER SERVING

1 serving		Percent of U.S. RDA	
Calories	75	Protein	2%
Protein, g	2	Vitamin A	*
Carbohydrate, g	8	Vitamin C	66%
Fat, g	4	Thiamin	2%
Unsaturated	3	Riboflavin	8%
Saturated	1	Niacin	6%
Dietary Fiber, g	2	Calcium	4%
Cholesterol, mg	0	Iron	4%
Sodium, mg	300		
Potassium, mg	480		

Tossed Salad with Apple Cider Dressing

Apple Cider Dressing (page 154)
2 cups bite-size pieces romaine lettuce
2 cups bite-size pieces spinach
1 cup bite-size pieces iceberg lettuce
1 cup shredded zucchini (about 1 medium)
½ cup chopped mushrooms (about 2 ounces)
½ cup chopped radishes (about 8 medium)
½ cup chopped red bell pepper (about 1 small)

Prepare Apple Cider Dressing in large bowl. Add remaining ingredients; toss. *6 servings*

FRUITY TOSSED SALAD WITH APPLE CIDER DRESS-ING: Omit shredded apple from dressing. Omit zucchini and radishes. Stir in 1 eating apple, chopped, and 1 can (11 ounces) mandarin orange segments, drained, with the remaining ingredients. Sprinkle with chopped walnuts if desired.

Wintery Root-Vegetable Salad

We've tossed cauliflower with three favorite root vegetables—parsnips, carrots and beets—to make a tasty salad perfect with soups and stews. The cauliflower and parsnips take on a rosy, warm glow from the beets.

Dill Vinaigrette (page 154)
1 cup chopped cooked parsnip (about 1 medium)
1 cup cooked cauliflowerets
½ cup chopped cooked beet (about 1 medium)
½ cup chopped carrot (about 1 medium)
2 tablespoons finely chopped shallot (about 1 large)

Toss all ingredients in large glass or plastic bowl. Cover and refrigerate about 2 hours or until chilled. *6 servings*

NUTRITION INFORMATION PER SERVING

1 serving		Percent of U.S. RDA	
Calories	50	Protein	2%
Protein, g	2	Vitamin A	26%
Carbohydrate, g	8	Vitamin C	50%
Fat, g	1	Thiamin	4%
Unsaturated	0	Riboflavin	6%
Saturated	1	Niacin	2%
Dietary Fiber, g	1	Calcium	4%
Cholesterol, mg	2	Iron	6%
Sodium, mg	150		
Potassium, mg	330		

NUTRITION INFORMATION PER SERVING

1 serving		Percent of U.S. RDA	
Calories	60	Protein	2%
Protein, g	1	Vitamin A	32%
Carbohydrate, g	9	Vitamin C	22%
Fat, g	2	Thiamin	2%
Unsaturated	2	Riboflavin	2%
Saturated	0	Niacin	2%
Dietary Fiber, g	2	Calcium	2%
Cholesterol, mg	0	Iron	4%
Sodium, mg	55		
Potassium, mg	230		

Sunchoke and Spinach Salad

Sunchokes, or Jerusalem artichokes, are paired with lime for a refreshing taste. When entertaining, serve on shredded lettuce, as we've suggested. For a more casual meal, toss the lettuce in with the other ingredients.

Lime-Yogurt Dressing (page 155)
2 cups shredded spinach
1 cup finely chopped peeled Jerusalem artichokes (about 4 medium)
1 cup chopped carrots (about 2 medium)
½ cup chopped red bell pepper (about 1 small)
½ cup finely chopped red onion (about ½ medium)
2 cups shredded lettuce

Prepare Lime-Yogurt Dressing in large glass or plastic bowl. Add remaining ingredients except lettuce; toss. Cover and refrigerate about 2 hours or until chilled. Serve on lettuce. *6 servings*

NUTRITION INFORMATION PER SERVING			
I serving		**Percent of U.S. RDA**	
Calories	65	Protein	4%
Protein, g	3	Vitamin A	44%
Carbohydrate, g	13	Vitamin C	48%
Fat, g	0	Thiamin	6%
Unsaturated	0	Riboflavin	6%
Saturated	0	Niacin	4%
Dietary Fiber, g	2	Calcium	8%
Cholesterol, mg	0	Iron	4%
Sodium, mg	220		
Potassium, mg	380		

Artichoke-Asparagus Salad

1 package (6 ounces) frozen artichoke hearts
Tangy Lemon Dressing (page 156)
1 can (15 ounces) white asparagus spears, drained, or 1 pound cooked fresh asparagus
1 cup sliced mushrooms (about 3 ounces)
6 Boston lettuce leaves
18 small pitted ripe olives

Cook artichoke hearts as directed on package; drain. Immediately rinse with cold water; drain. Prepare Tangy Lemon Dressing; pour over artichoke hearts, asparagus and mushrooms in glass or plastic bowl. Cover and refrigerate about 2 hours or until chilled. Remove vegetables with slotted spoon; reserve dressing. Arrange vegetables on lettuce on individual serving plates. Garnish with olives. Serve with remaining dressing. *6 servings*

NUTRITION INFORMATION PER SERVING			
I serving		**Percent of U.S. RDA**	
Calories	140	Protein	4%
Protein, g	3	Vitamin A	4%
Carbohydrate, g	7	Vitamin C	32%
Fat, g	10	Thiamin	4%
Unsaturated	8	Riboflavin	8%
Saturated	2	Niacin	6%
Dietary Fiber, g	3	Calcium	4%
Cholesterol, mg	0	Iron	12%
Sodium, mg	600		
Potassium, mg	300		

Spicy Bean and Cucumber Salad

Spicy Bean and Cucumber Salad

2 cups cooked chopped green beans (about 11 ounces)
1 cup finely chopped peeled cucumber (about 1 medium)
½ cup finely chopped red onion (about ½ medium)
2 tablespoons chopped fresh cilantro leaves
2 tablespoons red wine vinegar or cider vinegar
2 teaspoons chopped fresh hot green chile pepper or ¼ teaspoon crushed red pepper
1 teaspoon honey
½ teaspoon salt

Mix all ingredients. Cover and refrigerate about 2 hours or until chilled. *6 servings*

NUTRITION INFORMATION PER SERVING

1 serving		Percent of U.S. RDA	
Calories	30	Protein	*
Protein, g	1	Vitamin A	2%
Carbohydrate, g	6	Vitamin C	10%
Fat, g	0	Thiamin	2%
Unsaturated	0	Riboflavin	2%
Saturated	0	Niacin	*
Dietary Fiber, g	2	Calcium	2%
Cholesterol, mg	0	Iron	2%
Sodium, mg	190		
Potassium, mg	110		

Creamy Horseradish–Beet Salad

Creamy Horseradish Dressing (page 151)
3 cups ¼-inch slices peeled cooked beets
(about 3 medium)
¼ cup finely chopped onion (about 1 small)

Prepare Creamy Horseradish Dressing in large glass or plastic bowl. Add beets and onion; toss. Cover and refrigerate about 2 hours or until chilled. *6 servings*

CREAMY HORSERADISH–SQUASH SALAD: Substitute 1½ cups sliced uncooked zucchini and 1½ cups sliced uncooked yellow squash for the beets, and ¼ cup finely chopped red onion for the onion. Cover and refrigerate at least 1 hour.

CREAMY HORSERADISH–KOHLRABI SALAD: Substitute 3 cups sliced cooked kohlrabi bulbs for the beets and ¼ cup sliced green onions for the onions. Cover and refrigerate at least 1 hour.

NUTRITION INFORMATION PER SERVING

I serving		Percent of U.S. RDA	
Calories	85	Protein	6%
Protein, g	5	Vitamin A	2%
Carbohydrate, g	9	Vitamin C	8%
Fat, g	3	Thiamin	2%
Unsaturated	I	Riboflavin	4%
Saturated	2	Niacin	*
Dietary Fiber, g	2	Calcium	10%
Cholesterol, mg	10	Iron	4%
Sodium, mg	90		
Potassium, mg	340		

Sugar Snap Pea Salad

Sugar snap peas used to be a fleeting delight, found only in the summer. With the availability of frozen sugar snaps, this can be a year-round treat.

Cucumber Dressing (page 153)
2 cups cooked sugar snap peas (about 12 ounces)
½ cup shredded carrot (about 1 small)
6 Bibb lettuce leaves

Prepare Cucumber Dressing in large glass or plastic bowl. Mix in peas and carrot. Cover and refrigerate about 2 hours or until chilled. Serve on lettuce leaves. *6 servings*

NUTRITION INFORMATION PER SERVING

I serving		Percent of U.S. RDA	
Calories	45	Protein	4%
Protein, g	3	Vitamin A	16%
Carbohydrate, g	8	Vitamin C	48%
Fat, g	0	Thiamin	6%
Unsaturated	0	Riboflavin	6%
Saturated	0	Niacin	2%
Dietary Fiber, g	I	Calcium	6%
Cholesterol, mg	0	Iron	6%
Sodium, mg	25		
Potassium, mg	260		

Corn, Pea and Sun-dried Tomato Salad

This salad can also be a great topping! Omit the lettuce and use to top grilled chicken or fish.

1 cup cooked fresh, thawed frozen or drained canned whole kernel corn (about 2 medium ears)

1 cup cooked green peas

1/2 cup thinly sliced red onion (about 1/2 small)

1/2 cup chopped tomato (about 1 small)

1/3 cup chopped green onions (about 3 medium)

2 tablespoons chopped fresh parsley

1 tablespoon finely chopped sun-dried tomato (not oil-packed)

3 tablespoons lime juice

2 tablespoons white vinegar

1/2 teaspoon salt

1/4 teaspoon pepper

3 cups bite-size pieces lettuce (about 1/2 head)

Mix all ingredients except lettuce in glass or plastic bowl. Cover and refrigerate about 2 hours or until chilled. Serve on lettuce.
6 servings

NUTRITION INFORMATION PER SERVING

1 serving		Percent of U.S. RDA	
Calories	55	Protein	4%
Protein, g	2	Vitamin A	4%
Carbohydrate, g	12	Vitamin C	22%
Fat, g	0	Thiamin	10%
Unsaturated	0	Riboflavin	4%
Saturated	0	Niacin	4%
Dietary Fiber, g	3	Calcium	2%
Cholesterol, mg	0	Iron	4%
Sodium, mg	210		
Potassium, mg	220		

Corn, Pea and Sun-dried Tomato Salad

Curried Spaghetti Squash Salad

1 medium spaghetti squash (about 2½ pounds)
½ cup nonfat buttermilk
2 tablespoons lime juice
1 tablespoon Dijon mustard
1 teaspoon curry powder
¼ teaspoon pepper
1 cup chopped peeled pear (about 1 medium)
¼ cup finely chopped onion (about 1 small)
2 tablespoons chopped green onions
3 cups shredded lettuce (about ½ head)

Heat oven to 400°. Cut squash into halves. Place cut sides down in ungreased rectangular baking dish, 13×9×2 inches. Pour water into dish to ¼-inch depth. Cover and bake 30 to 40 minutes or until tender. Remove strands with two forks.

Mix buttermilk, lime juice, mustard, curry powder and pepper in large glass or plastic bowl. Add squash strands, pear, onion and green onions; toss. Cover and refrigerate about 2 hours or until chilled. Serve on lettuce.
6 servings

NUTRITION INFORMATION PER SERVING

1 serving		Percent of U.S. RDA	
Calories	65	Protein	2%
Protein, g	2	Vitamin A	20%
Carbohydrate, g	12	Vitamin C	16%
Fat, g	1	Thiamin	4%
Unsaturated	1	Riboflavin	4%
Saturated	0	Niacin	2%
Dietary Fiber, g	3	Calcium	4%
Cholesterol, mg	0	Iron	2%
Sodium, mg	60		
Potassium, mg	230		

Creamy Country Potato Salad

2½ cups cubed medium red potatoes (about 1 pound)
½ cup nonfat buttermilk
¼ cup lemon juice
2 tablespoons cholesterol-free reduced-calorie mayonnaise or salad dressing
1 tablespoon Dijon mustard
1 tablespoon chopped fresh or 1 teaspoon dried thyme leaves
½ teaspoon salt
½ cup chopped celery (about 1 medium stalk)
½ cup chopped green bell pepper (about 1 small)

Heat 1½ quarts water to boiling in 2-quart saucepan. Add potatoes. Cover and heat to boiling; reduce heat. Simmer 15 to 20 minutes or until tender; drain.

Mix buttermilk, lemon juice, mayonnaise, mustard, thyme and salt in large glass or plastic bowl. Add potatoes, celery and bell pepper; toss. Cover and refrigerate about 2 hours or until chilled. *6 servings*

NUTRITION INFORMATION PER SERVING

1 serving		Percent of U.S. RDA	
Calories	90	Protein	2%
Protein, g	2	Vitamin A	*
Carbohydrate, g	16	Vitamin C	12%
Fat, g	2	Thiamin	6%
Unsaturated	2	Riboflavin	2%
Saturated	0	Niacin	4%
Dietary Fiber, g	1	Calcium	4%
Cholesterol, mg	0	Iron	6%
Sodium, mg	270		
Potassium, mg	310		

Tangy Garbanzo Bean Salad

1 cup dried or 2 cans (15 ounces each)
   drained garbanzo beans
1/2 cup tomato juice
2 tablespoons chopped fresh parsley
2 teaspoons Dijon mustard
1/2 teaspoon salt
1/4 teaspoon pepper
1/4 cup chopped red onion
1/4 cup finely chopped carrot

Cook beans as directed on package—except omit salt; drain. (Do not cook canned beans.) Mix tomato juice, parsley, mustard, salt and pepper in large glass or plastic bowl. Stir in beans, onion and carrot. Cover and refrigerate about 2 hours or until chilled. *6 servings*

NUTRITION INFORMATION PER SERVING

1 serving		Percent of U.S. RDA	
Calories	125	Protein	10%
Protein, g	6	Vitamin A	8%
Carbohydrate, g	21	Vitamin C	12%
Fat, g	2	Thiamin	6%
Unsaturated	2	Riboflavin	2%
Saturated	0	Niacin	2%
Dietary Fiber, g	4	Calcium	4%
Cholesterol, mg	0	Iron	12%
Sodium, mg	280		
Potassium, mg	280		

Kidney Bean Salad

1/2 cup chopped orange sections (about 1
   medium orange)
1/2 cup chopped celery (about 1 medium
   stalk)
1/4 cup chopped onion (about 1 small)
1/3 cup orange juice (about 1 medium
   orange)
2 tablespoons red wine vinegar or cider
   vinegar
1/4 to 1/2 teaspoon ground cumin
1/4 teaspoon pepper
1 can (16 ounces) reduced-sodium kidney
   beans, drained

Mix all ingredients in glass or plastic bowl. Cover and refrigerate about 2 hours or until chilled. *6 servings*

NUTRITION INFORMATION PER SERVING

1 serving		Percent of U.S. RDA	
Calories	120	Protein	10%
Protein, g	7	Vitamin A	*
Carbohydrate, g	23	Vitamin C	32%
Fat, g	0	Thiamin	10%
Unsaturated	0	Riboflavin	4%
Saturated	0	Niacin	2%
Dietary Fiber, g	0	Calcium	4%
Cholesterol, mg	7	Iron	12%
Sodium, mg	160		
Potassium, mg	420		

Lentil Salad

Lentil Salad

Lentils are a wonderful source of soluble fiber, and while most people are familiar with the common green lentils, many don't know they also come in other colors, including white and orange. For a bit more zip, stir ¼ teaspoon crushed red pepper into the salad.

½ cup uncooked dried lentils
2 cups chicken broth
Creamy Tomato Dressing (page 151)
1 cup chopped red bell pepper (about 1
    medium)
½ cup chopped tomato (about 1 small)
⅓ cup chopped green onions (about 3
    medium)
¼ cup chopped red onion

Cover and cook lentils and broth in 2-quart saucepan over medium-low heat 25 minutes or until lentils are tender; drain. Prepare Creamy Tomato Dressing in large glass or plastic bowl. Mix in lentils and remaining ingredients. Cover and refrigerate about 2 hours or until chilled.
6 servings

NUTRITION INFORMATION PER SERVING			
I serving		**Percent of U.S. RDA**	
Calories	95	Protein	10%
Protein, g	7	Vitamin A	12%
Carbohydrate, g	14	Vitamin C	68%
Fat, g	1	Thiamin	8%
Unsaturated	1	Riboflavin	6%
Saturated	0	Niacin	10%
Dietary Fiber, g	3	Calcium	4%
Cholesterol, mg	0	Iron	12%
Sodium, mg	480		
Potassium, mg	390		

Chile Pasta Salad

4 ounces uncooked farfalle (bow-tie–shape)
   pasta (about 1⅓ cups)
½ cup plain low-fat yogurt
1 tablespoon Dijon mustard
½ teaspoon salt
1 jalapeño chile, seeded and finely chopped
3 plum tomatoes, cut lengthwise into halves
   and sliced
2 green onions, cut diagonally into ½-inch
   pieces
1 large clove garlic, crushed

Cook pasta as directed on package—except omit salt; drain. Rinse with cold water; drain. Mix pasta and remaining ingredients. Cover and refrigerate about 2 hours or until chilled. Serve on lettuce leaves if desired. *6 servings*

NUTRITION INFORMATION PER SERVING

1 serving		Percent of U.S. RDA	
Calories	100	Protein	6%
Protein, g	4	Vitamin A	24%
Carbohydrate, g	19	Vitamin C	84%
Fat, g	1	Thiamin	8%
Unsaturated	1	Riboflavin	6%
Saturated	0	Niacin	6%
Dietary Fiber, g	1	Calcium	4%
Cholesterol, mg	1	Iron	6%
Sodium, mg	230		
Potassium, mg	220		

Bulgur and Orange Salad

Bulgur is coarsely cut wheat berries that have been parboiled, toasted and partially debranned. Here, it adds chewiness and fiber to this lively citrus salad. If you like, substitute ¼ cup fresh mint leaves for a third of the parsley.

⅓ cup uncooked bulgur
¾ cup chopped orange sections (about 1
   large orange)
¾ cup chopped fresh parsley
½ cup chopped tomato (about 1 small)
½ cup chopped onion (about 1 medium)
2 tablespoons lemon juice
2 teaspoons grated orange peel
2 teaspoons olive or vegetable oil
½ teaspoon salt
¼ teaspoon pepper
⅛ teaspoon crushed red pepper

Cook bulgur as directed on package—except omit salt. Toss bulgur and remaining ingredients in glass or plastic bowl. Cover and refrigerate about 2 hours or until chilled.
6 servings

NUTRITION INFORMATION PER SERVING

1 serving		Percent of U.S. RDA	
Calories	90	Protein	4%
Protein, g	2	Vitamin A	6%
Carbohydrate, g	16	Vitamin C	52%
Fat, g	2	Thiamin	4%
Unsaturated	2	Riboflavin	2%
Saturated	0	Niacin	4%
Dietary Fiber, g	4	Calcium	2%
Cholesterol, mg	0	Iron	4%
Sodium, mg	190		
Potassium, mg	210		

Chile Pasta Salad

Asian Noodle Salad

Chinese egg noodles are the noodles used to make lo mein dishes. If they are not available, substitute thin egg noodles or spaghetti.

6 ounces Chinese-style egg noodles
⅓ cup chopped green onions (about 3 medium)
2 tablespoons chopped fresh cilantro leaves
2 tablespoons frozen (thawed) apple juice concentrate
1 tablespoon balsamic vinegar
1 tablespoon reduced-sodium soy sauce
2 teaspoons finely chopped gingerroot
½ teaspoon sesame oil
1 clove garlic, finely chopped (about ½ teaspoon)

Cook noodles as directed on package—except omit salt; drain. Toss noodles and remaining ingredients. Cover and refrigerate about 2 hours or until chilled. *6 servings*

NUTRITION INFORMATION PER SERVING

1 serving		Percent of U.S. RDA	
Calories	75	Protein	2%
Protein, g	1	Vitamin A	*
Carbohydrate, g	18	Vitamin C	4%
Fat, g	0	Thiamin	4%
Unsaturated	0	Riboflavin	*
Saturated	0	Niacin	4%
Dietary Fiber, g	1	Calcium	*
Cholesterol, mg	0	Iron	4%
Sodium, mg	100		
Potassium, mg	75		

Brown Rice Salad

½ cup uncooked brown rice
1½ cups chicken broth
1 cup finely chopped apple (about 1 medium)
⅓ cup raisins
¼ cup finely chopped onion (about 1 small)
¼ cup lemon juice
2 tablespoons chopped fresh parsley
1 teaspoon grated lemon peel
2 tablespoons frozen (thawed) apple juice concentrate
½ teaspoon pepper
¼ teaspoon ground ginger
¼ teaspoon ground nutmeg

Cook rice as directed on package—except substitute broth for the water and omit salt. Toss rice and remaining ingredients in glass or plastic bowl. Cover and refrigerate about 2 hours or until chilled. *6 servings*

NUTRITION INFORMATION PER SERVING

1 serving		Percent of U.S. RDA	
Calories	115	Protein	4%
Protein, g	2	Vitamin A	*
Carbohydrate, g	25	Vitamin C	10%
Fat, g	1	Thiamin	6%
Unsaturated	1	Riboflavin	2%
Saturated	1	Niacin	8%
Dietary Fiber, g	2	Calcium	2%
Cholesterol, mg	0	Iron	4%
Sodium, mg	25		
Potassium, mg	200		

Creamy Horseradish Dressing

³/₄ **cup nonfat ricotta cheese**

¹/₄ **cup low-fat buttermilk**

2 tablespoons malt vinegar or cider vinegar

1 teaspoon prepared horseradish

Mix all ingredients with fork or wire whisk. *About 1 cup dressing*

CREAMY DIJON DRESSING: Omit horseradish. Stir in 2 teaspoons Dijon mustard.

CREAMY TARRAGON–HORSERADISH DRESSING: Stir in 1 teaspoon chopped fresh or ¹/₄ teaspoon dried tarragon leaves.

NUTRITION INFORMATION PER SERVING

1 tablespoon		Percent of U.S. RDA	
Calories	15	Protein	2%
Protein, g	1	Vitamin A	*
Carbohydrate, g	1	Vitamin C	*
Fat, g	1	Thiamin	*
Unsaturated	0	Riboflavin	2%
Saturated	1	Niacin	*
Dietary Fiber, g	0	Calcium	4%
Cholesterol, mg	5	Iron	*
Sodium, mg	20		
Potassium, mg	25		

Creamy Tomato Dressing

This tangy dressing is wonderful on any tossed salad. For an intense tomato flavor, drizzle dressing over sliced ripe tomatoes, and top with fresh basil.

¹/₄ **cup plain nonfat yogurt**

¹/₄ **cup tomato juice**

3 tablespoons chopped fresh parsley

2 tablespoons red wine vinegar

¹/₂ **teaspoon salt**

¹/₄ **teaspoon pepper**

Mix all ingredients. *About ³/₄ cup dressing*

NUTRITION INFORMATION PER SERVING

1 tablespoon		Percent of U.S. RDA	
Calories	5	Protein	*
Protein, g	0	Vitamin A	*
Carbohydrate, g	1	Vitamin C	4%
Fat, g	0	Thiamin	*
Unsaturated	0	Riboflavin	*
Saturated	0	Niacin	*
Dietary Fiber, g	0	Calcium	*
Cholesterol, mg	0	Iron	*
Sodium, mg	110		
Potassium, mg	30		

Apple Kabob Salad (page 135) with Poppy Seed Dressing and Celeriac Salad (page 136)

Poppy Seed Dressing

Cholesterol-free egg product, which is pasteurized, adds body to this fruit salad dressing. Use it on all-fruit salads or on mixed green and fruit salads.

¼ cup low-fat sour cream

¼ cup cholesterol-free reduced-calorie
   mayonnaise or salad dressing

¼ cup finely chopped red onion

¼ cup cholesterol-free egg product

2 tablespoons poppy seed

2 tablespoons lemon juice

1 tablespoon Dijon mustard

1 teaspoon honey

½ teaspoon salt

Mix all ingredients with fork or wire whisk in glass or plastic bowl. Cover and refrigerate at least 1 hour until chilled. *About 1 cup dressing*

NUTRITION INFORMATION PER SERVING

1 tablespoon		Percent of U.S. RDA	
Calories	30	Protein	*
Protein, g	1	Vitamin A	*
Carbohydrate, g	2	Vitamin C	*
Fat, g	2	Thiamin	*
Unsaturated	2	Riboflavin	2%
Saturated	0	Niacin	*
Dietary Fiber, g	0	Calcium	2%
Cholesterol, mg	0	Iron	*
Sodium, mg	110		
Potassium, mg	30		

Cucumber Dressing

Unpeeled cucumber adds a pretty color to this dressing. However, if the cucumber skin has been waxed or tastes bitter, it is best to make the dressing with a peeled cucumber.

1 cup finely chopped seeded peeled cucumber (about 1 medium)
½ cup plain nonfat yogurt
½ teaspoon grated lime peel
2 tablespoons chopped fresh or 2 teaspoons freeze-dried chives
2 tablespoons lime juice
1 tablespoon low-fat sour cream
¼ teaspoon pepper

Mix all ingredients with fork or wire whisk. *About 1¾ cups dressing*

NUTRITION INFORMATION PER SERVING			
I tablespoon		**Percent of U.S. RDA**	
Calories	5	Protein	*
Protein, g	0	Vitamin A	*
Carbohydrate, g	1	Vitamin C	*
Fat, g	0	Thiamin	*
Unsaturated	0	Riboflavin	*
Saturated	0	Niacin	*
Dietary Fiber, g	0	Calcium	*
Cholesterol, mg	0	Iron	*
Sodium, mg	5		
Potassium, mg	20		

Tofu Mayonnaise

Try stirring in 1 to 2 tablespoons of your favorite chopped fresh herb for variety. This mayonnaise is excellent with hot or cold vegetables, and when thinned with 2 tablespoons of chicken broth, it becomes a creamy sauce for poultry and fish.

1 cup mashed soft tofu (about 8 ounces)
2 tablespoons lemon juice
1 tablespoon Dijon mustard
½ teaspoon salt
2 tablespoons finely chopped shallot (about 1 large)
1 clove garlic, finely chopped (about ½ teaspoon)
2 teaspoons vegetable oil

Place all ingredients except oil in blender or food processor. Cover and blend until smooth. With blender on, add oil by drops. Cover and refrigerate in glass or plastic container at least 1 hour until chilled. *About 1 cup mayonnaise*

NUTRITION INFORMATION PER SERVING			
I tablespoon		**Percent of U.S. RDA**	
Calories	20	Protein	2%
Protein, g	1	Vitamin A	*
Carbohydrate, g	1	Vitamin C	*
Fat, g	1	Thiamin	*
Unsaturated	1	Riboflavin	*
Saturated	0	Niacin	*
Dietary Fiber, g	0	Calcium	2%
Cholesterol, mg	0	Iron	4%
Sodium, mg	80		
Potassium, mg	30		

Apple Cider Dressing

¼ cup frozen (thawed) apple juice
    concentrate
2 tablespoons chopped fresh parsley or 2
    teaspoons dried parsley flakes
2 tablespoons finely shredded apple
3 tablespoons low-fat sour cream
3 tablespoons water
2 tablespoons cider vinegar
1 tablespoon Dijon mustard
¼ teaspoon salt
⅛ teaspoon pepper

Mix all ingredients with fork or wire whisk.
About 1 cup dressing

NUTRITION INFORMATION PER SERVING			
1 tablespoon		**Percent of U.S. RDA**	
Calories	10	Protein	*
Protein, g	0	Vitamin A	*
Carbohydrate, g	2	Vitamin C	*
Fat, g	0	Thiamin	*
Unsaturated	0	Riboflavin	*
Saturated	0	Niacin	*
Dietary Fiber, g	0	Calcium	*
Cholesterol, mg	0	Iron	*
Sodium, mg	50		
Potassium, mg	25		

Dill Vinaigrette

¼ cup water
2 tablespoons cider vinegar
1 tablespoon Dijon mustard
1 tablespoon chopped fresh or 1 teaspoon
    dried dill weed
2 teaspoons vegetable oil
¼ teaspoon pepper
⅛ teaspoon ground nutmeg

Shake all ingredients in tightly covered container. *About ½ cup vinaigrette*

MIXED HERB VINAIGRETTE: Substitute 1 tablespoon chopped fresh or 1 teaspoon dried parsley flakes for the dill weed and ¼ teaspoon coarsely-ground black pepper for the pepper. Omit nutmeg. Stir in 1 teaspoon chopped fresh or ¼ teaspoon dried basil leaves.

NUTRITION INFORMATION PER SERVING			
1 tablespoon		**Percent of U.S. RDA**	
Calories	15	Protein	*
Protein, g	0	Vitamin A	*
Carbohydrate, g	1	Vitamin C	*
Fat, g	1	Thiamin	*
Unsaturated	1	Riboflavin	*
Saturated	0	Niacin	*
Dietary Fiber, g	0	Calcium	*
Cholesterol, mg	0	Iron	*
Sodium, mg	25		
Potassium, mg	15		

Lime-Yogurt Dressing

The perfect dressing for Sunchoke and Spinach Salad (page 141), this is also delightful on any tossed green salad. If you like, try a salad of spinach and mandarin orange segments, and top with slivered almonds and Lime-Yogurt Dressing.

¾ cup plain nonfat yogurt
3 tablespoons chopped fresh parsley
2 tablespoons lime juice
2 tablespoons red wine vinegar or cider vinegar
½ teaspoon grated lime peel
½ teaspoon salt
¼ teaspoon pepper

Mix all ingredients with fork or wire whisk.
About 1 cup dressing

NUTRITION INFORMATION PER SERVING

1 tablespoon		Percent of U.S. RDA	
Calories	10	Protein	*
Protein, g	1	Vitamin A	*
Carbohydrate, g	1	Vitamin C	2%
Fat, g	0	Thiamin	*
Unsaturated	0	Riboflavin	2%
Saturated	0	Niacin	*
Dietary Fiber, g	0	Calcium	2%
Cholesterol, mg	0	Iron	*
Sodium, mg	75		
Potassium, mg	340		

Ricotta Dressing

¾ cup nonfat ricotta cheese
¼ cup finely chopped onion (about 1 small)
¼ cup low-fat buttermilk
2 tablespoons chopped fresh or 1 tablespoon freeze-dried chives
1 tablespoon sherry vinegar or cider vinegar
½ teaspoon salt
¼ teaspoon pepper

Mix all ingredients with fork or wire whisk.
About 1 cup dressing

NUTRITION INFORMATION PER SERVING

1 tablespoon		Percent of U.S. RDA	
Calories	20	Protein	2%
Protein, g	1	Vitamin A	*
Carbohydrate, g	1	Vitamin C	*
Fat, g	1	Thiamin	*
Unsaturated	0	Riboflavin	2%
Saturated	1	Niacin	*
Dietary Fiber, g	0	Calcium	4%
Cholesterol, mg	5	Iron	*
Sodium, mg	85		
Potassium, mg	25		

5

Meats

Meat has been much maligned when discussed as part of a healthy eating plan. Yes, meat is a source of fat and cholesterol. However, it is also a very good source of protein, iron and B vitamins, along with other nutrients. Because protein is not a problem nutrient for most Americans, the large portions of meat we eat are not necessary and just contribute added fat and cholesterol. The question for healthy eating is not should we eat meat but, rather how much meat. The meat recipes that follow generally call for about 4 ounces of uncooked meat per serving, or 1 pound for 4 servings. The new Food Guide Pyramid (page 14) recommends limiting a serving to 2 or 3 ounces of cooked meat. That may not sound like much for a main course but it is a healthy goal for the long run.

The beef and pork available in markets today are leaner than ever. It still pays, though, to shop wisely. Look for cuts that are naturally lower in fat, such as loins, rounds and flank cuts, or that have the least visible fat in them. When purchasing ground beef, look for the extra-lean variety. And, get in the habit of always trimming fat from meat before cooking.

When meat is used as part of a dish instead of as the main ingredient, it provides a good source of protein that can complement other less complete sources, such as grains, pastas or beans. Using less meat also controls the amount of fat and cholesterol in the dish. Adding bulgur to ground beef in Beef and Bulgur Stew (page 177) stretches the 1½ pounds of meat to 8 servings instead of 6. Garbanzo beans extend 1 pound of pork to 6 servings in Spicy Pork and Garbanzo Bean Salad (page 203). Another example is Asian Beef Salad (page 198), where a pound of beef is combined with rice stick noodles and cholesterol-free egg product for 6 servings.

But don't worry, you don't have to give up pot roast, steak or meatloaf. Beef Roast with Fruit (page 160) combines a beef pot roast with yams, peaches and pears instead of the more typical carrots and potatoes for a main dish that's under 300 calories per serving. Sliced broiled flank steak smothered with a red onion and bell pepper sauce provides less than 250 calories per serving in Steak with Onions and Peppers (page 162). Instead of using a whole egg to bind the meat mixture together, Healthy Meat Loaf (page 168) uses only the egg whites and also substitutes ground turkey for half of the ground beef, all for only 225 calories per serving.

From beef to lamb and stir-fries to sandwiches, enjoy these meat dishes as part of your healthy eating plan.

Preceding page: Beef with Tomatoes and Rice (page 159), Marinated Pork Chops with Cilantro-Mint Salsa (page 184)

Beef with Tomatoes and Rice

An easy main dish for a crowd, this simple roast is perked up with yellow rice and marinated tomatoes, all for under 350 calories a serving.

Marinated Tomatoes (right)
4-pound beef tip, bottom round or rolled
   rump roast
2⅓ cups uncooked regular long grain rice
4⅔ cups water
2 teaspoons salt
1 teaspoon ground turmeric
½ cup chopped fresh parsley

Prepare Marinated Tomatoes. Heat oven to 325°. Trim fat from beef roast. Place beef on rack in shallow roasting pan. Insert meat thermometer so tip is in center of thickest part of beef and does not rest in fat. Roast uncovered about 3 hours or until thermometer registers 160° (medium doneness).

About 30 minutes before beef is done, heat rice, water, salt and turmeric to boiling, stirring once or twice; reduce heat. Cover and simmer 14 minutes (do not lift cover or stir). Remove from heat; fluff rice lightly with fork. Cover and let steam 5 to 10 minutes. Stir parsley into rice. Cut beef into ¼-inch slices. Arrange beef and Marinated Tomatoes on rice. Spoon remaining tomato marinade over beef. *16 servings*

Marinated Tomatoes

4 medium tomatoes, cut into ¼-inch slices
2 tablespoons olive or vegetable oil
2 tablespoons red wine vinegar
⅛ teaspoon salt
3 drops red pepper sauce
2 cloves garlic, finely chopped

Place tomatoes in glass or plastic dish. Mix remaining ingredients; pour over tomatoes. Cover and let stand at room temperature about 3 hours.

NUTRITION INFORMATION PER SERVING			
I serving		**Percent of U.S. RDA**	
Calories	315	Protein	58%
Protein, g	38	Vitamin A	2%
Carbohydrate, g	23	Vitamin C	6%
Fat, g	8	Thiamin	18%
Unsaturated	5	Riboflavin	20%
Saturated	3	Niacin	40%
Dietary Fiber, g	I	Calcium	2%
Cholesterol, mg	95	Iron	24%
Sodium, mg	360		
Potassium, mg	610		

Beef Roast with Fruit

4-pound beef arm, blade or rib pot roast

½ teaspoon salt

¼ teaspoon pepper

1 cup dry white wine or beef broth

2 medium onions, sliced

1½ cups chopped tomatoes (about 2 medium)

2 medium yams or sweet potatoes, peeled and cut into ¼-inch slices

1 can (16 ounces) sliced peaches in juice, drained

1 can (16 ounces) sliced pears in juice, drained

1 tablespoon cornstarch

2 tablespoons cold water

Trim fat from beef roast. Cook beef in nonstick Dutch oven over medium heat until brown on all sides; drain. Sprinkle with salt and pepper.

Add wine, onions and tomatoes. Heat to boiling; reduce heat. Cover and simmer 3 hours.

Add yams. Cover and simmer 20 minutes; add peaches and pears. Cook about 10 minutes longer or until yams and meat are tender. Remove beef, fruit and vegetables; keep warm. Skim any fat from liquid in Dutch oven. If necessary, add enough water to liquid to measure 2 cups. Mix cornstarch and cold water; gradually stir into liquid. Heat to boiling, stirring constantly. Boil and stir 1 minute. Serve with beef, fruit and vegetables. Garnish with chopped fresh parsley if desired. *16 servings*

NUTRITION INFORMATION PER SERVING

1 serving		Percent of U.S. RDA	
Calories	275	Protein	50%
Protein, g	33	Vitamin A	32%
Carbohydrate, g	10	Vitamin C	6%
Fat, g	11	Thiamin	8%
Unsaturated	7	Riboflavin	16%
Saturated	4	Niacin	32%
Dietary Fiber, g	2	Calcium	2%
Cholesterol, mg	85	Iron	16%
Sodium, mg	150		
Potassium, mg	640		

Beef Roast with Fruit

Oriental Pot Roast

3-pound beef arm, blade or rib pot roast
1 large onion, sliced
1 can (15¼ ounces) pineapple chunks in
   juice, drained and juice reserved
3 tablespoons reduced-sodium soy sauce
1 teaspoon ground ginger
1 clove garlic, crushed
1 cup sliced celery (about 2 medium stalks)
1 package (10 ounces) frozen spinach
   leaves, thawed and drained
1 cup sliced mushrooms (about 4 ounces) or
   1 can (4 ounces) mushroom stems and
   pieces, drained

Trim fat from beef roast. Cook beef in nonstick Dutch oven over medium heat until brown on all sides; drain. Place onion on beef. Mix reserved pineapple juice, the soy sauce, ginger and garlic; pour over beef. Heat to boiling; reduce heat. Cover and simmer about 2 hours or until tender. Add celery. Cover and simmer 20 minutes. Add pineapple, spinach and mushrooms. Cover and simmer 5 minutes. Remove beef, pineapple and vegetables. Skim any fat from broth; serve broth with beef, pineapple and vegetables. *12 servings*

NUTRITION INFORMATION PER SERVING			
1 serving		Percent of U.S. RDA	
Calories	265	Protein	52%
Protein, g	33	Vitamin A	12%
Carbohydrate, g	8	Vitamin C	4%
Fat, g	11	Thiamin	10%
Unsaturated	7	Riboflavin	16%
Saturated	4	Niacin	32%
Dietary Fiber, g	2	Calcium	4%
Cholesterol, mg	85	Iron	18%
Sodium, mg	290		
Potassium, mg	600		

Three-Pepper Beef Tenderloin

1½-pound beef tenderloin
1 tablespoon freshly ground black pepper
2 teaspoons white pepper
2 teaspoons ground fennel seed
½ teaspoon salt
½ teaspoon ground thyme
¼ teaspoon ground red pepper (cayenne)

Trim fat from beef tenderloin. Mix remaining ingredients; rub over beef. Cover and refrigerate 2 hours.

Heat oven to 350°. Spray shallow roasting pan with nonstick cooking spray. Place beef in pan. Roast uncovered about 40 minutes for medium doneness (160°). Let stand 5 minutes. Cut beef across grain at slanted angle into thin slices. *6 servings*

NUTRITION INFORMATION PER SERVING			
1 serving		Percent of U.S. RDA	
Calories	230	Protein	50%
Protein, g	32	Vitamin A	*
Carbohydrate, g	1	Vitamin C	*
Fat, g	11	Thiamin	6%
Unsaturated	7	Riboflavin	14%
Saturated	4	Niacin	30%
Dietary Fiber, g	0	Calcium	2%
Cholesterol, mg	85	Iron	18%
Sodium, mg	260		
Potassium, mg	470		

Hearty Paprika Stew, Oat Bran Bread (page 95)

Easy Burgundy Stew

2-pound beef boneless bottom or top round,
   tip or chuck steak

2 cups sliced carrots (about 4 medium)

1 cup sliced celery (about 2 medium stalks)

2 medium onions, sliced

1 can (8 ounces) sliced water chestnuts,
   drained

2 cups sliced mushrooms (about 8 ounces)
   or 1 can (8 ounces) mushroom stems and
   pieces, drained

3 tablespoons all-purpose flour

1 tablespoon chopped fresh or 1 teaspoon
   dried thyme leaves

1 teaspoon ground mustard

½ teaspoon salt

¼ teaspoon pepper

1 cup water

1 cup dry red wine or beef broth

1 can (16 ounces) whole tomatoes,
   undrained

Heat oven to 325°. Trim fat from beef steak. Cut
beef into 1-inch cubes. Mix beef, carrots, celery, onions, water chestnuts and mushrooms in
Dutch oven. Mix flour, thyme, mustard, salt
and pepper; stir into beef mixture. Stir in remaining ingredients; break up tomatoes. Cover
and bake about 4 hours or until beef is tender
and stew is thickened. *8 servings*

NUTRITION INFORMATION PER SERVING

1 serving		Percent of U.S. RDA	
Calories	200	Protein	36%
Protein, g	23	Vitamin A	50%
Carbohydrate, g	16	Vitamin C	14%
Fat, g	4	Thiamin	12%
Unsaturated	3	Riboflavin	20%
Saturated	1	Niacin	28%
Dietary Fiber, g	4	Calcium	4%
Cholesterol, mg	55	Iron	18%
Sodium, mg	300		
Potassium, mg	750		

Hearty Paprika Stew

1½-pound lean beef chuck roast

3 cups sliced onions (about 3 large)

4 slices turkey bacon, finely chopped

2½ cups beef broth

1 tablespoon cider vinegar

2 teaspoons paprika

1 cup tomato juice

1 tablespoon tomato paste

1½ teaspoons chopped fresh or ½ teaspoon
    dried thyme leaves

¼ teaspoon pepper

1 clove garlic, finely chopped

1 bay leaf

1 tablespoon cornstarch

1 tablespoon cold water

3 cups hot cooked rice

Spray 12-inch skillet with nonstick cooking spray. Trim fat from beef roast. Cut beef into 1½-inch cubes. Cook onions, bacon, ½ cup of the broth and the vinegar in skillet over medium heat about 10 minutes or until liquid has evaporated. Stir in beef. Sprinkle with paprika. Cook 3 to 5 minutes, stirring occasionally, until beef is brown on all sides. Stir in remaining 2 cups broth, the tomato juice, tomato paste, thyme, pepper, garlic and bay leaf. Heat to boiling; reduce heat.

Cover and simmer about 1¾ hours, stirring occasionally, until beef is tender. Add additional water, about ¼ cup at a time, if liquid evaporates before beef is tender. Mix cornstarch and cold water; stir into stew. Cook about 3 minutes or until sauce thickens. Remove bay leaf. Serve over rice. *6 servings*

CHICKEN–GARBANZO PAPRIKA STEW: Substitute 1 pound skinless, boneless chicken breasts for the beef roast and 2½ cups chicken broth for the beef broth. Stir in 2 cups cooked garbanzo beans or 1 can (15 ounces) garbanzo beans, drained, with the remaining 2 cups broth. Substitute 3 cups hot cooked couscous for the rice.

NUTRITION INFORMATION PER SERVING			
I serving		**Percent of U.S. RDA**	
Calories	485	Protein	58%
Protein, g	38	Vitamin A	6%
Carbohydrate, g	41	Vitamin C	12%
Fat, g	19	Thiamin	22%
Unsaturated	12	Riboflavin	20%
Saturated	7	Niacin	34%
Dietary Fiber, g	3	Calcium	4%
Cholesterol, mg	95	Iron	30%
Sodium, mg	630		
Potassium, mg	800		

Beef with Bow-tie Pasta

1½ pounds beef boneless sirloin steak
3 cups 2-inch pieces asparagus (about 1
   pound)
1 cup sliced onions (about 2 medium)
1½ cups beef broth
4 cups cooked farfalle (bow-tie–shape) pasta
1 cup tomato puree
3 tablespoons chopped fresh or 1
   tablespoon dried basil leaves
3 tablespoons chopped sun-dried tomatoes
   (not oil-packed)
¼ teaspoon pepper
2 tablespoons freshly grated Parmesan
   cheese

Spray 12-inch skillet with nonstick cooking spray. Trim fat from beef steak. Cut beef into 2-inch strips. Cut strips crosswise into ⅛-inch slices. Heat skillet over medium heat until hot. Cook asparagus, onions and 1 cup of the broth 5 to 7 minutes, stirring occasionally, until liquid has evaporated. Remove from skillet.

Add beef to skillet; cook, stirring frequently, about 2 minutes or until beef is no longer pink. Return vegetables to skillet. Add remaining broth and ingredients except cheese; cook about 2 minutes, stirring frequently or until mixture is hot. Sprinkle with cheese. *6 servings*

NUTRITION INFORMATION PER SERVING

1 serving		Percent of U.S. RDA	
Calories	315	Protein	46%
Protein, g	30	Vitamin A	12%
Carbohydrate, g	37	Vitamin C	22%
Fat, g	5	Thiamin	24%
Unsaturated	3	Riboflavin	22%
Saturated	2	Niacin	36%
Dietary Fiber, g	4	Calcium	8%
Cholesterol, mg	55	Iron	26%
Sodium, mg	400		
Potassium, mg	800		

Healthy Meat Loaf

This meat loaf has been updated for today's tastes. Ground turkey replaces half of the beef, and egg whites (or cholesterol-free egg product) fill in for a whole egg. And as always, leftover meat loaf makes a great sandwich!

¾ pound lean ground turkey
¾ pound extra-lean ground beef
¾ cup chopped onion (about 1½ medium)
½ cup fresh bread crumbs
1 tablespoon tomato puree or ketchup
2 teaspoons Dijon mustard
½ teaspoon salt
¼ teaspoon white pepper
⅛ teaspoon ground nutmeg
⅛ teaspoon Worcestershire sauce
2 egg whites or ¼ cup cholesterol-free egg
   product
1 clove garlic, finely chopped

Heat oven to 375°. Spray loaf pan, 8½×4½×2½ inches, with nonstick cooking spray. Mix all ingredients. Spread evenly in pan. Bake about 1 hour or until no longer pink in center. Drain immediately. *6 servings*

NUTRITION INFORMATION PER SERVING

1 serving		Percent of U.S. RDA	
Calories	255	Protein	38%
Protein, g	25	Vitamin A	2%
Carbohydrate, g	9	Vitamin C	*
Fat, g	13	Thiamin	6%
Unsaturated	9	Riboflavin	16%
Saturated	4	Niacin	20%
Dietary Fiber, g	1	Calcium	2%
Cholesterol, mg	75	Iron	14%
Sodium, mg	350		
Potassium, mg	340		

Beef with Bow-tie Pasta

Stir-fried Beef

Just enough oil is used to coat the wok. If using a nonstick skillet, you can spray it with nonstick cooking spray and omit oil altogether. Serve this dish over brown rice if desired.

1-pound beef flank or boneless sirloin steak
1 teaspoon cornstarch
2 tablespoons reduced-sodium soy sauce
1/8 teaspoon pepper
4 large stalks bok choy
2 tablespoons cornstarch
2 tablespoons cold water
2 teaspoons vegetable oil
1 teaspoon finely chopped gingerroot
1 clove garlic, finely chopped
1 medium onion, thinly sliced
1 1/2 cups Chinese pea pods (about 4 ounces)
2 cups sliced mushrooms (about 6 ounces)
1/2 cup chicken broth
1 tablespoon reduced-sodium soy sauce

Trim fat from beef steak. Cut beef with grain into 2-inch strips. Cut strips across grain into 1/8-inch slices. (Beef is easier to slice if partially frozen.) Toss beef, 1 teaspoon cornstarch, 2 tablespoons soy sauce and the pepper in glass or plastic bowl. Cover and refrigerate 30 minutes. Separate bok choy leaves from stems. Cut leaves into 2-inch pieces; cut stems diagonally into 1/4-inch slices. (Do not combine leaves and stems.) Mix 2 tablespoons cornstarch and the cold water.

Heat oil in wok or 10-inch nonstick skillet over high heat until hot. Add beef mixture, gingerroot and garlic; stir-fry about 3 minutes or until beef is brown. Remove beef from wok with slotted spoon. Add bok choy stems and onion; stir-fry 3 minutes. Add bok choy leaves, pea pods and mushrooms; stir-fry 2 minutes. Stir in broth and 1 tablespoon soy sauce; heat to boiling. Stir in cornstarch mixture; cook and stir 1 minute. Stir in beef; heat just until beef is hot. *4 servings*

NUTRITION INFORMATION PER SERVING			
1 serving		**Percent of U.S. RDA**	
Calories	265	Protein	42%
Protein, g	28	Vitamin A	10%
Carbohydrate, g	14	Vitamin C	36%
Fat, g	11	Thiamin	14%
Unsaturated	7	Riboflavin	24%
Saturated	4	Niacin	36%
Dietary Fiber, g	3	Calcium	8%
Cholesterol, mg	60	Iron	22%
Sodium, mg	630		
Potassium, mg	770		

Curried Meat Loaf

1½ pounds extra-lean ground beef

¾ cup regular or quick-cooking oats

½ cup chopped onion (about 1 medium)

½ cup plain nonfat yogurt

2 teaspoons curry powder

1 teaspoon ground mustard

½ teaspoon salt

¼ teaspoon red pepper sauce

2 egg whites or ¼ cup cholesterol-free egg product

Vegetable Sauce (right)

Heat oven to 350°. Mix all ingredients except Vegetable Sauce. Spread evenly in ungreased loaf pan, 9×5×3 inches or 8½×4½×2½ inches. Bake uncovered about 1 to 1½ hours or until no longer pink in center. Serve with Vegetable Sauce. *6 servings*

Vegetable Sauce

¾ cup chopped seeded cucumber (about 1 small)

¾ cup chopped tomato (about 1 medium)

¼ cup sliced green onions (2 to 3 medium)

¼ cup plain nonfat yogurt

½ teaspoon curry powder

1 clove garlic, finely chopped

Mix all ingredients.

NUTRITION INFORMATION PER SERVING			
1 serving		**Percent of U.S. RDA**	
Calories	290	Protein	42%
Protein, g	28	Vitamin A	2%
Carbohydrate, g	13	Vitamin C	6%
Fat, g	14	Thiamin	12%
Unsaturated	9	Riboflavin	20%
Saturated	5	Niacin	18%
Dietary Fiber, g	2	Calcium	8%
Cholesterol, mg	70	Iron	18%
Sodium, mg	280		
Potassium, mg	560		

Curried Meat Loaf, Stuffed Cabbage with Parsley Sauce (page 176)

Giant Oven Burger

Giant Oven Burger

Tired of pressing out individual hamburger patties? Then this recipe's for you. One giant burger is cut into fun "burger wedges," great for a teen party, or any time you're serving hamburgers. Top it with your favorite burger fixings.

1½ pounds extra-lean ground beef
½ cup chopped bell pepper (about 1 small)
¼ cup chopped onion (about 1 small)
1 tablespoon prepared horseradish
1 tablespoon prepared mustard
½ teaspoon salt
⅓ cup chile sauce or ketchup
1 unsliced round loaf Italian or sourdough
   bread, 8 inches in diameter

Heat oven to 350°. Mix all ingredients except chile sauce and bread. Press beef mixture in ungreased pie plate, 9×1¼ inches. Spread chile sauce over top. Bake uncovered 45 to 50 minutes or until no longer pink in center; drain. Let stand 5 minutes. Cut bread crosswise into halves. Carefully place burger between halves. Cut into wedges. *6 servings*

NUTRITION INFORMATION PER SERVING

1 serving		Percent of U.S. RDA	
Calories	325	Protein	40%
Protein, g	26	Vitamin A	2%
Carbohydrate, g	26	Vitamin C	6%
Fat, g	13	Thiamin	8%
Unsaturated	8	Riboflavin	14%
Saturated	5	Niacin	24%
Dietary Fiber, g	1	Calcium	4%
Cholesterol, mg	70	Iron	20%
Sodium, mg	640		
Potassium, mg	430		

Hamburgers Ranchero

These burgers can also be served in hamburger buns with the shredded lettuce and Ranchero Sauce. Look for whole- or multi-grain buns when shopping.

Ranchero Sauce (right) or prepared salsa
1½ pounds extra-lean ground beef
½ cup chopped onion (about 1 medium)
1 tablespoon chopped fresh or 1 teaspoon dried oregano leaves
½ teaspoon salt
¼ teaspoon pepper
6 corn tortillas (6 inches in diameter)
3 cups shredded lettuce (about 1 small head)

Prepare Ranchero Sauce. Mix ground beef, onion, oregano, salt and pepper. Shape into 6 patties, each about ½ inch thick. Set oven control to broil. Spray broiler pan rack with non-stick cooking spray. Place patties on rack. Broil with tops about 3 inches from heat 4 to 6 minutes on each side for medium doneness.

Heat tortillas as directed on package. Top each tortilla with ½ cup lettuce and 1 patty. Spoon Ranchero Sauce over each patty. *6 servings*

Ranchero Sauce

1 teaspoon lemon juice
¼ teaspoon ground coriander
1 large clove garlic
1 small onion, cut up
1 can (28 ounces) whole tomatoes, well drained
1 jalapeño or green chile

Place all ingredients in blender or food processor. Cover and blend on medium speed about 5 seconds or until finely chopped.

CHICKEN BURGERS RANCHERO: Substitute 1½ pounds ground chicken for the ground beef and 6 flour tortillas (8 inches in diameter) for the corn tortillas. Sprinkle with chopped fresh cilantro if desired.

NUTRITION INFORMATION PER SERVING			
1 serving		Percent of U.S. RDA	
Calories	305	Protein	40%
Protein, g	26	Vitamin A	10%
Carbohydrate, g	19	Vitamin C	22%
Fat, g	14	Thiamin	12%
Unsaturated	9	Riboflavin	16%
Saturated	5	Niacin	22%
Dietary Fiber, g	4	Calcium	10%
Cholesterol, mg	70	Iron	22%
Sodium, mg	570		
Potassium, mg	760		

Manicotti

1 pound extra-lean ground beef

1 cup chopped onion (about 1 large)

2 cloves garlic, crushed

1 can (28 ounces) whole tomatoes, undrained

2 cups sliced mushrooms (about 8 ounces) or 1 can (8 ounces) mushroom stems and pieces, drained

¼ cup chopped fresh parsley

1 tablespoon chopped fresh or 1 teaspoon dried basil leaves

1 teaspoon fennel seed

¼ teaspoon salt

2 cups low-fat cottage cheese

⅓ cup grated Parmesan cheese

¼ teaspoon ground nutmeg

¼ teaspoon pepper

2 packages (10 ounces each) frozen chopped spinach, thawed and well drained

14 uncooked manicotti shells

2 tablespoons grated Parmesan cheese

Heat oven to 350°. Cook ground beef, onion and garlic in 10-inch nonstick skillet, stirring frequently, until beef is brown; drain. Stir in tomatoes, mushrooms, parsley, basil, fennel seed and salt; break up tomatoes. Heat to boiling; reduce heat. Cover and simmer 10 minutes. Spoon about one-third of the beef mixture into ungreased rectangular baking dish, 13×9×2 inches.

Mix cottage cheese, ⅓ cup Parmesan cheese, the nutmeg, pepper and spinach. Fill manicotti shells with spinach mixture; place shells on beef mixture in baking dish. Pour remaining beef mixture evenly over shells, covering shells completely. Sprinkle with 2 tablespoons Parmesan cheese. Cover and bake about 1½ hours or until manicotti shells are tender. *7 servings*

NUTRITION INFORMATION PER SERVING			
I serving		**Percent of U.S. RDA**	
Calories	340	Protein	46%
Protein, g	30	Vitamin A	52%
Carbohydrate, g	30	Vitamin C	24%
Fat, g	II	Thiamin	18%
Unsaturated	6	Riboflavin	30%
Saturated	5	Niacin	24%
Dietary Fiber, g	4	Calcium	24%
Cholesterol, mg	50	Iron	24%
Sodium, mg	700		
Potassium, mg	800		

Mostaccioli and Beef, Tossed Salad with Apple Cider Dressing (page 154)

Mostaccioli and Beef

6 ounces uncooked mostaccioli (about 1½ cups)

1 pound extra-lean ground beef

½ cup chopped onion (about 1 medium)

2 teaspoons chopped fresh or ½ teaspoon dried oregano leaves

¼ teaspoon salt

¼ teaspoon ground cinnamon

⅛ teaspoon ground nutmeg

1 can (8 ounces) tomato sauce

1 clove garlic, finely chopped

1 tablespoon margarine

2 tablespoons all-purpose flour

Dash of ground nutmeg

1½ cups low-fat milk

¼ cup grated Romano cheese

Cook mostaccioli as directed on package—except omit salt; drain. Cook ground beef and onion in 10-inch nonstick skillet, stirring frequently, until beef is brown; drain. Stir in oregano, salt, cinnamon, ⅛ teaspoon nutmeg, the tomato sauce and garlic.

Heat oven to 350°. Alternate layers of mostaccioli and beef mixture in ungreased 2-quart casserole. Heat margarine in 1-quart saucepan over low heat until melted. Stir in flour and dash of nutmeg. Cook over low heat, stirring constantly, until smooth and bubbly; remove from heat. Stir in milk. Heat to boiling, stirring constantly. Boil and stir 1 minute. Spoon sauce over mostaccioli and beef mixture. Sprinkle with cheese. Bake uncovered about 35 minutes or until cheese is light brown. *6 servings*

NUTRITION INFORMATION PER SERVING

1 serving		Percent of U.S. RDA	
Calories	335	Protein	36%
Protein, g	23	Vitamin A	10%
Carbohydrate, g	31	Vitamin C	4%
Fat, g	13	Thiamin	18%
Unsaturated	8	Riboflavin	20%
Saturated	5	Niacin	20%
Dietary Fiber, g	2	Calcium	14%
Cholesterol, mg	55	Iron	18%
Sodium, mg	580		
Potassium, mg	490		

Stuffed Cabbage with Parsley Sauce

To remove the leaves from the head of cabbage, cut out and discard the core, then hold the head under running hot water and gently peel off leaves one at a time. The sauce can be made up to three days ahead, then stored, covered, in the refrigerator.

12 green cabbage leaves (about 1 large head)

3 cups chicken broth

1 cup uncooked bulgur

1 pound extra-lean ground beef

2 egg whites or ¼ cup cholesterol-free egg product

2 teaspoons grated lemon peel

½ teaspoon ground cumin

¼ teaspoon pepper

Parsley Sauce (right)

Heat oven to 375°. Spray rectangular baking dish, 13×9×2 inches, with nonstick cooking spray. Cover cabbage leaves with boiling water. Let stand about 10 minutes or until leaves are limp; drain. Heat 1 cup of the broth to boiling in 3-quart saucepan. Stir in bulgur; remove from heat. Cover and let stand 10 minutes. Stir in remaining ingredients except remaining broth and Parsley Sauce.

Place about ⅓ cup beef mixture at stem end of each leaf. Roll leaf around mixture, tucking in sides. Place rolls, seam sides down, in baking dish. Pour remaining 2 cups broth over rolls. Cover with aluminum foil. Bake 45 to 50 minutes or until beef mixture is no longer pink in center. Prepare Parsley Sauce. Serve sauce with cabbage rolls. *6 servings*

Parsley Sauce

1 cup lightly packed parsley sprigs

⅓ cup chopped onion (about 1 small)

¼ cup low-fat sour cream

¼ cup nonfat buttermilk

2 tablespoons lemon juice

1 teaspoon honey

½ teaspoon salt

¼ teaspoon ground coriander

⅛ teaspoon crushed red pepper

1 clove garlic, chopped

Place all ingredients in blender or food processor. Cover and blend 30 seconds or until smooth. Cover and refrigerate up to 3 days.

NUTRITION INFORMATION PER SERVING			
1 serving		**Percent of U.S. RDA**	
Calories	340	Protein	40%
Protein, g	25	Vitamin A	10%
Carbohydrate, g	35	Vitamin C	100%
Fat, g	11	Thiamin	16%
Unsaturated	7	Riboflavin	20%
Saturated	4	Niacin	28%
Dietary Fiber, g	10	Calcium	16%
Cholesterol, mg	50	Iron	24%
Sodium, mg	690		
Potassium, mg	1080		

Barley-Beef Stew

1½ pounds extra-lean ground beef
1 cup chopped onion (about 1 large)
1 cup sliced celery (about 2 medium stalks)
1 cup uncooked pearl barley
2½ cups water
1 tablespoon chile powder
½ teaspoon salt
¼ teaspoon pepper
1 can (28 ounces) whole tomatoes,
   undrained

Cook ground beef, onion and celery in nonstick Dutch oven, stirring frequently, until beef is brown; drain. Stir in remaining ingredients; break up tomatoes. Heat to boiling; reduce heat. Cover and simmer about 1 hour or until barley is done and stew is desired consistency.
6 servings

NUTRITION INFORMATION PER SERVING

1 serving		Percent of U.S. RDA	
Calories	380	Protein	42%
Protein, g	28	Vitamin A	12%
Carbohydrate, g	35	Vitamin C	20%
Fat, g	14	Thiamin	14%
Unsaturated	9	Riboflavin	16%
Saturated	5	Niacin	30%
Dietary Fiber, g	7	Calcium	6%
Cholesterol, mg	70	Iron	24%
Sodium, mg	480		
Potassium, mg	820		

Beef and Bulgur Stew

1½ pounds extra-lean ground beef
½ cup chopped onion (about 1 medium)
1 cup uncooked bulgur
2 cups water
1 tablespoon chopped fresh or 1 teaspoon
   dried mint leaves
1 tablespoon chopped fresh or 1 teaspoon
   dried oregano leaves
½ teaspoon salt
1 small eggplant (about 1 pound), cut into
   1-inch pieces
1½ cups chopped tomatoes (about 2
   medium)
¼ cup grated Parmesan cheese

Cook ground beef and onion in nonstick Dutch oven, stirring frequently, until beef is brown; drain. Stir in bulgur, water, mint, oregano, salt and eggplant. Heat to boiling; reduce heat. Cover and simmer about 30 minutes, stirring occasionally, until bulgur is tender (add small amount of water if necessary). Stir in tomatoes and cheese. Heat about 5 minutes or just until tomatoes are hot. Serve with additional grated Parmesan cheese if desired. *8 servings*

NUTRITION INFORMATION PER SERVING

1 serving		Percent of U.S. RDA	
Calories	295	Protein	34%
Protein, g	22	Vitamin A	2%
Carbohydrate, g	27	Vitamin C	6%
Fat, g	11	Thiamin	12%
Unsaturated	7	Riboflavin	12%
Saturated	4	Niacin	22%
Dietary Fiber, g	6	Calcium	6%
Cholesterol, mg	55	Iron	16%
Sodium, mg	230		
Potassium, mg	560		

Veal Sauté

1-pound veal round steak, about ½ inch
  thick
2 tablespoons all-purpose flour
½ teaspoon paprika
¼ teaspoon salt
⅛ teaspoon pepper
2 teaspoons olive or vegetable oil
½ cup dry white wine or chicken broth
¼ cup water
1 teaspoon chopped fresh or ¼ teaspoon
  dried rosemary or thyme leaves
¼ teaspoon salt
¾ cup peeled tiny pearl onions (about 4
  ounces)
2 medium carrots, cut into julienne strips

Trim fat from veal steak. Cut veal into 4 serving pieces. Mix flour, paprika, ¼ teaspoon salt and the pepper. Coat veal with flour mixture; pound to ¼-inch thickness between waxed paper or plastic wrap.

Heat oil in 10-inch nonstick skillet over medium-high heat until hot. Cook veal in oil, turning once, until brown; drain. Add wine, water, rosemary, ¼ teaspoon salt, the onions and carrots. Heat to boiling; reduce heat. Cover and simmer about 45 minutes or until veal and vegetables are tender. (Add water if necessary.) Place veal and vegetables on platter; pour pan drippings over top. Sprinkle with chopped fresh parsley if desired. *4 servings*

NUTRITION INFORMATION PER SERVING			
1 serving		Percent of U.S. RDA	
Calories	170	Protein	28%
Protein, g	18	Vitamin A	56%
Carbohydrate, g	9	Vitamin C	4%
Fat, g	6	Thiamin	4%
Unsaturated	4	Riboflavin	16%
Saturated	2	Niacin	30%
Dietary Fiber, g	2	Calcium	4%
Cholesterol, mg	75	Iron	8%
Sodium, mg	340		
Potassium, mg	430		

Veal Sauté

Shredded Veal with Ginger

1-pound veal boneless sirloin steak
1 tablespoon cornstarch
¼ teaspoon salt
⅛ teaspoon white pepper
6 green onions
½ teaspoon cornstarch
½ teaspoon sugar
1 tablespoon chicken broth
1 teaspoon reduced-sodium soy sauce
2 teaspoons vegetable oil
1 tablespoon shredded gingerroot

Trim fat from veal steak. Cut veal lengthwise into 2-inch strips. Cut strips crosswise into ⅛-inch slices. Stack slices and cut into julienne strips. (Veal is easier to slice if partially frozen.) Toss veal, 1 tablespoon cornstarch, the salt and white pepper in glass or plastic bowl. Cover and refrigerate 30 minutes.

Cut onions diagonally into 1-inch pieces. Mix ½ teaspoon cornstarch, the sugar, broth and soy sauce. Heat oil in wok or 10-inch nonstick skillet over high heat until hot. Add veal and gingerroot; stir-fry until veal is white. Add onions; stir-fry 10 seconds. Stir in cornstarch mixture; heat to boiling, stirring constantly. Boil and stir 1 minute. *4 servings*

NUTRITION INFORMATION PER SERVING

1 serving		Percent of U.S. RDA	
Calories	145	Protein	28%
Protein, g	18	Vitamin A	*
Carbohydrate, g	5	Vitamin C	2%
Fat, g	6	Thiamin	4%
Unsaturated	4	Riboflavin	14%
Saturated	2	Niacin	28%
Dietary Fiber, g	1	Calcium	4%
Cholesterol, mg	75	Iron	6%
Sodium, mg	260		
Potassium, mg	310		

Italian Roasted Pork Loin

The fennel and garlic seasoning used on this pork loin combines well with the flavor of Tomato-Herb Loaf (page 102), for a delightful sandwich.

1½-pound pork boneless top loin roast
1 teaspoon olive or vegetable oil
½ teaspoon salt
½ teaspoon crushed fennel seed
¼ teaspoon pepper
1 garlic clove, finely chopped

Heat oven to 325°. Spray roasting pan rack with nonstick cooking spray. Trim fat from pork roast. Cut pork lengthwise almost into halves; open flat with cut side up. Mash remaining ingredients into a paste. Rub 2 teaspoons of the paste on inside of pork. Fold pork lengthwise into halves; rub remaining paste on outside of pork. Place pork on rack in shallow roasting pan. Roast uncovered 1 hour for medium doneness (160°). Cut into ¼-inch slices. *6 servings*

NUTRITION INFORMATION PER SERVING

1 serving		Percent of U.S. RDA	
Calories	275	Protein	46%
Protein, g	30	Vitamin A	*
Carbohydrate, g	0	Vitamin C	*
Fat, g	17	Thiamin	60%
Unsaturated	11	Riboflavin	24%
Saturated	6	Niacin	34%
Dietary Fiber, g	0	Calcium	*
Cholesterol, mg	100	Iron	6%
Sodium, mg	260		
Potassium, mg	420		

Zesty Pork Tenderloin

2 pork tenderloins, about ¾ pound each
¼ cup ketchup
1 tablespoon sugar
1 tablespoon white wine or water
1 tablespoon hoisin sauce
½ teaspoon salt
1 clove garlic, finely chopped

Trim fat from pork tenderloins. Mix remaining ingredients in shallow glass or plastic dish. Add pork; turn to coat with marinade. Cover and refrigerate at least 1 hour but no longer than 24 hours.

Heat oven to 375°. Place pork on rack in shallow roasting pan. Insert meat thermometer horizontally so tip is in thickest part of pork. Bake uncovered about 35 minutes for medium doneness (160°). *6 servings*

NUTRITION INFORMATION PER SERVING

1 serving		Percent of U.S. RDA	
Calories	205	Protein	50%
Protein, g	33	Vitamin A	*
Carbohydrate, g	5	Vitamin C	2%
Fat, g	6	Thiamin	72%
Unsaturated	4	Riboflavin	26%
Saturated	2	Niacin	28%
Dietary Fiber, g	0	Calcium	*
Cholesterol, mg	105	Iron	10%
Sodium, mg	390		
Potassium, mg	670		

Marinated Pork Chops with Cilantro-Mint Salsa

To grill pork chops, cover and grill them 5 to 6 inches from medium coals for 25 to 35 minutes, turning 3 or 4 times until done. Although fresh herbs have more flavor, dried herbs are an acceptable substitute here. However, cilantro (the leaves of fresh coriander, also known as Chinese parsley), is an exception. The dried version, is lacking in that fresh bite that only fresh cilantro can add to a dish, so we cannot recommend using dried cilantro in this dish, or any other.

4 pork loin or rib chops, about ¾ inch thick
   (about 1¼ pounds)
1 tablespoon olive or vegetable oil
1 tablespoon lime juice
½ teaspoon chile powder
1 clove garlic, crushed
Salt and pepper
Cilantro-Mint Salsa (right)

Trim fat from pork chops. Place pork in glass or plastic dish. Mix oil, lime juice, chile powder and garlic; rub into both sides of pork, using back of spoon. Cover and refrigerate at least 1 hour but no longer than 24 hours. Prepare Cilantro-Mint Salsa.

Set oven control to broil. Sprinkle pork with salt and pepper. Place pork on rack in broiler pan. Broil with tops 3 to 5 inches from heat 8 to 11 minutes, turning once, for medium doneness (160°). Serve with salsa. *4 servings*

Cilantro-Mint Salsa

1 cup chopped seeded tomato (about 1
　　large)
1 tablespoon chopped fresh cilantro leaves
1 tablespoon chopped fresh or 1 teaspoon
　　dried mint leaves
1 tablespoon chopped onion
½ teaspoon lime juice
1 jalapeño chile, seeded and finely chopped

Mix all ingredients in glass or plastic bowl.
Cover and let stand at least 1 hour before serving time.

NUTRITION INFORMATION PER SERVING

1 serving		Percent of U.S. RDA	
Calories	210	Protein	28%
Protein, g	19	Vitamin A	14%
Carbohydrate, g	4	Vitamin C	28%
Fat, g	13	Thiamin	38%
Unsaturated	9	Riboflavin	16%
Saturated	4	Niacin	22%
Dietary Fiber, g	1	Calcium	2%
Cholesterol, mg	60	Iron	6%
Sodium, mg	320		
Potassium, mg	410		

Pork Chops with Grapes

4 pork loin or rib chops, about ½ inch thick
　　(about 1 pound)
1 teaspoon chopped fresh or ¼ teaspoon
　　dried tarragon leaves
¼ teaspoon salt
⅛ teaspoon pepper
1 cup chicken broth
1 tablespoon lemon juice

1 clove garlic, finely chopped
2 teaspoons cornstarch
2 tablespoons cold water
1 cup seedless green grapes
1 can (4 ounces) mushroom stems and
　　pieces, drained

Trim fat from pork chops. Cook pork in 10-inch
nonstick skillet over medium heat, turning
once, until brown; drain. Sprinkle with tarragon, salt and pepper. Mix broth, lemon juice
and garlic; pour over pork. Heat to boiling;
reduce heat. Cover and simmer about 30 minutes or until pork is tender. Remove pork; keep
warm. Skim any fat from liquid in skillet. Mix
cornstarch and cold water; gradually stir into
liquid. Heat to boiling, stirring constantly. Boil
and stir 1 minute. Stir in grapes and mushrooms; heat just until hot. Serve sauce over
pork. *4 servings*

NUTRITION INFORMATION PER SERVING

1 serving		Percent of U.S. RDA	
Calories	215	Protein	30%
Protein, g	20	Vitamin A	*
Carbohydrate, g	11	Vitamin C	4%
Fat, g	10	Thiamin	40%
Unsaturated	6	Riboflavin	16%
Saturated	4	Niacin	26%
Dietary Fiber, g	1	Calcium	2%
Cholesterol, mg	60	Iron	6%
Sodium, mg	500		
Potassium, mg	420		

Pork with Apple and Parsnips

Pork with Apple and Parsnips

**4 pork loin or rib chops, about ¹/₂ inch thick
(about 1 pound)**

**3 medium parsnips, cut crosswise into
¹/₂-inch slices**

1 medium onion, sliced

¹/₂ cup chicken broth

1 teaspoon ground mustard

¹/₄ teaspoon salt

¹/₄ teaspoon ground allspice

¹/₈ teaspoon pepper

1 medium apple, cut into ¹/₄-inch wedges

2 tablespoons chopped fresh parsley

Trim fat from pork chops. Cook pork in 10-inch nonstick skillet over medium heat, turning once, until brown; drain. Place parsnips and onion on pork. Mix broth, mustard, salt, allspice and pepper; pour over vegetables and pork. Heat to boiling; reduce heat. Cover and simmer about 30 minutes or until pork is tender. Arrange apple on vegetables. Cover and simmer about 3 minutes or just until apple is tender. Sprinkle with parsley. *4 servings*

NUTRITION INFORMATION PER SERVING			
1 serving		**Percent of U.S. RDA**	
Calories	270	Protein	30%
Protein, g	20	Vitamin A	*
Carbohydrate, g	25	Vitamin C	14%
Fat, g	10	Thiamin	42%
Unsaturated	6	Riboflavin	18%
Saturated	4	Niacin	26%
Dietary Fiber, g	5	Calcium	4%
Cholesterol, mg	60	Iron	8%
Sodium, mg	290		
Potassium, mg	680		

Pork with Stuffed Yams

2 medium yams or sweet potatoes
4 pork loin or rib chops, about ¾ inch thick
½ teaspoon salt
¼ teaspoon paprika
⅛ teaspoon garlic powder
½ cup orange juice
2 tablespoons orange juice
½ cup chopped apple (about ½ medium)
2 tablespoons finely chopped onion
2 tablespoons finely chopped celery

Heat oven to 350°. Prick yams with fork to allow steam to escape. Bake 55 to 60 minutes or until tender. Trim fat from pork chops. About 30 minutes before yams are done, place pork in ungreased rectangular pan, 13×9×2 inches. Mix salt, paprika, garlic powder and pepper; sprinkle half of the salt mixture over pork. Turn pork; sprinkle with remaining salt mixture. Pour ½ cup orange juice into pan. Cover and bake 30 minutes.

Cut yam lengthwise in half. Scoop out pulp, leaving ¼-inch shell. Mash pulp; beat in 2 tablespoons orange juice until light and fluffy. Stir in apple, onion and celery. Fill shells with pulp mixture. Push pork to one end of pan; place yams in other end. Bake uncovered about 30 minutes or until pork is tender and yams are hot. *4 servings*

NUTRITION INFORMATION PER SERVING			
1 serving		**Percent of U.S. RDA**	
Calories	240	Protein	30%
Protein, g	19	Vitamin A	100%
Carbohydrate, g	21	Vitamin C	24%
Fat, g	9	Thiamin	40%
Unsaturated	6	Riboflavin	18%
Saturated	3	Niacin	22%
Dietary Fiber, g	2	Calcium	2%
Cholesterol, mg	60	Iron	6%
Sodium, mg	320		
Potassium, mg	630		

Sweet-Sour Pork 'n' Onions

4 pork loin or rib chops, about ½ inch thick
    (about 1 pound)
¼ teaspoon salt
⅛ teaspoon pepper
2 medium onions, cut into ¼-inch slices
½ cup dry white wine or chicken broth
2 tablespoons red wine vinegar
2 teaspoons sugar
⅛ teaspoon ground cloves
1 teaspoon cornstarch
2 tablespoons cold water

Trim fat from pork chops. Cook pork in 10-inch nonstick skillet over medium heat, turning once, until brown; drain. Sprinkle with salt and pepper. Arrange onions on pork. Mix wine, vinegar, sugar and cloves; pour over onions and pork. Heat to boiling; reduce heat. Cover and simmer about 30 minutes or until pork is tender. Remove pork and onions; keep warm. Skim any fat from liquid in skillet. Mix cornstarch and cold water; gradually stir into liquid. Heat to boiling, stirring constantly. Boil and stir 1 minute. Serve sauce over pork and onions. *4 servings*

NUTRITION INFORMATION PER SERVING			
1 serving		**Percent of U.S. RDA**	
Calories	200	Protein	28%
Protein, g	18	Vitamin A	*
Carbohydrate, g	8	Vitamin C	2%
Fat, g	9	Thiamin	36%
Unsaturated	6	Riboflavin	14%
Saturated	3	Niacin	20%
Dietary Fiber, g	1	Calcium	2%
Cholesterol, mg	60	Iron	6%
Sodium, mg	180		
Potassium, mg	370		

Ginger-Sherry Pork Chops

To grill pork chops, cover and grill them 4 to 5 inches from medium coals, brushing occasionally with marinade and turning them once, 14 to 16 minutes until done. Oriental Daikon Salad (page 138) would be a good accompaniment to these easy chops.

4 pork boneless butterfly loin chops, about
    1 inch thick (about 1 pound)
⅓ cup dry sherry or apple juice
1 tablespoon finely chopped gingerroot
2 tablespoons reduced-sodium soy sauce
1 teaspoon honey
1 clove garlic, finely chopped

Trim fat from pork chops. Mix remaining ingredients in shallow glass or plastic dish. Add pork; turn to coat with marinade. Cover and refrigerate at least 1 hour but no longer than 12 hours.

Set oven control to broil. Remove pork from marinade; reserve marinade. Place pork on rack in broiler pan. Brush with marinade. Broil with top about 4 inches from heat 7 minutes or until brown; turn. Brush with marinade. Broil 5 to 7 minutes longer for medium doneness (160°). *4 servings*

NUTRITION INFORMATION PER SERVING

1 serving		Percent of U.S. RDA	
Calories	190	Protein	28%
Protein, g	18	Vitamin A	*
Carbohydrate, g	5	Vitamin C	*
Fat, g	9	Thiamin	36%
Unsaturated	6	Riboflavin	14%
Saturated	3	Niacin	22%
Dietary Fiber, g	0	Calcium	*
Cholesterol, mg	60	Iron	6%
Sodium, mg	350		
Potassium, mg	290		

Pork Chops Smothered with Cabbage

8 cups coarsely shredded red cabbage
    (about 1½ pounds)
4 cups chopped apples (about 4 medium)
2 cups sliced red onion (about 1 large)
1½ cups chicken broth
¼ cup red wine vinegar or cider vinegar
2 teaspoons grated lemon peel
¼ teaspoon salt
¼ teaspoon pepper
1 bay leaf
6 pork rib or loin chops, about ¾ inch thick
    (about 1½ pounds)
1 cup cranberry juice cocktail
¼ cup chopped fresh parsley

Cover and cook all ingredients except pork chops, cranberry juice and parsley in Dutch oven over medium heat 10 minutes, stirring occasionally; reduce heat to medium-low. Cook 20 minutes, stirring occasionally. Trim fat from pork. Stir cranberry juice into cabbage mixture; add pork. Heat to boiling; reduce heat. Cover and simmer about 45 minutes or until pork is tender. Remove bay leaf. Serve cabbage over pork chops. Sprinkle with parsley. *6 servings*

NUTRITION INFORMATION PER SERVING

1 serving		Percent of U.S. RDA	
Calories	280	Protein	30%
Protein, g	20	Vitamin A	2%
Carbohydrate, g	28	Vitamin C	58%
Fat, g	10	Thiamin	40%
Unsaturated	6	Riboflavin	18%
Saturated	4	Niacin	24%
Dietary Fiber, g	4	Calcium	6%
Cholesterol, mg	55	Iron	10%
Sodium, mg	350		
Potassium, mg	710		

Pork Medallions with Asian Glaze

Don't limit the use of this flavorful glaze to pork. Try brushing it on chicken breasts or lean fish fillets (see page 266) when broiling.

Asian Glaze (below)
6 pork boneless loin or center-cut chops, about ½ inch thick (about 1½ pounds)

Set oven control to broil. Spray shallow roasting pan with nonstick cooking spray. Prepare Asian Glaze. Trim fat from pork chops. Place pork in pan. Brush with half of glaze. Broil with tops 7 inches from heat 5 minutes; turn. Brush remaining glaze over pork. Broil 5 to 6 minutes longer for medium doneness (160°). *6 servings*

Asian Glaze

½ cup tomato puree
2 tablespoons lemon juice
1 tablespoon rice vinegar or white vinegar
2 teaspoons grated lemon peel
2 teaspoons finely chopped gingerroot
2 teaspoons reduced-sodium soy sauce
1 teaspoon honey
½ teaspoon ground cinnamon
¼ teaspoon red pepper sauce
1 clove garlic, finely chopped
½ cup beef broth
2 teaspoons cornstarch

Cook all ingredients except broth and cornstarch in 1-quart saucepan over medium heat 2 minutes, stirring occasionally. Mix broth and cornstarch; stir into hot mixture. Cook about 2 minutes or until thickened.

NUTRITION INFORMATION PER SERVING

1 serving		Percent of U.S. RDA	
Calories	180	Protein	34%
Protein, g	22	Vitamin A	2%
Carbohydrate, g	5	Vitamin C	4%
Fat, g	8	Thiamin	38%
Unsaturated	5	Riboflavin	16%
Saturated	3	Niacin	20%
Dietary Fiber, g	0	Calcium	*
Cholesterol, mg	70	Iron	6%
Sodium, mg	250		
Potassium, mg	410		

Pork-Vegetable Stew

1½ pounds pork boneless shoulder
1 cup chopped onion (about 1 large)
½ cup water
1 tablespoon chopped fresh or 1 teaspoon
  dried rosemary leaves
½ teaspoon salt
¼ teaspoon pepper
⅛ teaspoon ground cloves
2 cloves garlic, finely chopped
1 can (10½ ounces) condensed chicken
  broth
3 cups 1-inch pieces rutabagas (about 2
  medium)
1 package (10 ounces) frozen baby Brussels
  sprouts
1 tablespoon cornstarch
2 tablespoons cold water

Spray nonstick Dutch oven with nonstick cooking spray. Trim fat from pork shoulder. Cut pork into 1-inch pieces. Cook pork in Dutch oven over medium heat, stirring occasionally, until brown; drain. Stir in onion, water, rosemary, salt, pepper, cloves, garlic and broth. Heat to boiling; reduce heat. Cover and simmer 30 minutes.

Stir rutabagas into pork mixture. Heat to boiling; reduce heat. Cover and simmer 20 minutes. Stir in frozen Brussels sprouts. Heat to boiling; reduce heat. Cover and simmer about 10 minutes or until Brussels sprouts are tender. Mix cornstarch and cold water; gradually stir into pork mixture. Heat to boiling, stirring constantly. Boil and stir 1 minute. *6 servings*

NUTRITION INFORMATION PER SERVING

1 serving		Percent of U.S. RDA	
Calories	345	Protein	54%
Protein, g	35	Vitamin A	2%
Carbohydrate, g	13	Vitamin C	30%
Fat, g	17	Thiamin	66%
Unsaturated	11	Riboflavin	30%
Saturated	6	Niacin	44%
Dietary Fiber, g	4	Calcium	6%
Cholesterol, mg	100	Iron	12%
Sodium, mg	590		
Potassium, mg	880		

Stir-fried Pork

1-pound pork tenderloin
2 cans (8 ounces each) pineapple chunks in
  juice, drained and juice reserved
3 tablespoons white vinegar
3 tablespoons mirin (rice wine), sweet white
  wine or water
3 tablespoons reduced-sodium soy sauce
2 teaspoons cornstarch
1 teaspoon sesame oil
¼ cup coarsely chopped onion (about 1
  small)
1 medium green bell pepper, cut into 1-inch
  pieces

Trim fat from pork tenderloin. Cut pork into 1-inch cubes. Mix reserved pineapple juice, the vinegar, mirin, soy sauce and cornstarch.

Spray wok or 12-inch nonstick skillet with nonstick cooking spray. Heat wok until hot. Add oil and pork; stir-fry 6 to 8 minutes or until pork is no longer pink. Remove pork from wok. Add onion and bell pepper to wok; stir-fry about 5 minutes or until onion is tender.

Stir pork, pineapple and cornstarch mixture into onion mixture. Heat to boiling. Boil about 45 seconds, stirring constantly, or until thickened. Serve over hot cooked rice or Chinese noodles if desired. *4 servings*

NUTRITION INFORMATION PER SERVING

1 serving		Percent of U.S. RDA	
Calories	300	Protein	52%
Protein, g	34	Vitamin A	2%
Carbohydrate, g	25	Vitamin C	24%
Fat, g	7	Thiamin	40%
Unsaturated	5	Riboflavin	28%
Saturated	2	Niacin	30%
Dietary Fiber, g	3	Calcium	4%
Cholesterol, mg	105	Iron	14%
Sodium, mg	530		
Potassium, mg	850		

Marinated-Pork Fried Rice

¹/₂-pound pork tenderloin

¹/₄ cup unsweetened pineapple juice

¹/₂ teaspoon grated gingerroot or ¹/₄
   teaspoon ground ginger

¹/₄ teaspoon red pepper sauce

1 clove garlic, crushed

¹/₂ cup chopped onion (about 1 medium)

¹/₂ cup chopped red bell pepper (about 1
   small)

2 tablespoons reduced-sodium soy sauce or
   fish sauce

3 cups cold cooked rice

Trim fat from pork tenderloin. Cut pork into ¹/₂-inch cubes. Mix pork, pineapple juice, gingerroot, pepper sauce and garlic in glass or plastic bowl. Cover and refrigerate at least 1 hour but no longer than 12 hours.

Spray wok or 12-inch nonstick skillet with nonstick cooking spray. Heat wok until hot. Remove pork from marinade; drain. Add pork to wok; stir-fry 5 to 10 minutes or until no longer pink. Remove pork from wok.

Add onion and bell pepper to wok; stir-fry about 8 minutes or until onion is tender. Stir in pork and remaining ingredients. Cook about 10 minutes, stirring constantly, until rice is hot and golden. Sprinkle with chopped fresh chives and serve with additional soy sauce if desired. *4 servings*

NUTRITION INFORMATION PER SERVING

1 serving		Percent of U.S. RDA	
Calories	305	Protein	32%
Protein, g	21	Vitamin A	4%
Carbohydrate, g	48	Vitamin C	16%
Fat, g	3	Thiamin	54%
Unsaturated	2	Riboflavin	14%
Saturated	1	Niacin	26%
Dietary Fiber, g	1	Calcium	2%
Cholesterol, mg	55	Iron	16%
Sodium, mg	340		
Potassium, mg	450		

Spicy Southwest Pork Burgers

Grill the patties about 4 inches from medium coals for 15 to 20 minutes, turning them once, until pork is done. If you'd like a more casual meal, spread the salsa and low-fat sour cream on whole-wheat buns and serve like hamburgers.

1 pound ground pork
2 tablespoons finely chopped onion
1 teaspoon chile powder
¹/₂ teaspoon salt
¹/₂ teaspoon ground cumin
¹/₈ teaspoon pepper
1 jalapeño chile, seeded and finely chopped
Salsa
Low-fat sour cream

Set oven control to broil. Spray broiler pan rack with nonstick cooking spray. Mix all ingredients except salsa and sour cream. Shape into 4 patties, each about ¹/₂ inch thick. Place patties on rack in broiler pan. Broil with tops 3 to 5 inches from heat 10 to 15 minutes, turning once, until pork is well done (170°). Top with salsa and sour cream. Sprinkle with chopped fresh cilantro if desired. *4 servings*

NUTRITION INFORMATION PER SERVING			
1 serving		Percent of U.S. RDA	
Calories	315	Protein	34%
Protein, g	22	Vitamin A	16%
Carbohydrate, g	5	Vitamin C	20%
Fat, g	23	Thiamin	36%
Unsaturated	14	Riboflavin	16%
Saturated	9	Niacin	22%
Dietary Fiber, g	1	Calcium	4%
Cholesterol, mg	75	Iron	6%
Sodium, mg	420		
Potassium, mg	460		

Pork Kabobs with Chile Barbecue Sauce

Chile Barbecue Sauce (below)
1¹/₂-pound pork tenderloin

Prepare Chile Barbecue Sauce. Trim fat from pork tenderloin. Cut pork into 1¹/₂-inch cubes. Mix pork and 1¹/₄ cups of the sauce in large glass or plastic bowl. Cover and refrigerate at least 4 hours but no longer than 24 hours. Cover and refrigerate remaining sauce.

Set oven control to broil. Thread pork on six 10-inch skewers.* Spray broiler pan rack with nonstick cooking spray. Place pork on rack in broiler pan. Broil with tops 3 inches from heat 5 minutes; turn. Brush with ¹/₄ cup of the sauce. Broil about 5 minutes longer or until pork is no longer pink. Serve with remaining sauce over steamed shredded cabbage if desired. *6 servings*

Chile Barbecue Sauce

1¹/₂ cups tomato puree
³/₄ cup finely chopped onions (about 1¹/₂ medium)
¹/₄ cup molasses
2 tablespoons red wine vinegar or cider vinegar
2 tablespoons finely chopped pickled hot chiles
1 tablespoon tomato paste
1 tablespoon Dijon mustard
2 cloves garlic, finely chopped

Heat all ingredients to boiling over medium heat; reduce heat to medium-low. Cook uncovered 15 minutes, stirring occasionally.

* If using bamboo skewers, soak skewers in water at least 30 minutes before using to prevent burning.

Pork Kabobs with Chile Barbecue Sauce

NUTRITION INFORMATION PER SERVING

1 serving		Percent of U.S. RDA	
Calories	265	Protein	52%
Protein, g	34	Vitamin A	12%
Carbohydrate, g	19	Vitamin C	16%
Fat, g	6	Thiamin	76%
Unsaturated	4	Riboflavin	30%
Saturated	2	Niacin	32%
Dietary Fiber, g	2	Calcium	6%
Cholesterol, mg	105	Iron	18%
Sodium, mg	380		
Potassium, mg	1190		

Glazed Lamb Chops

6 lamb loin chops, 1 inch thick (about 1½
    pounds)
¼ cup apricot spreadable fruit
2 tablespoons red wine vinegar or cider
    vinegar
2 tablespoons Dijon mustard
½ teaspoon reduced-sodium soy sauce
¼ teaspoon pepper

Trim fat from lamb chops. Mix remaining ingredients. Brush lamb with ⅓ cup apricot mixture; reserve remaining mixture. Let stand 20 minutes at room temperature or cover and refrigerate up to 12 hours.

Set oven control to broil. Spray broiler pan rack with nonstick cooking spray. Place lamb on rack in broiler pan. Brush with reserved apricot mixture. Broil with tops 5 inches from heat about 5 minutes or until brown; turn. Brush with pan drippings. Broil 6 to 9 minutes longer for medium doneness (160°). *6 servings*

NUTRITION INFORMATION PER SERVING

1 serving		Percent of U.S. RDA	
Calories	150	Protein	28%
Protein, g	18	Vitamin A	*
Carbohydrate, g	6	Vitamin C	*
Fat, g	6	Thiamin	4%
Unsaturated	4	Riboflavin	10%
Saturated	2	Niacin	20%
Dietary Fiber, g	0	Calcium	*
Cholesterol, mg	55	Iron	8%
Sodium, mg	120		
Potassium, mg	230		

Mint-Wine Lamb Chops

**8 lamb rib or loin chops, about 1 inch thick
(about 2 pounds)**
2 tablespoons dry white wine or apple juice
2 tablespoons honey
**1 teaspoon chopped fresh or ¼ teaspoon
dried mint leaves**
¼ teaspoon salt
⅛ teaspoon pepper

Set oven control to broil. Trim fat from lamb
chops. Mix remaining ingredients. Brush lamb
with wine mixture. Place lamb on rack in
broiler pan. Broil with tops 3 to 4 inches from
heat about 4 minutes or until brown. Brush with
wine mixture. Turn lamb; brush with wine mixture. Broil 5 to 7 minutes longer for medium
doneness (160°). *8 servings*

NUTRITION INFORMATION PER SERVING			
I serving		**Percent of U.S. RDA**	
Calories	185	Protein	30%
Protein, g	20	Vitamin A	*
Carbohydrate, g	4	Vitamin C	*
Fat, g	10	Thiamin	4%
Unsaturated	6	Riboflavin	10%
Saturated	4	Niacin	24%
Dietary Fiber, g	0	Calcium	2%
Cholesterol, mg	70	Iron	8%
Sodium, mg	130		
Potassium, mg	250		

Mustard Lamb Chops

**6 lamb sirloin or shoulder chops, about ¾
inch thick (about 2 pounds)**
**1 tablespoon chopped fresh or 1 teaspoon
dried thyme leaves**
2 tablespoons Dijon mustard
¼ teaspoon salt

Set oven control to broil. Trim fat from lamb
chops. Place lamb on rack in broiler pan. Mix
thyme, mustard and salt; brush half of the mustard mixture evenly over lamb. Broil with tops
about 3 to 4 inches from heat about 4 minutes or
until brown; turn. Brush remaining mustard
mixture over lamb. Broil 5 to 7 minutes longer
for medium doneness (160°). *6 servings*

NUTRITION INFORMATION PER SERVING			
I serving		**Percent of U.S. RDA**	
Calories	150	Protein	34%
Protein, g	22	Vitamin A	*
Carbohydrate, g	0	Vitamin C	*
Fat, g	7	Thiamin	6%
Unsaturated	4	Riboflavin	14%
Saturated	3	Niacin	24%
Dietary Fiber, g	0	Calcium	*
Cholesterol, mg	70	Iron	12%
Sodium, mg	210		
Potassium, mg	270		

*Opposite: Lamburgers with Rosemary-Mint Sauce,
Lemon-Chive Fettuccine (page 126)*

Lamburgers with Rosemary-Mint Sauce

These burgers can be shaped up to 8 hours ahead of time. Store them covered in the refrigerator until ready to cook.

1½ pounds lean ground lamb
¼ cup finely chopped onion (about 1 small)
1 tablespoon chopped fresh mint leaves
½ teaspoon salt
¼ teaspoon pepper
2 cloves garlic, finely chopped
Rosemary-Mint Sauce (right)

Spray 12-inch skillet with nonstick cooking spray. Mix all ingredients except Rosemary-Mint Sauce. Heat skillet over medium heat. Shape meat mixture into 6 patties. Cook patties in skillet 5 minutes; turn. Cook 3 to 5 minutes longer until no longer pink in center. Serve with Rosemary-Mint Sauce. *6 servings*

Rosemary-Mint Sauce

1 cup plain nonfat yogurt
2 tablespoons chopped fresh mint leaves
2 tablespoons red wine vinegar or cider vinegar
1 teaspoon fresh or ½ teaspoon dried rosemary leaves, crushed
¼ teaspoon salt
¼ teaspoon pepper
¼ teaspoon ground cumin

Mix all ingredients.

NUTRITION INFORMATION PER SERVING			
1 serving		Percent of U.S. RDA	
Calories	240	Protein	30%
Protein, g	20	Vitamin A	*
Carbohydrate, g	4	Vitamin C	*
Fat, g	16	Thiamin	6%
Unsaturated	9	Riboflavin	16%
Saturated	7	Niacin	24%
Dietary Fiber, g	0	Calcium	10%
Cholesterol, mg	75	Iron	10%
Sodium, mg	350		
Potassium, mg	320		

Asian Beef Salad

Though this salad requires alot of chopping, it looks quite impressive when arranged on a platter and is also quite delicious. It's a great dish for company, or when you'd like to set a pretty table.

Tomato-Ginger Sauce (below)
1 package (about 7 ounces) rice stick
   noodles
Egg Strips (right)
2 cups 2-inch strips cooked lean beef steak
   (about 1 pound)
1½ cups sliced seeded peeled cucumbers
   (about 1½ medium)
2 tablespoons finely chopped unsalted
   roasted peanuts

Prepare Tomato-Ginger Sauce. Cook noodles as directed on package; drain. Prepare Egg Strips. Arrange noodles in center of plate or platter; top with sauce. Arrange beef, cucumbers and Egg Strips around noodles on plate. Sprinkle with peanuts. *6 servings*

Tomato-Ginger Sauce

2 cups chopped tomatoes (about 2 large)
⅓ cup chopped green onions (about 3
   medium)
2 tablespoons chopped fresh cilantro
1 tablespoon balsamic vinegar
2 teaspoons finely chopped gingerroot
1 teaspoon sesame oil
¼ teaspoon crushed red pepper
1 clove garlic, finely chopped

Mix all ingredients in glass or plastic bowl. Cover and refrigerate 1 hour.

Egg Strips

½ cup cholesterol-free egg product or Egg
   Substitute (page 28)
1 tablespoon chopped fresh cilantro
⅛ teaspoon salt

Spray 8-inch skillet with nonstick cooking spray. Heat skillet over medium heat. Mix all ingredients. Pour ¼ cup egg mixture into skillet. Cook until egg mixture is set. Turn out onto cutting board; cut into 6 strips. Repeat with remaining egg mixture.

NUTRITION INFORMATION PER SERVING			
1 serving		**Percent of U.S. RDA**	
Calories	250	Protein	30%
Protein, g	20	Vitamin A	8%
Carbohydrate, g	25	Vitamin C	40%
Fat, g	8	Thiamin	14%
Unsaturated	5	Riboflavin	14%
Saturated	3	Niacin	24%
Dietary Fiber, g	2	Calcium	4%
Cholesterol, mg	40	Iron	16%
Sodium, mg	130		
Potassium, mg	580		

Asian Beef Salad (front), *Summer Garden Beef Salad* (back) (*page 201*)

Warm Beef Salad

If you like, use bite-size pieces of lettuce instead of the shredded lettuce here. Arrange the meat mixture on lettuce beds just before serving, as the warmth wilts the lettuce immediately. You can also make fajitas with this recipe. Just wrap the meat and lettuce in tortillas.

Roasted Garlic Dressing (right)
6 reserved roasted garlic cloves (from dressing)
12 strips red bell pepper, 3×½×¼ inch (about 1 large)
12 strips zucchini, 3×½×¼ inch (about 1 large)
6 green onions, cut into 2-inch pieces
1½ pounds beef flank steak or tenderloin, cut into 3×½×¼-inch strips
6 cups shredded romaine lettuce (about 1 large head)

Prepare Roasted Garlic Dressing. Mix ⅔ cup of the dressing and the remaining ingredients except romaine in glass or plastic bowl. Cover and refrigerate 1 hour. Cover and refrigerate remaining dressing.

Set oven control to broil. Spray shallow roasting pan with nonstick cooking spray. Place beef mixture in pan. Broil with top 5 inches from heat 7 to 10 minutes or until beef is no longer pink. Serve on romaine. Top with remaining dressing. *6 servings*

Roasted Garlic Dressing

12 unpeeled garlic cloves
3 tablespoons cholesterol-free reduced-calorie mayonnaise or salad dressing
⅔ cup plain nonfat yogurt
¼ cup lemon juice
2 tablespoons balsamic vinegar
½ teaspoon salt
¼ teaspoon pepper

Heat oven to 375°. Wrap garlic cloves in aluminum foil. Bake 1 hour. Cool slightly. Slip skins off cloves. Reserve 6 cloves for salad. Mash remaining 6 cloves; mix with remaining dressing ingredients.

NUTRITION INFORMATION PER SERVING			
1 serving		Percent of U.S. RDA	
Calories	255	Protein	42%
Protein, g	27	Vitamin A	20%
Carbohydrate, g	12	Vitamin C	46%
Fat, g	11	Thiamin	14%
Unsaturated	7	Riboflavin	18%
Saturated	4	Niacin	24%
Dietary Fiber, g	2	Calcium	12%
Cholesterol, mg	65	Iron	18%
Sodium, mg	310		
Potassium, mg	780		

Summer Garden Beef Salad

Make this salad when you have access to fresh basil, either from the garden or the farmer's market. Resist the urge to make it if fresh basil is not available, as dried basil just doesn't deliver the needed flavor in this dish.

Green Onion Dressing (right)
3 cups julienne strips cooked lean roast
    beef (about 1½ pounds)
2 cups cooked fresh, frozen (thawed) or
    canned (drained) whole kernel corn
    (about 4 medium ears)
1 cup julienne strips cooked Chinese pea
    pods (about 4 ounces)
1 cup julienne strips roma (plum) tomatoes
1 cup julienne strips zucchini (about 1
    medium)
1 cup julienne strips yellow bell pepper
    (about 1 small)
¼ cup chopped fresh basil leaves
6 Bibb or Boston lettuce leaves
1 tablespoon chopped fresh chives

Prepare Green Onion Dressing. Toss dressing and remaining ingredients except lettuce leaves and chives. Serve salad on lettuce leaves. Sprinkle with chives. *6 servings*

Green Onion Dressing

½ cup chopped green onions (about 5
    medium)
½ cup nonfat plain yogurt
¼ cup white wine or apple juice
¼ cup beef broth
2 tablespoons lemon juice
¼ teaspoon salt
¼ teaspoon pepper

Place all ingredients in blender. Cover and blend about 30 seconds or until smooth.

NUTRITION INFORMATION PER SERVING			
1 serving		Percent of U.S. RDA	
Calories	360	Protein	52%
Protein, g	34	Vitamin A	14%
Carbohydrate, g	16	Vitamin C	90%
Fat, g	18	Thiamin	16%
Unsaturated	11	Riboflavin	22%
Saturated	7	Niacin	26%
Dietary Fiber, g	2	Calcium	10%
Cholesterol, mg	90	Iron	26%
Sodium, mg	220		
Potassium, mg	830		

Minty Couscous and Pork Salad

A small amount of pork is extended with cous-cous in this refreshing main dish salad. You can also make it without the meat for an excellent salad to serve with Mediterranean Chicken Ka-bobs (page 225).

Minty Dressing (right)
3 cups cooked couscous
2 cups cut-up cooked pork tenderloin (about ¾ pound)
1½ cups finely chopped green bell peppers (about 1½ medium)
1 cup finely chopped carrots (about 2 medium)
½ cup sliced red onion (about ½ small)
½ cup golden raisins

Mix all ingredients in glass or plastic bowl. Cover and refrigerate at least 2 hours but no longer than 3 days. *6 servings*

Minty Dressing

¼ cup chopped fresh or 1 tablespoon dried mint leaves
¼ cup chopped fresh parsley
¼ cup lemon juice
¼ cup orange juice
2 tablespoons olive or vegetable oil
½ teaspoon salt
½ teaspoon ground cinnamon
½ teaspoon pepper

Mix all ingredients.

MINTY MIXED BEAN AND COUSCOUS SALAD: Omit pork. Stir in 2 cups cooked great northern beans or 1 can (about 15 ounces) great northern, can-nellini or navy beans, drained, and 2 cups cooked garbanzo beans or 1 can (15 ounces) garbanzo beans, drained.

NUTRITION INFORMATION PER SERVING			
1 serving		**Percent of U.S. RDA**	
Calories	305	Protein	32%
Protein, g	21	Vitamin A	30%
Carbohydrate, g	37	Vitamin C	24%
Fat, g	8	Thiamin	42%
Unsaturated	6	Riboflavin	16%
Saturated	2	Niacin	20%
Dietary Fiber, g	3	Calcium	2%
Cholesterol, mg	55	Iron	10%
Sodium, mg	230		
Potassium, mg	620		

Spicy Pork and Garbanzo Bean Salad

The tomatillos used in this dressing are the basis for most Mexican green salsas. They can be found in the produce section of supermarkets or ethnic grocery stores. See page 320 to learn more about garbanzo beans.

Green Salsa Dressing (right)
3 cups cubed cooked pork (about 1 pound)
1 cup grapefruit section halves (about 1 medium)
1 cup chopped celery (about 2 medium stalks)
1/2 cup coarsely chopped onion (about 1 medium)
1/4 cup chopped fresh cilantro
1 can (15 ounces) garbanzo beans, rinsed and drained
12 Bibb or Boston lettuce leaves

Prepare Green Salsa Dressing. Mix dressing and remaining ingredients except lettuce leaves in glass or plastic bowl. Cover and refrigerate 1 hour. Serve on lettuce leaves. *6 servings*

Green Salsa Dressing

1/3 cup chopped green onions (about 3 medium)
1/4 cup grapefruit juice
2 teaspoons chopped jalapeño chiles
1 teaspoon vegetable oil
1 teaspoon honey
1/2 teaspoon salt
1/4 teaspoon pepper
1 can (11 ounces) tomatillos, drained
1 clove garlic, finely chopped

Place all ingredients in blender or food processor. Cover and blend about 30 seconds or until smooth.

NUTRITION INFORMATION PER SERVING			
I serving		Percent of U.S. RDA	
Calories	340	Protein	40%
Protein, g	27	Vitamin A	6%
Carbohydrate, g	31	Vitamin C	62%
Fat, g	13	Thiamin	48%
Unsaturated	9	Riboflavin	20%
Saturated	4	Niacin	26%
Dietary Fiber, g	6	Calcium	8%
Cholesterol, mg	65	Iron	20%
Sodium, mg	340		
Potassium, mg	800		

Garbanzo-Rice Chile

1½ pound beef round steak

2 teaspoons vegetable oil

1½ cups chopped bell peppers

1 cup chopped onion (about 1 large)

⅓ cup chopped fresh parsley

1½ cups water

1 tablespoon chopped fresh or 1 teaspoon
 dried oregano leaves

2 teaspoons paprika

1 teaspoon ground cumin

½ teaspoon salt

½ teaspoon crushed red pepper

½ teaspoon ground coriander

1 can (10½ ounces) condensed beef broth

1 clove garlic, finely chopped

1 bay leaf

3 cups cooked rice

1 can (15 ounces) garbanzo beans, drained,
 except 2 tablespoons

Trim fat from beef steak. Cut beef into ½-inch cubes. Cook beef in oil in nonstick Dutch oven over medium heat, stirring occasionally, until light brown; drain. Stir in remaining ingredients except rice and beans. Heat to boiling; reduce heat. Cover and simmer 1 hour, stirring occasionally. Uncover and simmer about 30 minutes longer, stirring occasionally, until mixture is thickened and beef is tender. Remove bay leaf. Mix rice and beans. Heat over low heat, stirring occasionally, just until hot. Divide rice mixture among 8 serving bowls. Spoon beef mixture over rice. *8 servings*

NUTRITION INFORMATION PER SERVING

	1 serving		Percent of U.S. RDA	
Calories	305	Protein		38%
Protein, g	25	Vitamin A		6%
Carbohydrate, g	40	Vitamin C		14%
Fat, g	5	Thiamin		18%
Unsaturated	3	Riboflavin		12%
Saturated	2	Niacin		24%
Dietary Fiber, g	4	Calcium		6%
Cholesterol, mg	40	Iron		26%
Sodium, mg	490			
Potassium, mg	550			

Garbanzo-Rice Chile

Portuguese Kale Soup with Ham

Low-sodium chicken broth is combined with ham to cut the amount of sodium.

1 cup finely chopped onion (about 1 large)

1 pound potatoes, peeled and cut into ½-inch cubes

3 cans (14½ ounces each) low-sodium chicken broth or water

1 pound kale, collard greens or turnip greens, stems removed and leaves finely shredded

1½ cups ½-inch cubes fully cooked smoked lean ham (about ½ pound)

½ teaspoon salt

Spray nonstick Dutch oven with nonstick cooking spray. Cook onion in Dutch oven over medium heat about 10 minutes, stirring frequently, until tender. Stir in potatoes and broth. Heat to boiling; reduce heat. Cover and simmer 20 to 25 minutes or until potatoes are tender. Carefully mash potatoes with potato masher.

Stir in remaining ingredients. Simmer uncovered about 5 minutes or until kale is tender and ham is hot. *6 servings*

NUTRITION INFORMATION PER SERVING

1 serving		Percent of U.S. RDA	
Calories	160	Protein	18%
Protein, g	12	Vitamin A	14%
Carbohydrate, g	21	Vitamin C	18%
Fat, g	3	Thiamin	26%
Unsaturated	2	Riboflavin	12%
Saturated	1	Niacin	22%
Dietary Fiber, g	3	Calcium	2%
Cholesterol, mg	20	Iron	10%
Sodium, mg	690		
Potassium, mg	540		

Vegetable-Ham Soup with Pasta

1 cup chopped fennel bulb

¼ cup chopped onion (about 1 small)

1 cup uncooked rotini, rigatoni or other medium pasta

½ cup thinly sliced carrot (about 1 medium)

1 cup water

2 teaspoons chopped fresh or ½ teaspoon dried oregano leaves

⅛ teaspoon crushed red pepper

2 cans (14½ ounces each) reduced-sodium chicken broth

2 cups julienne strips fully cooked smoked lean ham (about ½ pound)

Spray 3-quart nonstick saucepan with nonstick cooking spray. Cook fennel and onion in saucepan over medium heat about 10 minutes, stirring frequently, until onion is tender. Stir in remaining ingredients except ham. Heat to boiling; reduce heat. Cover and simmer about 10 minutes or until pasta is tender. Stir in ham. Heat 1 to 2 minutes or until ham is hot. Sprinkle with chopped fresh parsley is desired. *4 servings*

NUTRITION INFORMATION PER SERVING

1 serving		Percent of U.S. RDA	
Calories	235	Protein	42%
Protein, g	18	Vitamin A	24%
Carbohydrate, g	30	Vitamin C	12%
Fat, g	5	Thiamin	42%
Unsaturated	4	Riboflavin	16%
Saturated	1	Niacin	30%
Dietary Fiber, g	2	Calcium	2%
Cholesterol, mg	30	Iron	16%
Sodium, mg	740		
Potassium, mg	360		

Open-face Pork Sandwich with Watercress Salad

To prepare the pork ahead of time, brush the oil mixture on both sides of the pork slices. Cover and refrigerate no longer than 24 hours.

Watercress Salad (right)
1-pound pork tenderloin
1 tablespoon olive or vegetable oil
1 tablespoon raspberry vinegar
1 teaspoon chopped fresh or ½ teaspoon
    crushed dried rosemary leaves
1 teaspoon Dijon mustard
¼ teaspoon salt
6 diagonally cut ½-inch slices whole-grain
    or white French bread, toasted

Prepare Watercress Salad. Trim fat from pork tenderloin. Cut pork crosswise into 6 pieces. Place pork, cut sides up, between plastic wrap or waxed paper. Flatten to ¼-inch thickness. Place pork on rack in broiler pan. Mix oil, vinegar, rosemary, mustard and salt; brush half of mixture on top side of pork.

Set oven control to broil. Broil pork with tops 3 to 5 inches from heat 5 minutes; turn. Brush remaining oil mixture over pork. Broil about 5 minutes or until medium doneness (160°).

Place pork on toast. Top with Watercress Salad. Garnish with fresh raspberries, carrot curls or cherry tomatoes if desired. *6 servings*

Watercress Salad

2 tablespoons olive or vegetable oil
1 tablespoon raspberry vinegar
½ teaspoon ground mustard
Dash of salt
Dash of pepper
3 cups watercress or shredded mixed
    greens
⅓ cup thinly sliced green onions

Mix oil, vinegar, mustard, salt and pepper in large bowl. Add watercress and onions; toss until evenly coated. Cover and refrigerate until serving time.

NUTRITION INFORMATION PER SERVING			
1 serving		**Percent of U.S. RDA**	
Calories	270	Protein	40%
Protein, g	26	Vitamin A	8%
Carbohydrate, g	17	Vitamin C	8%
Fat, g	11	Thiamin	54%
Unsaturated	8	Riboflavin	20%
Saturated	3	Niacin	22%
Dietary Fiber, g	2	Calcium	6%
Cholesterol, mg	70	Iron	12%
Sodium, mg	420		
Potassium, mg	590		

Opposite: Open-face Pork Sandwich with Watercress Salad

Meatball Pita Pockets

1½ pounds extra-lean ground beef

⅓ cup plain nonfat yogurt

⅓ cup finely chopped shallots (about 2
   large)

¼ cup chopped fresh parsley

¼ teaspoon salt

¼ teaspoon pepper

1 can (15 ounces) tomato puree

1½ cups sliced mushrooms (about 4 ounces)

⅔ cup plain nonfat yogurt

2 teaspoons prepared horseradish

1 cup shredded lettuce

1 cup chopped tomato (about 1 large)

4 whole wheat pita breads (about 6 inches
   in diameter), cut into halves to form
   pockets

Spray 12-inch skillet with nonstick cooking
spray. Mix ground beef, ⅓ cup yogurt, the shallots, parsley, salt and pepper. Shape into 24
meatballs, each about 1½ inches. Cook meatballs in skillet over medium heat about 5 minutes or until light brown on all sides. Stir in
tomato puree and mushrooms; turn meatballs to
coat with sauce.

Cook about 20 minutes, turning occasionally,
until meatballs are no longer pink in center.
Remove meatballs from skillet. Cool sauce 5
minutes; stir in ⅔ cup yogurt and the horseradish. Divide meatballs, lettuce, tomatoes and
sauce among pita breads. *8 servings*

NUTRITION INFORMATION PER SERVING			
1 serving		**Percent of U.S. RDA**	
Calories	320	Protein	38%
Protein, g	25	Vitamin A	10%
Carbohydrate, g	33	Vitamin C	14%
Fat, g	10	Thiamin	22%
Unsaturated	6	Riboflavin	24%
Saturated	4	Niacin	28%
Dietary Fiber, g	5	Calcium	12%
Cholesterol, mg	50	Iron	22%
Sodium, mg	590		
Potassium, mg	760		

Vegetable-Beef Burgers

1½ pounds extra-lean ground beef
1 cup bean sprouts, coarsely chopped
¼ cup chopped bell pepper
¼ cup chopped onion (about 1 small)
¼ cup shredded carrot
¼ cup chopped celery
½ teaspoon salt
¼ teaspoon pepper
6 whole-grain hamburger buns, split
2 medium tomatoes, each cut into 3 slices
1½ cups alfalfa sprouts

Mix all ingredients except buns, tomatoes and alfalfa sprouts. Shape into 6 patties, each about ½ inch thick. Set oven control to broil. Spray broiler pan rack with nonstick cooking spray. Place patties on rack in broiler pan. Broil with tops about 3 inches from heat 3 to 5 minutes on each side for medium doneness (160°). Serve each patty on bun with 1 tomato slice and ¼ cup alfalfa sprouts. *6 servings*

NUTRITION INFORMATION PER SERVING

1 serving		Percent of U.S. RDA	
Calories	340	Protein	42%
Protein, g	28	Vitamin A	10%
Carbohydrate, g	25	Vitamin C	10%
Fat, g	14	Thiamin	14%
Unsaturated	9	Riboflavin	16%
Saturated	5	Niacin	24%
Dietary Fiber, g	3	Calcium	6%
Cholesterol, mg	70	Iron	22%
Sodium, mg	470		
Potassium, mg	570		

Vegetable-Beef Burgers, Vegetable-Ham Soup with Pasta (page 205)

6
Poultry

6

Poultry

Chicken and turkey are available in many forms and lend themselves well to a variety of uses. From whole birds to pieces or bone-in to boned, chicken and turkey are low-fat, high-quality protein sources. Most of the fat in chicken and turkey is in the skin, which means it's easy to remove. Poultry can be cooked with the skin on to prevent the meat from drying out, but remove the skin before eating. Turkey is a bit leaner than chicken, and light poultry meat has somewhat less fat than dark meat, although the cholesterol content is similar. Even though duck and goose are traditionally included in the poultry category, we have not included them here because of their high fat content.

The subtle flavor of chicken makes it suitable for so many kinds of dishes. In Gingered Chicken with Vegetables (page 212), a whole chicken is roasted with the skin on to maintain moistness, then a flavorful mixture of vegetables and spices is served with the mild, skinned meat, all for under 250 calories per serving. Skinless, boneless chicken breast halves soak up the zest of lemon and dill in Lemon-Dill Chicken (page 223) for only 150 calories and 4 grams of fat per serving. Nonfat plain yogurt can be used in a marinade, for Roast Chicken with Spiced Yogurt (page 213), as a sauce in Drumsticks with Yogurt Sauce (page 231) and in salad dressing in Crunchy Chicken and Pear Salad (page 250).

Turkey is just as versatile as chicken and is available fresh in several forms. Turkey tenderloins are marinated, baked and served with a saucy salsa in Asian Turkey (page 244). Turkey Breakfast Sausage (page 249) seasons ground turkey with applesauce, shallots, lemon juice and cloves for a healthy take on an old favorite. As you can see, there are many ways to add flavor and excitement to poultry without adding fat. Herbs, spices, flavored vinegars, garlic and chiles are but some of the many seasonings you'll find in these poultry recipes.

Preceding page: Rice-stuffed Chicken, Tropical Chicken Rolls (page 222)

Rice-stuffed Chicken

1½ cups cooked brown or regular rice
1 cup chopped apple (about 1 medium)
½ cup chopped prunes
½ cup chopped dried apricots
¼ cup chopped celery (about 1 small stalk)
2 tablespoons margarine, melted
1 teaspoon ground ginger
½ teaspoon grated lemon peel
¼ teaspoon salt
¼ teaspoon garlic powder
3- to 3½-pound broiler-fryer chicken

Heat oven to 375°. Mix all ingredients except chicken. Fill wishbone area of chicken with stuffing first. Fasten neck skin to back with skewer. Fold wings across back with tips touching. Fill body cavity lightly with stuffing. Tie or skewer drumsticks to tail. Place chicken, breast side up, on rack in shallow roasting pan.

Roast uncovered 1½ to 1¾ hours or until juices of chicken run clear. Let stand 10 minutes before carving. Remove and discard skin. Cover and refrigerate any remaining chicken and stuffing separately. *6 servings*

NUTRITION INFORMATION PER SERVING

1 serving		Percent of U.S. RDA	
Calories	310	Protein	56%
Protein, g	25	Vitamin A	16%
Carbohydrate, g	30	Vitamin C	2%
Fat, g	10	Thiamin	8%
Unsaturated	7	Riboflavin	12%
Saturated	3	Niacin	36%
Dietary Fiber, g	3	Calcium	4%
Cholesterol, mg	70	Iron	12%
Sodium, mg	210		
Potassium, mg	540		

Chicken-Potato Roast

3- to 3½-pound broiler-fryer chicken
1 medium apple, cut into fourths
1 medium onion, cut into fourths
2 cloves garlic, cut into fourths
6 medium baking potatoes
2 tablespoons margarine, melted
1 teaspoon dried thyme leaves
1 teaspoon paprika
½ teaspoon salt

Heat oven to 375°. Fold wings of chicken across back with tips touching. Place apple, onion and garlic in body cavity. Tie or skewer drumsticks to tail. Place chicken, breast side up, on rack in shallow roasting pan. Cut potatoes crosswise into ¼-inch slices about three quarters of the way through. Place on rack around chicken.

Mix remaining ingredients; brush over chicken and potatoes. Roast uncovered 1 to 1¼ hours, brushing chicken and potatoes with margarine mixture every 30 minutes, until juices of chicken run clear and potatoes are tender. Let chicken stand 10 minutes before carving; keep potatoes warm. Discard apple, onion and garlic. Remove and discard chicken skin. *6 servings*

NUTRITION INFORMATION PER SERVING

1 serving		Percent of U.S. RDA	
Calories	375	Protein	42%
Protein, g	27	Vitamin A	8%
Carbohydrate, g	47	Vitamin C	20%
Fat, g	9	Thiamin	16%
Unsaturated	7	Riboflavin	12%
Saturated	2	Niacin	42%
Dietary Fiber, g	4	Calcium	4%
Cholesterol, mg	70	Iron	22%
Sodium, mg	300		
Potassium, mg	970		

Country-style Chicken

Country-style Chicken

3- to 3½-pound broiler-fryer chicken

1 tablespoon margarine or butter

1 can (10½ ounces) condensed chicken broth

¾ teaspoon chopped fresh or ¼ teaspoon dried thyme leaves

¼ teaspoon pepper

8 medium carrots, cut into fourths

8 whole small white onions

4 medium turnips, cut into fourths

½ cup dry white wine or chicken broth

2 tablespoons cold water

1 tablespoon cornstarch

Fold wings of chicken across back with tips touching. Tie or skewer drumsticks to tail. Heat margarine in nonstick Dutch oven until melted. Cook chicken in margarine over medium heat until brown on all sides; drain.

Heat oven to 375°. Pour broth over chicken in Dutch oven. Sprinkle with thyme and pepper.

Cover and bake 45 minutes. Arrange carrots, onions and turnips around chicken. Cover and bake 1 to 1¼ hours longer or until juices of chicken run clear. Remove chicken and vegetables from Dutch oven; keep warm.

Skim fat from pan juices in Dutch oven. Stir wine into juices. Heat to boiling. Mix cold water and cornstarch; stir into wine mixture. Heat to boiling, stirring constantly. Boil and stir 1 minute. Remove and discard chicken skin. Serve chicken and vegetables with sauce. *6 servings*

NUTRITION INFORMATION PER SERVING

1 serving		Percent of U.S. RDA	
Calories	280	Protein	44%
Protein, g	28	Vitamin A	100%
Carbohydrate, g	24	Vitamin C	20%
Fat, g	8	Thiamin	14%
Unsaturated	6	Riboflavin	16%
Saturated	2	Niacin	42%
Dietary Fiber, g	7	Calcium	8%
Cholesterol, mg	70	Iron	14%
Sodium, mg	490		
Potassium, mg	890		

Wine-sauced Chicken

3- to 3½-pound broiler-fryer chicken
1 cup dry red wine
½ cup finely chopped onion (about 1
    medium)
2 large cloves garlic, finely chopped
1 tablespoon chopped fresh or 1 teaspoon
    dried basil leaves
½ teaspoon salt
1 can (8 ounces) tomato sauce

Heat oven to 375°. Fold wings of chicken across back with tips touching. Tie or skewer drumsticks to tail. Place chicken, breast side up, on rack in shallow roasting pan. Roast uncovered 1 to 1¼ hours or until juices run clear. Let stand 10 minutes before carving. Remove and discard skin.

Meanwhile, mix remaining ingredients in 1½-quart saucepan. Heat to boiling, stirring occasionally; reduce heat. Cover and simmer 30 minutes. Serve with chicken. *6 servings*

NUTRITION INFORMATION PER SERVING

1 serving		Percent of U.S. RDA	
Calories	180	Protein	38%
Protein, g	24	Vitamin A	4%
Carbohydrate, g	5	Vitamin C	4%
Fat, g	5	Thiamin	6%
Unsaturated	3	Riboflavin	10%
Saturated	2	Niacin	30%
Dietary Fiber, g	1	Calcium	4%
Cholesterol, mg	70	Iron	10%
Sodium, mg	470		
Potassium, mg	430		

Rosemary-Lemon Chicken

¼ cup finely chopped shallots (about 2
    large)
1 teaspoon grated lemon peel
½ teaspoon salt
½ teaspoon dried rosemary leaves, crushed
¼ teaspoon pepper
1 garlic clove, finely chopped
3- to 3½-pound broiler-fryer chicken
1 lemon, cut into halves
½ teaspoon paprika

Heat oven to 350°. Mix all ingredients except chicken, lemon and paprika. Gently loosen breast skin from chicken with fingers, reaching as far back as possible without tearing skin. Spread herb mixture over breast meat; cover with skin. Squeeze lemon halves over outside of chicken and inside body cavity; place lemon halves in cavity. Fold wings across back with tips touching. Tie or skewer drumsticks to tail. Sprinkle paprika over chicken.

Place chicken, breast side up, on rack in shallow roasting pan. Roast uncovered about 1½ hours or until juices run clear. Let stand 10 minutes before carving. Remove and discard lemon and skin. *6 servings*

NUTRITION INFORMATION PER SERVING

1 serving		Percent of U.S. RDA	
Calories	140	Protein	36%
Protein, g	23	Vitamin A	2%
Carbohydrate, g	1	Vitamin C	*
Fat, g	5	Thiamin	4%
Unsaturated	3	Riboflavin	8%
Saturated	2	Niacin	28%
Dietary Fiber, g	0	Calcium	2%
Cholesterol, mg	70	Iron	8%
Sodium, mg	240		
Potassium, mg	250		

Herbed Chicken and Vegetables

Basil, oregano and marjoram simmer with chicken, olives, carrots, onions and potatoes for a savory, satisfying dish.

3- to 3½-pound cut-up broiler-fryer chicken

¼ cup all-purpose flour

1 tablespoon chopped fresh or 1 teaspoon dried basil leaves

1½ teaspoons chopped fresh or ½ teaspoon dried oregano leaves

1 teaspoon paprika

¾ teaspoon chopped fresh or ¼ teaspoon dried marjoram leaves

¼ teaspoon pepper

2 tablespoons vegetable oil

1 cup chicken broth or dry white wine

12 small pitted ripe olives

8 medium carrots, cut into fourths

8 whole small onions

4 medium baking potatoes, cut into fourths

1 tablespoon cornstarch

1 tablespoon cold water

Remove skin and fat from chicken pieces. Mix flour, basil, oregano, paprika, marjoram and pepper. Coat chicken with flour mixture. Heat oil in nonstick Dutch oven or 12-inch skillet until hot. Cook chicken in oil about 15 minutes or until light brown on all sides; remove chicken and drain. Stir in broth, olives, carrots, onions and potatoes; add chicken. Heat to boiling; reduce heat. over and simmer 35 to 40 minutes or until juices of chicken run clear.

Remove chicken and vegetables; keep warm. Mix cornstarch and cold water; stir into liquid in Dutch oven. Heat to boiling, stirring constantly. Boil and stir 1 minute. Serve with chicken and vegetables. *6 servings*

NUTRITION INFORMATION PER SERVING			
1 serving		**Percent of U.S. RDA**	
Calories	355	Protein	42%
Protein, g	28	Vitamin A	100%
Carbohydrate, g	36	Vitamin C	16%
Fat, g	11	Thiamin	18%
Unsaturated	8	Riboflavin	16%
Saturated	3	Niacin	42%
Dietary Fiber, g	6	Calcium	8%
Cholesterol, mg	70	Iron	16%
Sodium, mg	290		
Potassium, mg	940		

Chicken with Lentils (back) *(page 218), Herbed Chicken and Vegetables* (front)

Chicken with Lentils

3- to 3¹/₂-pound cut-up broiler-fryer
  chicken
2 tablespoons vegetable oil
1 cup dried lentils (about 7 ounces)
³/₄ cup sliced celery (about 1 large stalk)
¹/₂ cup chopped onion (about 1 medium)
¹/₂ cup dry white wine or apple juice
¹/₄ teaspoon salt
1¹/₂ teaspoons chopped fresh or ¹/₂ teaspoon
  dried thyme leaves
1 tablespoon chopped fresh parsley
1 can (16 ounces) whole tomatoes,
  undrained
1 large clove garlic, finely chopped

Remove skin and fat from chicken pieces. Heat
oil in nonstick Dutch oven or 12-inch skillet
until hot. Cook chicken in oil over medium heat
about 15 minutes or until light brown on all
sides; drain. Stir in remaining ingredients except parsley; break up tomatoes. Heat to boiling; reduce heat. Cover and simmer 35 to 40
minutes or until juices of chicken run clear and
the lentils are tender. Sprinkle with parsley.
6 servings

NUTRITION INFORMATION PER SERVING

1 serving		Percent of U.S. RDA	
Calories	255	Protein	42%
Protein, g	27	Vitamin A	6%
Carbohydrate, g	12	Vitamin C	12%
Fat, g	10	Thiamin	10%
Unsaturated	8	Riboflavin	12%
Saturated	2	Niacin	34%
Dietary Fiber, g	3	Calcium	6%
Cholesterol, mg	70	Iron	18%
Sodium, mg	370		
Potassium, mg	590		

Pepper Chicken

3- to 3¹/₂-pound cut-up broiler-fryer
  chicken
¹/₄ cup reduced-sodium soy sauce
1 tablespoon water
¹/₂ teaspoon garlic powder or 1 clove garlic,
  finely chopped
1 can (8 ounces) sliced water chestnuts,
  drained
1 medium green bell pepper, cut into 1-inch
  pieces
2 teaspoons cornstarch
2 tablespoons water

Remove skin and fat from chicken pieces. Place
chicken in nonstick Dutch oven or 12-inch skillet. Mix soy sauce, 1 tablespoon water and the
garlic powder; pour over chicken. Heat chicken
and soy sauce mixture to boiling; reduce heat.
Cover and simmer 50 minutes. Stir in water
chestnuts and bell pepper. Cover and simmer 5
to 10 minutes or until juices of chicken run
clear. Remove chicken; keep warm. Mix cornstarch and 2 tablespoons water; stir into liquid
in Dutch oven. Heat to boiling, stirring constantly, until mixture thickens and boils. Boil
and stir 1 minute. Serve chicken with sauce.
6 servings

NUTRITION INFORMATION PER SERVING

1 serving		Percent of U.S. RDA	
Calories	175	Protein	38%
Protein, g	24	Vitamin A	*
Carbohydrate, g	8	Vitamin C	10%
Fat, g	5	Thiamin	4%
Unsaturated	3	Riboflavin	10%
Saturated	2	Niacin	32%
Dietary Fiber, g	1	Calcium	2%
Cholesterol, mg	70	Iron	10%
Sodium, mg	470		
Potassium, mg	330		

Chicken with Apricots

3- to 3¹/₂-pound cut-up broiler-fryer
  chicken
¹/₂ cup water
¹/₄ cup apricot brandy or apricot nectar
2 tablespoons currants
1 package (6 ounces) dried apricots (about
  1¹/₄ cups)
2 tablespoons vegetable oil
1¹/₂ teaspoons chopped fresh or ¹/₂ teaspoon
  dried thyme leaves
¹/₂ teaspoon salt
¹/₄ teaspoon pepper
1 lemon, thinly sliced

Remove skin and fat from chicken pieces. Mix water, brandy, currants and apricots. Let stand 15 minutes.

Heat oil in nonstick Dutch oven or 12-inch skillet until hot. Cook chicken in oil over medium heat about 15 minutes or until light brown on all sides; drain. Sprinkle thyme, salt and pepper over chicken. Add apricot mixture and lemon. Heat to boiling; reduce heat. Cover and simmer 35 to 40 minutes, spooning pan juices over chicken occasionally, until juices of chicken run clear. *6 servings*

NUTRITION INFORMATION PER SERVING

1 serving		Percent of U.S. RDA	
Calories	285	Protein	38%
Protein, g	24	Vitamin A	20%
Carbohydrate, g	23	Vitamin C	*
Fat, g	10	Thiamin	4%
Unsaturated	8	Riboflavin	12%
Saturated	2	Niacin	32%
Dietary Fiber, g	2	Calcium	2%
Cholesterol, mg	70	Iron	16%
Sodium, mg	250		
Potassium, mg	640		

Oat-baked Chicken

3- to 3¹/₂-pound cut-up broiler-fryer
  chicken
2 tablespoons margarine
1 cup quick-cooking oats
¹/₄ cup grated Parmesan cheese
1 teaspoon paprika
¹/₂ teaspoon pepper
2 egg whites

Heat oven to 375°. Remove skin and fat from chicken pieces. Heat margarine in rectangular pan, 13×9×2 inches, in oven until melted. Mix remaining ingredients except egg whites. Dip chicken into egg whites; coat with oat mixture. Place meaty sides down in pan. Bake uncovered 30 minutes; turn. Bake 20 to 30 minutes longer or until juices run clear. *6 servings*

NUTRITION INFORMATION PER SERVING

1 serving		Percent of U.S. RDA	
Calories	250	Protein	44%
Protein, g	28	Vitamin A	8%
Carbohydrate, g	10	Vitamin C	*
Fat, g	11	Thiamin	10%
Unsaturated	8	Riboflavin	14%
Saturated	3	Niacin	30%
Dietary Fiber, g	1	Calcium	6%
Cholesterol, mg	70	Iron	10%
Sodium, mg	190		
Potassium, mg	300		

Cornmeal Chicken

3- to 3½-pound cut-up broiler-fryer
chicken
2 tablespoons margarine
2 tablespoons stone-ground or
degerminated cornmeal
¾ teaspoon chopped fresh or ¼ teaspoon
dried oregano leaves
½ teaspoon chile powder
Casera Sauce (below)

Heat oven to 375°. Remove skin and fat from chicken pieces. Heat margarine in rectangular pan, 13×9×2 inches, in oven until melted. Mix cornmeal, oregano and chile powder. Coat chicken with cornmeal mixture. Place meaty sides down in pan. Bake uncovered 30 minutes; turn. Bake 20 to 30 minutes longer or until brown and juices run clear. Serve with Casera Sauce.

Casera Sauce

¾ cup finely chopped tomato (about 1
medium)
¼ cup chopped onion (about 1 small)
2 teaspoons chopped fresh cilantro or
parsley
2 teaspoons lemon juice
¾ teaspoon chopped fresh or ¼ teaspoon
dried oregano leaves
1 small clove garlic, crushed
1 canned green chile or jalapeño chile,
seeded and finely chopped

Mix all ingredients.

NUTRITION INFORMATION PER SERVING			
I serving		Percent of U.S. RDA	
Calories	195	Protein	36%
Protein, g	24	Vitamin A	8%
Carbohydrate, g	5	Vitamin C	6%
Fat, g	9	Thiamin	6%
Unsaturated	7	Riboflavin	10%
Saturated	2	Niacin	30%
Dietary Fiber, g	1	Calcium	2%
Cholesterol, mg	70	Iron	8%
Sodium, mg	130		
Potassium, mg	300		

Wine-poached Chicken Breasts

4 skinless boneless chicken breast halves
(about 1 pound)
½ cup dry white wine or chicken broth
1 tablespoon lemon juice
¼ teaspoon salt

Remove excess fat from chicken; place chicken and remaining ingredients in 10-inch nonstick skillet. Heat to boiling; reduce heat. Cover and simmer until chicken is done, about 10 minutes.
4 servings

NUTRITION INFORMATION PER SERVING			
I serving		Percent of U.S. RDA	
Calories	150	Protein	40%
Protein, g	26	Vitamin A	*
Carbohydrate, g	1	Vitamin C	*
Fat, g	3	Thiamin	4%
Unsaturated	2	Riboflavin	6%
Saturated	1	Niacin	42%
Dietary Fiber, g	0	Calcium	2%
Cholesterol, mg	65	Iron	6%
Sodium, mg	200		
Potassium, mg	270		

Tarragon Chicken and Leeks

4 skinless boneless chicken breast halves
   (about 1 pound)
1 cup sliced leeks (about 2 medium)
¾ cup evaporated skimmed milk
1 tablespoon Dijon mustard
1½ teaspoons chopped fresh or ½ teaspoon
   dried tarragon leaves
1 teaspoon cornstarch

Spray 10-inch skillet with nonstick cooking spray. Cook chicken breast halves in skillet over medium heat 12 to 14 minutes, turning once, until juices run clear. Remove chicken from skillet; keep warm.

Cook leeks in skillet about 3 minutes, stirring frequently, until crisp-tender. Mix remaining ingredients; stir into leeks. Heat to boiling, stirring occasionally. Boil and stir about 1 minute or until slightly thickened. Add chicken; heat through. *4 servings*

NUTRITION INFORMATION PER SERVING

1 serving		Percent of U.S. RDA	
Calories	190	Protein	46%
Protein, g	30	Vitamin A	6%
Carbohydrate, g	8	Vitamin C	4%
Fat, g	4	Thiamin	4%
Unsaturated	3	Riboflavin	16%
Saturated	1	Niacin	42%
Dietary Fiber, g	0	Calcium	16%
Cholesterol, mg	70	Iron	8%
Sodium, mg	170		
Potassium, mg	460		

Creamy Spinach and Chicken Sauté

6 skinless boneless chicken breast halves
   (about 1½ pounds)
1 cup low-fat milk
½ cup chicken broth
½ cup chopped onion (about 1 medium)
7 cups chopped spinach (about 9 ounces)
¼ teaspoon salt
¼ teaspoon pepper
¼ teaspoon ground nutmeg

Spray 12-inch skillet with nonstick cooking spray. Heat skillet over medium heat. Cook chicken in skillet 2 minutes on each side. Reduce heat to medium-low. Add milk, broth and onion. Cook 5 minutes, turning chicken occasionally, until onion is tender. Add spinach. Cook 3 to 4 minutes, stirring occasionally, until spinach is completely wilted and juices of chicken run clear. Remove chicken from skillet; keep warm. Increase heat to medium. Cook spinach mixture about 3 minutes or until liquid has almost evaporated. Stir in salt, pepper and nutmeg. Serve chicken on top of spinach. *6 servings*

NUTRITION INFORMATION PER SERVING

1 serving		Percent of U.S. RDA	
Calories	170	Protein	44%
Protein, g	28	Vitamin A	56%
Carbohydrate, g	6	Vitamin C	16%
Fat, g	4	Thiamin	8%
Unsaturated	2	Riboflavin	16%
Saturated	2	Niacin	42%
Dietary Fiber, g	2	Calcium	12%
Cholesterol, mg	65	Iron	16%
Sodium, mg	280		
Potassium, mg	690		

Tropical Chicken Rolls

4 skinless boneless chicken breast halves
  (about 1 pound)
1 cup finely chopped bell pepper (about 1
  medium)
3 tablespoons grated Parmesan cheese
2 tablespoons pine nuts, finely chopped
1 tablespoon vegetable oil
⅛ teaspoon salt
⅛ teaspoon pepper
1 clove garlic, finely chopped
Mango-Papaya Relish (below)

Flatten each chicken breast half to ¼-inch thickness between plastic wrap or waxed paper. Mix remaining ingredients except Mango-Papaya Relish. Spread one quarter of bell pepper mixture on each chicken breast half to within ½ inch of edges. Roll up tightly; secure with toothpicks.

Set oven control to broil. Place chicken, seam sides down, on rack in broiler pan. Broil with tops 4 to 5 inches from heat 25 to 30 minutes or until juices of chicken run clear. Remove toothpicks. Cut each roll into ½-inch slices. Serve with Mango-Papaya Relish. *4 servings*

Mango-Papaya Relish

1 jalapeño chile, seeded and finely chopped
2 tablespoons sliced green onions
2 tablespoons chopped fresh cilantro
1 tablespoon finely chopped gingerroot
2 tablespoons lime juice
1 large mango, peeled and chopped
1 large papaya, peeled, seeded and chopped

Mix all ingredients.

NUTRITION INFORMATION PER SERVING			
1 serving		Percent of U.S. RDA	
Calories	310	Protein	46%
Protein, g	29	Vitamin A	36%
Carbohydrate, g	24	Vitamin C	100%
Fat, g	11	Thiamin	12%
Unsaturated	8	Riboflavin	12%
Saturated	3	Niacin	46%
Dietary Fiber, g	5	Calcium	10%
Cholesterol, mg	70	Iron	10%
Sodium, mg	210		
Potassium, mg	720		

Tangy Pineapple Chicken

This wonderfully refreshing salsa serves as both marinade and accompaniment. Pineapple salsa is also delicious served with tuna.

6 skinless boneless chicken breast halves
  (about 1½ pounds)
Pineapple Salsa (right)
¼ cup pineapple juice or water

Place chicken in shallow glass or plastic dish. Prepare Pineapple Salsa. Place 1 cup of the salsa in blender. Add pineapple juice. Cover and blend about 30 seconds or until pureed; pour over chicken. Cover and refrigerate at least 2 hours. Cover and refrigerate remaining salsa.

Set oven control to broil. Spray broiler pan with nonstick cooking spray. Remove chicken from marinade; place in pan. Broil chicken with tops 5 to 7 inches from heat 7 to 10 minutes or until juices run clear. Serve with salsa. *6 servings*

Pineapple Salsa

2 cups chopped fresh pineapple

2 tablespoons chopped green onions

1 tablespoon finely chopped fresh hot chile

1 tablespoon chopped fresh cilantro

2 teaspoons finely chopped gingerroot

1 teaspoon grated lemon peel

1/2 teaspoon salt

1/2 teaspoon ground cumin

Mix all ingredients. Cover and refrigerate until serving time.

FANCY PINEAPPLE-PASTA SALAD: Omit chicken. Prepare Pineapple Salsa in large glass or plastic bowl. Stir in the pineapple juice (do not use water) and 3 cups cooked tricolor pasta spirals (about 8 ounces uncooked). Cover and refrigerate about 2 hours or until chilled.

NUTRITION INFORMATION PER SERVING			
I serving		Percent of U.S. RDA	
Calories	170	Protein	40%
Protein, g	26	Vitamin A	2%
Carbohydrate, g	8	Vitamin C	10%
Fat, g	4	Thiamin	6%
Unsaturated	3	Riboflavin	8%
Saturated	1	Niacin	42%
Dietary Fiber, g	1	Calcium	2%
Cholesterol, mg	65	Iron	8%
Sodium, mg	240		
Potassium, mg	330		

Lemon-Dill Chicken

1/2 cup chopped onion (about 1 medium)

1/2 cup chicken broth

1/4 cup lemon juice

2 teaspoons dried dill weed

1/4 teaspoon salt

1/4 teaspoon pepper

2 cloves garlic, finely chopped

6 skinless boneless chicken breast halves (about 1 1/2 pounds)

Mix all ingredients except chicken breast halves in glass or plastic dish. Add chicken; turn to coat with marinade. Cover and refrigerate at least 3 hours but no longer than 24 hours.

Set oven control to broil. Spray broiler pan with nonstick cooking spray. Remove chicken from marinade; reserve marinade. Place chicken in pan. Broil chicken with tops 5 to 7 inches from heat 7 minutes; turn. Brush with marinade. Broil about 7 minutes longer or until juices run clear. *6 servings*

NUTRITION INFORMATION PER SERVING			
I serving		Percent of U.S. RDA	
Calories	150	Protein	60%
Protein, g	27	Vitamin A	*
Carbohydrate, g	2	Vitamin C	2%
Fat, g	4	Thiamin	4%
Unsaturated	3	Riboflavin	6%
Saturated	1	Niacin	42%
Dietary Fiber, g	0	Calcium	2%
Cholesterol, mg	65	Iron	6%
Sodium, mg	220		
Potassium, mg	300		

Curried Chicken Breasts

6 skinless boneless chicken breast halves
  (about 1½ pounds)
⅔ cup plain nonfat yogurt
1 teaspoon ground coriander
1 teaspoon ground ginger
1 teaspoon sesame seed
¼ teaspoon ground red pepper (cayenne)
⅛ teaspoon ground turmeric
4 cloves garlic, crushed
3 large onions, thinly sliced
1 tablespoon margarine
Paprika
1 small cucumber

Place chicken in ungreased rectangular baking dish, 13×9×2 inches. Mix yogurt, coriander, ginger, sesame seed, red pepper, turmeric and garlic; pour over chicken. Turn chicken to coat with marinade. Cover and refrigerate at least 4 hours, but no longer than 24 hours.

Heat oven to 350°. Cook onions in margarine in 10-inch nonstick skillet over medium heat about 10 minutes, stirring frequently, until onions are tender. Remove chicken from baking dish; stir onions into yogurt mixture in baking dish. Place chicken on onion mixture. Sprinkle with paprika. Bake uncovered about 1 hour or until juices of chicken run clear. Cut cucumber lengthwise into halves; remove seeds. Chop cucumber; sprinkle over chicken. *6 servings*

NUTRITION INFORMATION PER SERVING

1 serving		Percent of U.S. RDA	
Calories	210	Protein	44%
Protein, g	29	Vitamin A	4%
Carbohydrate, g	10	Vitamin C	6%
Fat, g	6	Thiamin	6%
Unsaturated	4	Riboflavin	10%
Saturated	2	Niacin	42%
Dietary Fiber, g	2	Calcium	8%
Cholesterol, mg	70	Iron	8%
Sodium, mg	110		
Potassium, mg	470		

Curried Chicken Breasts

Broiled Sage Chicken

Polenta Sauté (page 127) is a great side dish to serve with this chicken.

2 tablespoons chopped fresh or 2 teaspoons
    dried sage leaves
2 tablespoons chopped shallot (about 1
    large)
2 tablespoons low-fat sour cream
2 tablespoons lime juice
2 teaspoons Dijon mustard
½ teaspoon salt
¼ teaspoon pepper
6 skinless boneless chicken breast halves
    (about 1½ pounds)

Mix all ingredients except chicken breast halves in large glass or plastic dish. Add chicken; turn to coat with marinade. Cover and refrigerate at least 3 hours.

Set oven control to broil. Spray broiler pan with nonstick cooking spray. Place chicken in pan. Broil chicken with tops 5 to 7 inches from heat 5 minutes; turn. Broil about 5 minutes longer or until juices run clear. *6 servings*

NUTRITION INFORMATION PER SERVING

1 serving		Percent of U.S. RDA	
Calories	150	Protein	58%
Protein, g	26	Vitamin A	2%
Carbohydrate, g	2	Vitamin C	*
Fat, g	4	Thiamin	4%
Unsaturated	3	Riboflavin	6%
Saturated	1	Niacin	42%
Dietary Fiber, g	0	Calcium	2%
Cholesterol, mg	70	Iron	6%
Sodium, mg	270		
Potassium, mg	270		

Mediterranean Chicken Kabobs

24 chicken tenders (about 1½ pounds)
¾ cup white wine or apple juice
¼ cup chopped fresh parsley
¼ cup chicken broth
1 tablespoon chopped fresh or 1 teaspoon
    dried marjoram leaves
2 tablespoons cholesterol-free reduced-
    calorie mayonnaise or salad dressing
2 teaspoons honey
½ teaspoon salt
¼ teaspoon pepper

Place chicken tenders in shallow glass or plastic dish. Place remaining ingredients in blender. Cover and blend 30 seconds; pour over chicken. Cover and refrigerate 1 to 2 hours.

Set oven control to broil. Spray rack of broiler pan with nonstick cooking spray. Remove chicken from marinade; reserve marinade. Thread 2 chicken tenders on each of twelve 10-inch skewers.* Place skewers on rack in pan. Broil chicken with tops 5 to 7 inches from heat 3 minutes; turn. Spoon marinade over chicken. Broil about 3 minutes longer or until chicken is white. *6 servings*

* If using bamboo skewers, soak in water at least 30 minutes before using to prevent burning.

NUTRITION INFORMATION PER SERVING

1 serving		Percent of U.S. RDA	
Calories	160	Protein	54%
Protein, g	25	Vitamin A	2%
Carbohydrate, g	3	Vitamin C	2%
Fat, g	5	Thiamin	2%
Unsaturated	4	Riboflavin	6%
Saturated	1	Niacin	40%
Dietary Fiber, g	0	Calcium	2%
Cholesterol, mg	60	Iron	6%
Sodium, mg	300		
Potassium, mg	270		

Spring Chicken Pasta

Spring Chicken Pasta

8 ounces uncooked spaghetti

1 pound asparagus, cut into 2-inch pieces

8 chopped sun-dried tomatoes (not oil-
packed)

2 cloves garlic, finely chopped

1½ cups chopped yellow bell peppers
(about 1½ medium)

¾ cup chopped red onion (about 1 medium)

2 cups chicken broth

1½ pounds skinless boneless chicken breast
halves, cut into ½-inch strips

¾ cup nonfat ricotta cheese

⅓ cup chopped fresh basil leaves

2 tablespoons low-fat sour cream

½ teaspoon salt

¼ teaspoon pepper

Cook spaghetti as directed on package—except omit salt; drain. Cook asparagus, tomatoes, garlic, bell peppers, onion and broth in 3-quart saucepan over medium heat 5 minutes. Stir in chicken. Cook 2 to 3 minutes, stirring constantly, until asparagus is crisp-tender and chicken is white. Stir in spaghetti and remaining ingredients. Toss about 30 seconds or until heated through. *6 servings*

NUTRITION INFORMATION PER SERVING

1 serving		Percent of U.S. RDA	
Calories	370	Protein	56%
Protein, g	37	Vitamin A	24%
Carbohydrate, g	40	Vitamin C	52%
Fat, g	7	Thiamin	22%
Unsaturated	4	Riboflavin	20%
Saturated	3	Niacin	56%
Dietary Fiber, g	3	Calcium	16%
Cholesterol, mg	75	Iron	20%
Sodium, mg	540		
Potassium, mg	620		

Stir-fried Chicken and Vegetables

To make slicing raw chicken easier, partially freeze it for about 1½ hours.

4 skinless boneless chicken breast halves (about 1 pound), cut into 1½×¼-inch strips
1 egg white
1 teaspoon cornstarch
1 teaspoon reduced-sodium soy sauce
6 ounces Chinese pea pods or 1 package (6 ounces) frozen Chinese pea pods, partially thawed
1 tablespoon vegetable oil
2 cloves garlic, finely chopped
1 teaspoon finely chopped gingerroot
3 cups ¼-inch diagonal slices celery (about 6 medium stalks)
2 cups sliced mushrooms (about 6 ounces)
1 can (8 ounces) sliced water chestnuts, drained
1 can (8 ounces) sliced bamboo shoots, drained
1 tablespoon vegetable oil
¾ cup chicken broth
½ teaspoon sugar
¼ cup cold water
2 tablespoons cornstarch
1 teaspoon reduced-sodium soy sauce

Mix chicken, egg white, 1 teaspoon cornstarch and 1 teaspoon soy sauce in glass or plastic bowl. Cover and refrigerate 30 minutes.

Meanwhile, remove strings from fresh pea pods or rinse frozen pea pods with cold water to separate; drain. Heat 1 tablespoon oil in wok or 12-inch nonstick skillet until hot. Add garlic and gingerroot; stir-fry over medium heat until light brown. Add pea pods and celery; stir-fry 1 minute. Add mushrooms, water chestnuts and bamboo shoots; stir-fry 1 minute. Remove vegetables with slotted spoon.

Heat 1 tablespoon oil in wok until hot. Add chicken; stir-fry over high heat about 2 minutes or until white. Stir in broth and sugar. Heat to boiling; reduce heat. Cover and simmer 2 minutes, stirring occasionally. Mix cold water, 2 tablespoons cornstarch and 1 teaspoon soy sauce; stir into chicken mixture. Heat to boiling, stirring constantly. Boil and stir 1 minute. Add vegetables; cook and stir 1 to 2 minutes or until hot. *4 servings*

NUTRITION INFORMATION PER SERVING			
1 serving		**Percent of U.S. RDA**	
Calories	315	Protein	50%
Protein, g	32	Vitamin A	2%
Carbohydrate, g	22	Vitamin C	24%
Fat, g	11	Thiamin	12%
Unsaturated	9	Riboflavin	24%
Saturated	2	Niacin	56%
Dietary Fiber, g	5	Calcium	8%
Cholesterol, mg	65	Iron	18%
Sodium, mg	390		
Potassium, mg	840		

Chicken Satay with Cucumber Sauce

Satay, marinated meat broiled or grilled on skewers, is becoming an American favorite as Thai and Indonisian cuisines become more popular. Here it's served as a main dish, but it can also easily make 8 appetizer servings.

3 tablespoons lime juice
1 teaspoon curry powder
2 teaspoons honey
½ teaspoon ground coriander
½ teaspoon ground cumin
⅛ teaspoon salt
2 cloves garlic, finely chopped
1 pound skinless boneless chicken breast
   halves, cut into 1-inch cubes
Cucumber Sauce (right)

Mix all ingredients except chicken and Cucumber Sauce in medium glass or plastic bowl. Stir in chicken. Cover and refrigerate at least 2 hours, stirring occasionally. Prepare Cucumber Sauce.

Set oven control to broil. Spray broiler pan rack with nonstick cooking spray. Remove chicken from marinade; reserve marinade. Thread chicken on eight 8-inch skewers,* leaving space between each piece. Place skewers on rack in broiler pan. Broil with tops about 3 inches from heat 4 minutes; turn. Brush with marinade. Broil 4 to 5 minutes longer or until chicken is white. Serve with sauce. *4 servings*

Cucumber Sauce

1 tablespoon sugar
2 tablespoons rice wine vinegar
1 tablespoon water
Dash of ground red pepper (cayenne)
¾ cup shredded seeded peeled cucumber
¼ cup finely chopped red or green bell
   pepper

Heat sugar, vinegar, water and red pepper to boiling in 1-quart saucepan; remove from heat. Stir in cucumber and bell pepper; cool.

* If using bamboo skewers, soak in water at least 30 minutes before using to prevent burning.

NUTRITION INFORMATION PER SERVING			
1 serving		Percent of U.S. RDA	
Calories	165	Protein	38%
Protein, g	25	Vitamin A	4%
Carbohydrate, g	9	Vitamin C	12%
Fat, g	3	Thiamin	4%
Unsaturated	2	Riboflavin	6%
Saturated	1	Niacin	40%
Dietary Fiber, g	0	Calcium	2%
Cholesterol, mg	60	Iron	8%
Sodium, mg	130		
Potassium, mg	300		

*Stir-fried Chicken and Vegetables (page 227),
Chicken Satay with Cucumber Sauce*

Sichuan Chicken

4 skinless boneless chicken breast halves
   (about 1 pound), cut into ¼-inch pieces
1 egg white
1 teaspoon cornstarch
1 teaspoon reduced-sodium soy sauce
1 tablespoon cornstarch
1 tablespoon cold water
1 tablespoon reduced-sodium soy sauce
1 tablespoon vegetable oil
1 tablespoon vegetable oil
1 medium onion, cut into 1-inch pieces
2 cloves garlic, finely chopped
1 large green bell pepper, cut into 1-inch
   pieces
1 can (8 ounces) sliced bamboo shoots,
   drained
2 tablespoons chile sauce
1 teaspoon finely chopped dried chile or ¼
   teaspoon crushed red pepper
¼ cup chicken broth

Mix chicken, egg white, 1 teaspoon cornstarch and 1 teaspoon soy sauce in glass or plastic bowl. Cover and refrigerate 20 minutes.

Mix 1 tablespoon cornstarch, the cold water and 1 tablespoon soy sauce; reserve. Heat 1 tablespoon oil in wok or 12-inch nonstick skillet over medium-high heat until hot. Add chicken; stir-fry until white. Remove chicken from wok.

Heat 1 tablespoon oil in wok until hot. Add onion and garlic; stir-fry until garlic is light brown. Add chicken, bell pepper, bamboo shoots, chile sauce and chile; stir-fry 1 minute. Stir in broth. Heat to boiling. Stir in cornstarch mixture; cook and stir about 30 seconds or until thickened. Sprinkle with chopped green onions if desired. *4 servings*

NUTRITION INFORMATION PER SERVING			
1 serving		Percent of U.S. RDA	
Calories	260	Protein	44%
Protein, g	29	Vitamin A	4%
Carbohydrate, g	11	Vitamin C	22%
Fat, g	11	Thiamin	8%
Unsaturated	9	Riboflavin	12%
Saturated	2	Niacin	46%
Dietary Fiber, g	2	Calcium	4%
Cholesterol, mg	65	Iron	10%
Sodium, mg	420		
Potassium, mg	460		

Chicken Pilaf

If you'd like, omit the chicken and you'll have a savory rice side dish.

1 cup uncooked regular long grain rice
1½ cups chopped onions (about 3 medium)
1 cup dry white wine or apple juice
1 tablespoon chopped fresh or 1 teaspoon
   dried thyme leaves
¼ teaspoon pepper
3 to 3½ cups chicken broth*
1½ pounds skinless boneless chicken breast
   halves, cut into 2-inch pieces
1 package (10 ounces) frozen green peas,
   separated
3 tablespoons chopped fresh parsley

Spray 3-quart saucepan with nonstick cooking spray. Heat pan over medium-high heat. Heat rice in pan about 5 minutes, stirring occasionally, until light brown; reduce heat to medium. Stir in onions, wine, thyme and pepper. Cook 2 minutes or until liquid has evaporated. Stir in 1 cup of the broth. Cook 4 to 5 minutes, stirring occasionally, until liquid has evaporated. Stir in additional 1 cup broth. Cook 4 to 5 minutes, stirring occasionally, until liquid has evaporated.

Stir in chicken, peas and 1 cup of the remaining broth. Cover and cook 5 minutes. Stir in remaining ½ cup broth if needed to keep rice from sticking. Cover and cook about 5 minutes or until liquid has evaporated and rice is tender and chicken is white; remove from heat. Stir in parsley. *6 servings*

* The amount of broth will vary depending on the absorbency of the rice.

NUTRITION INFORMATION PER SERVING

1 serving		Percent of U.S. RDA	
Calories	330	Protein	48%
Protein, g	32	Vitamin A	4%
Carbohydrate, g	35	Vitamin C	6%
Fat, g	4	Thiamin	22%
Unsaturated	3	Riboflavin	12%
Saturated	1	Niacin	56%
Dietary Fiber, g	4	Calcium	6%
Cholesterol, mg	60	Iron	20%
Sodium, mg	490		
Potassium, mg	540		

Drumsticks with Yogurt Sauce

8 chicken drumsticks (about 1¾ pounds)
2 teaspoons margarine
½ teaspoon paprika
¼ teaspoon salt
½ teaspoon fresh or ¼ teaspoon dried
    dill weed
⅓ cup chicken broth
1 medium onion, sliced

½ cup plain nonfat yogurt
1½ teaspoons cornstarch
¼ cup cold water

Remove skin and fat from chicken drumsticks. Cook drumsticks in margarine in 10-inch nonstick skillet over medium heat until brown on all sides; drain. Sprinkle with paprika, salt and dill weed. Pour broth over chicken; add onion. Heat to boiling; reduce heat. Cover and simmer about 30 minutes or until juices of chicken run clear.

Remove drumsticks from skillet; keep warm. Stir yogurt into liquid in skillet. Mix cornstarch and cold water; gradually stir into yogurt mixture. Heat to boiling, stirring constantly. Boil and stir 1 minute. Pour yogurt sauce over drumsticks. *4 servings*

NUTRITION INFORMATION PER SERVING

1 serving		Percent of U.S. RDA	
Calories	195	Protein	44%
Protein, g	29	Vitamin A	4%
Carbohydrate, g	6	Vitamin C	2%
Fat, g	6	Thiamin	4%
Unsaturated	4	Riboflavin	10%
Saturated	2	Niacin	44%
Dietary Fiber, g	1	Calcium	8%
Cholesterol, mg	70	Iron	6%
Sodium, mg	310		
Potassium, mg	390		

Southwestern Drumsticks with Casera Sauce (page 220) and Corn Bread (page 81)

Wheat-stuffed Drumsticks

¾ **cup uncooked cracked wheat**

¾ **cup cold water**

⅓ **cup chopped green onions (about 3 medium)**

¼ **teaspoon salt**

¼ **teaspoon ground sage**

⅛ **teaspoon pepper**

8 **chicken drumsticks (about 1¾ pounds)**

2 **tablespoons margarine**

½ **cup whole wheat flour**

1 **teaspoon paprika**

¼ **teaspoon salt**

¼ **teaspoon ground sage**

¼ **teaspoon pepper**

Cover cracked wheat with cold water. Let stand 1 hour.

Heat oven to 375°. Mix cracked wheat mixture, onions, ¼ teaspoon salt, ¼ teaspoon sage and ⅛ teaspoon pepper. Carefully separate skin from meat all around each chicken drumstick, beginning at wide end. Fill opening between meat and skin with wheat mixture. Wipe off excess filling on outside of drumstick.

Heat margarine in rectangular pan, 13×9×2 inches, in oven until melted. Mix flour, paprika, ¼ teaspoon salt, ¼ teaspoon sage and ¼ teaspoon pepper. Coat drumsticks with flour mixture; place in pan. Bake uncovered 30 minutes; turn. Bake about 30 minutes longer or until juices of chicken run clear. *4 servings*

NUTRITION INFORMATION PER SERVING			
I serving		**Percent of U.S. RDA**	
Calories	330	Protein	50%
Protein, g	32	Vitamin A	12%
Carbohydrate, g	28	Vitamin C	*
Fat, g	10	Thiamin	14%
Unsaturated	8	Riboflavin	12%
Saturated	2	Niacin	54%
Dietary Fiber, g	4	Calcium	4%
Cholesterol, mg	70	Iron	16%
Sodium, mg	270		
Potassium, mg	440		

Southwestern Drumsticks

☒

No doubt about it, these drumsticks really are best when served with Casera Sauce (page 220).

8 chicken drumsticks (about 1¾ pounds)
⅔ cup stone-ground or degerminated
   cornmeal
1 teaspoon ground cumin
1 teaspoon chile powder
¼ teaspoon salt
⅓ cup nonfat buttermilk
¼ teaspoon red pepper sauce
2 teaspoons vegetable oil
Casera Sauce (page 220), if desired

Heat oven to 400°. Spray rectangular pan, 13×9×2 inches, with nonstick cooking spray. Remove skin and fat from chicken drumsticks. Mix cornmeal, cumin, chile powder and salt in large plastic bag. Mix buttermilk and pepper sauce in medium bowl. Dip drumsticks in buttermilk mixture; shake in bag to coat with cornmeal mixture. Place in pan. Drizzle with 2 teaspoons oil or spray lightly with oil. Bake uncovered 40 to 45 minutes or until juices run clear. Serve with Casera Sauce if desired.
4 servings

NUTRITION INFORMATION PER SERVING			
1 serving		Percent of U.S. RDA	
Calories	250	Protein	44%
Protein, g	29	Vitamin A	4%
Carbohydrate, g	19	Vitamin C	*
Fat, g	6	Thiamin	14%
Unsaturated	4	Riboflavin	14%
Saturated	2	Niacin	48%
Dietary Fiber, g	1	Calcium	4%
Cholesterol, mg	70	Iron	14%
Sodium, mg	230		
Potassium, mg	330		

Balsamic Chicken

☒

½ cup white wine or apple juice
½ cup chicken broth
1 tablespoon chopped fresh or ½ teaspoon
   dried thyme leaves
2 tablespoons lemon juice
2 tablespoons balsamic vinegar
2 teaspoons grated lemon peel
1 teaspoon paprika
½ teaspoon salt
¼ teaspoon pepper
12 skinless boneless chicken thighs or 6
   breast halves (about 1½ pounds)

Mix all ingredients except chicken thighs in shallow glass or plastic dish. Add chicken; turn to coat with marinade. Cover and refrigerate at least 2 hours.

Place chicken and marinade in 10-inch nonstick skillet. Heat to boiling; reduce heat. Cover and simmer 15 to 20 minutes or until juices of chicken run clear. Remove chicken; keep warm. Heat marinade to boiling. Boil about 6 minutes or until liquid is reduced by half. Pour over chicken. *6 servings*

NUTRITION INFORMATION PER SERVING			
1 serving		Percent of U.S. RDA	
Calories	210	Protein	46%
Protein, g	29	Vitamin A	2%
Carbohydrate, g	1	Vitamin C	*
Fat, g	9	Thiamin	4%
Unsaturated	6	Riboflavin	16%
Saturated	3	Niacin	28%
Dietary Fiber, g	0	Calcium	2%
Cholesterol, mg	95	Iron	12%
Sodium, mg	330		
Potassium, mg	330		

Tarragon-Garlic Chicken

🔲

¹⁄₃ cup chopped red onion (about ¹⁄₂ small)

¹⁄₂ cup nonfat buttermilk

2 tablespoons chopped fresh or 2 teaspoons
dried tarragon leaves

1 tablespoon tarragon vinegar or wine
vinegar

¹⁄₂ teaspoon salt

¹⁄₄ teaspoon pepper

¹⁄₈ teaspoon crushed red pepper

2 cloves garlic, finely chopped

12 skinless boneless chicken thighs (about
1¹⁄₂ pounds)

Mix all ingredients except chicken thighs in
large glass or plastic dish. Add chicken; turn to
coat with marinade. Cover and refrigerate at
least 3 hours.

Set oven control to broil. Spray broiler pan with
nonstick cooking spray. Remove chicken from
marinade; reserve marinade. Place chicken in
pan. Broil chicken with tops 5 to 7 inches from
heat 5 minutes; turn. Brush with marinade.
Broil about 5 minutes longer or until juices run
clear. *6 servings*

NUTRITION INFORMATION PER SERVING			
1 serving		Percent of U.S. RDA	
Calories	210	Protein	66%
Protein, g	30	Vitamin A	*
Carbohydrate, g	2	Vitamin C	*
Fat, g	9	Thiamin	6%
Unsaturated	6	Riboflavin	16%
Saturated	3	Niacin	26%
Dietary Fiber, g	0	Calcium	4%
Cholesterol, mg	95	Iron	10%
Sodium, mg	290		
Potassium, mg	330		

Tarragon-Garlic Chicken

Rosemary-Mustard Chicken

Savory Focaccia (page 107) and a tossed green salad dressed with Creamy Tomato Dressing (page 151) are all you need to serve with this dish for a memorable meal.

3 tablespoons low-fat sour cream
3 tablespoons Dijon mustard
2 teaspoons fresh or 1 teaspoon dried rosemary leaves, crushed
¼ teaspoon white pepper
12 skinless boneless chicken thighs (about 1½ pounds)

Mix all ingredients except chicken thighs in large glass or plastic dish. Add chicken; turn to coat with marinade. Cover and refrigerate at least 3 hours.

Heat oven to 400°. Spray rectangular pan, 13×9×2 inches, with nonstick cooking spray. Place chicken in pan. Bake about 20 minutes or until juices run clear. Serve with low-fat sour cream and crushed rosemary if desired. *6 servings*

NUTRITION INFORMATION PER SERVING			
1 serving		**Percent of U.S. RDA**	
Calories	220	Protein	66%
Protein, g	30	Vitamin A	2%
Carbohydrate, g	2	Vitamin C	*
Fat, g	10	Thiamin	4%
Unsaturated	7	Riboflavin	16%
Saturated	3	Niacin	26%
Dietary Fiber, g	0	Calcium	4%
Cholesterol, mg	95	Iron	12%
Sodium, mg	190		
Potassium, mg	300		

Crispy Deviled Chicken

⅓ cup cholesterol-free egg product or Egg Substitute (page 28)
2 tablespoons chicken broth
1 tablespoon Dijon mustard
1 clove garlic, finely chopped
1½ cups dry whole wheat or white bread crumbs
3 tablespoons fresh or 1 tablespoon dried basil leaves
1 teaspoon paprika
¼ teaspoon white pepper
12 skinless boneless chicken thighs (about 1½ pounds)

Heat oven to 400°. Spray shallow roasting pan with nonstick cooking spray. Mix egg product, broth, mustard and garlic in small bowl. In separate container, mix bread crumbs, basil, paprika and white pepper. Dip each chicken thigh into egg mixture and shake to remove excess. Coat with bread crumb mixture. Place in pan. Bake uncovered about 20 minutes or until juices run clear. *6 servings*

NUTRITION INFORMATION PER SERVING			
1 serving		**Percent of U.S. RDA**	
Calories	305	Protein	74%
Protein, g	34	Vitamin A	4%
Carbohydrate, g	20	Vitamin C	*
Fat, g	10	Thiamin	12%
Unsaturated	7	Riboflavin	22%
Saturated	3	Niacin	32%
Dietary Fiber, g	1	Calcium	8%
Cholesterol, mg	95	Iron	20%
Sodium, mg	350		
Potassium, mg	370		

Chicken Enchiladas

Chicken Enchiladas

Depending on your preference, use mild or hot bottled salsa for these lime-spiced enchiladas.

1 cup bottled mild green taco sauce or salsa

¼ cup cilantro sprigs

¼ cup parsley sprigs

1 tablespoon lime juice

2 cloves garlic

2 cups chopped cooked chicken or turkey

¾ cup shredded part-skim mozzarella cheese

6 flour tortillas (7 inches in diameter)

Heat oven to 350°. Spray rectangular baking dish, 11×7×1½ inches, with nonstick cooking spray. Place taco sauce, cilantro, parsley, lime juice and garlic in blender or food processor. Cover and blend on high speed about 30 seconds or until smooth. Reserve half of mixture.

Mix remaining salsa mixture, the chicken and ¼ cup of the cheese. Spoon about ¼ cup chicken mixture onto each tortilla. Roll tortilla around filling; place seam side down in baking dish. Pour remaining sauce over enchiladas. Sprinkle with remaining cheese. Bake uncovered 20 to 25 minutes or until hot. Serve with lime wedges if desired. *6 servings*

NUTRITION INFORMATION PER SERVING			
I serving		**Percent of U.S. RDA**	
Calories	320	Protein	34%
Protein, g	22	Vitamin A	8%
Carbohydrate, g	36	Vitamin C	6%
Fat, g	10	Thiamin	18%
Unsaturated	6	Riboflavin	16%
Saturated	4	Niacin	28%
Dietary Fiber, g	2	Calcium	16%
Cholesterol, mg	50	Iron	20%
Sodium, mg	750		
Potassium, mg	340		

Chicken Spaghetti

1 cup chopped onion (about 1 large)
1 cup water
1 tablespoon chopped fresh or 1 teaspoon
dried oregano leaves
2 teaspoons chopped fresh or ¾ teaspoon
dried basil leaves
1½ teaspoons chopped fresh or ½ teaspoon
dried marjoram leaves
1 teaspoon sugar
¾ teaspoon chopped fresh or ¼ teaspoon
dried rosemary leaves
1 clove garlic, crushed
1 bay leaf
1 can (8 ounces) tomato sauce
1 can (6 ounces) tomato paste
1½ cups cut-up cooked chicken or turkey
4 cups hot cooked spaghetti

Heat all ingredients except chicken and spaghetti to boiling in 10-inch skillet; reduce heat. Cover and simmer 30 minutes, stirring occasionally. Stir in chicken. Cover and simmer 30 minutes longer, stirring occasionally. Remove bay leaf. Serve sauce over spaghetti. *6 servings*

NUTRITION INFORMATION PER SERVING

1 serving		Percent of U.S. RDA	
Calories	245	Protein	26%
Protein, g	16	Vitamin A	10%
Carbohydrate, g	38	Vitamin C	14%
Fat, g	3	Thiamin	20%
Unsaturated	2	Riboflavin	14%
Saturated	1	Niacin	28%
Dietary Fiber, g	3	Calcium	4%
Cholesterol, mg	30	Iron	18%
Sodium, mg	610		
Potassium, mg	580		

Spicy Citrus Hens

3 Rock Cornish hens (about 1 pound each)
½ cup unsweetened grape juice or red wine
½ cup orange juice
½ cup lemon juice
2 tablespoons chopped fresh cilantro leaves
2 tablespoons chopped green onions
1 tablespoon grated orange peel
1 tablespoon grated lemon peel
1½ teaspoons chopped fresh or ½ teaspoon
dried oregano leaves
1 teaspoon ground cumin
½ teaspoon salt
¼ teaspoon crushed red pepper
Orange slices, if desired

Cut each hen into halves along backbone from tail to neck with kitchen scissors. Remove and discard skin and excess fat from hens. Place hens in shallow glass or plastic dish. Mix remaining ingredients; pour over hens. Cover and refrigerate at least 3 hours.

Heat oven to 375°. Spray rack in shallow roasting pan with nonstick cooking spray. Remove hens from marinade; place on rack. Reserve marinade. Bake 50 to 55 minutes, brushing with marinade every 15 minutes, until juices run clear. Serve with orange slices, if desired. *6 servings*

NUTRITION INFORMATION PER SERVING

1 serving		Percent of U.S. RDA	
Calories	240	Protein	56%
Protein, g	37	Vitamin A	2%
Carbohydrate, g	5	Vitamin C	14%
Fat, g	8	Thiamin	8%
Unsaturated	6	Riboflavin	14%
Saturated	2	Niacin	46%
Dietary Fiber, g	0	Calcium	4%
Cholesterol, mg	105	Iron	12%
Sodium, mg	280		
Potassium, mg	440		

Turkey with Vegetable Stuffing

1 cup sliced celery (about 2 medium stalks)

½ cup chopped onion (about 1 medium)

2 tablespoons margarine

¼ cup chopped fresh parsley

1 tablespoon chopped fresh or 1 teaspoon dried sage leaves

1½ teaspoons chopped fresh or ½ teaspoon dried marjoram leaves

¾ teaspoon chopped fresh or ¼ teaspoon dried tarragon leaves

½ teaspoon salt

7 cups soft bread cubes

1½ cups shredded carrots (about 2 medium)

1 cup shredded zucchini (about 1 medium)

1 cup chopped mushrooms (about 4 ounces)

12-pound turkey

Heat oven to 325°. Cook celery and onion in margarine in 10-inch nonstick skillet, stirring frequently, until onion is tender. Stir in parsley, sage, marjoram, tarragon and salt. Mix bread cubes, carrots, zucchini and mushrooms in large bowl. Add celery mixture; toss.

Fill wishbone area of turkey with stuffing first. Fasten neck skin to back with skewer. Fold wings across back with tips touching. Fill body cavity lightly with stuffing. (Place any remaining stuffing in small ungreased baking dish; cover and refrigerate. Place in oven with turkey the last 30 minutes of roasting.) Tuck drumsticks under band of skin at tail, or tie together with heavy string, then tie to tail. Place turkey, breast side up, on rack in shallow roasting pan. Insert meat thermometer so tip is in thickest part of inside thigh muscle or thickest part of breast meat and does not touch bone.

Roast uncovered 3½ to 4½ hours or until thermometer registers 180° or drumstick moves easily and juices of turkey run clear. When ⅔ done, cut band of skin or string holding legs. Place a tent of aluminum foil loosely over turkey when it begins to turn golden brown. Let turkey stand 20 minutes before carving. Remove and discard skin. Cover and refrigerate any remaining turkey and stuffing separately. *24 servings*

NUTRITION INFORMATION PER SERVING			
1 serving		Percent of U.S. RDA	
Calories	315	Protein	100%
Protein, g	48	Vitamin A	12%
Carbohydrate, g	6	Vitamin C	2%
Fat, g	11	Thiamin	10%
Unsaturated	8	Riboflavin	20%
Saturated	3	Niacin	62%
Dietary Fiber, g	1	Calcium	4%
Cholesterol, mg	135	Iron	16%
Sodium, mg	230		
Potassium, mg	520		

Braised Turkey Breast

4½- to 5-pound turkey breast
¼ cup all-purpose flour
1 tablespoon vegetable oil
½ cup chopped onion (about 1 medium)
½ cup chopped carrot (about 1 medium)
½ cup chopped celery (about 1 medium stalk)
1 cup chicken broth
½ cup dry white wine or chicken broth
1½ teaspoons chopped fresh or ½ teaspoon dried marjoram leaves
¼ teaspoon salt
¼ teaspoon pepper
1 clove garlic, finely chopped
1 bay leaf
2 tablespoons chopped fresh parsley
1 teaspoon grated lemon peel
1 clove garlic, finely chopped
1 tablespoon plus 1 teaspoon cornstarch
¼ cup cold water

Coat turkey breast with flour. Heat oil in non-stick Dutch oven until hot. Cook turkey in oil over medium heat about 20 minutes or until light brown on all sides; drain. Add onion, carrot, celery, broth, wine, marjoram, salt, pepper, 1 clove garlic and the bay leaf. Heat to boiling; reduce heat. Cover and simmer 2 to 2½ hours or until juices of turkey run clear. Mix parsley, lemon peel and 1 clove garlic; reserve. Remove turkey and vegetables from Dutch oven. Keep turkey and vegetables warm.

Remove bay leaf from pan drippings. Pour drippings into measuring cup; skim off fat. Add enough water to drippings, if necessary, to measure 2 cups; return to Dutch oven. Heat to boiling. Mix cornstarch and cold water; stir into drippings. Boil and stir 1 minute. Remove and discard turkey skin. Sprinkle parsley mixture over turkey. Serve turkey with sauce. *8 servings*

NUTRITION INFORMATION PER SERVING			
1 serving		**Percent of U.S. RDA**	
Calories	345	Protein	92%
Protein, g	59	Vitamin A	14%
Carbohydrate, g	7	Vitamin C	2%
Fat, g	9	Thiamin	10%
Unsaturated	6	Riboflavin	16%
Saturated	3	Niacin	96%
Dietary Fiber, g	1	Calcium	4%
Cholesterol, mg	145	Iron	16%
Sodium, mg	310		
Potassium, mg	650		

Turkey with Pineapple

4½- to 5-pound turkey breast

1 pineapple or 8 slices canned pineapple,
   cut into halves

½ cup dry white wine or pineapple juice

2 tablespoons honey

2 tablespoons reduced-sodium soy sauce

1 teaspoon finely chopped gingerroot or ½
   teaspoon ground ginger

1 large clove garlic, finely chopped

2 teaspoons cornstarch

2 tablespoons cold water

Heat oven to 325°. Place turkey breast, skin side up, on rack in shallow roasting pan. Insert meat thermometer so tip is in thickest part of meat and does not touch bone. Roast uncovered 1 hour.

Peel pineapple. Cut lengthwise into halves and remove core. Cut each half crosswise into 8 slices. Arrange pineapple on rack around turkey. Mix wine, honey, soy sauce, gingerroot and garlic; brush over turkey and pineapple. Roast uncovered about 1 hour longer, brushing turkey and pineapple frequently with wine mixture, until thermometer registers 170° or juices of turkey run clear. Remove turkey and pineapple from pan; keep warm.

Pour pan drippings into measuring cup; skim off fat. Add enough water to drippings to measure 1 cup. Heat drippings to boiling in 1-quart saucepan. Mix cornstarch and cold water; stir into drippings. Boil and stir 1 minute. Remove and discard turkey skin. Serve turkey with sauce. *8 servings*

NUTRITION INFORMATION PER SERVING

1 serving		Percent of U.S. RDA	
Calories	295	Protein	72%
Protein, g	47	Vitamin A	*
Carbohydrate, g	13	Vitamin C	14%
Fat, g	6	Thiamin	10%
Unsaturated	4	Riboflavin	12%
Saturated	2	Niacin	76%
Dietary Fiber, g	1	Calcium	2%
Cholesterol, mg	120	Iron	12%
Sodium, mg	260		
Potassium, mg	520		

Lemon Rice with Turkey

Brown rice has a hearty flavor that blends well with lemon. You may want to decrease the lemon juice to ¼ cup if using white rice.

1 cup chopped green onions (about 9 medium)
1 cup chicken broth
2 cloves garlic, finely chopped
1½-pound turkey breast, cut into 3×¼×¼-inch strips
3 cups cooked brown or white rice
⅓ cup lemon juice
1 tablespoon capers, rinsed and drained
2 teaspoons grated lemon peel
¼ teaspoon pepper
3 tablespoons chopped fresh parsley

Cook onions, broth and garlic in 12-inch skillet over medium heat 3 minutes, stirring occasionally, until onions are tender. Stir in turkey. Cook 3 minutes. Stir in remaining ingredients except parsley. Cook about 3 minutes or until rice is hot and turkey is white; remove from heat. Stir in parsley. *6 servings*

NUTRITION INFORMATION PER SERVING			
1 serving		Percent of U.S. RDA	
Calories	265	Protein	46%
Protein, g	30	Vitamin A	2%
Carbohydrate, g	25	Vitamin C	16%
Fat, g	5	Thiamin	10%
Unsaturated	4	Riboflavin	8%
Saturated	1	Niacin	52%
Dietary Fiber, g	2	Calcium	4%
Cholesterol, mg	65	Iron	10%
Sodium, mg	200		
Potassium, mg	390		

Fruit-stuffed Turkey Breast

1 package (6 ounces) diced dried fruits and raisins
½ cup apple cider or apple juice
1½ teaspoons chopped fresh or ½ teaspoon dried mint leaves
⅛ teaspoon salt
4- to 5-pound turkey breast

Heat oven to 375°. Heat dried fruits, apple cider, mint and salt to boiling in 1½-quart saucepan; reduce heat. Simmer uncovered 6 to 8 minutes or until fruit absorbs cider.

Gently loosen turkey breast skin with fingers, reaching as far back as possible without tearing skin. Spread fruit mixture over breast meat; cover with skin.

Place turkey, skin side up, in shallow roasting pan. Insert meat thermometer so tip is in thickest part of meat and does not touch bone. Cover tightly with aluminum foil. Bake 1 hour 45 minutes to 1 hour 55 minutes or until thermometer registers 170° or juices run clear. Let stand 15 minutes before carving. Remove and discard skin. Cut into 16 slices. Skim off fat from pan drippings. Serve drippings with turkey.
16 servings

NUTRITION INFORMATION PER SERVING			
1 serving		Percent of U.S. RDA	
Calories	145	Protein	46%
Protein, g	21	Vitamin A	2%
Carbohydrate, g	8	Vitamin C	*
Fat, g	3	Thiamin	2%
Unsaturated	2	Riboflavin	6%
Saturated	1	Niacin	34%
Dietary Fiber, g	1	Calcium	2%
Cholesterol, mg	55	Iron	6%
Sodium, mg	70		
Potassium, mg	280		

Fruit-stuffed Turkey Breast

Fettuccine with Turkey Marinara Sauce (page 247), Eggplant-Turkey Parmigiana

Eggplant-Turkey Parmigiana

½ cup fine dry bread crumbs

2 teaspoons chopped fresh or ½ teaspoon dried oregano leaves

6 turkey breast slices, ¼ inch thick (about 1½ pounds)

2 egg whites, slightly beaten

2 cups cubed peeled eggplant

1½ cups low-fat spaghetti sauce

½ cup shredded part-skim mozzarella cheese

½ cup grated Parmesan cheese

Heat oven to 375°. Spray 10-inch nonstick skillet with nonstick cooking spray. Mix bread crumbs and oregano. Dip turkey breast slices into egg whites; coat with bread crumb mixture. Heat skillet about 30 seconds. Cook half of turkey slices in skillet 3 to 4 minutes, turning once, until light brown. Repeat with remaining turkey.

Spray rectangular baking dish, 13×9×2 inches, with nonstick cooking spray. Place turkey in single layer in baking dish. Top with eggplant, spaghetti sauce and cheeses. Bake uncovered about 20 minutes or until cheese is bubbly and mixture is heated through. *6 servings*

NUTRITION INFORMATION PER SERVING			
1 serving		Percent of U.S. RDA	
Calories	210	Protein	40%
Protein, g	26	Vitamin A	8%
Carbohydrate, g	13	Vitamin C	6%
Fat, g	6	Thiamin	8%
Unsaturated	3	Riboflavin	14%
Saturated	3	Niacin	34%
Dietary Fiber, g	2	Calcium	18%
Cholesterol, mg	55	Iron	10%
Sodium, mg	670		
Potassium, mg	500		

Turkey with Confetti Vegetables

6 turkey breast slices, ¼ inch thick (about 1½ pounds)

¼ cup apple juice

3 cups broccoli flowerets

1 cup finely chopped red bell pepper (about 1 medium)

1 cup thinly sliced onion (about ½ medium)

½ cup apple juice

¼ teaspoon salt

¼ teaspoon pepper

2 tablespoons finely chopped fresh chives

Heat oven to 350°. Spray square pan, 9×9×2 inches, with nonstick cooking spray. Place turkey breast slices in pan. Pour ¼ cup apple juice over turkey. Cover with aluminum foil and bake about 20 minutes or until juices of turkey run clear.

Meanwhile, cook remaining ingredients except chives in 12-inch skillet over medium heat 8 to 12 minutes, stirring occasionally, until broccoli is tender and liquid has evaporated. Stir in chives. Serve over turkey. Sprinkle with lemon pepper if desired. *6 servings*

NUTRITION INFORMATION PER SERVING

1 serving		Percent of U.S. RDA	
Calories	185	Protein	42%
Protein, g	28	Vitamin A	14%
Carbohydrate, g	9	Vitamin C	56%
Fat, g	4	Thiamin	6%
Unsaturated	3	Riboflavin	10%
Saturated	1	Niacin	44%
Dietary Fiber, g	2	Calcium	4%
Cholesterol, mg	65	Iron	8%
Sodium, mg	160		
Potassium, mg	470		

Turkey with Confetti Vegetables and biscuits

Turkey with Peppers

2 turkey thighs (about 2 pounds)
1 tablespoon vegetable oil
½ cup water
2 tablespoons chopped fresh parsley
2 tablespoons reduced-sodium soy sauce
1½ teaspoons chopped fresh or ½ teaspoon dried thyme leaves
½ teaspoon chopped fresh or ¼ teaspoon dried rosemary leaves
2 medium green bell peppers, cut into ¼-inch strips
¼ cup sliced green onions (2 to 3 medium)
1 teaspoon cornstarch
1 tablespoon cold water

Remove skin and bones from turkey. Cut turkey into strips, 2×1 inch. Cook turkey in oil in 10-inch nonstick skillet about 6 minutes, stirring occasionally, until turkey is white; drain.

Stir ½ cup water, the parsley, soy sauce, thyme and rosemary into turkey. Heat to boiling; reduce heat. Cover and simmer about 30 minutes or until turkey is tender. Stir in bell peppers and onions. Cover and simmer about 5 minutes or until peppers are crisp-tender. Mix cornstarch and 1 tablespoon cold water; stir into turkey mixture. Heat to boiling, stirring constantly. Boil and stir 1 minute. *6 servings*

NUTRITION INFORMATION PER SERVING

1 serving		Percent of U.S. RDA	
Calories	205	Protein	40%
Protein, g	26	Vitamin A	2%
Carbohydrate, g	3	Vitamin C	20%
Fat, g	10	Thiamin	6%
Unsaturated	7	Riboflavin	14%
Saturated	3	Niacin	24%
Dietary Fiber, g	1	Calcium	2%
Cholesterol, mg	80	Iron	12%
Sodium, mg	280		
Potassium, mg	320		

Roast Turkey Tenderloins

After rubbing it with the spice mixture, place the turkey in a heavy, resealable plastic food-storage bag and refrigerate up to 12 hours for a stronger flavor. This mixture is also good on beef. To serve the meat cold, drizzle slices with Creamy Horseradish Dressing (page 151).

1 teaspoon dried rosemary leaves
1 teaspoon dried thyme leaves
½ teaspoon salt
½ teaspoon dried sage leaves
½ teaspoon ground fennel seed
¼ teaspoon pepper
1½ pounds turkey tenderloins

Heat oven to 350°. Spray rectangular pan, 13×9×2 inches, with nonstick cooking spray. Mix all ingredients except turkey tenderloins. Rub half of the herb mixture over each tenderloin. Bake 35 to 40 minutes or until the juices run clear. Cut diagonally into thin slices. *6 servings*

NUTRITION INFORMATION PER SERVING

1 serving		Percent of U.S. RDA	
Calories	130	Protein	58%
Protein, g	26	Vitamin A	*
Carbohydrate, g	0	Vitamin C	*
Fat, g	3	Thiamin	4%
Unsaturated	2	Riboflavin	6%
Saturated	1	Niacin	42%
Dietary Fiber, g	0	Calcium	2%
Cholesterol, mg	65	Iron	8%
Sodium, mg	240		
Potassium, mg	240		

Glazed Turkey Tenderloins

1 pound turkey tenderloins
1/3 cup orange marmalade spreadable fruit
1 teaspoon finely chopped gingerroot or 1/2
　teaspoon ground ginger
1 teaspoon Worcestershire sauce

Spray 10-inch nonstick skillet with nonstick cooking spray. Cook turkey tenderloins in skillet over medium heat about 5 minutes or until brown on 1 side; turn turkey. Stir in remaining ingredients; reduce heat. Cover and simmer about 15 minutes, stirring sauce occasionally, until juices of turkey run clear and sauce is thickened. Cut turkey into thin slices. Spoon sauce over turkey. *4 servings*

NUTRITION INFORMATION PER SERVING

1 serving		Percent of U.S. RDA	
Calories	205	Protein	40%
Protein, g	26	Vitamin A	*
Carbohydrate, g	18	Vitamin C	*
Fat, g	3	Thiamin	4%
Unsaturated	2	Riboflavin	6%
Saturated	1	Niacin	40%
Dietary Fiber, g	0	Calcium	2%
Cholesterol, mg	65	Iron	8%
Sodium, mg	75		
Potassium, mg	260		

Fettuccine with Turkey Marinara Sauce

1 1/2 cups chopped onions (about 3 medium)
3/4 cup chopped carrots (about 1 1/2 medium)
3/4 cup chopped celery (about 1 large stalk)
1 1/2 cups chicken broth
2 cloves garlic, finely chopped
1 1/2 pounds ground turkey
1 tablespoon chopped fresh or 1 1/2
　teaspoons dried thyme leaves
1 1/2 teaspoons fennel seed
1/4 teaspoon pepper
1/2 cup red wine or unsweetened grape juice
1 tablespoon tomato paste
1 can (28 ounces) Italian plum tomatoes,
　drained
2 tablespoons chopped fresh parsley
3 cups hot cooked fettuccine

Cook onions, carrots, celery, broth and garlic in 3-quart saucepan over medium heat 5 to 7 minutes, stirring frequently, until onion is tender. Stir in turkey, thyme, fennel seed and pepper. Cook over medium heat about 3 minutes, stirring occasionally, until turkey is white. Stir in wine, tomato paste and tomatoes; break up tomatoes. Cover and simmer over low heat 20 minutes, stirring occasionally. Uncover and cook 5 to 7 minutes longer or until sauce thickens. Stir in parsley. Serve over fettuccine. *6 servings*

NUTRITION INFORMATION PER SERVING

1 serving		Percent of U.S. RDA	
Calories	330	Protein	50%
Protein, g	32	Vitamin A	34%
Carbohydrate, g	33	Vitamin C	22%
Fat, g	7	Thiamin	20%
Unsaturated	5	Riboflavin	18%
Saturated	2	Niacin	48%
Dietary Fiber, g	5	Calcium	10%
Cholesterol, mg	95	Iron	24%
Sodium, mg	720		
Potassium, mg	830		

Chicken and Plum Salad

Fennel Seed Dressing (below)
4 skinless boneless chicken breast halves
  (about 1 pound)
2 teaspoons vegetable oil
4 plums, sliced
1 cup sliced celery (about 2 medium stalks)
2 cups small cauliflowerets
Lettuce leaves or bite-size pieces lettuce

NUTRITION INFORMATION PER SERVING			
1 serving		Percent of U.S. RDA	
Calories	190	Protein	28%
Protein, g	18	Vitamin A	4%
Carbohydrate, g	9	Vitamin C	26%
Fat, g	9	Thiamin	6%
Unsaturated	7	Riboflavin	8%
Saturated	2	Niacin	30%
Dietary Fiber, g	2	Calcium	2%
Cholesterol, mg	45	Iron	6%
Sodium, mg	240		
Potassium, mg	450		

Prepare Fennel Seed Dressing. Cook chicken breast halves in oil in 10-inch nonstick skillet about 6 minutes on each side or until juices run clear. Cool slightly; cut into thin slices. Toss plums, celery, cauliflowerets and dressing in large bowl. Carefully stir in chicken. Cover and refrigerate at least 4 hours. Spoon onto lettuce leaves. *6 servings*

Fennel Seed Dressing

1/4 cup dry white wine or apple juice
2 tablespoons vegetable oil
1 teaspoon fennel seed
1 teaspoon sugar
1 teaspoon chopped fresh or 1/4 teaspoon
  dried rosemary leaves
1 teaspoon chopped fresh or 1/4 teaspoon
  dried tarragon leaves
1/2 teaspoon salt
Dash of ground red pepper (cayenne)

Shake all ingredients in tightly covered container.

Crunchy Chicken and Pear Salad

The firmness and tartness of a Bosc pear are just what this salad requires. We found the softer Anjou pear does not hold up as well.

Lemon-Mayonnaise Dressing (right)
3 cups cubed cooked chicken or turkey
2 cups chopped firm pears (about 2
  medium)
3/4 cup sliced red onion (about 1 small)
3/4 cup chopped celery (about 1 large stalk)
3/4 cup chopped mushrooms (about 3
  ounces)
1/2 cup chopped green onions (about 5
  medium)
2 tablespoons chopped fresh or 2 teaspoons
  dried tarragon leaves
Lettuce leaves

Prepare Lemon-Mayonnaise Dressing in large bowl. Add remaining ingredients except lettuce leaves; toss. Cover and refrigerate at least 1 hour. Serve on lettuce leaves. *6 servings*

Lemon-Mayonnaise Dressing

½ cup plain nonfat yogurt

2 tablespoons cholesterol-free reduced-calorie mayonnaise or salad dressing

2 teaspoons grated lemon peel

2 tablespoons lemon juice

1 tablespoon rice vinegar or white wine vinegar

1 tablespoon Dijon mustard

½ teaspoon salt

¼ teaspoon pepper

Mix all ingredients in a glass or plastic bowl.

CRUNCHY BEAN AND PEAR SALAD: Omit chicken. Stir in 4 cups cooked kidney beans or 2 cans (about 15 ounces) kidney beans, drained.

NUTRITION INFORMATION PER SERVING

I serving		Percent of U.S. RDA	
Calories	200	Protein	36%
Protein, g	24	Vitamin A	4%
Carbohydrate, g	15	Vitamin C	18%
Fat, g	5	Thiamin	6%
Unsaturated	4	Riboflavin	12%
Saturated	1	Niacin	36%
Dietary Fiber, g	3	Calcium	8%
Cholesterol, mg	55	Iron	8%
Sodium, mg	320		
Potassium, mg	490		

Chile-Chicken Salad

Salad Dressing (below)

3 cups cut-up cooked chicken or turkey

2 tablespoons finely chopped onion

¼ teaspoon salt

1 can (4 ounces) chopped green chiles, drained

6 cups bite-size pieces lettuce (about 1 medium head)

2 medium tomatoes, cut into thin wedges

Prepare Salad Dressing. Mix chicken, onion, salt, chiles and Salad Dressing in large bowl. Add lettuce and tomatoes; toss. *8 servings*

Salad Dressing

¼ cup vinegar

2 tablespoons sugar

2 tablespoons vegetable oil

½ teaspoon salt

½ teaspoon ground cumin

Shake all ingredients in tightly covered container.

NUTRITION INFORMATION PER SERVING

I serving		Percent of U.S. RDA	
Calories	150	Protein	24%
Protein, g	16	Vitamin A	2%
Carbohydrate, g	6	Vitamin C	26%
Fat, g	7	Thiamin	4%
Unsaturated	5	Riboflavin	6%
Saturated	2	Niacin	20%
Dietary Fiber, g	0	Calcium	2%
Cholesterol, mg	45	Iron	6%
Sodium, mg	410		
Potassium, mg	250		

Chicken-Grapefruit Salad

Grapefruit Dressing (below)

3 cups cubed cooked chicken or turkey

3 cups chopped apples (about 3 medium)

2 cups red grapefruit sections (about 2
large grapefruit)

¾ cup chopped peeled cucumber (about 1
medium)

5 cups watercress sprigs (about 2 large
bunches)

Prepare Grapefruit Dressing in large bowl. Add remaining ingredients except watercress; toss. Cover and refrigerate about 1 hour or until chilled. Serve on watercress. *6 servings*

Grapefruit Dressing

⅔ cup plain nonfat yogurt

½ cup finely chopped peeled cucumber
(about ½ medium)

3 tablespoons grapefruit juice (about ½
medium grapefruit)

2 tablespoons cholesterol-free reduced-
calorie mayonnaise or salad dressing

1 teaspoon prepared horseradish

¼ teaspoon pepper

Mix all ingredients in glass or plastic bowl.

NUTRITION INFORMATION PER SERVING			
1 serving		**Percent of U.S. RDA**	
Calories	350	Protein	68%
Protein, g	45	Vitamin A	20%
Carbohydrate, g	30	Vitamin C	100%
Fat, g	7	Thiamin	12%
Unsaturated	5	Riboflavin	16%
Saturated	2	Niacin	30%
Dietary Fiber, g	4	Calcium	15%
Cholesterol, mg	60	Iron	15%
Sodium, mg	170		
Potassium, mg	910		

Chicken-Grapefruit Salad, Chicken and Plum Salad (page 250)

Chicken-Vermicelli Salad

8 ounces uncooked vermicelli
Ginger Dressing (below)
2 cups cut-up cooked chicken or turkey
1½ cups shredded carrots
1 cup coarsely chopped cucumber
½ cup coarsely chopped jícama or water
  chestnuts
¼ cup chopped fresh cilantro or parsley

Break vermicelli into halves. Cook vermicelli as directed on package—except omit salt; drain. Rinse with cold water; drain. Prepare Ginger Dressing in large bowl. Add vermicelli and remaining ingredients; toss. Spoon onto salad greens if desired. *6 servings*

Ginger Dressing

⅓ cup cholesterol-free reduced-calorie
  mayonnaise or salad dressing
⅓ cup plain nonfat yogurt
1 tablespoon reduced-sodium soy sauce
1 teaspoon sugar
½ teaspoon ground ginger
Dash red pepper sauce

Mix all ingredients.

NUTRITION INFORMATION PER SERVING

1 serving		Percent of U.S. RDA	
Calories	305	Protein	32%
Protein, g	20	Vitamin A	38%
Carbohydrate, g	38	Vitamin C	16%
Fat, g	8	Thiamin	20%
Unsaturated	6	Riboflavin	14%
Saturated	2	Niacin	28%
Dietary Fiber, g	2	Calcium	6%
Cholesterol, mg	40	Iron	14%
Sodium, mg	380		
Potassium, mg	370		

Turkey Salad with Fruit

3 cups cut-up cooked turkey or chicken
1 can (11 ounces) mandarin orange
  segments, drained
1 can (8 ounces) sliced water chestnuts,
  drained
1 cup thinly sliced celery (about 2 medium
  stalks)
¾ cup sliced green grapes
2 green onions, thinly sliced
1 container (6 ounces) peach, orange or
  lemon yogurt (⅔ cup)
2 tablespoons reduced-sodium soy sauce
Mixed salad greens

Mix turkey, orange segments, water chestnuts, grapes, celery and onions in large glass or plastic bowl. Mix yogurt and soy sauce. Pour over chicken mixture; toss. Cover and refrigerate at least 2 hours. Serve on salad greens. *6 servings*

NUTRITION INFORMATION PER SERVING

1 serving		Percent of U.S. RDA	
Calories	235	Protein	36%
Protein, g	23	Vitamin A	4%
Carbohydrate, g	24	Vitamin C	34%
Fat, g	5	Thiamin	8%
Unsaturated	3	Riboflavin	14%
Saturated	2	Niacin	28%
Dietary Fiber, g	2	Calcium	8%
Cholesterol, mg	60	Iron	10%
Sodium, mg	290		
Potassium, mg	520		

Curried Turkey and Rice Salad

½ cup cholesterol-free reduced-calorie
   mayonnaise or salad dressing
½ cup plain nonfat yogurt
¾ teaspoon curry powder
½ teaspoon ground ginger
¼ teaspoon salt
¼ teaspoon ground red pepper (cayenne)
3 cups cold cooked rice
2 cups cut-up cooked turkey or chicken
1 cup sliced celery (about 2 medium stalks)
½ cup chopped bell pepper (about 1 small)
1 can (15¼ ounces) pineapple chunks in
   juice, drained
Salad greens
2 medium tomatoes, cut into wedges

Mix mayonnaise, yogurt, curry powder, ginger, salt and red pepper in large glass or plastic bowl. Stir in rice, turkey, celery, bell pepper and pineapple. Cover and refrigerate about 2 hours or until chilled. Just before serving, line 6 salad plates with salad greens. Divide salad evenly among plates. Garnish with tomato wedges. *6 servings*

NUTRITION INFORMATION PER SERVING

I serving		Percent of U.S. RDA	
Calories	340	Protein	28%
Protein, g	18	Vitamin A	4%
Carbohydrate, g	45	Vitamin C	38%
Fat, g	10	Thiamin	20%
Unsaturated	8	Riboflavin	10%
Saturated	2	Niacin	28%
Dietary Fiber, g	3	Calcium	8%
Cholesterol, mg	40	Iron	14%
Sodium, mg	660		
Potassium, mg	480		

Turkey-Pesto Salad

Pesto (below)
2 cups cut-up cooked turkey or chicken
¾ cup chopped tomato (about 1 medium)
2 tablespoons sliced green onions
1 can (8 ounces) sliced water chestnuts,
   drained
4 cups shredded Bibb lettuce
2 tablespoons crumbled feta cheese

Prepare Pesto. Mix turkey, tomato, onions and water chestnuts. Serve on lettuce. Spoon Pesto over salad. Sprinkle with cheese. *4 servings*

Pesto

¾ cup firmly packed fresh basil leaves
¼ cup grated Parmesan cheese
1 tablespoon pine nuts
2 tablespoons olive or vegetable oil
1 tablespoon plain nonfat yogurt
1 tablespoon lemon juice
2 cloves garlic

Place all ingredients in blender or food processor. Cover and blend on medium speed about 2 minutes, stopping occasionally to scrape sides, until almost smooth.

NUTRITION INFORMATION PER SERVING

I serving		Percent of U.S. RDA	
Calories	300	Protein	40%
Protein, g	26	Vitamin A	8%
Carbohydrate, g	15	Vitamin C	27%
Fat, g	15	Thiamin	10%
Unsaturated	11	Riboflavin	14%
Saturated	4	Niacin	30%
Dietary Fiber, g	3	Calcium	22%
Cholesterol, mg	65	Iron	20%
Sodium, mg	210		
Potassium, mg	630		

Turkey-Macaroni Salad

1½ cups uncooked elbow or spiral
    macaroni (about 6 ounces)

1 package (10 ounces) frozen green peas

2 cups cut-up cooked turkey or chicken

¾ cup cholesterol-free reduced-calorie
    mayonnaise or salad dressing

½ cup shredded reduced-fat Cheddar
    cheese

½ cup sliced green onions (about 5
    medium)

½ cup sliced celery (about 1 medium stalk)

⅓ cup sweet pickle relish

3 cups bite-size pieces lettuce (about ½
    medium head)

Cook macaroni as directed on package—
except omit salt; drain. Rinse with cold water;
drain. Rinse frozen peas with cold water to
separate; drain. Mix macaroni, peas and remaining ingredients except lettuce. Cover and
refrigerate about 4 hours or until chilled. Serve
on lettuce. *6 servings*

NUTRITION INFORMATION PER SERVING

1 serving		Percent of U.S. RDA	
Calories	375	Protein	34%
Protein, g	23	Vitamin A	6%
Carbohydrate, g	37	Vitamin C	14%
Fat, g	15	Thiamin	22%
Unsaturated	11	Riboflavin	14%
Saturated	4	Niacin	28%
Dietary Fiber, g	4	Calcium	10%
Cholesterol, mg	45	Iron	16%
Sodium, mg	500		
Potassium, mg	370		

Turkey-Macaroni Salad

Turkey–Green Bean Salad

3 cups cubed cooked turkey or chicken

3 cups 1-inch pieces cooked green beans (about 1 pound)

1 cup sliced jicama (about $\frac{1}{2}$ medium)

1 cup plain nonfat yogurt

$\frac{1}{4}$ cup chopped fresh cilantro leaves

$\frac{1}{3}$ cup lemon juice

2 tablespoons frozen (thawed) apple juice concentrate

$\frac{1}{2}$ teaspoon salt

$\frac{1}{4}$ teaspoon pepper

3 cups chopped lettuce (about $\frac{1}{2}$ medium head)

Mix all ingredients except lettuce in large glass or plastic bowl. Cover and refrigerate at least 1 hour. Serve on lettuce. *6 servings*

NUTRITION INFORMATION PER SERVING			
I serving		**Percent of U.S. RDA**	
Calories	180	Protein	38%
Protein, g	25	Vitamin A	6%
Carbohydrate, g	13	Vitamin C	30%
Fat, g	3	Thiamin	8%
Unsaturated	2	Riboflavin	14%
Saturated	1	Niacin	36%
Dietary Fiber, g	3	Calcium	14%
Cholesterol, mg	55	Iron	10%
Sodium, mg	280		
Potassium, mg	510		

Chicken-Cabbage Soup

5 cups finely chopped green cabbage

2 cups $\frac{1}{4}$-inch slices carrots (about 4 medium)

1 cup chopped celery (about 2 medium stalks)

3 cups eight-vegetable juice

2 cups chicken broth

$\frac{1}{4}$ teaspoon pepper

1 medium onion, sliced

3- to $3\frac{1}{2}$-pound cut-up broiler-fryer chicken

$\frac{1}{2}$ teaspoon paprika

Heat all ingredients except chicken and paprika to boiling in Dutch oven; reduce heat. Cover and simmer 30 minutes.

Meanwhile, remove skin and fat from chicken pieces. Sprinkle chicken with paprika. Spray 10-inch skillet with nonstick cooking spray. Cook chicken in skillet over medium-high heat about 15 minutes or until light brown on all sides; drain. Add chicken to cabbage mixture. Heat to boiling; reduce heat. Cover and simmer 35 to 40 minutes or until juices of chicken run clear. *6 servings*

NUTRITION INFORMATION PER SERVING			
I serving		**Percent of U.S. RDA**	
Calories	230	Protein	42%
Protein, g	27	Vitamin A	90%
Carbohydrate, g	17	Vitamin C	62%
Fat, g	6	Thiamin	12%
Unsaturated	4	Riboflavin	16%
Saturated	2	Niacin	42%
Dietary Fiber, g	4	Calcium	8%
Cholesterol, mg	70	Iron	14%
Sodium, mg	810		
Potassium, mg	930		

Chicken Soup with French Bread

The soup, including whole chicken pieces, is ladled over toasted slices of French bread. If you'd like, remove and discard bones from chicken before adding the bell pepper.

3- to 3½-pound cut-up broiler-fryer
   chicken
2 tablespoons vegetable oil
2 large onions, thinly sliced and separated
   into rings
2 cloves garlic, finely chopped
1 cup water
1 cup dry white wine or apple juice
1 tablespoon sugar
1 tablespoon chopped fresh or 1 teaspoon
   dried thyme leaves
¼ teaspoon pepper
1 can (16 ounces) whole tomatoes,
   undrained
1 can (10½ ounces) condensed chicken
   broth
1 medium green bell pepper, cut into ¼-
   inch strips
6 slices French bread, toasted
Chopped fresh parsley

Remove skin and fat from chicken pieces. Heat oil in nonstick Dutch oven. Cook chicken in oil about 15 minutes or until light brown on all sides. Remove chicken from Dutch oven; keep warm. Cook onions and garlic in Dutch oven, stirring frequently, until onions are tender; drain off fat. Return chicken to Dutch oven. Stir in water, wine, sugar, thyme, pepper, tomatoes and broth; break up tomatoes. Heat to boiling; reduce heat. Cover and simmer 35 to 40 minutes or until juices of chicken run clear.

Skim fat from chicken mixture. Stir in bell pepper. Heat to boiling; reduce heat. Cover and simmer 5 to 10 minutes or just until bell pepper is tender. Place 1 slice bread in each soup bowl. Spoon chicken and broth over bread. Sprinkle with parsley. *6 servings*

NUTRITION INFORMATION PER SERVING			
1 serving		**Percent of U.S. RDA**	
Calories	335	Protein	44%
Protein, g	29	Vitamin A	6%
Carbohydrate, g	26	Vitamin C	22%
Fat, g	11	Thiamin	8%
Unsaturated	8	Riboflavin	14%
Saturated	3	Niacin	44%
Dietary Fiber, g	3	Calcium	8%
Cholesterol, mg	70	Iron	18%
Sodium, mg	660		
Potassium, mg	640		

Broccoli-Chicken Soup

1 cup water

1 tablespoon lemon juice

2 cups coarsely chopped broccoli (about 12 ounces)

½ cup chopped celery (about 1 medium stalk)

¼ cup chopped onion (about 1 small)

1 tablespoon margarine

1 tablespoon all-purpose flour

1¼ cups chicken broth

Dash of ground nutmeg

1½ cups cut-up cooked chicken or turkey

¾ cup low-fat milk

Heat water and lemon juice to boiling in 3-quart saucepan. Stir in broccoli, celery and onion. Cover and heat to boiling; reduce heat. Simmer about 15 minutes or until vegetables are tender; do not drain. Place in blender. Cover and blend on medium speed about 45 seconds, stopping blender frequently to scrape sides, until mixture is uniform consistency.

Heat margarine in 3-quart saucepan over low heat until melted. Stir in flour. Cook, stirring constantly, until mixture is smooth and bubbly; remove from heat. Stir in broth. Heat to boiling, stirring constantly. Boil and stir 1 minute. Stir in broccoli mixture and nutmeg. Heat just to boiling. Stir in chicken and milk. Heat just until hot (do not boil). *4 servings*

NUTRITION INFORMATION PER SERVING

1 serving		Percent of U.S. RDA	
Calories	185	Protein	30%
Protein, g	20	Vitamin A	12%
Carbohydrate, g	8	Vitamin C	36%
Fat, g	8	Thiamin	6%
Unsaturated	6	Riboflavin	14%
Saturated	2	Niacin	26%
Dietary Fiber, g	2	Calcium	10%
Cholesterol, mg	50	Iron	8%
Sodium, mg	360		
Potassium, mg	490		

Harvest Chicken Stew

4 cups 1-inch cubes peeled eggplant (about 1 pound)

4 cups ⅛-inch slices small red potatoes (about 8)

2 cups sliced carrots (about 4 medium)

3 medium onions, cut into fourths

⅔ cup chopped fresh parsley

3 cups chicken broth

2 tablespoons chopped fresh or 2 teaspoons dried thyme leaves

¼ teaspoon salt

¼ teaspoon pepper

½ cup cold water

2 tablespoons all-purpose flour

6 skinless boneless chicken breast halves (about 1½ pounds), cut into fourths

¼ cup tomato paste

2 tablespoons lemon juice

Heat oven to 350°. Mix eggplant, potatoes, carrots, onions, parsley, broth, thyme, salt and pepper in Dutch oven. Cover and bake 50 minutes. Shake cold water and flour in tightly covered container. Stir flour mixture, chicken, tomato paste and lemon juice into stew. Cover and bake about 20 minutes or until potatoes are tender and juices of chicken run clear. *6 servings*

HARVEST VEGETABLE STEW: Omit chicken. Increase eggplant and red potatoes to 6 cups each. Increase carrots to 3 cups.

NUTRITION INFORMATION PER SERVING

1 serving		Percent of U.S. RDA	
Calories	375	Protein	52%
Protein, g	34	Vitamin A	70%
Carbohydrate, g	49	Vitamin C	32%
Fat, g	5	Thiamin	22%
Unsaturated	4	Riboflavin	16%
Saturated	1	Niacin	66%
Dietary Fiber, g	7	Calcium	8%
Cholesterol, mg	65	Iron	26%
Sodium, mg	650		
Potassium, mg	1350		

Turkey and Wild Rice Soup

2 turkey drumsticks (about 1½ pounds)
2 cups chopped tomatoes (about 2 large)
1 cup sliced celery with leaves (about 2 medium stalks)
½ cup chopped onion (about 1 medium)
½ cup uncooked wild rice
3½ cups water
2 teaspoons chicken bouillon granules
2 bay leaves

Remove skin from turkey drumsticks and discard. Mix turkey and remaining ingredients in Dutch oven. Heat to boiling; reduce heat. Cover and simmer 50 to 60 minutes or until juices of turkey run clear and wild rice is tender. Remove turkey from Dutch oven; cool about 5 minutes. Remove turkey meat from bones; cut meat into bite-size pieces. Stir turkey into soup. Heat until hot. Remove bay leaves. *6 servings*

NUTRITION INFORMATION PER SERVING

1 serving		Percent of U.S. RDA	
Calories	200	Protein	32%
Protein, g	20	Vitamin A	4%
Carbohydrate, g	17	Vitamin C	10%
Fat, g	6	Thiamin	8%
Unsaturated	4	Riboflavin	14%
Saturated	2	Niacin	22%
Dietary Fiber, g	1	Calcium	2%
Cholesterol, mg	55	Iron	10%
Sodium, mg	670		
Potassium, mg	430		

Turkey and White Bean Chile

Turkey and White Bean Chile

This chile holds the heat well and is perfect for a winter buffet. Serve pieces of Barley-Corn Bread (page 81) in a bun warmer if you like.

1½ pounds ground turkey

1 cup chopped onion (about 1 large)

1½ cups chicken broth

2 teaspoons ground cumin

1½ teaspoons chopped fresh or ½ teaspoon dried oregano leaves

1 teaspoon ground cinnamon

1 teaspoon chile powder

⅛ teaspoon ground red pepper (cayenne)

3 cloves garlic, finely chopped

1 can (4 ounces) chopped mild green chiles, drained

1 cup chopped red bell pepper (about 1 medium)

1 can (15 ounces) great northern beans, rinsed and drained

¾ cup plain nonfat yogurt

2 tablespoons chopped fresh cilantro leaves

¾ cup salsa

½ cup reduced-fat Cheddar cheese

Cook ground turkey, onion and ¾ cup of the broth in 3-quart saucepan over medium heat 5 minutes, stirring occasionally, until turkey is white and onion is tender. Stir in remaining broth, the cumin, oregano, cinnamon, chile powder, red pepper, garlic and green chiles; reduce heat. Cover and simmer 15 minutes.

Stir in bell pepper and beans. Cook uncovered over low heat 20 to 30 minutes or until most of the liquid has evaporated. Mix yogurt and cilantro. Serve chile topped with yogurt mixture, salsa and cheese. *6 servings*

NUTRITION INFORMATION PER SERVING			
I serving		**Percent of U.S. RDA**	
Calories	340	Protein	58%
Protein, g	38	Vitamin A	16%
Carbohydrate, g	29	Vitamin C	42%
Fat, g	8	Thiamin	14%
Unsaturated	5	Riboflavin	20%
Saturated	3	Niacin	38%
Dietary Fiber, g	6	Calcium	24%
Cholesterol, mg	75	Iron	30%
Sodium, mg	1050		
Potassium, mg	990		

Chicken Calzones

1 package regular active dry yeast

1 cup warm water (105° to 115°)

1 tablespoon sugar

2 teaspoons vegetable oil

½ teaspoon salt

1½ cups all-purpose flour

1¼ to 1¾ cups whole wheat flour

Chicken-Mushroom Filling (right)

1 egg white, beaten, or 1 tablespoon
   cholesterol-free egg product

Dissolve yeast in warm water in large bowl. Stir in sugar, oil, salt and all-purpose flour. Beat until smooth. Mix in enough whole wheat flour to make dough easy to handle. Turn dough onto lightly floured surface; gently roll in flour to coat. Knead about 5 minutes or until smooth and elastic. Cover with bowl and let rest 5 minutes.

Heat oven to 375°. Prepare Chicken-Mushroom Filling; reserve. Spray large cookie sheet with nonstick cooking spray. Divide dough into 6 equal parts. Roll or pat each part into 7-inch circle on lightly floured surface, turning dough over occasionally to coat with flour.

Place about ⅓ cup filling on half of each circle; spread to within 1 inch of edge. Fold dough over filling; press edge with fork to seal, or fold edge up and pinch securely to seal. Place on cookie sheet; brush with egg white. Cut several slits in top surface of dough to vent steam. Bake 25 to 30 minutes or until golden brown. *6 servings*

Chicken-Mushroom Filling

1 cup cut-up cooked chicken

1 cup chopped mushrooms (about 4 ounces)

¾ cup shredded reduced-fat mozzarella
   cheese

¼ cup chopped onion (about 1 small)

⅓ cup pizza sauce

2 tablespoons grated Parmesan cheese

Mix all ingredients.

NUTRITION INFORMATION PER SERVING			
I serving		**Percent of U.S. RDA**	
Calories	330	Protein	30%
Protein, g	19	Vitamin A	4%
Carbohydrate, g	48	Vitamin C	2%
Fat, g	7	Thiamin	28%
Unsaturated	4	Riboflavin	26%
Saturated	3	Niacin	30%
Dietary Fiber, g	5	Calcium	14%
Cholesterol, mg	30	Iron	18%
Sodium, mg	400		
Potassium, mg	360		

Cajun Turkey Burgers

Serving burgers open-face on slices of Italian bread makes for a welcome change. However, they can certainly be served on multi-grain or white hamburger buns if desired.

Tomato Mayonnaise (right)
1 pound ground turkey or chicken
¼ cup chopped green onions (2 to 3 medium)
2 tablespoons wheat germ
2 tablespoons chopped fresh parsley
⅛ teaspoon salt
⅛ teaspoon ground red pepper (cayenne)
⅛ teaspoon pepper
1 clove garlic, finely chopped
4 slices Italian bread, about 1 inch thick

Prepare Tomato Mayonnaise; reserve. Mix remaining ingredients except bread. Shape into 4 patties, each about ½ inch thick. Set oven control to broil. Place patties on rack in broiler pan. Broil with tops 3 to 4 inches from heat about 7 minutes on each side, turning once. Place on bread slices. Serve open-face with Tomato Mayonnaise. *4 servings*

Tomato Mayonnaise

1 cup chopped tomato (about 1 large)
¼ cup cholesterol-free reduced-calorie mayonnaise or salad dressing
1 tablespoon chopped fresh parsley

Mix all ingredients.

NUTRITION INFORMATION PER SERVING			
1 serving		Percent of U.S. RDA	
Calories	345	Protein	42%
Protein, g	27	Vitamin A	6%
Carbohydrate, g	19	Vitamin C	12%
Fat, g	18	Thiamin	14%
Unsaturated	13	Riboflavin	18%
Saturated	5	Niacin	28%
Dietary Fiber, g	2	Calcium	4%
Cholesterol, mg	75	Iron	18%
Sodium, mg	340		
Potassium, mg	430		

**7
Seafood**

7

Seafood

Fresh fish is increasingly available across the country as it grows in popularity as a healthy food choice. Although fish can be categorized by fat content, both fin fish and shellfish tend to be leaner than red meat. The Fat Content of Fish table (right) gives you information on the fat in fish. Most fish are less fatty than lean ground meat, which is about 15 percent fat. Lean fish are mild-flavored and tender and lend themselves well to poaching. (See Poaching, page 25.) Fattier fish such as coho salmon and lake trout stand up well to grilling and broiling. Whatever the cooking method, fish is delicate and tender, so overcooking should be avoided. Cook fish until it flakes easily with a fork. To test, insert a fork at an angle into the thickest part of the fish and twist gently. For food safety reasons we recommend cooking to an internal temperature of 160°.

Shellfish are higher in cholesterol than fin fish. Eaten in moderation, they too can be part of a healthy eating plan. Shrimp are higher in cholesterol than other shellfish but can be enjoyed if combined with other healthy ingredients as in Shrimp and Zucchini (page 295); although 1 serving has 120 milligrams of cholesterol, it boasts only 140 calories and 1 gram of fat. Whether enjoyed individually or combined, as in Mediterranean Fish Stew (page 308), fin fish and shellfish lend themselves to many cooking methods and embrace many flavors, as you will discover in this chapter.

FAT CONTENT OF FISH

Individual fish have different percentages of fat that vary with the season, stage of maturity, locale, species and the diet of each fish. You can substitute one type of fish for another of the same classification when preparing recipes in this chapter.

Lean	Medium–Fat	Fatty
Bass, sea	Anchovy	Butterfish
Bass, striped	Bluefish	Carp
Cod	Catfish	Eel
Cusk	Croaker	Herring
Flounder	Mullet	Mackerel,
Grouper	Porgy	Atlantic
Haddock	Redfish	Mackerel,
Hake	Salmon, pink	Pacific
Halibut	Shark	Mackerel,
Lingcod	Swordfish	Spanish
Mackerel, king	Trout, rainbow	Pompano
Mahimahi	Trout, sea	Sablefish
Monkfish	Tuna, bluefin	Salmon,
Orange roughy	Turbot	Chinook
Perch, ocean	Whitefish	Salmon, coho
Pike, northern		Salmon,
Pollock		sockeye
Red snapper		Sardines
Rockfish		Shad
Scrod		Trout, lake
Smelt		Tuna, albacore
Sole		
Tilefish		
Tuna, skipjack		
Tuna, yellowfin		
Whiting		

Preceding page: Seafood Stew with Rosamarina (page 281), Southwestern Stir-fried Shrimp (page 295)

266

Risotto with Sea Bass and Zucchini

Arborio is the traditional rice for risotto. Different brands of rice have different absorption levels and may require an additional 5 minutes cooking time or up to ½ cup of additional broth.

2¼ to 2½ cups chicken broth

½ cup chopped celery (about 1 medium stalk)

¼ cup finely chopped shallots (about 2 large)

1 teaspoon grated lemon peel

1 cup uncooked Arborio or other short grain rice

½ cup dry white wine or apple juice

2 teaspoons tomato paste

1½ cups chopped zucchini (about 1 medium)

1½ pound bass or other lean fish fillet, cut into 1½-inch pieces

2 tablespoons sliced green onions

1 tablespoon chopped fresh or 1 teaspoon dried dill weed

6 lemon wedges

Heat 1 cup of the broth, the celery, shallots and lemon peel to boiling in 3-quart saucepan; reduce heat. Simmer uncovered over medium heat about 10 minutes, stirring occasionally, until liquid has almost evaporated. Stir in rice, ¾ cup of the broth, the wine and tomato paste. Heat to boiling; reduce heat. Simmer uncovered 15 minutes, stirring occasionally.

Stir in zucchini, fish and ½ cup of the broth. Cover and simmer about 20 minutes or until rice is tender and fish flakes easily with fork, adding remaining broth, if necessary, to prevent sticking. Stir in onions and dill weed; remove from heat. Cover and let stand 5 minutes. Stir rice mixture. Serve with lemon wedges.
6 servings

NUTRITION INFORMATION PER SERVING			
I serving		**Percent of U.S. RDA**	
Calories	250	Protein	40%
Protein, g	26	Vitamin A	2%
Carbohydrate, g	30	Vitamin C	4%
Fat, g	2	Thiamin	16%
Unsaturated	1	Riboflavin	8%
Saturated	1	Niacin	24%
Dietary Fiber, g	1	Calcium	4%
Cholesterol, mg	60	Iron	10%
Sodium, mg	380		
Potassium, mg	590		

Asian Fish Rolls in Rice-Paper Wrappers

Rice paper wrappers are available in the foreign foods section of some supermarkets and in international markets. If rice paper wrappers are unavailable, substitute lettuce leaves. Dip each lettuce leaf in boiling water 30 to 60 seconds, or until wilted; shake off as much water as possible, then assemble and wrap as directed.

Tomato-Ginger Dipping Sauce (right)
2 cups bean sprouts
2 cups shredded napa (Chinese) cabbage
2 cups Chinese pea pods, cut into julienne strips
18 six-inch rice-paper wrappers
2 cups finely chopped cooked sea bass or whitefish (about ¾ pound)
⅓ cup chopped fresh cilantro leaves
3 tablespoons finely chopped unsalted roasted peanuts

Prepare Tomato-Ginger Dipping Sauce. Heat 1 inch water to boiling, or place steamer basket in ½ inch water (water should not touch bottom of basket) and heat to boiling. Add bean sprouts. Cover and cook or steam 2 minutes. Immediately rinse in cold water; drain. Repeat with cabbage and pea pods.

Place rice-paper wrappers, 2 at a time, in bowl of hot water 45 seconds. Remove and place on plate. When completely soft, separate wrappers. Place about 2 tablespoons fish, 1 tablespoon each bean sprouts, cabbage and pea pods, 1 teaspoon cilantro and ½ teaspoon peanuts in center of each wrapper. Fold one end of wrapper up about 1 inch over filling; fold right and left sides in, over folded end. Fold remaining end down, wrapping around roll. Serve with sauce. *6 servings*

Tomato-Ginger Dipping Sauce

¾ cup tomato puree
2 tablespoons lime juice
1 teaspoon grated gingerroot
1 teaspoon reduced-sodium soy sauce
½ teaspoon sesame oil
½ teaspoon chile paste or 1 teaspoon finely chopped hot chile

Mix all ingredients in small glass or plastic bowl. Cover and refrigerate until serving time.

NUTRITION INFORMATION PER SERVING			
1 serving		**Percent of U.S. RDA**	
Calories	145	Protein	24%
Protein, g	15	Vitamin A	8%
Carbohydrate, g	10	Vitamin C	42%
Fat, g	5	Thiamin	10%
Unsaturated	4	Riboflavin	12%
Saturated	1	Niacin	22%
Dietary Fiber, g	3	Calcium	8%
Cholesterol, mg	30	Iron	16%
Sodium, mg	330		
Potassium, mg	680		

Asian Fish Rolls in Rice-Paper Wrappers

Zesty Fish Stew

1 medium onion, thinly sliced
2 cloves garlic, finely chopped
1 tablespoon chile powder
3 cups chicken broth
1 can (4 ounces) chopped green chiles,
    undrained
3 cups coarsely chopped tomatoes (about 4
    medium)
1 cup chopped green bell pepper (about 1
    medium)
1 cup frozen cooked cleaned shrimp
1 pound frozen cod or other lean fish fillet,
    partially thawed and cut into 1-inch
    pieces
1½ cups plain nonfat yogurt
Chopped fresh cilantro or parsley leaves

Spray nonstick Dutch oven with nonstick cooking spray. Cook onion and garlic in Dutch oven
about 5 minutes, stirring frequently, until onion
is tender. Stir in chile powder. Cook 2 minutes,
stirring frequently. Stir in broth and chiles.
Heat to boiling; reduce heat. Cover and simmer
20 minutes.

Stir in tomatoes, bell pepper, shrimp and fish.
Heat to boiling; reduce heat. Cover and simmer
about 5 minutes or until fish flakes easily with
fork and shrimp are heated through. Gradually
stir in yogurt; heat just until hot (do not boil).
Sprinkle with cilantro. *8 servings*

NUTRITION INFORMATION PER SERVING			
I serving		**Percent of U.S. RDA**	
Calories	135	Protein	30%
Protein, g	19	Vitamin A	10%
Carbohydrate, g	10	Vitamin C	28%
Fat, g	2	Thiamin	8%
Unsaturated	1	Riboflavin	14%
Saturated	1	Niacin	16%
Dietary Fiber, g	1	Calcium	12%
Cholesterol, mg	60	Iron	8%
Sodium, mg	590		
Potassium, mg	600		

Baked Flounder Teriyaki

6 small flounder or other lean fish fillets
(about 1½ pounds)
⅓ cup dry sherry or apple juice
3 tablespoons lemon juice
2 tablespoons chopped green onions
2 teaspoons finely chopped gingerroot
2 teaspoons honey
1 teaspoon vegetable oil
¼ teaspoon pepper
2 cloves garlic, finely chopped

Spray rectangular pan, 13×9×2 inches, with nonstick cooking spray. Place fish fillets in pan. Mix remaining ingredients; spoon over fish. Cover with aluminum foil and refrigerate 1 hour.

Heat oven to 375°. Bake covered 15 to 20 minutes or until fish flakes easily with fork. *6 servings*

NUTRITION INFORMATION PER SERVING

1 serving		Percent of U.S. RDA	
Calories	150	Protein	42%
Protein, g	27	Vitamin A	*
Carbohydrate, g	4	Vitamin C	2%
Fat, g	3	Thiamin	6%
Unsaturated	2	Riboflavin	8%
Saturated	1	Niacin	12%
Dietary Fiber, g	0	Calcium	2%
Cholesterol, mg	75	Iron	2%
Sodium, mg	120		
Potassium, mg	420		

Baked Fish with Tomatoes and Spices

1 large onion, sliced
2 cloves garlic, chopped
2 jalapeño chiles, seeded and chopped
1 can (16 ounces) whole tomatoes, drained
and chopped
2 tablespoons white vinegar
1¼ teaspoons ground cumin
¾ teaspoon ground coriander
4 halibut or other lean fish steaks, about 1
inch thick (about 2 pounds)

Heat oven to 350°. Spray 10-inch nonstick skillet with nonstick cooking spray. Cook onion, garlic and chiles in skillet over medium heat, stirring frequently, until onion is tender; reduce heat. Stir in remaining ingredients except fish steaks. Simmer uncovered over low heat 5 minutes, stirring occasionally.

Arrange fish in ungreased rectangular baking dish, 11×7×1½ inches. Spoon tomato mixture over fish. Bake uncovered 25 to 30 minutes or until fish flakes easily with fork. Sprinkle with chopped fresh cilantro if desired. *4 servings*

NUTRITION INFORMATION PER SERVING

1 serving		Percent of U.S. RDA	
Calories	250	Protein	100%
Protein, g	45	Vitamin A	30%
Carbohydrate, g	11	Vitamin C	52%
Fat, g	3	Thiamin	14%
Unsaturated	2	Riboflavin	14%
Saturated	1	Niacin	24%
Dietary Fiber, g	2	Calcium	8%
Cholesterol, mg	120	Iron	12%
Sodium, mg	370		
Potassium, mg	1010		

Halibut-Asparagus Stir-fry

1 pound fresh asparagus, cut into 1-inch pieces, or 1 package (10 ounces) frozen asparagus cuts, thawed and drained

1-pound halibut or other lean fish steak, cut into 1-inch pieces

1 medium onion, thinly sliced

3 cloves garlic, finely chopped

1 teaspoon finely chopped gingerroot

1 cup sliced mushrooms (about 4 ounces) or 1 jar (4½ ounces) sliced mushrooms, drained

2 tablespoons reduced-sodium soy sauce

1 tablespoon lemon juice

1 medium tomato, cut into thin wedges

Spray 10-inch nonstick skillet with nonstick cooking spray. Heat over medium-high heat. Stir-fry asparagus 2 minutes. Add fish, onion, garlic and gingerroot; stir-fry 2 to 3 minutes or until fish almost flakes with fork. Carefully stir in remaining ingredients. Cook until heated through and fish flakes easily with fork. Serve with additional reduced-sodium soy sauce if desired. *4 servings*

NUTRITION INFORMATION PER SERVING

1 serving		Percent of U.S. RDA	
Calories	160	Protein	38%
Protein, g	25	Vitamin A	6%
Carbohydrate, g	10	Vitamin C	18%
Fat, g	2	Thiamin	10%
Unsaturated	1	Riboflavin	10%
Saturated	1	Niacin	16%
Dietary Fiber, g	3	Calcium	4%
Cholesterol, mg	60	Iron	6%
Sodium, mg	510		
Potassium, mg	600		

Halibut-Asparagus Stir-fry

Salmon with Mint Couscous

Mint Sauce (right)

1½-pound pink salmon or other medium-fat fish fillet, cut into 6 serving pieces

1 teaspoon grated lemon peel

½ teaspoon salt

¼ teaspoon pepper

3 cups hot cooked couscous

2 tablespoons finely chopped fresh or 2 teaspoons dried mint leaves

Prepare Mint Sauce. Sprinkle fish fillets with lemon peel, salt and pepper. Set oven control to broil. Spray broiler pan rack with nonstick cooking spray. Place fish on rack in broiler pan. Broil with tops about 4 inches from heat 5 to 6 minutes or until fish flakes easily with fork.

Mix couscous and mint. Serve fish over couscous with Mint Sauce. *6 servings*

Mint Sauce

¾ cup plain nonfat yogurt

1 tablespoon finely chopped fresh or 1 teaspoon dried mint leaves

1 tablespoon cholesterol-free reduced-calorie mayonnaise or salad dressing

1 teaspoon grated orange peel

1 clove garlic, finely chopped (about ½ teaspoon)

Mix all ingredients.

SALMON WITH DILL COUSCOUS: Substitute 1½ teaspoons chopped fresh or ½ teaspoon dried dill weed for the mint in the sauce. Omit orange peel. Substitute 1 tablespoon chopped fresh or 1 teaspoon dried dill weed for the mint stirred into the couscous.

NUTRITION INFORMATION PER SERVING

1 serving		Percent of U.S. RDA	
Calories	290	Protein	46%
Protein, g	30	Vitamin A	2%
Carbohydrate, g	24	Vitamin C	*
Fat, g	8	Thiamin	16%
Unsaturated	6	Riboflavin	16%
Saturated	2	Niacin	42%
Dietary Fiber, g	1	Calcium	10%
Cholesterol, mg	45	Iron	6%
Sodium, mg	470		
Potassium, mg	620		

Salmon with Mint Couscous

Basil-poached Salmon with Red Pepper Sauce

Red Pepper Sauce (below)

¼ cup chopped shallots (about 2 large)

2½ cups water

½ cup dry white wine or apple juice

2 tablespoons chopped fresh or 2 teaspoons dried basil leaves

½ teaspoon salt

¼ teaspoon white pepper

1 bay leaf

6 small salmon or other fatty fish steaks, about 1 inch thick (about 2 pounds)

Prepare Red Pepper Sauce. Heat remaining ingredients except fish steaks to boiling in 6-quart Dutch oven; reduce heat. Cover and simmer 5 minutes. Place fish in Dutch oven and add water, if necessary, to cover. Heat to boiling; reduce heat. Cover and simmer 10 to 12 minutes or until fish flakes easily with fork. Carefully remove fish with slotted spatula; drain on wire rack. Remove skin. Cover and refrigerate about 4 hours or until chilled. Serve with Red Pepper Sauce. *6 servings*

Red Pepper Sauce

1 large red bell pepper, roasted (page 41)

1 tablespoon chopped fresh or 1 teaspoon dried basil leaves

2 tablespoons chopped green onions

2 tablespoons balsamic vinegar

2 tablespoons lemon juice

2 tablespoons plain nonfat yogurt

½ teaspoon salt

¼ teaspoon pepper

Place bell pepper and remaining ingredients in blender or food processor. Cover and blend on high about 30 seconds or until smooth. Cover and refrigerate about 4 hours or until chilled.

NUTRITION INFORMATION PER SERVING			
1 serving		Percent of U.S. RDA	
Calories	230	Protein	50%
Protein, g	33	Vitamin A	12%
Carbohydrate, g	3	Vitamin C	30%
Fat, g	9	Thiamin	16%
Unsaturated	7	Riboflavin	14%
Saturated	2	Niacin	50%
Dietary Fiber, g	0	Calcium	8%
Cholesterol, mg	60	Iron	8%
Sodium, mg	300		
Potassium, mg	710		

Baked Scrod with Corn Bread Stuffing

¾ cup chicken broth

2 cups soft corn bread crumbs

1 cup finely chopped green onions (about 9 medium)

1 cup cooked fresh, frozen (thawed) or canned (drained) whole kernel corn (about 2 medium ears)

½ cup finely chopped green bell pepper (about 1 small)

½ cup finely chopped celery (about 1 medium stalk)

¼ cup cholesterol-free egg product or 2 egg whites

¼ teaspoon salt

¼ teaspoon pepper

6 small scrod or other lean fish fillets (about 1½ pounds)

½ teaspoon paprika

Heat oven to 375°. Spray rectangular baking dish, 13×9×2 inches, with nonstick cooking spray. Reserve ¼ cup of the broth. Mix remaining broth and ingredients except fish fillets and paprika. Spread corn bread mixture in dish.

Bake uncovered about 15 minutes or until brown. Arrange fish on corn bread mixture in dish. Bake uncovered about 15 minutes or until brown. Arrange fish on corn bread mixture. Mix reserved broth and the paprika; brush on fish. Cover and bake 15 to 18 minutes or until fish flakes easily with fork. *6 servings*

NUTRITION INFORMATION PER SERVING

1 serving		Percent of U.S. RDA	
Calories	255	Protein	42%
Protein, g	27	Vitamin A	6%
Carbohydrate, g	23	Vitamin C	10%
Fat, g	6	Thiamin	16%
Unsaturated	4	Riboflavin	18%
Saturated	2	Niacin	18%
Dietary Fiber, g	2	Calcium	12%
Cholesterol, mg	80	Iron	10%
Sodium, mg	490		
Potassium, mg	540		

Seafood Stew with Rosamarina

To devein shrimp, make a shallow cut along the outside length of the shrimp with a small knife. Remove the black vein and wash.

½ cup chopped green onions (about 5 medium)

1 clove garlic, finely chopped

1 cup coarsely chopped tomato (about 1 large)

½ cup thinly sliced carrot (about 1 medium)

⅓ cup uncooked rosamarina (orzo) pasta

1¾ cups chicken broth

1 bottle (8 ounces) clam juice

½ cup dry white wine

1 tablespoon chopped fresh or 1 teaspoon dried thyme leaves

2 teaspoons chopped fresh or ½ teaspoon dried dill weed

6 drops red pepper sauce

½-pound red snapper or other lean fish fillet, skinned and cut into ½-inch pieces

8 mussels, scrubbed and debearded

8 raw medium shrimp, peeled and deveined

½ cup sliced mushrooms (about 2 ounces)

Chopped fresh parsley

Lemon wedges

Spray nonstick Dutch oven with nonstick cooking spray. Cook onions and garlic in Dutch oven over medium heat about 5 minutes, stirring occasionally. Stir in tomato, carrot, pasta, broth, clam juice, wine, thyme, dill weed and pepper sauce. Heat to boiling; reduce heat. Cover and simmer about 20 minutes, stirring occasionally, until pasta is almost tender.

Stir in fish, mussels, shrimp and mushrooms. Cover and heat to boiling; reduce heat. Simmer 6 to 8 minutes, stirring occasionally, until fish flakes easily with fork and mussels open, removing mussels as they open, reserve. Discard any unopened mussels. Return reserved mussels to stew. Sprinkle with parsley. Serve with lemon wedges. *4 servings*

NUTRITION INFORMATION PER SERVING

1 serving		Percent of U.S. RDA	
Calories	190	Protein	34%
Protein, g	22	Vitamin A	42%
Carbohydrate, g	18	Vitamin C	28%
Fat, g	2	Thiamin	14%
Unsaturated	1	Riboflavin	16%
Saturated	1	Niacin	24%
Dietary Fiber, g	2	Calcium	6%
Cholesterol, mg	60	Iron	38%
Sodium, mg	720		
Potassium, mg	750		

Sole with Apples and Mint, Rice Stir-fry (page 129)

Sole with Apples and Mint

4 cups chopped eating apples (about 4
   medium)
½ cup cranberry juice cocktail
2 tablespoons lemon juice
½ cup shredded eating apple
¼ cup dry bread crumbs
2 tablespoons finely chopped onion
1 tablespoon finely chopped fresh or 1
   teaspoon dried mint leaves
1 teaspoon grated lemon peel
¼ teaspoon salt
¼ teaspoon pepper
1 egg white
6 small sole or other lean fish fillets (about
   1½ pounds)

Heat oven to 375°. Spray rectangular pan,
13×9×2 inches, with nonstick cooking spray.
Cover and cook chopped apples, cranberry
juice and lemon juice in 3-quart saucepan over
medium heat 10 minutes or until apples are
almost tender.

Mix remaining ingredients except fish fillets.
Place 2 tablespoons bread crumb mixture on
center of each fish fillet; fold ends of fish over
mixture. Place fish, seam sides down in pan.
Cover with aluminum foil and bake 10 to 12
minutes or until fish flakes easily with fork.
Serve fish with apples. *6 servings*

NUTRITION INFORMATION PER SERVING			
1 serving		**Percent of U.S. RDA**	
Calories	175	Protein	44%
Protein, g	20	Vitamin A	*
Carbohydrate, g	19	Vitamin C	10%
Fat, g	2	Thiamin	6%
Unsaturated	2	Riboflavin	8%
Saturated	0	Niacin	10%
Dietary Fiber, g	2	Calcium	2%
Cholesterol, mg	55	Iron	2%
Sodium, mg	210		
Potassium, mg	390		

Broiled Caribbean Swordfish

The Papaya Salsa is also a refreshing addition to grilled chicken. And, as you can see from the variation, it's also the great beginning of a meatless salad.

Papaya Salsa (right)
¼ cup lime juice
¼ cup grapefruit juice
1 tablespoon grated lime peel
¼ teaspoon salt
1 clove garlic, crushed
4 swordfish or shark steaks, about 1 inch thick (about 1½ pounds)

Prepare Papaya Salsa. Mix remaining ingredients except fish steaks in ungreased square baking dish, 8×8×2 inches. Add fish steaks; turn to coat with marinade. Cover and refrigerate at least 2 hours.

Set oven control to broil. Spray broiler pan rack with nonstick cooking spray. Remove fish from marinade; reserve marinade. Place fish on rack in broiler pan. Broil with tops about 4 inches from heat about 16 minutes, turning and brushing with marinade after 8 minutes, until fish flakes easily with fork. Serve fish with salsa.
4 servings

Papaya Salsa

2 cups chopped seeded peeled papaya
  (about 1 large)
¼ cup finely chopped red bell pepper
1 tablespoon finely chopped green onion
1 tablespoon chopped fresh cilantro leaves
2 to 3 tablespoons grapefruit juice
⅛ teaspoon salt

Mix all ingredients. Cover and refrigerate until serving time.

BROWN RICE–PAPAYA SALAD: Omit swordfish. Prepare Papaya Salsa in large glass or plastic bowl, substituting ¼ cup orange juice for the grapefruit juice. Stir in 4 cups cooked brown rice (about 1 cup uncooked). Cover and refrigerate at least 2 hours or until chilled.

NUTRITION INFORMATION PER SERVING			
1 serving		**Percent of U.S. RDA**	
Calories	240	Protein	50%
Protein, g	33	Vitamin A	10%
Carbohydrate, g	14	Vitamin C	76%
Fat, g	6	Thiamin	10%
Unsaturated	5	Riboflavin	18%
Saturated	1	Niacin	44%
Dietary Fiber, g	3	Calcium	14%
Cholesterol, mg	90	Iron	18%
Sodium, mg	280		
Potassium, mg	1110		

Swordfish with White Beans

1-pound swordfish or other medium-fat fish
steak, cut into 1-inch cubes

2 tablespoons lemon juice

1 teaspoon fresh or ½ teaspoon dried
rosemary leaves, crushed

¼ teaspoon salt

1 clove garlic, finely chopped

4 cups cooked cannellini or navy beans
(page 320) or 2 cans (about 15 ounces
each) cannellini or navy beans, drained

1 cup chopped tomato (about 1 large)

½ cup chopped onion (about ½ medium)

1⅓ cups chicken broth

1½ teaspoons fresh or ¾ teaspoon dried
rosemary leaves, crushed

¼ teaspoon pepper

2 tablespoons chopped fresh parsley

Mix fish, lemon juice, ½ teaspoon rosemary, the salt and garlic in medium glass or plastic bowl. Cover and refrigerate 30 minutes.

Meanwhile, cook remaining ingredients except parsley in 3-quart saucepan over medium-low heat 15 minutes, stirring occasionally. Stir in fish mixture. Cover and cook over medium heat 10 to 12 minutes, stirring occasionally, or until fish flakes easily with fork. Stir in parsley.
6 servings

NUTRITION INFORMATION PER SERVING

1 serving		Percent of U.S. RDA	
Calories	290	Protein	44%
Protein, g	29	Vitamin A	4%
Carbohydrate, g	37	Vitamin C	8%
Fat, g	3	Thiamin	14%
Unsaturated	2	Riboflavin	12%
Saturated	1	Niacin	24%
Dietary Fiber, g	8	Calcium	18%
Cholesterol, mg	40	Iron	36%
Sodium, mg	600		
Potassium, mg	1240		

Swordfish with White Beans, Ginger-glazed Carrots (page 116)

Summer Swordfish with Citrus and Basil

6 small swordfish or other medium-fat fish
  steaks, about 1 inch thick (about 1½
  pounds)
1 cup orange juice
¼ cup chopped fresh basil leaves
2 tablespoons lemon juice
2 tablespoons lime juice
1 teaspoon grated lemon peel
1 teaspoon grated lime peel
1 teaspoon olive or vegetable oil
½ teaspoon salt
¼ teaspoon pepper
Lemon wedges

Place fish steaks in shallow glass or plastic dish.
Mix remaining ingredients except lemon
wedges; pour over fish. Cover and refrigerate at
least 30 minutes.

Heat oven to 375°. Place fish with marinade in
ungreased rectangular pan, 13×9×2 inches.
Cover with aluminum foil and bake 10 to 15
minutes or until fish flakes easily with fork.
Serve with lemon wedges. *6 servings*

NUTRITION INFORMATION PER SERVING

1 serving		Percent of U.S. RDA	
Calories	155	Protein	34%
Protein, g	22	Vitamin A	4%
Carbohydrate, g	7	Vitamin C	20%
Fat, g	4	Thiamin	6%
Unsaturated	3	Riboflavin	12%
Saturated	1	Niacin	30%
Dietary Fiber, g	1	Calcium	14%
Cholesterol, mg	60	Iron	18%
Sodium, mg	210		
Potassium, mg	710		

Sautéed Tuna with Creamy Tarragon Sauce

6 small yellowfin tuna or other lean fish
  steaks, about 1 inch thick (about 1½
  pounds)
¾ cup apple juice
3 tablespoons low-fat sour cream
2 tablespoons chopped fresh or 2 teaspoons
  dried tarragon leaves
¼ teaspoon ground mustard

Spray 10-inch skillet with nonstick cooking
spray. Cook fish steaks in skillet over medium-
high heat 5 minutes; turn. Cover and cook 5 to 6
minutes longer or until fish flakes easily with
fork. Mix apple juice, sour cream, tarragon and
mustard.

Remove fish from skillet; keep warm. Add apple juice mixture to skillet; heat to boiling. Boil
5 to 6 minutes or until reduced to ½ cup. Serve
over fish. *6 servings*

NUTRITION INFORMATION PER SERVING

1 serving		Percent of U.S. RDA	
Calories	180	Protein	42%
Protein, g	27	Vitamin A	70%
Carbohydrate, g	5	Vitamin C	*
Fat, g	6	Thiamin	18%
Unsaturated	4	Riboflavin	18%
Saturated	2	Niacin	48%
Dietary Fiber, g	0	Calcium	2%
Cholesterol, mg	45	Iron	6%
Sodium, mg	50		
Potassium, mg	340		

Seafood Marinara with Linguine

8 ounces uncooked linguine

¾ cup tomato puree

¾ cup white wine or apple juice

2 cloves garlic, finely chopped

1 teaspoon olive or vegetable oil

1 can (14½ ounces) whole tomatoes, undrained

1-pound yellowfin tuna or other lean fish fillet, cut into 1-inch pieces

3 tablespoons chopped fresh or 1 tablespoon dried basil leaves

1 teaspoon grated lemon peel

2 tablespoons lemon juice

2 teaspoons capers

¼ teaspoon pepper

Cook pasta according to package directions—except omit salt; drain. Cook tomato puree, wine, garlic, oil and tomatoes in 2-quart saucepan over medium heat 10 minutes, breaking up tomatoes and stirring occasionally. Stir in fish. Cover and simmer 7 minutes or until fish flakes easily with fork. Stir in cooked linguine and remaining ingredients. *6 servings*

NUTRITION INFORMATION PER SERVING

1 serving		Percent of U.S. RDA	
Calories	300	Protein	36%
Protein, g	24	Vitamin A	54%
Carbohydrate, g	38	Vitamin C	14%
Fat, g	5	Thiamin	30%
Unsaturated	4	Riboflavin	20%
Saturated	1	Niacin	46%
Dietary Fiber, g	2	Calcium	6%
Cholesterol, mg	30	Iron	18%
Sodium, mg	420		
Potassium, mg	590		

Tuna and Artichoke Pasta

1 package (9 ounces) frozen artichoke hearts

1 package (10 ounces) frozen green peas

1 medium onion, sliced

½ cup diagonally sliced celery (about 1 medium stalk)

¼ cup water

1 teaspoon fresh or ¼ teaspoon dried tarragon leaves

¼ teaspoon pepper

2 cans (6⅛ ounces each) tuna in water, drained and flaked

1 jar (2 ounces) diced pimientos, drained

1 tablespoon lemon juice

3 cups hot cooked fettuccine

Rinse artichoke hearts and peas in cold water to separate; drain. Spray 10-inch nonstick skillet with nonstick cooking spray. Cook onion and celery in skillet about 5 minutes, stirring frequently, until onion is tender. Stir in artichoke hearts, peas, water, tarragon and pepper. Heat to boiling; reduce heat. Cover and simmer about 10 minutes or until vegetables are tender. Stir in tuna, pimientos and lemon juice. Heat uncovered just until tuna is hot. Toss with fettuccine. *6 servings*

NUTRITION INFORMATION PER SERVING

1 serving		Percent of U.S. RDA	
Calories	250	Protein	36%
Protein, g	24	Vitamin A	8%
Carbohydrate, g	34	Vitamin C	16%
Fat, g	2	Thiamin	22%
Unsaturated	1	Riboflavin	12%
Saturated	1	Niacin	46%
Dietary Fiber, g	6	Calcium	6%
Cholesterol, mg	35	Iron	24%
Sodium, mg	420		
Potassium, mg	500		

Soft Fish Tacos

Who said tacos had to be made with ground meat? Although the Spicy Fresh Chile Sauce is wonderful, you can also substitute bottled salsa. Finely chopped cucumbers, radishes and green peppers are tasty additions.

Spicy Fresh Chile Sauce (right)
2 tablespoons lime juice
1 teaspoon vegetable oil
1 pound yellowfin tuna or other lean fish steaks
8 flour tortillas (8 inches in diameter), warmed
¾ cup shredded lettuce (about ¼ small head)
¾ cup finely chopped red bell pepper (about 1 small)
½ cup finely chopped onion (about 1 medium)

Prepare Spicy Fresh Chile Sauce. Set oven control to broil. Spray broiler pan rack with non-stick cooking spray. Mix lime juice and oil; brush over fish steaks. Place fish on rack in broiler pan. Broil with tops about 4 inches from heat 5 minutes; turn. Broil 5 to 8 minutes longer or until fish flakes easily with fork.

Break fish into large flakes or cut into 1-inch cubes. Spoon scant ½ cup fish onto center of each tortilla. Top with lettuce, bell pepper and onion. Roll up tortilla. Serve with sauce. *4 servings*

Spicy Fresh Chile Sauce

¾ cup finely chopped tomato (about 1 medium)
⅓ cup sliced green onions (about 3 medium)
1 tablespoon finely chopped hot green chile (about 1 small)
1 tablespoon chopped fresh cilantro leaves
¼ teaspoon ground cumin
1 clove garlic, finely chopped

Mix all ingredients.

NUTRITION INFORMATION PER SERVING			
I serving		Percent of U.S. RDA	
Calories	445	Protein	48%
Protein, g	31	Vitamin A	18%
Carbohydrate, g	53	Vitamin C	46%
Fat, g	12	Thiamin	28%
Unsaturated	8	Riboflavin	24%
Saturated	4	Niacin	48%
Dietary Fiber, g	3	Calcium	14%
Cholesterol, mg	75	Iron	34%
Sodium, mg	360		
Potassium, mg	870		

Fluffy Fish Frittata

This frittata is low-fat, low-cholesterol, low-sodium and under 350 calories. Serve with Triple Wheat–Honey Muffins (page 68) and it will be high-fiber too! This dish is nice at a brunch along with Mixed Summer Fruit Freeze (page 391).

½ cup chopped cooked baking potato
  (about 1 small)
¼ cup finely chopped onion (about 1 small)
¼ cup chicken broth
¼ teaspoon pepper
½ cup cholesterol-free egg product
2 egg whites
1½ cups chopped cooked whitefish or other
  medium-fat fish fillets (about ½ pound)

Spray 10-inch skillet with nonstick cooking spray. Cook potato, onion, broth and pepper in skillet over medium heat 3 minutes, stirring occasionally.

Mix egg product and egg whites with fork or wire whisk. Stir fish into potato mixture in skillet. Pour egg mixture over fish mixture. Rotate skillet to spread egg mixture evenly. Cook 5 minutes or until egg mixture is set; remove from heat. Cool slightly. Cut into 6 wedges.
6 servings

NUTRITION INFORMATION PER SERVING

1 serving		Percent of U.S. RDA	
Calories	70	Protein	24%
Protein, g	11	Vitamin A	2%
Carbohydrate, g	3	Vitamin C	2%
Fat, g	1	Thiamin	12%
Unsaturated	1	Riboflavin	12%
Saturated	0	Niacin	12%
Dietary Fiber, g	0	Calcium	4%
Cholesterol, mg	20	Iron	6%
Sodium, mg	100		
Potassium, mg	2		

Warm Mahimahi Salad

⅓ cup thinly sliced green onions
½ cup orange juice
2 tablespoons lemon juice
1 teaspoon finely chopped gingerroot
2 teaspoons reduced-sodium soy sauce
¼ teaspoon pepper
1½ pounds mahimahi fillets, skinned, cut
  into 6 serving pieces
6 cups bite-size pieces spinach
3 medium oranges, peeled and thinly sliced
1 small cucumber, sliced
1 tablespoon vegetable oil

Mix onions, orange juice, lemon juice, gingerroot, soy sauce and pepper in shallow glass or plastic dish. Add fish fillets; turn to coat with marinade. Cover and refrigerate at least 2 hours.

Set oven control to broil. Spray broiler pan rack with nonstick cooking spray. Remove fish from marinade; reserve marinade. Place fish on rack in broiler pan. Broil with tops about 4 inches from heat 4 minutes; turn. Broil 5 to 7 minutes longer or until fish flakes easily with fork. Arrange spinach, oranges and cucumber on dinner plates. Place fish on spinach mixture. Pour marinade and oil into 1-quart saucepan. Boil until reduced to ½ cup. Pour over fish. *6 servings*

NUTRITION INFORMATION PER SERVING

1 serving		Percent of U.S. RDA	
Calories	140	Protein	38%
Protein, g	25	Vitamin A	80%
Carbohydrate, g	6	Vitamin C	24%
Fat, g	2	Thiamin	10%
Unsaturated	2	Riboflavin	16%
Saturated	0	Niacin	14%
Dietary Fiber, g	3	Calcium	12%
Cholesterol, mg	60	Iron	18%
Sodium, mg	240		
Potassium, mg	920		

Summer Scallops with Melon Relish

1½ cups finely chopped cantaloupe (about ½ medium)

1½ cups finely chopped honeydew melon (about ½ small)

3 tablespoons chopped fresh cilantro leaves

2 tablespoons finely chopped shallot (about 1 large)

2 tablespoons lemon juice

½ teaspoon salt

⅛ teaspoon pepper

⅛ teaspoon crushed red pepper

1 pound sea scallops

Mix all ingredients except scallops; reserve 2 cups. Mix remaining relish and the scallops in glass or plastic bowl. Cover and refrigerate scallop mixture and 2 cups reserved relish separately at least 1 hour.

Set oven control to broil. Spray broiler pan rack with nonstick cooking spray. Remove scallops from marinade. Thread scallops on six 11-inch skewers.* Broil with tops about 4 inches from heat 3 minutes; turn. Broil about 3 minutes longer or until scallops are firm. Serve reserved relish over scallops. *6 servings*

* If using bamboo skewers, soak in water at least 30 minutes before using to prevent burning.

NUTRITION INFORMATION PER SERVING

	I serving		Percent of U.S. RDA
Calories	115	Protein	38%
Protein, g	17	Vitamin A	16%
Carbohydrate, g	10	Vitamin C	52%
Fat, g	1	Thiamin	4%
Unsaturated	1	Riboflavin	4%
Saturated	0	Niacin	6%
Dietary Fiber, g	1	Calcium	10%
Cholesterol, mg	25	Iron	14%
Sodium, mg	390		
Potassium, mg	620		

Summer Scallops with Melon Relish

Shrimp and Artichoke Pizza

Shrimp and Artichoke Pizza

½ pound raw large shrimp, peeled and deveined (about 12)

½ package (9-ounce size) frozen artichoke hearts, thawed (about 1 cup)

1 cup chopped tomato (about 1 large)

3 tablespoons chopped fresh or 1 tablespoon dried basil leaves

1 tablespoon lemon juice

1 teaspoon olive or vegetable oil

¼ teaspoon pepper

Herbed Pizza Crust (page 108)

1 tablespoon stone-ground or degerminated cornmeal

½ cup shredded part-skim mozzarella cheese

2 tablespoons grated Parmesan cheese

Cut shrimp lengthwise into halves. Mix shrimp, artichoke hearts, tomato, basil, lemon juice, oil and pepper in large glass or plastic bowl. Cover and refrigerate. Prepare Herbed Pizza Crust dough.

Heat oven to 425°. Sprinkle 12-inch pizza pan with cornmeal. Roll pizza crust dough into 12-inch circle on lightly floured surface; ease into pan. Sprinkle with mozzarella cheese. Top with shrimp-artichoke mixture. Sprinkle with Parmesan cheese. Bake 15 to 20 minutes or until crust is golden brown. *6 slices*

NUTRITION INFORMATION PER SERVING			
1 slice		Percent of U.S. RDA	
Calories	250	Protein	20%
Protein, g	13	Vitamin A	6%
Carbohydrate, g	38	Vitamin C	10%
Fat, g	5	Thiamin	24%
Unsaturated	3	Riboflavin	18%
Saturated	2	Niacin	20%
Dietary Fiber, g	4	Calcium	12%
Cholesterol, mg	40	Iron	18%
Sodium, mg	210		
Potassium, mg	340		

Southwestern Stir-fried Shrimp

2 tablespoons lime juice

2 teaspoons cornstarch

¹/₂ teaspoon ground cumin

¹/₄ teaspoon salt

¹/₄ teaspoon pepper

1¹/₂ pounds raw large shrimp, peeled and deveined (about 24)

1¹/₂ cups chopped yellow bell pepper (about 1¹/₂ medium)

1¹/₂ cups chopped red bell pepper (about 1¹/₂ medium)

1 cup chopped red onion (about 1 medium)

¹/₃ cup chicken broth

2 cloves garlic, finely chopped

¹/₈ teaspoon ground red pepper (cayenne)

2 tablespoons chopped fresh cilantro leaves

Mix lime juice, cornstarch, cumin, salt and pepper in medium glass or plastic bowl. Stir in shrimp. Cover and refrigerate 1 hour.

Spray 12-inch skillet with nonstick cooking spray. Cook bell peppers, onion, broth, garlic, red pepper and cilantro in skillet over medium heat 2 minutes, stirring constantly. Stir in shrimp mixture. Cook 3 to 4 minutes, stirring constantly, until shrimp are pink. *6 servings*

NUTRITION INFORMATION PER SERVING			
I serving		Percent of U.S. RDA	
Calories	110	Protein	28%
Protein, g	18	Vitamin A	34%
Carbohydrate, g	7	Vitamin C	84%
Fat, g	1	Thiamin	4%
Unsaturated	1	Riboflavin	2%
Saturated	0	Niacin	12%
Dietary Fiber, g	1	Calcium	4%
Cholesterol, mg	160	Iron	16%
Sodium, mg	320		
Potassium, mg	310		

Shrimp and Zucchini

1 can (8 ounces) pineapple chunks in juice, drained and juice reserved

1 package (12 ounces) frozen uncooked peeled and deveined medium shrimp

1 tablespoon cornstarch

2 tablespoons cold water

1 clove garlic, finely chopped

1 medium onion, sliced

2 cups ¹/₄-inch slices zucchini (about 1 medium)

1 tablespoon reduced-sodium soy sauce

1 teaspoon sugar

¹/₄ teaspoon ground ginger

2 medium tomatoes, cut into wedges

Add enough water to reserved pineapple juice to measure ¹/₂ cup. Rinse frozen shrimp with cold water to separate; drain. Mix cornstarch and cold water.

Spray 10-inch nonstick skillet with nonstick cooking spray. Heat over medium-high heat until hot. Cook shrimp, garlic, onion and zucchini in skillet about 3 minutes, stirring frequently, until vegetables are crisp-tender. Stir in pineapple juice, soy sauce, sugar and ginger. Heat to boiling. Stir in cornstarch mixture. Cook and stir 10 seconds. Stir in pineapple and tomatoes; heat just until hot. *4 servings*

NUTRITION INFORMATION PER SERVING			
I serving		Percent of U.S. RDA	
Calories	140	Protein	22%
Protein, g	15	Vitamin A	8%
Carbohydrate, g	18	Vitamin C	20%
Fat, g	1	Thiamin	10%
Unsaturated	1	Riboflavin	4%
Saturated	0	Niacin	12%
Dietary Fiber, g	3	Calcium	4%
Cholesterol, mg	120	Iron	16%
Sodium, mg	300		
Potassium, mg	490		

Cod Salad with Thai Sauce

A daikon is a large white radish with a mild flavor. It's used here to balance the bite of the red radish. If red radishes don't agree with you, replace them with thinly sliced carrots or chopped apple.

Thai Sauce (right)

3 cups shredded lettuce (about 1 small head)

3 cups 1-inch pieces cooked cod or whitefish (about 1½ pounds)

1 cup sliced red radishes (about 12 medium)

1 cup sliced daikon white radish (about 1 medium)

1 tablespoon chopped fresh cilantro leaves

1 tablespoon flaked coconut

Prepare Thai Sauce. Divide lettuce among 6 plates. Top with fish and radishes. Sprinkle with cilantro and coconut. Serve with sauce.
6 servings

Thai Sauce

½ cup chicken broth

2 tablespoons lime juice

1 teaspoon chopped fresh or ¼ teaspoon dried mint leaves

1 teaspoon chopped fresh or ¼ teaspoon dried basil leaves

1 teaspoon finely chopped fresh gingerroot

1 teaspoon finely chopped hot chile

2 teaspoons reduced-sodium soy sauce

Mix all ingredients.

CHICKEN SALAD WITH THAI SAUCE: Substitute 3 cups shredded cabbage for the lettuce, 3 cups cubed cooked chicken or turkey for the cod and 1 cup thinly sliced carrots for the red radishes.

NUTRITION INFORMATION PER SERVING			
I serving		**Percent of U.S. RDA**	
Calories	100	Protein	26%
Protein, g	17	Vitamin A	2%
Carbohydrate, g	3	Vitamin C	22%
Fat, g	2	Thiamin	4%
Unsaturated	1	Riboflavin	6%
Saturated	1	Niacin	10%
Dietary Fiber, g	1	Calcium	2%
Cholesterol, mg	45	Iron	4%
Sodium, mg	220		
Potassium, mg	400		

Wild Rice and Walleye Salad, Warm Mahimahi Salad (page 290)

Wild Rice and Walleye Salad

¾ cup frozen (thawed) cranberry juice cocktail concentrate

3 tablespoons cider vinegar

¼ teaspoon salt

¼ teaspoon pepper

3 cups 1-inch pieces cooked walleye pike or other lean fish fillets (about 1 pound)

3 cups cooked wild rice

2 cups shredded spinach

1½ cups chopped celery (about 2 large stalks)

¾ cup sliced onions (about 2 small)

¾ cup finely chopped carrots (about 1½ medium)

¼ cup chopped dried cranberries or raisins

2 tablespoons chopped fresh chives

Mix juice concentrate, vinegar, salt and pepper in large bowl. Add remaining ingredients; toss. Cover and refrigerate at least 1 hour. *6 servings*

NUTRITION INFORMATION PER SERVING

1 serving		Percent of U.S. RDA	
Calories	260	Protein	30%
Protein, g	19	Vitamin A	44%
Carbohydrate, g	42	Vitamin C	46%
Fat, g	2	Thiamin	10%
Unsaturated	2	Riboflavin	12%
Saturated	0	Niacin	14%
Dietary Fiber, g	3	Calcium	6%
Cholesterol, mg	40	Iron	10%
Sodium, mg	480		
Potassium, mg	610		

Salmon-Pasta Salad with Spinach Pesto

Spinach is used in place of the traditional fresh basil for a colorful dish full of flavor. For a tasty change, serve with Whole Wheat Popovers (page 71) instead of garlic toast.

Spinach Pesto (below)
3 cups 1½-inch pieces cooked salmon or other fatty fish fillets (about 1 pound)
3 cups cooked ziti pasta
2 cups cooked cut green beans (about 11 ounces)
2 cups shredded zucchini (about 2 medium)
2 cups chopped roma (plum) tomatoes (about 8 medium)
1 cup cooked fresh, frozen (thawed) or canned (drained) whole kernel corn (about 2 medium ears)

Prepare Spinach Pesto. Mix pesto and remaining ingredients in large glass or plastic bowl. Cover and refrigerate at least 2 hours. *6 servings*

Spinach Pesto

1 cup fresh parsley sprigs
¾ cup cooked chopped spinach
½ cup chicken broth
2 tablespoons lemon juice
1 teaspoon olive or vegetable oil
¼ teaspoon salt
¼ teaspoon pepper
1 garlic clove, cut into halves

Place all ingredients in blender or food processor. Cover and blend on high 30 seconds or until smooth.

NUTRITION INFORMATION PER SERVING			
1 serving		Percent of U.S. RDA	
Calories	280	Protein	36%
Protein, g	23	Vitamin A	32%
Carbohydrate, g	33	Vitamin C	64%
Fat, g	6	Thiamin	26%
Unsaturated	5	Riboflavin	18%
Saturated	1	Niacin	38%
Dietary Fiber, g	4	Calcium	10%
Cholesterol, mg	30	Iron	18%
Sodium, mg	330		
Potassium, mg	820		

Fresh Tuna and Red Potato Salad

Mix the ingredients while the potatoes are still hot—their warmth releases the flavors of the dressing, allowing the potatoes to absorb more flavor. In fact, if the potatoes and tuna are both hot, you can eat this immediately as a warm salad.

3 cups ½-inch cubes cooked red potatoes (about 1 pound)
3 cups 1-inch pieces grilled yellowfin tuna or other lean fish fillets (about 1 pound)
2 cups chopped celery (about 4 medium stalks)
1 cup plain nonfat yogurt
¼ cup chopped fresh parsley
2 tablespoons red wine vinegar or cider vinegar
½ teaspoon salt
½ teaspoon ground cumin
¼ teaspoon pepper

Mix all ingredients in glass or plastic bowl. Cover and refrigerate about 2 hours, or until chilled. *6 servings*

NUTRITION INFORMATION PER SERVING			
I serving		**Percent of U.S. RDA**	
Calories	185	Protein	30%
Protein, g	20	Vitamin A	2%
Carbohydrate, g	20	Vitamin C	12%
Fat, g	3	Thiamin	10%
Unsaturated	2	Riboflavin	14%
Saturated	1	Niacin	26%
Dietary Fiber, g	2	Calcium	16%
Cholesterol, mg	45	Iron	12%
Sodium, mg	270		
Potassium, mg	880		

Asparagus and Trout Salad with Horseradish Sauce

Horseradish Sauce (below)
6 cups torn Boston lettuce (about 1 large
   head)
1 pound asparagus spears (about 24),
   cooked
6 small trout or other medium-fat fish
   fillets (about 1½ pounds), cooked

Prepare Horseradish Sauce. Divide lettuce among 6 plates. Arrange asparagus and fish on lettuce. Spoon sauce over top or serve as an accompaniment. *6 servings*

Horseradish Sauce

¾ cup plain nonfat yogurt
⅓ cup chopped hard-cooked egg whites
   (about 2)
1 tablespoon chopped sweet pickle

1 tablespoon chopped fresh or 1 teaspoon
   dried tarragon leaves
1 tablespoon white wine vinegar or cider
   vinegar
1 tablespoon cholesterol-free reduced-
   calorie mayonnaise or salad dressing
1 tablespoon prepared horseradish
¼ teaspoon pepper

Mix all ingredients in glass or plastic bowl. Cover and refrigerate at least 2 hours.

NUTRITION INFORMATION PER SERVING			
I serving		**Percent of U.S. RDA**	
Calories	210	Protein	42%
Protein, g	28	Vitamin A	6%
Carbohydrate, g	6	Vitamin C	10%
Fat, g	8	Thiamin	14%
Unsaturated	6	Riboflavin	20%
Saturated	2	Niacin	38%
Dietary Fiber, g	1	Calcium	12%
Cholesterol, mg	45	Iron	8%
Sodium, mg	125		
Potassium, mg	730		

Marinated Shrimp Kabob Salad

The salad greens can vary from all of one kind to a mixture of several. See Seafood Stew with Rosamarina (page 281) for directions on deveining shrimp.

1 tablespoon grated orange peel

½ cup orange juice

2 tablespoons vegetable oil

½ teaspoon crushed red pepper

¼ teaspoon salt

2 cloves garlic, crushed

16 large raw shrimp, peeled and deveined

8 ounces jícama, peeled and cut into 1-inch pieces

1 medium red bell pepper, cut into 1½-inch pieces

½ small pineapple, peeled and cut into chunks

4 cups bite-size pieces salad greens

Mix orange peel, orange juice, oil, red pepper, salt and garlic in large glass or plastic bowl. Reserve ⅓ cup orange juice mixture; cover and refrigerate. Toss shrimp and remaining orange juice mixture in bowl. Cover and refrigerate at least 2 hours but no longer than 24 hours.

Set oven control to broil. Remove shrimp from marinade; reserve marinade. Thread shrimp, jícama, bell pepper and pineapple alternately on each of eight 10-inch skewers.* Place on rack in broiler pan.

Broil with tops about 4 inches from heat about 8 minutes, turning and brushing once with marinade, until shrimp are pink. Arrange salad greens on 4 plates. Top each with 2 kabobs; remove skewers. Serve with reserved orange juice mixture. *4 servings*

* If using bamboo skewers, soak in water at least 30 minutes before using to prevent burning.

NUTRITION INFORMATION PER SERVING			
I serving		**Percent of U.S. RDA**	
Calories	170	Protein	12%
Protein, g	7	Vitamin A	14%
Carbohydrate, g	17	Vitamin C	100%
Fat, g	8	Thiamin	10%
Unsaturated	6	Riboflavin	4%
Saturated	2	Niacin	6%
Dietary Fiber, g	2	Calcium	4%
Cholesterol, mg	55	Iron	10%
Sodium, mg	200		
Potassium, mg	390		

Poached Shrimp and Fennel Salad

This salad, combining the flavors of white wine, fennel and shrimp, is also nice served on a bed of Boston lettuce leaves.

3 cups sliced fennel bulbs (about 2 medium)
2 cups chopped tomatoes (about 2 large)
½ cup sliced red onion (about ½ medium)
1 tablespoon chopped fresh or 1 teaspoon dried dill weed
3 tablespoons lemon juice
1 tablespoon olive or vegetable oil
½ teaspoon salt
¼ teaspoon pepper
1½ cups white wine or apple juice
1 teaspoon grated lemon peel
1½ pounds raw large shrimp, peeled and deveined (about 24)

Mix all ingredients except wine, lemon peel, and shrimp in large glass or plastic bowl. Heat wine and lemon peel to boiling in 12-inch skillet; reduce heat. Stir in shrimp. Simmer 3 to 4 minutes, turning once, until shrimp are pink; remove from heat. Stir shrimp and 1 cup hot cooking liquid into fennel mixture. Cool 10 minutes. Cover and refrigerate at least 1 hour. *6 servings*

NUTRITION INFORMATION PER SERVING

1 serving		Percent of U.S. RDA	
Calories	145	Protein	40%
Protein, g	18	Vitamin A	8%
Carbohydrate, g	5	Vitamin C	12%
Fat, g	3	Thiamin	4%
Unsaturated	2	Riboflavin	4%
Saturated	1	Niacin	12%
Dietary Fiber, g	1	Calcium	4%
Cholesterol, mg	160	Iron	16%
Sodium, mg	370		
Potassium, mg	360		

Shrimp and Mushroom-Pasta Salad

3 cups sliced mushrooms (about 8 ounces)
½ cup chopped onion (about 1 medium)
1 cup chicken broth
2 cloves garlic, finely chopped
12 raw jumbo shrimp, peeled, deveined and cut into halves (about 1 pound)
3 cups cooked radiatore or other small pasta
¼ cup chopped green onions (2 to 3 medium)
2 tablespoons lemon juice
2 tablespoons low-fat sour cream
¼ teaspoon salt
¼ teaspoon pepper
3 cups shredded romaine (about ½ large head)

Heat mushrooms, onion, broth and garlic to boiling in 3-quart saucepan; reduce heat. Simmer uncovered 3 minutes. Stir in shrimp. Simmer about 4 minutes or until shrimp are pink; remove from heat. Cool 5 minutes.

Stir remaining ingredients except romaine into shrimp mixture in glass or plastic bowl. Cover and refrigerate 2 hours or until chilled. Serve on romaine. *6 servings*

NUTRITION INFORMATION PER SERVING

1 serving		Percent of U.S. RDA	
Calories	200	Protein	32%
Protein, g	21	Vitamin A	10%
Carbohydrate, g	25	Vitamin C	8%
Fat, g	2	Thiamin	14%
Unsaturated	1	Riboflavin	16%
Saturated	1	Niacin	26%
Dietary Fiber, g	2	Calcium	6%
Cholesterol, mg	150	Iron	6%
Sodium, mg	500		
Potassium, mg	420		

Scallop and Shrimp Minestrone

2 cups chopped onions (about 2 large)
¹/₂ cup chopped carrot (about 1 medium)
1 cup chicken broth
1 clove garlic, finely chopped
1¹/₂ cups tomato juice
2 tablespoons lemon juice
1 can (14¹/₂ ounces) whole tomatoes, cut up and undrained
1 bay leaf
¹/₂ cup uncooked medium pasta shells
1 cup chopped mushrooms (about 4 ounces)
¹/₂ cup chopped yellow summer squash
¹/₂ cup chopped zucchini
2 tablespoons chopped fresh parsley
¹/₄ teaspoon salt
12 raw large shrimp, peeled and deveined
6 ounces sea scallops

Cook onions, carrots, broth and garlic in 2-quart saucepan over medium heat 5 minutes, stirring occasionally. Stir in tomato juice, lemon juice, tomatoes and bay leaf. Reduce heat. Simmer covered 10 minutes.

Stir in pasta. Cook 7 minutes. Stir in remaining ingredients. Cover and cook 5 minutes, stirring occasionally, until shrimp are pink. *6 servings*

NUTRITION INFORMATION PER SERVING			
1 serving		Percent of U.S. RDA	
Calories	180	Protein	26%
Protein, g	17	Vitamin A	30%
Carbohydrate, g	23	Vitamin C	26%
Fat, g	2	Thiamin	12%
Unsaturated	1	Riboflavin	10%
Saturated	1	Niacin	18%
Dietary Fiber, g	3	Calcium	8%
Cholesterol, mg	65	Iron	18%
Sodium, mg	690		
Potassium, mg	750		

Hot Open-faced Creole Sandwiches

¹/₂ cup chopped onion (about 1 medium)
¹/₂ cup chopped red bell pepper (about 1 small)
¹/₂ cup chopped green bell pepper (about 1 small)
¹/₂ cup chicken broth
¹/₄ cup tomato puree
1 teaspoon margarine
¹/₄ teaspoon filé powder
1-pound catfish or other medium-fat fish fillet, cut into 1¹/₂-inch pieces
1 tablespoon tomato paste
Few drops red pepper sauce, if desired
6 pieces Corn Bread (page 81)

Cook onion, bell peppers, broth, tomato puree, margarine and filé powder in 10-inch skillet over medium heat 5 minutes, stirring frequently, until vegetables are tender. Stir in fish and tomato paste. Cook 7 to 10 minutes, stirring constantly, until fish flakes easily with fork and sauce has thickened. Stir in pepper sauce. Split each piece corn bread into halves. Spoon fish mixture over corn bread. *6 servings*

NUTRITION INFORMATION PER SERVING			
1 serving		Percent of U.S. RDA	
Calories	325	Protein	34%
Protein, g	23	Vitamin A	8%
Carbohydrate, g	33	Vitamin C	20%
Fat, g	11	Thiamin	22%
Unsaturated	8	Riboflavin	24%
Saturated	3	Niacin	32%
Dietary Fiber, g	2	Calcium	18%
Cholesterol, mg	45	Iron	18%
Sodium, mg	510		
Potassium, mg	660		

Savory M[...]

*Fresh or only sligh[...]
this strata, which [...]
hours in advance. [...]
dill and parsley m[...]
in place of the ros[...]*

1 cup chopped m[...]
1 cup nonfat cott[...]
¼ cup chopped g[...]
1 teaspoon chopp[...]
dried rosemar[...]
1 clove garlic, fir[...]
12 slices whole g[...]
1½ cups low-fat [...]
1 cup cholesterol[...]
whites
¼ cup shredded [...]
Monterey Jacl[...]

Spray square bak[...]
nonstick cooking [...]
tage cheese, onio[...]
4 of the bread slic[...]

Mariner's Salad Sandwiches

Spread the buns with a little cholesterol-free reduced-calorie mayonnaise or salad dressing if desired. The fish mixture can also be used to stuff a tomato or served on its own with whole-grain crackers.

1 cup nonfat ricotta cheese
2 tablespoons lemon juice
1½ cups chopped cooked whitefish or other medium-fat fish (about ½ pound)
½ cup chopped celery (about 1 medium stalk)
¼ cup chopped green onions (2 to 3 medium)
2 tablespoons plain nonfat yogurt
½ teaspoon salt
¼ teaspoon pepper
6 whole wheat hamburger buns, warmed

6 tomato slices
1½ cups shredded lettuce (about ½ small head)
6 red onion slices, each ⅛ inch thick

Place cheese and lemon juice in blender. Cover and blend about 30 seconds or until smooth. Mix cheese mixture, fish, celery, green onions, yogurt, salt and pepper. Place ½ cup fish mixture on each bun bottom. Top with tomato, lettuce and red onion. Top with bun top. *6 servings*

NUTRITION INFORMATION PER SERVING

1 serving		Percent of U.S. RDA	
Calories	240	Protein	28%
Protein, g	19	Vitamin A	8%
Carbohydrate, g	27	Vitamin C	18%
Fat, g	6	Thiamin	12%
Unsaturated	3	Riboflavin	14%
Saturated	3	Niacin	18%
Dietary Fiber, g	3	Calcium	20%
Cholesterol, mg	40	Iron	14%
Sodium, mg	490		
Potassium, mg	540		

Mariner's Salad Sandwiches, Creamy Slaw (page 136)

Twice-baked Cheese Potatoes

This hearty potato needs only a light soup or salad, such as Tossed Salad with Apple Cider Dressing (page 154), to make a satisfying meal. The potatoes may be prepared and refrigerated up to 24 hours ahead of time; increase the baking time by 5 to 10 minutes.

3 medium baking potatoes
1 cup cooked great northern beans or ½ can (about 15-ounce size) great northern, cannellini or navy beans, drained
3 cups chopped spinach (about 4 ounces)
1 cup nonfat ricotta cheese
1 cup shredded reduced-fat Cheddar cheese (4 ounces)
¾ cup chopped onion (about 1 large)
½ cup cholesterol-free egg product or 3 egg whites
2 tablespoons chopped fresh chives
2 tablespoons low-fat sour cream
2 teaspoons margarine, softened
1 teaspoon caraway seed
2 tablespoons low-fat sour cream
2 tablespoons chopped fresh chives

Heat oven to 375°. Bake potatoes 1 to 1¼ hours or until tender. Cool just until easy to handle. Cut potatoes lengthwise into halves; scoop out pulp, leaving thin shells. Mash potato pulp and beans. (Or place potato pulp and beans in blender or food processor; cover and blend until smooth.) Mix potato mixture and remaining ingredients except 2 tablespoons sour cream and 2 tablespoons chives. Divide mixture among potato shells. Place in ungreased rectangular pan, 13°9°2 inches. Bake uncovered 15 to 20 minutes or until hot and light brown. Top with sour cream and chives. *6 servings*

Oriental Stew

Look in the foreign food section of your supermarket or in international markets for buckwheat noodles. They bring their own hearty flavor to the dish, but any long thin pasta, such as vermicelli, can be substituted.

1 teaspoon vegetable oil
1 tablespoon grated gingerroot
1 clove garlic, crushed
½ cup chopped red bell pepper (about 1 small)
4 cups shredded napa (Chinese) cabbage
1 cup sliced mushrooms (about 3 ounces)
1 cup sugar snap peas
1 cup fresh or frozen peas
1 cup 1-inch cubes firm tofu
3 cups Vegetable Stock (page 349)*
2 tablespoons reduced-sodium soy sauce
1 package (8 ounces) buckwheat noodles (soba)

If the first thi
think of mea
think again! Y
here and som
Three-Squash
Beans and Ri
(page 335) an
Sauce (page :
savory dishe
eggs, vegetab
ing dishes in
the meat. Inc
eating plan b
week, then in
only a way to
terol, it's an e
bohydrates ar
  Eating eno
problem for
many of us ge
cially from n
vegetables, n
plete protein,
of the protein
acids) necess

Cook oil, gingerroot, garlic and bell pepper in Dutch oven over medium heat about 2 minutes, stirring frequently, until bell pepper is tender. Stir in remaining ingredients. Heat to boiling. Cook about 5 minutes, stirring frequently, until noodles are tender; reduce heat. Cover and simmer about 5 minutes or until vegetables are tender. *6 servings*

* 3 cups hot water and 1 tablespoon vegetable or chicken bouillon granules can be substituted for the Vegetable Stock.

NUTRITION INFORMATION PER SERVING

I serving		Percent of U.S. RDA	
Calories	280	Protein	24%
Protein, g	16	Vitamin A	34%
Carbohydrate, g	40	Vitamin C	50%
Fat, g	6	Thiamin	22%
Unsaturated	5	Riboflavin	14%
Saturated	1	Niacin	14%
Dietary Fiber, g	8	Calcium	20%
Cholesterol, mg	0	Iron	44%
Sodium, mg	410		
Potassium, mg	580		

Veggie Burgers

Pineapple Limeade (page 60) is just right for these carrot-studded burgers, whether served with or without regular hamburger "fixings."

8 ounces firm tofu
½ cup chopped carrot (about 1 medium)
¼ cup chopped green onions (2 to 3 medium)
1 teaspoon fennel seed
1 teaspoon paprika

¼ teaspoon ground ginger
¼ teaspoon pepper
1⅓ cups soft whole grain or white bread crumbs
½ cup cholesterol-free egg product or 3 egg whites
2 tablespoons chopped fresh parsley
½ teaspoon Worcestershire sauce

Heat oven to 425°. Spray rectangular pan, 13×9×2 inches, with nonstick cooking spray. Place tofu, carrot, onions, fennel seed, paprika, ginger and pepper in blender or food processor. Cover and blend about 15 seconds or until smooth. Add remaining ingredients. Cover and process about 10 seconds or until smooth. Shape mixture by about ½ cupfuls into 6 patties. Place in pan. Bake uncovered about 14 minutes, turning patties after 7 minutes, until brown. *6 burgers*

NUTRITION INFORMATION PER SERVING

I burger		Percent of U.S. RDA	
Calories	170	Protein	16%
Protein, g	11	Vitamin A	22%
Carbohydrate, g	20	Vitamin C	2%
Fat, g	5	Thiamin	10%
Unsaturated	4	Riboflavin	12%
Saturated	1	Niacin	6%
Dietary Fiber, g	3	Calcium	12%
Cholesterol, mg	0	Iron	28%
Sodium, mg	210		
Potassium, mg	220		

Know Your Beans

Collectively known as legumes because they come from leguminous plants (ones that produce pods with one row of seeds), beans, peas and lentils are a dietary staple all over the world. Loaded with soluble fiber, they combine well with grains, especially corn, wheat and rice, for a complete protein.

Legumes (except lentils) need to be boiled uncovered 2 minutes before cooking. Boiling destroys an enzyme that can cause some people to become ill. Soaking is not necessary but does allow for more uniform swelling. To prevent beans from foaming when cooking, add 1 tablespoon margarine or vegetable oil to the cooking water; drain and rinse. Salt and acid tend to toughen beans. Add salt and acidic foods such as lemon juice, vinegar, tomatoes and tomato sauce, paste or juice only after the beans are soft, or the beans may not soften. Dried beans triple in volume as they cook, so be sure to use a sufficiently large casserole or pan. Beans of similar sizes can easily be interchanged in recipes.

Black Beans, also called turtle beans, are found in the cuisines of South and Central America as well as the Caribbean. They are often served with rice because the combination makes a complete protein. Their popularity has grown in recent years and they can be found canned and dried in many supermarkets. If not, look for them in health and ethnic food stores.

Butter Beans are cream-colored, large lima beans. They can be found both canned and dried. Often served as a vegetable side dish, they can be added to soups, main dishes and salads.

Canellini Beans are large white kidney beans. Originally from South America, they have been adopted by Italy and are often mixed with pasta. Look for them with other canned beans.

Fava Beans are large, flat beans that look brown and wrinkly when dried. Sometime available fresh or canned in ethnic food stores, they have an earthy flavor and are the bean of choice for the Middle Eastern specialty, falafel.

Garbanzo Beans, also called chick-peas, are used in many dishes. Tan, bumpy and round, they have a firm texture and need long, slow cooking. They stand up well to a variety of dishes and are a good addition to soups, stews, casseroles and salads. Garbanzos are used in the popular Middle Eastern dip, hummus. They are available both canned and dried.

Great Northern Beans are kidney-shaped white beans. They are traditionally used in making baked beans and bean soup, and are commonly available canned and dried.

Kidney Beans are widely available both canned and dried in dark and light red. Used mainly to add color and texture to many dishes, we love them best in chile and red beans and rice.

Lentils are truly an ancient food, known to have been eaten in southwestern Asia around 7,000 B.C. The small grayish-green lentil we are familiar with is only one of the many types and colors of lentils used around the world. They are also available dried in white, yellow, red and black. Lentils are handy because they do not require soaking and cook in a relatively short time.

Lima Beans are available in 2 sizes—regular and baby. Green limas are good by themselves as a vegetable dish but also make a wonderful addition to multi-bean salads, soups and casseroles. Limas are occasionally available fresh, otherwise they can be found frozen and dried. (*See also* Butter Beans.)

Navy Beans, so called because they fed many a sailor in the early 1800s, are white beans available canned and dried. They are also known as pea beans. Smaller than great northern and canellini beans, they can be used in place of great northern and kidney beans.

Pinto Beans are two-toned, kidney-shaped beans that are widely used in Central and South American cooking. They turn a uniform pink when cooked, and are used for the Mexican staple, refried beans. They're readily available canned and dried.

Soy Beans are not widely eaten in this country as beans. However, we process much of the soy bean harvest into oil. Tofu is another product of soy beans with which we have become more familiar. The bland, solid bean curd is used in many meatless dishes and combines well with flavorful seasonings.

Split Peas are available dried, both green and yellow. They do not require soaking and cook relatively quickly. Used mostly in soups, the yellow version is particularly known for "pease porridge," referred to in the British nursery rhyme.

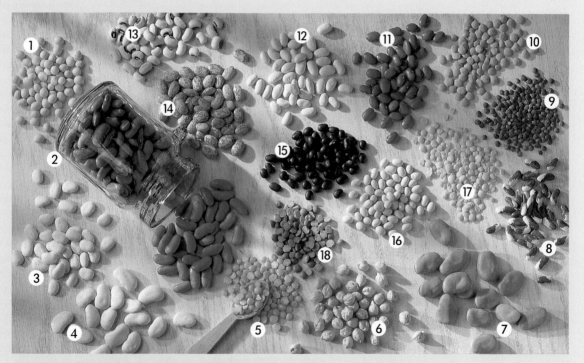

1) soybeans; 2) red kidney beans; 3) lima beans; 4) butter beans; 5) yellow split peas; 6) garbanzo beans; 7) fava beans; 8) appaloosa beans; 9) green lentils; 10) lentils; 11) small red beans (small reds); 12) great northern beans; 13) black-eyed peas; 14) pinto beans; 15) black turtle beans; 16) navy beans; 17) red lentils; 18) green split peas

Lentil Stew

2 teaspoons vegetable oil

1 cup chopped onion (about 1 large)

1 clove garlic, finely chopped

2 cups coarsely chopped potatoes (about 2
   medium)

1 cup dried lentils

¼ cup chopped fresh parsley

3 cups water

½ teaspoon salt

½ teaspoon ground cumin

¼ teaspoon pepper

¼ teaspoon ground mace

8 ounces small mushrooms, cut into halves

1 can (28 ounces) whole tomatoes,
   undrained

Heat oil in Dutch oven over medium-high heat.
Cook onion and garlic in oil, stirring frequently, until onion is tender. Stir in remaining
ingredients; break up tomatoes. Heat to boiling;
reduce heat. Cover and simmer about 40 minutes, stirring occasionally, until potatoes are
tender. *6 servings*

NUTRITION INFORMATION PER SERVING

1 serving		Percent of U.S. RDA	
Calories	210	Protein	18%
Protein, g	11	Vitamin A	8%
Carbohydrate, g	37	Vitamin C	24%
Fat, g	2	Thiamin	20%
Unsaturated	2	Riboflavin	16%
Saturated	0	Niacin	20%
Dietary Fiber, g	8	Calcium	6%
Cholesterol, mg	0	Iron	26%
Sodium, mg	400		
Potassium, mg	960		

Indian Lentils and Rice

½ cup chopped green onions

1 tablespoon finely chopped gingerroot

⅛ teaspoon crushed red pepper

2 cloves garlic, finely chopped

5¼ cups Vegetable Stock (page 349)*

1½ cups dried lentils

1 teaspoon ground turmeric

½ teaspoon salt

1 cup chopped tomato (about 1 large)

¼ cup shredded coconut

2 tablespoons chopped fresh mint leaves

3 cups hot cooked rice

1½ cups plain nonfat yogurt

Spray 3-quart saucepan with nonstick cooking
spray. Cook onions, gingerroot, red pepper and
garlic in saucepan over medium heat, stirring
occasionally, 3 to 5 minutes until onions are
tender. Stir in 5 cups of the Vegetable Stock, the
lentils, turmeric and salt. Heat to boiling; reduce
heat. Cover and simmer about 25 to 30 minutes,
adding remaining stock if needed, until lentils
are tender. Stir in tomato, coconut and mint.
Serve over rice, with yogurt. *6 servings*

* 5¼ cups hot water and 2 tablespoons vegetable or
chicken bouillon granules can be substituted for the Vegetable Stock.

NUTRITION INFORMATION PER SERVING

1 serving		Percent of U.S. RDA	
Calories	405	Protein	36%
Protein, g	24	Vitamin A	2%
Carbohydrate, g	66	Vitamin C	8%
Fat, g	5	Thiamin	30%
Unsaturated	2	Riboflavin	20%
Saturated	3	Niacin	30%
Dietary Fiber, g	9	Calcium	18%
Cholesterol, mg	0	Iron	38%
Sodium, mg	910		
Potassium, mg	1020		

Three-Squash Stew

1 tablespoon olive or vegetable oil
1 cup sliced onion (about 1 large)
1 clove garlic, crushed
1 jalapeño chile, finely chopped
4 cups sliced yellow squash (about 1 pound)
4 cups ½-inch pieces zucchini (about 2 medium)
4 cups 1-inch pieces pattypan squash
3 cups 1-inch pieces green beans (about 1 pound)
1 cup fresh or frozen whole kernel corn
1 tablespoon chopped fresh or 1 teaspoon dried thyme leaves
2 cans (15 ounces each) kidney beans, undrained

Heat oil in Dutch oven. Cook onion, garlic and chile in oil about 2 minutes or until tender. Stir in remaining ingredients. Cook over low heat 10 to 15 minutes, stirring frequently, until squash is tender. *6 servings*

NUTRITION INFORMATION PER SERVING

1 serving		Percent of U.S. RDA	
Calories	310	Protein	26%
Protein, g	17	Vitamin A	20%
Carbohydrate, g	52	Vitamin C	38%
Fat, g	4	Thiamin	30%
Unsaturated	3	Riboflavin	14%
Saturated	1	Niacin	12%
Dietary Fiber, g	18	Calcium	12%
Cholesterol, mg	0	Iron	34%
Sodium, mg	360		
Potassium, mg	1390		

Hearty Bean and Macaroni Stew

1 cup coarsely chopped tomato (about 1 large)
¾ cup uncooked medium macaroni shells
¼ cup chopped onion (about 1 small)
¼ cup chopped green bell pepper
1¾ cups Vegetable Stock (page 349)*
1 tablespoon chopped fresh or 1 teaspoon dried basil leaves
1 teaspoon Worcestershire sauce
1 clove garlic, finely chopped
1 can (16 ounces) kidney beans, drained
½ can (15-ounce size) garbanzo beans, drained

Mix all ingredients in 2-quart saucepan. Heat to boiling, stirring occasionally; reduce heat. Cover and simmer about 15 minutes, stirring occasionally, until pasta is tender. *4 servings*

* 1¾ cups hot water and 2 teaspoons vegetable or chicken bouillon granules can be substituted for the Vegetable Stock.

NUTRITION INFORMATION PER SERVING

1 serving		Percent of U.S. RDA	
Calories	350	Protein	28%
Protein, g	18	Vitamin A	4%
Carbohydrate, g	64	Vitamin C	14%
Fat, g	3	Thiamin	28%
Unsaturated	2	Riboflavin	12%
Saturated	1	Niacin	12%
Dietary Fiber, g	15	Calcium	8%
Cholesterol, mg	0	Iron	34%
Sodium, mg	430		
Potassium, mg	790		

Cuban Black Beans and Rice (page 326), Tortilla Casserole

Tortilla Casserole

Baked Tortilla Chips (page 44) or 4 cups
light tortilla chips
2 cups cooked kidney beans or 1 can (15
ounces) kidney beans, drained
½ cup low-fat milk
¼ cup cholesterol-free egg product or 2 egg
whites
2 tablespoons chopped fresh cilantro leaves
1 cup chopped onion (about 1 large)
1 cup chopped green bell pepper (about 1
medium)
½ cup Vegetable Stock (page 349)*
2 cloves garlic, finely chopped

2 cans (4 ounces each) chopped mild green
chiles, drained
2 tablespoons chopped fresh cilantro leaves
1 cup shredded reduced-fat Cheddar cheese
(4 ounces)
Spicy Fresh Chile Sauce (page 287)

Prepare Baked Tortilla Chips. Heat oven to
375°. Spray 2-quart casserole with nonstick
cooking spray. Mash beans and milk until
smooth; stir in egg product and 2 tablespoons
cilantro; reserve. (Or place beans, milk, egg
product and 2 tablespoons cilantro in blender or
food processor. Cover and blend until smooth.)
Cook onion, bell pepper, Vegetable Stock, garlic and chiles in 10-inch skillet over medium
heat about 5 minutes, stirring occasionally, until onion is tender. Stir in remaining cilantro.

Coarsely chop half of tortilla chips; place 1 cup
of the chopped chips in bottom of casserole.
Spread reserved bean mixture over chips.
Spread vegetable mixture over bean mixture.
Sprinkle with ½ cup of the cheese. Top with

remaining chopped chips. Sprinkle with remaining cheese. Bake 30 to 35 minutes until hot and cheese is golden brown. Serve with Spicy Fresh Chile Sauce, the remaining chips and, if desired, low-fat sour cream. *6 servings*

* ½ cup hot water and ½ teaspoon vegetable or chicken bouillon granules can be substituted for the Vegetable Stock.

NUTRITION INFORMATION PER SERVING

1 serving		Percent of U.S. RDA	
Calories	250	Protein	24%
Protein, g	16	Vitamin A	12%
Carbohydrate, g	35	Vitamin C	44%
Fat, g	5	Thiamin	14%
Unsaturated	2	Riboflavin	16%
Saturated	3	Niacin	8%
Dietary Fiber, g	8	Calcium	26%
Cholesterol, mg	10	Iron	18%
Sodium, mg	640		
Potassium, mg	600		

Kidney Bean and Macaroni Supper

8 cups chopped mustard greens or Swiss chard (about 1 large bunch)

1 cup Vegetable Stock (page 349)* or water

2 tablespoons tomato paste

4 cups water

2 cups cooked kidney beans or 1 can (15 ounces) kidney beans, drained

1 cup chopped onion (about 1 large)

1 cup chopped tomato (about 1 large)

½ cup chopped carrot (about 1 medium)

2 cloves garlic, finely chopped

3 cups water

2 cups uncooked small shell or elbow macaroni (about 6 ounces)

1 cup chopped green bell pepper (about 1 medium)

¼ cup freshly grated Parmesan cheese

Heat mustard greens, Vegetable Stock and tomato paste to boiling in 3-quart saucepan over medium heat; reduce heat. Simmer uncovered about 5 minutes or until greens are wilted. Stir in 4 cups water, the beans, onion, tomato, carrot and garlic. Heat to boiling; reduce heat. Simmer uncovered, stirring occasionally, 30 minutes.

Place 2 cups of the bean mixture in blender. Cover and blend until smooth. Return to saucepan. Stir in 3 cups water, the macaroni and bell pepper. Heat to boiling; reduce heat. Cover and simmer 15 minutes, stirring occasionally, until macaroni is tender. Sprinkle with cheese. *6 servings*

* 1 cup hot water and 1 teaspoon vegetable or chicken bouillon granules can be subsituted for the Vegetable Stock.

NUTRITION INFORMATION PER SERVING

1 serving		Percent of U.S. RDA	
Calories	260	Protein	18%
Protein, g	12	Vitamin A	64%
Carbohydrate, g	46	Vitamin C	38%
Fat, g	3	Thiamin	22%
Unsaturated	2	Riboflavin	12%
Saturated	1	Niacin	12%
Dietary Fiber, g	9	Calcium	20%
Cholesterol, mg	5	Iron	22%
Sodium, mg	150		
Potassium, mg	650		

Native American Vegetable Stew

³/₄ cup chopped onions (about 1¹/₂ medium)

1 clove garlic, finely chopped

2 tablespoons vegetable oil

1 large red bell pepper, cut into 2×¹/₂-inch strips

2 medium poblano or Anaheim chiles, seeded and cut into 2×¹/₂-inch strips

1 jalapeño chile, seeded and chopped

1 cup cubed Hubbard or acorn squash (about ¹/₂ pound)

2¹/₄ cups Vegetable Stock (page 349)*

¹/₂ teaspoon salt

¹/₂ teaspoon pepper

¹/₂ teaspoon ground coriander

1 cup thinly sliced zucchini (about 1 small)

1 cup thinly sliced yellow squash (about 1 small)

1 can (17 ounces) whole kernel corn, drained

1 can (16 ounces) pinto beans, drained

Cook onions and garlic in oil in Dutch oven over medium heat, stirring frequently, until onions are tender. Stir in bell pepper and poblano and jalapeño chiles. Cook uncovered 15 minutes, stirring occasionally.

Stir in Hubbard squash, Vegetable Stock, salt, pepper and coriander. Heat to boiling; reduce heat. Cover and simmer about 5 minutes or until squash is tender. Stir in remaining ingredients. Cook uncovered about 10 minutes, stirring occasionally, until zucchini is tender. *6 servings*

* 2¹/₄ cups hot water and 2¹/₂ teaspoons vegetable or chicken bouillon granules can be substituted for the Vegetable Stock.

NUTRITION INFORMATION PER SERVING			
1 serving		**Percent of U.S. RDA**	
Calories	280	Protein	16%
Protein, g	10	Vitamin A	52%
Carbohydrate, g	46	Vitamin C	84%
Fat, g	6	Thiamin	18%
Unsaturated	5	Riboflavin	12%
Saturated	1	Niacin	10%
Dietary Fiber, g	10	Calcium	8%
Cholesterol, mg	0	Iron	22%
Sodium, mg	730		
Potassium, mg	900		

Cuban Black Beans and Rice

Crunchy Sunchoke and Spinach Salad (page 141) is just the right side dish for this comforting dish, rich with the flavors of spices and black beans.

1 cup chopped onion (about 1 large)

1 cup chopped green bell pepper (about 1 medium)

³/₄ cup chopped carrots (about 1¹/₂ medium)

1 cup orange juice

2 teaspoons paprika

1 teaspoon ground coriander

¹/₈ teaspoon crushed red pepper

1 can (14¹/₂ ounces) whole tomatoes, undrained

2 cloves garlic, finely chopped

2 cups cooked black beans or 1 can (15 ounces) black beans, rinsed and drained

4 cups hot cooked brown rice

1 cup plain nonfat yogurt

1 lime, cut into 6 wedges

Heat onion, bell pepper, carrots, orange juice, paprika, coriander, red pepper, tomatoes and garlic to boiling in 2-quart saucepan; reduce heat. Cover and simmer about 45 minutes, stirring occasionally, until thick; remove from heat. Stir in beans. Place 1 cup of the bean mixture in blender or food processor. Cover and blend about 30 seconds or until smooth. Stir blended mixture into bean mixture in saucepan. Cook over medium heat about 3 minutes or until hot. Serve over rice and with yogurt and lime wedges. *6 servings*

NUTRITION INFORMATION PER SERVING

1 serving		Percent of U.S. RDA	
Calories	320	Protein	20%
Protein, g	13	Vitamin A	38%
Carbohydrate, g	63	Vitamin C	42%
Fat, g	2	Thiamin	26%
Unsaturated	2	Riboflavin	12%
Saturated	0	Niacin	16%
Dietary Fiber, g	9	Calcium	18%
Cholesterol, mg	0	Iron	16%
Sodium, mg	160		
Potassium, mg	780		

Mushroom and Mozzarella Risotto

Risotto is an Italian rice dish made by slowly stirring hot liquid into rice until it is creamy. Arborio rice holds up well to this technique and is the rice of choice, but regular short-grain rice also works well.

2 cups chopped mushrooms (about 8 ounces)
2 cups chopped onions (about 2 large)
2 cups uncooked Arborio or other short grain rice
2 cups white wine or apple juice

5½ to 6 cups hot Vegetable Stock (page 349)*
½ cup shredded part-skim mozzarella cheese
2 tablespoons grated Parmesan cheese
2 tablespoons chopped fresh chives

Spray 3-quart saucepan with nonstick cooking spray. Cook mushrooms and onions in saucepan over medium heat about 5 minutes, stirring occasionally, until onions are tender. Stir in rice. Cook 3 minutes, stirring constantly.

Stir in wine and 2 cups of the Vegetable Stock. Heat to boiling; reduce heat to medium. Cook uncovered about 5 minutes, stirring occasionally, until most liquid is absorbed. Stir in 1 cup of the stock. Cook uncovered, stirring occasionally, until most liquid is absorbed. Repeat with remaining stock, 1 cup at a time, until rice is tender and mixture is slightly thickened. Stir in remaining ingredients. *6 servings*

* 6 cups hot water and 2 tablespoons vegetable or chicken bouillon granules can be substituted for the Vegetable Stock.

NUTRITION INFORMATION PER SERVING

1 serving		Percent of U.S. RDA	
Calories	335	Protein	22%
Protein, g	14	Vitamin A	2%
Carbohydrate, g	61	Vitamin C	4%
Fat, g	4	Thiamin	22%
Unsaturated	2	Riboflavin	14%
Saturated	2	Niacin	34%
Dietary Fiber, g	3	Calcium	14%
Cholesterol, mg	5	Iron	18%
Sodium, mg	810		
Potassium, mg	520		

Mixed Bean Stew with Cottage Dumplings

Cottage Dumplings (right)

2 cups cooked great northern beans or 1 can (about 15 ounces) great northern, cannellini or navy beans, drained

2 cups cooked or 1 can (15 ounces) black beans, rinsed and drained

1 cup chopped red bell pepper (about 1 medium)

2 tablespoons chopped fresh or 2 teaspoons dried basil leaves

2 teaspoons olive or vegetable oil

¼ teaspoon pepper

2 cloves garlic, finely chopped

1 can (15 ounces) tomato sauce

Prepare Cottage Dumplings. Heat remaining ingredients to boiling in 3-quart saucepan; reduce heat. Shape dumpling mixture into 12 balls, using about 2 tablespoonfuls each. Carefully slide balls onto beans in simmering stew (do not drop directly into liquid). Cook uncovered 10 minutes. Cover and cook 10 minutes longer or until dumplings are firm. *6 servings*

Cottage Dumplings

1 cup shredded reduced-fat Monterey Jack cheese (4 ounces)

⅔ cup cooked fresh, frozen (thawed) or canned (drained) whole kernel corn (about 1½ ears)

½ cup all-purpose flour

½ cup nonfat cottage cheese

⅓ cup soft whole grain or white bread crumbs

⅓ cup stone-ground or degerminated cornmeal

2 egg whites

Mix all ingredients.

NUTRITION INFORMATION PER SERVING			
I serving		**Percent of U.S. RDA**	
Calories	390	Protein	36%
Protein, g	24	Vitamin A	20%
Carbohydrate, g	60	Vitamin C	36%
Fat, g	6	Thiamin	28%
Unsaturated	3	Riboflavin	22%
Saturated	3	Niacin	14%
Dietary Fiber, g	11	Calcium	28%
Cholesterol, mg	10	Iron	32%
Sodium, mg	700		
Potassium, mg	990		

Mixed Bean Stew with Cottage Dumplings, Native American Vegetable Stew (page 326)

Golden Risotto with Lima Beans

½ cup chopped onion (about 1 medium)

2 tablespoons chopped shallot (about 1 large)

1 cup uncooked Arborio or other short grain rice

1 clove garlic, crushed

3½ cups hot Vegetable Stock (page 349)*

⅛ teaspoon saffron threads or ground turmeric

1 package (10 ounces) frozen lima beans

¼ cup grated Parmesan cheese

Freshly ground pepper

2 tablespoons chopped fresh parsley

Spray 3-quart nonstick saucepan with nonstick cooking spray. Cook onion and shallot in saucepan over medium heat about 5 minutes, stirring frequently, until onion is tender.

Stir in rice and garlic. Cook 2 minutes. Stir in about 1½ cups of the Vegetable Stock and the saffron. Heat to boiling; reduce heat. Simmer uncovered, stirring occasionally, until most of the liquid is absorbed. Stir in half of the remaining Vegetable Stock and the lima beans. Simmer uncovered, stirring occasionally, until most of the liquid is absorbed. Stir in remaining Vegetable Stock. Simmer uncovered about 15 minutes, stirring occasionally, until rice is tender (add more stock if necessary). Stir in cheese. Sprinkle with pepper and parsley.

4 servings

* 3½ cups hot water and 1 tablespoon vegetable or chicken bouillon granules can be substituted for the Vegetable Stock.

NUTRITION INFORMATION PER SERVING			
1 serving		Percent of U.S. RDA	
Calories	320	Protein	18%
Protein, g	12	Vitamin A	28%
Carbohydrate, g	64	Vitamin C	28%
Fat, g	2	Thiamin	24%
Unsaturated	1	Riboflavin	8%
Saturated	1	Niacin	18%
Dietary Fiber, g	7	Calcium	16%
Cholesterol, mg	5	Iron	24%
Sodium, mg	390		
Potassium, mg	690		

Vegetable and Brown Rice Stew

2 cups chopped fresh or 1 package (10 ounces) frozen cut okra

2 cups cooked or 1 package (10 ounces) frozen lima beans

1½ cups uncooked quick-cooking brown rice

1 cup cauliflowerets

¾ cup chopped onions (about 1½ medium)

1¾ cups Vegetable Stock (page 349)*

1½ teaspoons chopped fresh or ½ teaspoon dried thyme leaves

1 teaspoon paprika

½ teaspoon ground mustard

⅛ teaspoon ground red pepper (cayenne)

1 can (28 ounces) whole tomatoes, undrained

2 cloves garlic, finely chopped

¾ cup shredded reduced-fat Cheddar cheese

Heat all ingredients except cheese to boiling in 3-quart saucepan, breaking up tomatoes; reduce heat. Cover and simmer about 15 minutes, stirring occasionally, until rice and vegetables are tender. Sprinkle with cheese. *6 servings*

* 1¾ cups hot water and 2 teaspoons vegetable or chicken bouillon granules can be substituted for the Vegetable Stock.

NUTRITION INFORMATION PER SERVING

1 serving		Percent of U.S. RDA	
Calories	345	Protein	22%
Protein, g	15	Vitamin A	16%
Carbohydrate, g	60	Vitamin C	38%
Fat, g	5	Thiamin	22%
Unsaturated	3	Riboflavin	14%
Saturated	2	Niacin	26%
Dietary Fiber, g	10	Calcium	22%
Cholesterol, mg	10	Iron	16%
Sodium, mg	460		
Potassium, mg	870		

Fruit-stuffed Squash

Whether made with cranberries or the fruit and raisins, this is a wonderful companion for naturally sweet buttercup squash. The cranberry version is lovely for the holidays.

½ cup uncooked brown rice

1 cup dried cranberries or diced dried fruit and raisin mixture

1 cup chopped all-purpose apple (about 1 medium)

½ cup finely chopped onion (about 1 medium)

½ cup chopped pecans

1 cup apple juice

½ teaspoon ground nutmeg

¼ teaspoon salt

2 buttercup squashes (about 2½ pounds each)

Cook rice as directed on package—except omit salt. Heat oven to 350°. Mix remaining ingredients except squashes in large bowl. Stir in rice.

Cut tops off squashes; scoop out seeds. Fill squashes with rice mixture. Place squashes in ungreased rectangular pan, 13×9×2 inches. Pour water into pan until ¼ inch deep. Cover pan tightly with aluminum foil. Bake about 1¼ hours or until squash is tender. Cut each squash into halves to serve. *4 servings*

NUTRITION INFORMATION PER SERVING

1 serving		Percent of U.S. RDA	
Calories	570	Protein	12%
Protein, g	8	Vitamin A	152%
Carbohydrate, g	103	Vitamin C	40%
Fat, g	14	Thiamin	40%
Unsaturated	12	Riboflavin	12%
Saturated	2	Niacin	24%
Dietary Fiber, g	16	Calcium	10%
Cholesterol, mg	0	Iron	18%
Sodium, mg	160		
Potassium, mg	1270		

Winter Fruit Couscous, Indian Lentils and Rice (page 322)

Winter Fruit Couscous

2 tablespoons vegetable oil

½ cup chopped onion (about 1 medium)

1½ cups uncooked bulgur or brown rice

1 cup dried apricots

1 cup golden raisins

1 cup chopped prunes

1 cup chopped dried apples

4 cups Vegetable Stock (page 349)*

½ teaspoon ground nutmeg

½ teaspoon ground cinnamon

¼ teaspoon ground coriander

Heat oven to 350°. Heat oil in Dutch oven over medium heat. Cook onion in oil about 2 min-utes, stirring frequently, until tender. Stir in bulgur. Cook about 5 minutes, stirring occa-sionally, or until bulgur is golden brown. Stir in remaining ingredients. Cover and bake 50 to 60 minutes or until bulgur is tender. *6 servings*

* 4 cups hot water and 1 tablespoon plus 1 teaspoon vegetable or chicken bouillon granules can be substituted for the Vegetable Stock.

NUTRITION INFORMATION PER SERVING			
1 serving		Percent of U.S. RDA	
Calories	530	Protein	16%
Protein, g	10	Vitamin A	40%
Carbohydrate, g	109	Vitamin C	16%
Fat, g	6	Thiamin	16%
Unsaturated	5	Riboflavin	14%
Saturated	1	Niacin	24%
Dietary Fiber, g	18	Calcium	10%
Cholesterol, mg	0	Iron	28%
Sodium, mg	230		
Potassium, mg	1230		

Sweet and Sour Vegetable Stew

1 cup orange juice

2 tablespoons chopped fresh or 2 teaspoons dried mint leaves

2 tablespoons cider vinegar

2 tablespoons orange marmalade spreadable fruit

2 teaspoons vegetable oil

1/4 teaspoon pepper

2 cups finely chopped potatoes (about 2 medium)

1 cup chopped carrots (about 2 medium)

1 cup chopped celery (about 2 medium stalks)

1 cup sliced onion (about 1 large)

1 cup Vegetable Stock (page 349)*

2 cups chopped yellow squash (about 2 large)

1 cup Chinese pea pods, cut into julienne strips

3 cups hot cooked bulgur

Mix 1/2 cup of the orange juice, the mint, vinegar, marmalade, oil and pepper; reserve. Heat remaining orange juice, potatoes, carrots, celery, onion and 1/2 cup of the Vegetable Stock to boiling in 10-inch skillet; reduce heat to medium. Cover and cook 12 to 15 minutes or until potatoes are tender. Stir in squash and remaining 1/2 cup stock. Cook uncovered 3 to 5 minutes or until squash is tender. Stir in reserved orange juice mixture and pea pods. Heat to boiling. Boil and stir about 1 minute or until thickened. Serve over bulgur. *6 servings*

* 1 cup hot water and 1 teaspoon vegetable or chicken bouillon granules can be substituted for the Vegetable Stock.

NUTRITION INFORMATION PER SERVING

	1 serving		Percent of U.S. RDA
Calories	210	Protein	10%
Protein, g	6	Vitamin A	38%
Carbohydrate, g	42	Vitamin C	34%
Fat, g	2	Thiamin	14%
Unsaturated	2	Riboflavin	6%
Saturated	0	Niacin	14%
Dietary Fiber, g	7	Calcium	4%
Cholesterol, mg	0	Iron	12%
Sodium, mg	170		
Potassium, mg	710		

Vegetable Couscous

2 cups chopped tomatoes (about 2 large)

1 can (15 ounces) garbanzo beans

1/2 cup chopped red bell pepper

1/2 cup chopped green onions

1 tablespoon chopped fresh oregano

1 teaspoon paprika

1 teaspoon olive or vegetable oil

1 clove garlic, finely chopped

5 cups hot cooked couscous

1/4 cup grated Parmesan cheese

Heat all ingredients except couscous and cheese to boiling in 2-quart saucepan. Serve over couscous. Sprinkle with cheese. *6 servings*

NUTRITION INFORMATION PER SERVING

	1 serving		Percent of U.S. RDA
Calories	285	Protein	18%
Protein, g	12	Vitamin A	12%
Carbohydrate, g	50	Vitamin C	24%
Fat, g	4	Thiamin	10%
Unsaturated	3	Riboflavin	6%
Saturated	1	Niacin	12%
Dietary Fiber, g	5	Calcium	10%
Cholesterol, mg	5	Iron	12%
Sodium, mg	90		
Potassium, mg	380		

Baked Spinach Polenta

6 cups water

2 teaspoons tomato paste

1½ cups stone-ground polenta or
degerminated yellow cornmeal

2 cups chopped mushrooms (about 8
ounces)

½ cup chopped onion (about 1 medium)

⅓ cup Vegetable Stock (page 349)* or
water

1 teaspoon chopped fresh or ½ teaspoon
dried dill weed

¼ teaspoon pepper

⅛ teaspoon ground nutmeg

1 package (10 ounces) frozen chopped
spinach, thawed and well drained

½ cup shredded part-skim mozzarella
cheese

Heat oven to 375°. Spray rectangular pan, 11×7×1½ inches, with nonstick cooking spray. Heat water and tomato paste to boiling in 2-quart saucepan; reduce heat to medium-low. Stir in polenta. Simmer uncovered about 10 minutes, stirring frequently, until mixture thickens and pulls away from side of saucepan. Spread in pan.

Cook mushrooms, onion and Vegetable Stock in 10-inch skillet over medium heat about 10 minutes or until liquid has almost evaporated. Stir in remaining ingredients except cheese. Cook and stir 2 to 3 minutes until spinach is hot. Spread spinach mixture over polenta. Sprinkle with cheese. Bake uncovered about 40 minutes until hot and cheese is lightly browned.

6 servings

* ⅓ cup hot water and ½ teaspoon vegetable or chicken bouillon granules can be substituted for the Vegetable Stock.

NUTRITION INFORMATION PER SERVING

1 serving		Percent of U.S. RDA	
Calories	175	Protein	12%
Protein, g	7	Vitamin A	28%
Carbohydrate, g	32	Vitamin C	4%
Fat, g	2	Thiamin	20%
Unsaturated	1	Riboflavin	20%
Saturated	1	Niacin	16%
Dietary Fiber, g	3	Calcium	12%
Cholesterol, mg	5	Iron	12%
Sodium, mg	140		
Potassium, mg	300		

Barley-Eggplant Pilaf

4 cups 1-inch pieces eggplant (about 1
pound)

¾ cup chopped red onion (about 1 medium)

½ cup apple juice

1 cup cooked fresh, frozen (thawed) or
canned (drained) whole kernel corn
(about 2 medium ears)

1 cup chopped yellow bell pepper (about 1
medium)

½ cup chopped celery

½ cup Vegetable Stock (page 349)* or
water

2 tablespoons chopped fresh or 2 teaspoons
dried basil leaves

2 tablespoons tomato paste

¼ teaspoon pepper

⅛ teaspoon saffron threads, if desired

6 cups cooked pearl barley

1 cup soft whole grain or white bread
crumbs

½ cup finely chopped green onions

¼ cup grated Parmesan cheese

Heat oven to 400°. Spray rectangular pan, 13×9×2 inches, with nonstick cooking spray. Place eggplant and red onion in pan; pour apple juice over top. Bake uncovered 20 minutes. Meanwhile, cook corn, bell pepper, celery, Vegetable Stock, basil, tomato paste, pepper and saffron threads in 2-quart saucepan over medium heat 10 minutes, stirring occasionally, until liquid has evaporated. Stir in eggplant mixture and barley.

Wash and dry pan; spray with nonstick cooking spray. Spread barley mixture in pan. Mix bread crumbs, green onions and cheese; sprinkle over top. Bake uncovered 15 minutes or until hot and topping is golden brown. *6 servings*

* ½ cup hot water and ½ teaspoon vegetable or chicken bouillon granules can be substituted for the Vegetable Stock.

NUTRITION INFORMATION PER SERVING

1 serving		Percent of U.S. RDA	
Calories	350	Protein	18%
Protein, g	11	Vitamin A	4%
Carbohydrate, g	71	Vitamin C	16%
Fat, g	3	Thiamin	18%
Unsaturated	1	Riboflavin	12%
Saturated	2	Niacin	22%
Dietary Fiber, g	11	Calcium	12%
Cholesterol, mg	5	Iron	16%
Sodium, mg	260		
Potassium, mg	550		

Eggplant Lasagne

1 package (8 ounces) lasagne noodles
1 medium eggplant (about 1 pound)
Creamy Sauce (right)
1 cup nonfat ricotta cheese
1 cup cholesterol-free egg product or 1
    whole egg plus 4 egg whites
½ cup chopped green onions
½ cup shredded part-skim mozzarella
    cheese

Heat oven to 350°. Spray rectangular pan, 13×9×2 inches, with nonstick cooking spray. Cook noodles as directed on package—except omit salt and cook for only 5 minutes; drain. Cut eggplant lengthwise into halves; cut halves crosswise into ¼-inch slices. Prepare Creamy Sauce. Mix ricotta cheese, egg product and onions.

Spread ½ cup of the Creamy Sauce in pan. Top with 3 noodles. Arrange half of the eggplant slices over noodles. Sprinkle with ¼ cup mozzarella cheese. Spread half the ricotta mixture over mozzarella cheese. Top with 4 noodles. Spread ½ cup of the sauce over noodles. Top with remaining eggplant slices, ricotta mixture, noodles, sauce and mozzarella cheese. Bake uncovered 50 to 60 minutes until hot and bubbly. Let stand 5 minutes before cutting. *6 servings*

Creamy Sauce

4 cups low-fat milk
2 tablespoons cornstarch
¼ teaspoon ground nutmeg

Heat all ingredients to boiling in 2-quart saucepan, stirring frequently. Reduce heat to medium. Cook 7 to 10 minutes, stirring frequently, until thickened.

NUTRITION INFORMATION PER SERVING

1 serving		Percent of U.S. RDA	
Calories	330	Protein	34%
Protein, g	22	Vitamin A	16%
Carbohydrate, g	49	Vitamin C	2%
Fat, g	5	Thiamin	24%
Unsaturated	2	Riboflavin	38%
Saturated	3	Niacin	12%
Dietary Fiber, g	3	Calcium	40%
Cholesterol, mg	60	Iron	12%
Sodium, mg	240		
Potassium, mg	630		

Lemon-Basil Vegetables and Noodles

Soba *means "noodles" in Japanese, and any of the thin Japanese noodles would work well for this recipe.*

2 cups chopped broccoli flowerets (about ¾ pound)

2 cups chopped cauliflowerets (about ¾ pound)

1 cup chopped onion (about 1 large)

1 cup Vegetable Stock (page 349)*

1 teaspoon grated lemon peel

2 cups chopped zucchini (about 1 large)

2 cups cooked Japanese noodles (soba) or vermicelli

2 tablespoons chopped fresh or 2 teaspoons dried basil leaves

2 tablespoons lemon juice

1 teaspoon olive or vegetable oil

¼ teaspoon pepper

1 package (9 ounces) frozen artichoke hearts, thawed

Cook broccoli flowerets, cauliflowerets, onion, ½ cup of the Vegetable Stock and the lemon peel in 12-inch skillet over medium heat 7 to 10 minutes, stirring frequently, until cauliflowerets are crisp-tender. Stir in remaining stock and ingredients. Cook about 5 minutes, stirring frequently, until vegetables are tender.
6 servings

* 1 cup hot water and 1 teaspoon vegetable or chicken bouillon granules can be substituted for the Vegetable Stock.

NUTRITION INFORMATION PER SERVING

1 serving		Percent of U.S. RDA	
Calories	145	Protein	10%
Protein, g	7	Vitamin A	6%
Carbohydrate, g	25	Vitamin C	54%
Fat, g	2	Thiamin	14%
Unsaturated	2	Riboflavin	10%
Saturated	0	Niacin	12%
Dietary Fiber, g	5	Calcium	6%
Cholesterol, mg	0	Iron	12%
Sodium, mg	190		
Potassium, mg	630		

Lemon-Basil Vegetables and Noodles, Soba Noodles with Ginger Sauce (page 338), Whole Wheat Popovers (page 71)

Soba Noodles with Ginger Sauce

As with Oriental Stew (page 318), vermicelli can be substituted for the buckwheat soba noodles.

Ginger Sauce (below)
½ cup cholesterol-free egg product or Egg
Substitute (page 28)
1 package (8 ounces) buckwheat soba
noodles
1 cup frozen green peas
1 cup shredded spinach leaves

Prepare Ginger Sauce. Spray 10-inch nonstick skillet with nonstick cooking spray; heat over medium heat. Pour ¼ cup of the egg product into skillet; rotate skillet to cover bottom. Cook about 1 minute or until egg product is set. Roll up cooked egg product. Remove from skillet; cool. Repeat with remaining egg product.

Cook noodles as directed on package—except add peas during last 3 minutes of cooking; drain. Finely shred egg rolls. Toss egg, noodles and remaining ingredients until evenly coated. *4 servings*

Ginger Sauce

3 tablespoons reduced-sodium soy sauce
2 tablespoons lemon juice
1 tablespoon vegetable or olive oil
2 teaspoons finely chopped gingerroot
⅛ teaspoon red pepper sauce
1 clove garlic, crushed

Mix all ingredients.

NUTRITION INFORMATION PER SERVING			
1 serving		**Percent of U.S. RDA**	
Calories	275	Protein	20%
Protein, g	13	Vitamin A	16%
Carbohydrate, g	47	Vitamin C	8%
Fat, g	4	Thiamin	20%
Unsaturated	3	Riboflavin	14%
Saturated	1	Niacin	10%
Dietary Fiber, g	7	Calcium	6%
Cholesterol, mg	0	Iron	18%
Sodium, mg	560		
Potassium, mg	270		

Pasta with White Beans and Eggplant

With only 25 milligrams of cholesterol, this dish is already very low in cholesterol. To eliminate the cholesterol entirely, use no-cholesterol noodles for the pasta. The sauce may be made a day ahead and reheated with the cooked pasta.

4 cups cubed peeled eggplant (about 1
pound)
2 cups cooked great northern beans or 1
can (about 15 ounces) great northern,
cannellini or navy beans, drained
¾ cup chopped celery (about 1 large stalk)
¾ cup chopped red onion (about 1 medium)
½ cup white wine or apple juice
2 tablespoons chopped fresh or 2 teaspoons
dried basil leaves
2 tablespoons capers
2 cloves garlic, finely chopped
1 can (28 ounces) whole tomatoes,
undrained
6 ounces uncooked rotini or other spiral
pasta (about 2⅓ cups)

Heat all ingredients except rotini to boiling in Dutch oven, breaking up tomatoes; reduce heat to medium. Cover and cook about 30 minutes, stirring occasionally. Meanwhile, cook rotini as directed on package—except omit salt; drain. Stir rotini into eggplant mixture; heat just to boiling. *6 servings*

NUTRITION INFORMATION PER SERVING

1 serving		Percent of U.S. RDA	
Calories	255	Protein	18%
Protein, g	11	Vitamin A	10%
Carbohydrate, g	48	Vitamin C	20%
Fat, g	2	Thiamin	24%
Unsaturated	2	Riboflavin	10%
Saturated	0	Niacin	14%
Dietary Fiber, g	8	Calcium	12%
Cholesterol, mg	25	Iron	26%
Sodium, mg	240		
Potassium, mg	970		

Vegetable Manicotti

8 uncooked manicotti shells

1 can (8 ounces) tomato sauce

1 teaspoon olive or vegetable oil

½ cup shredded carrot (about 1 small)

½ cup shredded zucchini (about 1 small)

½ cup sliced mushrooms (about 2 ounces)

¼ cup sliced green onions (2 to 3 medium)

1 clove garlic, finely chopped

2 cups nonfat ricotta cheese (about 15 ounces)

¼ cup grated Parmesan cheese

2 tablespoons chopped fresh or 2 teaspoons dried basil leaves

2 egg whites

½ cup shredded part-skim mozzarella cheese

Heat oven to 350°. Spray rectangular baking dish, 11×7×1½ inches, with nonstick cooking spray. Cook manicotti shells as directed on package—except omit salt; drain. Pour ⅓ cup of the tomato sauce into baking dish.

Heat oil in 10-inch nonstick skillet over medium-high heat. Cook carrot, zucchini, mushrooms, onions and garlic in oil, stirring frequently, until vegetables are crisp-tender. Stir in remaining ingredients except mozzarella cheese. Fill manicotti shells with vegetable mixture; place in baking dish. Pour remaining tomato sauce over manicotti. Sprinkle with mozzarella cheese. Cover and bake 40 to 45 minutes or until hot and bubbly. *4 servings*

NUTRITION INFORMATION PER SERVING

1 serving		Percent of U.S. RDA	
Calories	300	Protein	40%
Protein, g	30	Vitamin A	52%
Carbohydrate, g	33	Vitamin C	18%
Fat, g	7	Thiamin	14%
Unsaturated	5	Riboflavin	30%
Saturated	2	Niacin	12%
Dietary Fiber, g	3	Calcium	54%
Cholesterol, mg	28	Iron	14%
Sodium, mg	730		
Potassium, mg	590		

Baked Ziti and Bean Casserole, Cajun Zucchini (page 124)

Baked Ziti and Bean Casserole

1 can (28 ounces) whole tomatoes, drained

1 cup nonfat ricotta cheese

¼ cup chopped red onion

1 tablespoon chopped fresh parsley

1 tablespoon chopped fresh or 1 teaspoon dried thyme leaves

½ teaspoon salt

¼ teaspoon crushed red pepper

4 cups hot cooked ziti or penne pasta

1 can (15 ounces) great northern beans, rinsed and drained

3 slices part-skim mozzarella cheese, about 6½×4 inches

Grated Parmesan cheese, if desired

Heat oven to 400°. Spray rectangular baking dish, 11×7×1½ inches, with nonstick cooking spray. Break up tomatoes in large bowl. Stir in ricotta cheese, onion, parsley, thyme, salt and red pepper. Carefully fold in pasta and beans.

Pour pasta mixture into baking dish, spreading evenly. Arrange mozzarella cheese on top. Bake uncovered about 30 minutes or until mixture is hot and cheese is golden brown. Sprinkle with Parmesan cheese. *6 servings*

NUTRITION INFORMATION PER SERVING			
1 serving		Percent of U.S. RDA	
Calories	335	Protein	32%
Protein, g	21	Vitamin A	14%
Carbohydrate, g	54	Vitamin C	18%
Fat, g	4	Thiamin	24%
Unsaturated	2	Riboflavin	16%
Saturated	2	Niacin	14%
Dietary Fiber, g	8	Calcium	30%
Cholesterol, mg	55	Iron	32%
Sodium, mg	690		
Potassium, mg	810		

Baked Shells Alfredo

2 cups low-fat milk
1 tablespoon cornstarch
1 tablespoon Dijon mustard
¼ teaspoon pepper
⅛ teaspoon ground nutmeg
5 cups hot cooked small shell macaroni
2 cups finely chopped zucchini (about 1
    large)
2 cups chopped cooked green beans (about
    ¾ pound)
2 cups chopped seeded tomatoes (about 2
    large)
1 cup finely chopped onion (about 1 large)
1 cup soft whole grain or white bread
    crumbs
¼ cup grated Parmesan cheese
2 tablespoons chopped fresh or 2 teaspoons
    dried basil leaves

Heat oven to 400°. Spray 3-quart casserole with nonstick cooking spray. Heat milk, cornstarch, mustard, pepper and nutmeg to boiling in 2-quart saucepan over medium heat; reduce heat. Simmer about 2 minutes, stirring constantly, until slightly thickened.

Mix sauce, macaroni, zucchini, green beans, tomatoes and onion. Pour macaroni mixture in casserole. Mix remaining ingredients; sprinkle over top. Bake uncovered about 30 minutes or until hot and topping is golden brown. Let stand 5 minutes before serving. *6 servings*

NUTRITION INFORMATION PER SERVING

1 serving		Percent of U.S. RDA	
Calories	350	Protein	22%
Protein, g	15	Vitamin A	12%
Carbohydrate, g	60	Vitamin C	18%
Fat, g	6	Thiamin	30%
Unsaturated	3	Riboflavin	22%
Saturated	3	Niacin	18%
Dietary Fiber, g	6	Calcium	24%
Cholesterol, mg	55	Iron	22%
Sodium, mg	290		
Potassium, mg	560		

Baked Shells Alfredo, tossed salad with Dill Vinaigrette (page 154)

Pasta with Tomato-Lentil Sauce

1 cup chopped onion (about 1 large)

½ cup chopped celery (about 1 medium stalk)

½ cup chopped carrot (about 1 medium)

½ cup Vegetable Stock (page 349)*

2 cloves garlic, finely chopped

½ cup dried lentils

1 tablespoon chopped fresh or 1 teaspoon dried basil leaves

1½ teaspoons chopped fresh or ½ teaspoon dried thyme leaves

1 bay leaf

1 can (8 ounces) tomato sauce

12 ounces uncooked spiral macaroni (about 4 cups)

1 package (10 ounces) frozen chopped spinach, thawed and drained

2 tablespoons grated Parmesan cheese

Cook onion, celery, carrot, Vegetable Stock and garlic in 2-quart saucepan over medium heat about 10 minutes or until liquid has evaporated. Stir in remaining ingredients except macaroni, spinach and cheese. Heat to boiling; reduce heat. Cover and simmer 25 to 30 minutes, stirring occasionally, until lentils are tender. Meanwhile, cook macaroni as directed on package—except omit salt; drain.

Stir spinach into lentil mixture. Cook and stir 3 minutes or until spinach is hot. Remove bay leaf. Serve over macaroni and sprinkle with cheese. *6 servings*

* ½ cup hot water and ½ teaspoon vegetable or chicken bouillon granules can be substituted for the Vegetable Stock.

NUTRITION INFORMATION PER SERVING			
1 serving		**Percent of U.S. RDA**	
Calories	330	Protein	22%
Protein, g	15	Vitamin A	46%
Carbohydrate, g	63	Vitamin C	10%
Fat, g	2	Thiamin	30%
Unsaturated	2	Riboflavin	16%
Saturated	0	Niacin	20%
Dietary Fiber, g	7	Calcium	12%
Cholesterol, mg	0	Iron	28%
Sodium, mg	370		
Potassium, mg	600		

Black Bean, Corn and Tortilla Salad

Part of the tortillas are stirred into the salad, just for fun. They can also be "arranged" on each serving when the salad is served.

4 cups cooked black beans or 3 cans (15 ounces each) black beans, rinsed and drained

2 cups cooked fresh, frozen (thawed) or canned (drained) whole kernel corn (about 4 medium ears)

½ cup chopped green bell pepper (about 1 small)

⅓ cup sliced green onions

¼ cup lime juice

¼ cup chopped fresh cilantro leaves

¼ cup chopped fresh parsley

½ teaspoon pepper

½ teaspoon ground cumin

⅛ teaspoon ground red pepper (cayenne)

2 cloves garlic, finely chopped

3 corn tortillas (6 inches in diameter), each cut into 6 wedges

Mix all ingredients except tortillas in glass or plastic bowl. Cover and refrigerate at least 1 hour. Heat oven to 350°. Place tortilla wedges on ungreased cookie sheet. Bake about 10 minutes or until crisp. Stir 12 wedges into salad. Garnish salad with remaining wedges. *6 servings*

NUTRITION INFORMATION PER SERVING

1 serving		Percent of U.S. RDA	
Calories	260	Protein	20%
Protein, g	13	Vitamin A	4%
Carbohydrate, g	50	Vitamin C	16%
Fat, g	1	Thiamin	20%
Unsaturated	1	Riboflavin	8%
Saturated	0	Niacin	8%
Dietary Fiber, g	12	Calcium	12%
Cholesterol, mg	0	Iron	22%
Sodium, mg	30		
Potassium, mg	620		

Spanish Rice Salad

1 tablespoon olive or vegetable oil
½ cup finely chopped red onion (about ½ medium)
1 clove garlic, crushed
1½ cups uncooked brown rice
¼ teaspoon ground turmeric
¼ teaspoon crushed red pepper
4 cups Vegetable Stock (page 349)*
1 cup cooked fresh or frozen peas
½ cup sliced ripe olives
½ cup chopped red bell pepper (about 1 small)

1 medium tomato, cut into wedges
1 can (15 ounces) garbanzo beans, drained
1 can (about 15 ounces) artichoke hearts, drained and cut into eighths
½ cup spicy tomato juice or tomato juice
2 tablespoons lemon juice
Lemon wedges, if desired

Heat oil in 2-quart saucepan over medium heat. Cook onion and garlic in oil 2 to 3 minutes, stirring frequently, until onion begins to soften. Stir in rice, turmeric and red pepper; stir to coat rice with oil. Stir in Vegetable Stock. Heat to boiling; reduce heat. Cover and simmer 45 to 50 minutes or until rice is tender.

Carefully mix rice mixture and remaining ingredients except tomato juice, lemon juice and lemon wedges in large bowl. Pour tomato and lemon juices over rice mixture; toss. Cover and refrigerate about 3 hours or until chilled. Serve with lemon wedges. *6 servings*

* 4 cups hot water and 1 tablespoon plus 1 teaspoon vegetable or chicken bouillon granules can be substituted for the Vegetable Stock.

NUTRITION INFORMATION PER SERVING

1 serving		Percent of U.S. RDA	
Calories	425	Protein	24%
Protein, g	15	Vitamin A	30%
Carbohydrate, g	76	Vitamin C	82%
Fat, g	7	Thiamin	28%
Unsaturated	6	Riboflavin	12%
Saturated	1	Niacin	22%
Dietary Fiber, g	12	Calcium	14%
Cholesterol, mg	0	Iron	32%
Sodium, mg	630		
Potassium, mg	890		

Black Bean, Corn and Tortilla Salad (page 342), Rice-Taco Salad

Rice-Taco Salad

3 flour tortillas (8 inches in diameter)

³/₄ cup uncooked long grain white rice

1¹/₂ cups water

1 to 2 teaspoons chile powder

¹/₂ teaspoon salt

¹/₄ teaspoon garlic powder

¹/₄ teaspoon ground red pepper (cayenne)

1 can (8 ounces) kidney beans, drained

5 cups shredded lettuce

1 cup chopped tomato (about 1 large)

¹/₂ cup shredded reduced-fat Monterey Jack cheese

¹/₄ cup chopped onion (about 1 small)

¹/₄ cup reduced-calorie Thousand Island dressing

¹/₄ cup low-fat sour cream

4 pitted ripe olives, sliced

Heat oven to 400°. Cut tortillas into 12 wedges or strips, about 3×¹/₄ inch. Place in ungreased jelly roll pan, 15¹/₂×10¹/₂×1 inch. Bake uncovered 6 to 8 minutes, stirring at least once, until golden brown and crisp; cool.

Heat rice, water, chile powder, salt, garlic powder and red pepper to boiling in 1¹/₂-quart saucepan, stirring occasionally; reduce heat. Cover and simmer 14 minutes (do not lift cover or stir); remove from heat. Fluff rice lightly with fork. Cover and let steam 5 minutes. Stir in kidney beans.

Mix lettuce, tomato, cheese and onion in large bowl. Add dressing; toss. Divide lettuce mixture among 4 plates. Top each salad with about ¹/₂ cup rice mixture. Arrange tortilla wedges around salad. Garnish with sour cream and olives. *4 servings*

NUTRITION INFORMATION PER SERVING

I serving		Percent of U.S. RDA	
Calories	415	Protein	24%
Protein, g	16	Vitamin A	12%
Carbohydrate, g	68	Vitamin C	22%
Fat, g	9	Thiamin	30%
Unsaturated	5	Riboflavin	14%
Saturated	4	Niacin	16%
Dietary Fiber, g	7	Calcium	18%
Cholesterol, mg	15	Iron	16%
Sodium, mg	810		
Potassium, mg	610		

Wheat Berry Salad with Vinaigrette Dressing

This salad is very versatile. Change the look and flavor by substituting other cooked whole grains for the wheat berries, or other beans for the garbanzos. See page 320 for more information on wheat berries and other grains.

1 cup uncooked wheat berries
2¹/₂ cups water
1¹/₂ cups broccoli flowerets
¹/₂ cup chopped green onions (about 5 medium)
¹/₂ cup chopped carrot (about 1 medium)
1 can (15 ounces) garbanzo beans, drained
Vinaigrette Dressing (right)

Heat wheat berries and water to boiling in 2-quart saucepan, stirring once or twice; reduce heat. Cover and simmer 50 to 60 minutes or until wheat berries are tender but still chewy; drain. Toss wheat berries and remaining ingredients in glass or plastic bowl. Cover and refrigerate at least 1 hour. *4 servings*

Vinaigrette Dressing

¹/₄ cup balsamic or cider vinegar
2 tablespoons olive or vegetable oil
1 tablespoon chopped fresh or 1 teaspoon dried basil leaves
¹/₄ teaspoon paprika
¹/₈ teaspoon salt
1 clove garlic, crushed

Mix all ingredients.

WHEAT BERRY-TOFU SALAD: Omit Vinaigrette Dressing. Toss remaining salad ingredients with ¹/₂ cup Tofu Mayonnaise (page 153).

NUTRITION INFORMATION PER SERVING

I serving		Percent of U.S. RDA	
Calories	350	Protein	20%
Protein, g	13	Vitamin A	26%
Carbohydrate, g	52	Vitamin C	24%
Fat, g	10	Thiamin	18%
Unsaturated	8	Riboflavin	10%
Saturated	2	Niacin	14%
Dietary Fiber, g	10	Calcium	8%
Cholesterol, mg	0	Iron	26%
Sodium, mg	240		
Potassium, mg	590		

Spicy Brown Rice and Pinto Bean Salad

The crisp crunch of vegetables stands up well to the fresh flavor of this dressing. Serve the salad with a slotted spoon and place it on a bed of shredded lettuce or in lettuce cups for a more elegant presentation.

4 cups cooked brown rice

2 cups cooked pinto beans or 1 can (15 ounces) pinto beans, drained

1 cup chopped tomato (about 1 large)

1 cup chopped cucumber (about 1 medium)

1 cup chopped jícama (about ½ medium)

½ cup chopped green bell pepper (about 1 small)

¼ cup chopped pepperocini (Italian bottled peppers) or green chiles

3 tablespoons chopped fresh cilantro leaves

2 tablespoons lemon juice

1 tablespoon Dijon mustard

1 teaspoon vegetable oil

½ teaspoon salt

2 ounces hot pepper Monterey Jack or Cheddar cheese, cut into ¼-inch cubes

Mix all ingredients in glass or plastic bowl. Cover and refrigerate at least 2 hours or until chilled. *6 servings*

NUTRITION INFORMATION PER SERVING			
I serving		Percent of U.S. RDA	
Calories	315	Protein	18%
Protein, g	12	Vitamin A	6%
Carbohydrate, g	53	Vitamin C	28%
Fat, g	6	Thiamin	20%
Unsaturated	3	Riboflavin	8%
Saturated	3	Niacin	14%
Dietary Fiber, g	8	Calcium	10%
Cholesterol, mg	10	Iron	16%
Sodium, mg	280		
Potassium, mg	580		

Summer Split Pea Salad (page 344), Spicy Brown Rice and Pinto Bean Salad

Creamy Broccoli-Swiss Soup

The Vegetable Stock (right) makes more than what is needed for this soup. Refrigerate the remainder tightly covered up to 1 week for use in other recipes. Or, freeze in ice cube trays and use in gravies and sauces or as a substitute for chicken broth. Stir the stock just before measuring so the spices are well distributed.

3 cups Vegetable Stock (right)*
2 cups chopped carrots (about 4 medium)
1 cup chopped celery (about 2 medium stalks)
½ cup chopped onion (about 1 medium)
1 package (10 ounces) frozen chopped broccoli
½ teaspoon salt
¼ teaspoon pepper
2 cups low-fat milk
¼ cup all-purpose flour
1½ cups shredded reduced-fat Swiss cheese (6 ounces)

Prepare Vegetable Stock. Heat carrots, celery, onion, Vegetable Stock, broccoli, salt and pepper to boiling in Dutch oven; reduce heat. Cover and simmer 10 minutes; remove from heat. Shake milk and flour in tightly covered container; gradually stir into vegetable mixture. Heat to boiling, stirring constantly. Boil and stir 1 minute; remove from heat. Divide cheese among 4 soup bowls; ladle hot soup over cheese. *4 servings*

Vegetable Stock

6 cups coarsely chopped mild vegetables (bell peppers, carrots, celery, leeks, mushroom stems, potatoes, spinach, zucchini)
½ cup coarsely chopped onion (about 1 medium)
½ cup parsley sprigs
8 cups cold water
2 tablespoons chopped fresh or 2 teaspoons dried basil leaves
2 tablespoons chopped fresh or 2 teaspoons dried thyme leaves
1 teaspoon salt
¼ teaspoon cracked black pepper
4 cloves garlic, chopped
2 bay leaves

Heat all ingredients to boiling in Dutch oven or stockpot; reduce heat. Cover and simmer about 1 hour, stirring occasionally. Cool slightly. Strain and refrigerate. Stir before measuring. About 8 cups stock.

NOTE: Use strong vegetables, such as broccoli, cabbage, cauliflower, turnips and rutabagas sparingly combined with mild vegetables.

* 3 cups hot water and 1 tablespoon vegetable or chicken boullion granules can be substituted for the Vegetable Stock.

NUTRITION INFORMATION PER SERVING			
1 serving		Percent of U.S. RDA	
Calories	310	Protein	50%
Protein, g	23	Vitamin A	154%
Carbohydrate, g	34	Vitamin C	46%
Fat, g	9	Thiamin	20%
Unsaturated	4	Riboflavin	34%
Saturated	5	Niacin	12%
Dietary Fiber, g	7	Calcium	30%
Cholesterol, mg	25	Iron	14%
Sodium, mg	664		
Potassium, mg	970		

Chile-Corn Chowder

If spicy foods are your style, use hot green chiles instead of mild.

3 cups chopped baking potatoes (about 2 large)

1 cup chopped onion (about 1 large)

¾ cup chopped carrots (about 1½ medium)

½ cup chopped celery (about 1 medium stalk)

2 cups water

1 can (14½ ounces) whole tomatoes, undrained

1 can (4 ounces) chopped mild green chiles, drained

1 cup shredded reduced-fat Cheddar cheese (4 ounces)

1½ cups cooked fresh, frozen (thawed) or canned (drained) whole kernel corn (about 3 medium ears)

6 slices Whole Wheat Baguette (page 100) or French bread

Heat potatoes, onion, carrots, celery, water, tomatoes and chiles to boiling in 2-quart saucepan; reduce heat. Cover and simmer 20 to 25 minutes or until potatoes are tender. Place half the mixture in blender or food processor; add cheese. Cover and blend until smooth. Repeat with remaining mixture.

Return mixture to saucepan; stir in corn. Heat about 5 minutes, just until corn is heated through. (Do not boil to prevent mixture from curdling.) Serve chowder over bread slices.
6 servings

NUTRITION INFORMATION PER SERVING			
1 serving		Percent of U.S. RDA	
Calories	250	Protein	18%
Protein, g	11	Vitamin A	38%
Carbohydrate, g	43	Vitamin C	30%
Fat, g	4	Thiamin	16%
Unsaturated	2	Riboflavin	16%
Saturated	2	Niacin	16%
Dietary Fiber, g	6	Calcium	20%
Cholesterol, mg	10	Iron	12%
Sodium, mg	520		
Potassium, mg	720		

Winter Squash and Lentil Bisque

3 cups chopped butternut squash (about 2 medium)

2 cups chopped green apples (about 2 medium)

¾ cup chopped red onion (about 1 medium)

½ cup unsweetened applesauce

2 cups Vegetable Stock (page 349)*

1 cup apple juice

¼ teaspoon ground nutmeg

⅛ teaspoon ground red pepper (cayenne)

½ cup dried lentils

¾ cup shredded reduced-fat Monterey Jack cheese (6 ounces)

6 slices French bread, ¼ inch thick

Heat squash, apples, onion, applesauce, 1 cup of the Vegetable Stock, the apple juice, nutmeg and red pepper to boiling in 3-quart saucepan, stirring occasionally; reduce heat. Cover and simmer 20 minutes. Place mixture in blender or food processor. Cover and process until smooth. Return mixture to saucepan. Stir in lentils and remaining stock. Heat to boiling; reduce heat. Cover and simmer 25 to 30 minutes, stirring occasionally, or until lentils are tender.

Set oven control to broil. Sprinkle cheese on bread slices. Broil bread with tops 3 inches from heat about 2 minutes or until cheese is bubbly. Top each serving of soup with a piece of cheese bread. Garnish with chopped chives if desired. *6 servings*

* 2 cups hot water and 2 teaspoons vegetable or chicken bouillon granules can be substituted for the Vegetable Stock.

NUTRITION INFORMATION PER SERVING

1 serving		Percent of U.S. RDA	
Calories	265	Protein	18%
Protein, g	12	Vitamin A	44%
Carbohydrate, g	45	Vitamin C	14%
Fat, g	4	Thiamin	14%
Unsaturated	2	Riboflavin	8%
Saturated	2	Niacin	16%
Dietary Fiber, g	8	Calcium	16%
Cholesterol, mg	10	Iron	16%
Sodium, mg	430		
Potassium, mg	610		

Winter Squash and Lentil Bisque (left), *Vegetable Barley Soup* (right) (*page 356*)

Three-Bean and Barley Soup

2 small onions, cut into halves and thinly sliced
2 cloves garlic, finely chopped
1 teaspoon ground cumin
1 tablespoon olive or vegetable oil
½ cup uncooked instant barley
3 cups water
½ teaspoon salt
1 can (about 14½ ounces) stewed tomatoes
1 can (15 ounces) garbanzo beans, undrained
1 can (15 ounces) black beans, rinsed and drained
1 package (10 ounces) frozen lima beans or 1 can (15 ounces) lima beans, drained
2 tablespoons chopped fresh cilantro leaves

Cook onions, garlic and cumin in oil in Dutch oven 4 to 5 minutes, stirring occasionally, until onions are tender. Stir in remaining ingredients except cilantro. Heat to boiling; reduce heat. Cover and simmer about 10 minutes or until lima beans are tender. Stir in cilantro. *5 servings*

Vegetable Barley Soup

1 tablespoon vegetable oil
1 cup finely chopped onion (about 1 large)
2 cups diced peeled parsnips (about 2 medium)
1 cup uncooked pearl barley
1 cup cauliflowerets
1 cup sliced carrots (about 2 medium)
1 cup chopped bell pepper (about 1 medium)
3 cups Vegetable Stock (page 349)*
½ cup dry red wine or tomato juice
1 teaspoon ground cinnamon
1 medium turnip, peeled and diced
1 can (15 ounces) garbanzo beans, drained
½ cup chopped fresh parsley

Heat oil in Dutch oven over medium heat. Cook onion in oil about 2 minutes, stirring frequently, until tender. Stir in remaining ingredients except parsley. Heat to boiling; reduce heat. Simmer uncovered 35 to 45 minutes or until barley is done and vegetables are tender. Sprinkle with parsley. *6 servings*

* 1 cup hot water and 1 teaspoon vegetable or beef bouillon granules can be substituted for the Vegetable Stock.

NUTRITION INFORMATION PER SERVING			
1 serving		**Percent of U.S. RDA**	
Calories	475	Protein	32%
Protein, g	21	Vitamin A	10%
Carbohydrate, g	82	Vitamin C	26%
Fat, g	8	Thiamin	28%
Unsaturated	6	Riboflavin	12%
Saturated	2	Niacin	16%
Dietary Fiber, g	17	Calcium	14%
Cholesterol, mg	0	Iron	36%
Sodium, mg	840		
Potassium, mg	1120		

NUTRITION INFORMATION PER SERVING			
1 serving		**Percent of U.S. RDA**	
Calories	335	Protein	18%
Protein, g	11	Vitamin A	44%
Carbohydrate, g	62	Vitamin C	38%
Fat, g	5	Thiamin	16%
Unsaturated	4	Riboflavin	8%
Saturated	1	Niacin	14%
Dietary Fiber, g	12	Calcium	10%
Cholesterol, mg	0	Iron	24%
Sodium, mg	250		
Potassium, mg	760		

Minestrone

Minestrone

1 cup thinly sliced celery (about 2 medium
    stalks)
1 cup sliced zucchini (about 1 small)
1 cup shredded cabbage
¹/₂ cup chopped onion (about 1 medium)
¹/₂ cup uncooked elbow macaroni or broken
    spaghetti
1¹/₄ cups water
2 teaspoons vegetable bouillon granules
1 teaspoon Italian seasoning
1 clove garlic, crushed
1 can (28 ounces) whole tomatoes,
    undrained
1 can (15 ounces) great northern beans,
    undrained
1 can (8 ounces) kidney beans, undrained

1 can (about 8 ounces) whole kernel corn,
    undrained
Grated Parmesan cheese

Heat all ingredients except cheese to boiling in
Dutch oven, breaking up tomatoes; reduce heat.
Cover and simmer about 15 minutes, stirring
occasionally, until macaroni is tender. Serve
with cheese. *6 servings*

NUTRITION INFORMATION PER SERVING			
1 serving		**Percent of U.S. RDA**	
Calories	305	Protein	26%
Protein, g	17	Vitamin A	10%
Carbohydrate, g	52	Vitamin C	28%
Fat, g	3	Thiamin	20%
Unsaturated	2	Riboflavin	12%
Saturated	1	Niacin	12%
Dietary Fiber, g	10	Calcium	20%
Cholesterol, mg	5	Iron	30%
Sodium, mg	1140		
Potassium, mg	1100		

Bean Burgers with Horseradish Sauce

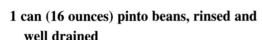

1 can (16 ounces) pinto beans, rinsed and well drained
½ cup shredded reduced-fat Cheddar cheese
¼ cup dry bread crumbs
2 tablespoons chopped green onions
1 teaspoon Worcestershire sauce
¼ teaspoon pepper
⅛ teaspoon salt
1 egg white or 2 tablespoons cholesterol-free egg product
4 whole wheat hamburger buns, split
Horseradish Sauce (below)
4 slices tomato
4 lettuce leaves

Spray 10-inch nonstick skillet with nonstick cooking spray. Mash beans in medium bowl. Mix in cheese, bread crumbs, onions, Worcestershire sauce, pepper, salt and egg white. Shape into 4 patties. Cook in skillet over medium heat about 10 minutes, turning once, until light brown. Serve on buns with Horseradish Sauce, tomato and lettuce. *4 servings*

Horseradish Sauce

½ cup plain nonfat yogurt
2 teaspoons prepared horseradish

Mix ingredients.

NUTRITION INFORMATION PER SERVING			
1 serving		**Percent of U.S. RDA**	
Calories	315	Protein	30%
Protein, g	19	Vitamin A	2%
Carbohydrate, g	51	Vitamin C	4%
Fat, g	4	Thiamin	22%
Unsaturated	2	Riboflavin	18%
Saturated	2	Niacin	8%
Dietary Fiber, g	9	Calcium	26%
Cholesterol, mg	10	Iron	24%
Sodium, mg	670		
Potassium, mg	750		

Bean and Cheese Tacos

Red Salsa (right) or salsa
1 can (8 ounces) kidney beans, drained and liquid reserved
1 clove garlic, finely chopped
4 flour tortillas (about 8 inches in diameter)
1 cup nonfat ricotta cheese
¼ cup grated Parmesan cheese
¼ cup chopped green onions (2 to 3 medium)
1 tablespoon chopped fresh cilantro leaves

Prepare Red Salsa. Heat oven to 350°. Mash beans and garlic. (Add 1 to 2 tablespoons reserved bean liquid if beans are dry.) Place tortillas on ungreased cookie sheet. Spread about ¼ cup of the bean mixture on half of each tortilla to within ½ inch of edge. Mix cheeses, onions and cilantro; spread over beans. Fold tortillas over filling. Bake about 10 minutes or until tortillas begin to brown and filling is hot. Serve with salsa. *4 servings*

Northern Italian White Bean Salad (page 344), Bean and Cheese Tacos

Red Salsa

1 cup chopped tomato (about 1 large)

¼ cup chopped green onions (2 to 3 medium)

2 to 3 teaspoons chopped jalapeño chile (about ½ small)

1½ teaspoons chopped fresh cilantro, if desired

1½ teaspoons lemon juice

1 teaspoon chopped fresh or ½ teaspoon dried oregano leaves

1 large clove garlic, finely chopped

Mix all ingredients in glass or plastic bowl. Cover and refrigerate at least 1 hour.

NUTRITION INFORMATION PER SERVING

1 serving		Percent of U.S. RDA	
Calories	535	Protein	44%
Protein, g	29	Vitamin A	36%
Carbohydrate, g	89	Vitamin C	100%
Fat, g	7	Thiamin	40%
Unsaturated	6	Riboflavin	46%
Saturated	1	Niacin	26%
Dietary Fiber, g	21	Calcium	74%
Cholesterol, mg	15	Iron	74%
Sodium, mg	540		
Potassium, mg	2220		

9

Desserts

If you think healthy eating means a sentence of plain fruit or angel food cake for dessert, these recipes will change your mind! Nearly all of them are only 250 or fewer calories per serving, and the majority of them are also low in fat, cholesterol and sodium. What we did leave in is flavor, and lots of it!

You'll find all your favorite kinds of desserts here—fruits, puddings, cakes, pies, cookies and bars. Reduced-fat dairy products and other non- or reduced-fat and cholesterol ingredients can be used very successfully to produce guilt-free treats. Apple-Noodle Pudding (page 386) combines nonfat ricotta, nonfat yogurt, cholesterol-free egg product, an egg white and cholesterol-free noodles with the natural sweetness of apples and raisins for a family-pleasing dessert. Forget the fat and calories found in pie crust; when it comes to Pumpkin Pie (page 401), our version calls for a sprinkling of brown sugar, rolled oats and a small amount of margarine over the top of the pie instead. Miniature chocolate chips replace the standard-size chips in Chocolate Chip Cookies (page 413) for loads of pleasure, without paying the price in calories.

Along with the standard desserts, you will also find many new and enticing ideas. Whichever recipes you choose, we know that you will be delighted with the results.

Preceding page: Phyllo Tartlets with Winter Apples (page 403), Cheesecake with Strawberry Topping (page 392); Above: New and unusual fruits; 1) papaya; 2) mango; 3) pepino melon; 4) star fruit; 5) pomegranate; 6) persimmon; 7) Asian pear; 8) horned melon; 9) plantain

Berries with Warm Custard Sauce

½ cup sweetened applesauce
⅔ cup cholesterol-free egg product or Egg
  Substitute (page 28)
1 teaspoon vanilla
¼ teaspoon almond extract
1 egg white
2 pints fresh berries

Mix all ingredients except berries in heavy 2-quart saucepan. Heat over low heat, stirring constantly, just until mixture is warm. Beat on medium speed 10 minutes or until mixture is doubled in volume. Serve immediately over berries. *8 servings*

NUTRITION INFORMATION PER SERVING

I serving		Percent of U.S. RDA	
Calories	45	Protein	4%
Protein, g	2	Vitamin A	*
Carbohydrate, g	9	Vitamin C	70%
Fat, g	0	Thiamin	2%
Unsaturated	0	Riboflavin	8%
Saturated	0	Niacin	*
Dietary Fiber, g	I	Calcium	2%
Cholesterol, mg	0	Iron	4%
Sodium, mg	45		
Potassium, mg	160		

Blueberry–Lemon Meringue Dessert

3 egg whites
¼ teaspoon cream of tartar
¾ cup sugar

1½ cups fresh or frozen (thawed and
  drained) blueberries
1 package (4-serving size) lemon instant
  pudding and pie filling
Low-fat milk
¼ package (5.2-ounce size) whipped
  topping mix (1 envelope)
Low-fat milk

Heat oven to 275°. Line cookie sheet with cooking parchment paper or aluminum foil. Beat egg whites and cream of tartar in medium bowl until foamy. Beat in sugar, 1 tablespoon at a time; continue beating until stiff and glossy. Do not underbeat. Shape meringue on cookie sheet into 9-inch circle with back of spoon, building up side. Bake 1 hour. Turn off oven; leave meringue in oven with door closed 1½ hours. Remove from oven. Cool completely at room temperature.

Arrange blueberries in meringue shell. Prepare pudding and pie filling as directed on package for pudding, using low-fat milk. Spread pudding over blueberries. Prepare whipped topping mix as directed on package, using low-fat milk. Spread whipped topping over pudding. Refrigerate at least 1 hour or until set. Garnish with additional blueberries and lemon twists if desired. *8 servings*

NUTRITION INFORMATION PER SERVING

I serving		Percent of U.S. RDA	
Calories	200	Protein	4%
Protein, g	4	Vitamin A	2%
Carbohydrate, g	41	Vitamin C	6%
Fat, g	2	Thiamin	2%
Unsaturated	0	Riboflavin	8%
Saturated	2	Niacin	*
Dietary Fiber, g	0	Calcium	8%
Cholesterol, mg	5	Iron	*
Sodium, mg	240		
Potassium, mg	180		

Strawberry-Chocolate Meringues

Strawberry-Chocolate Meringues

3 egg whites
¹⁄₄ teaspoon cream of tartar
³⁄₄ cup sugar
1 ounce unsweetened chocolate, coarsely grated
2 cups sliced strawberries (about 1 pint)
1 quart strawberry nonfat frozen yogurt

Heat oven to 275°. Line cookie sheet with cooking parchment paper or aluminum foil. Beat egg whites and cream of tartar in medium bowl until foamy. Beat in sugar, 1 tablespoon at a time; continue beating until stiff and glossy. Do not underbeat. Fold in chocolate. Drop meringue by ¹⁄₃ cupfuls onto cookie sheet. Shape into about 3-inch circles, building up sides.

Bake 1 hour. Turn off oven; leave meringues in oven with door closed 1¹⁄₂ hours. Remove from oven. Cool completely at room temperature.

Place strawberries in blender or food processor. Cover and blend until smooth. Fill each meringue with about ¹⁄₂ cup frozen yogurt. Top with strawberry mixture. *8 servings*

NUTRITION INFORMATION PER SERVING			
I serving		**Percent of U.S. RDA**	
Calories	200	Protein	12%
Protein, g	5	Vitamin A	8%
Carbohydrate, g	40	Vitamin C	36%
Fat, g	2	Thiamin	4%
Unsaturated	1	Riboflavin	16%
Saturated	1	Niacin	4%
Dietary Fiber, g	1	Calcium	12%
Cholesterol, mg	2	Iron	6%
Sodium, mg	65		
Potassium, mg	290		

Honey-glazed Ruby Grapefruit

Additional fruit can be added to garnish the plate of grapefruit pieces if you like. To serve as grapefruit halves, section the grapefruit with a grapefruit knife before brushing with the honey mixture; serve with grapefruit spoons. The grapefruit is also delicious served cold, in pieces or halves.

3 red grapefruit, cut into halves
2 tablespoons honey
2 tablespoons low-fat sour cream

Set oven control to broil. Cut thin slice from bottom of each grapefruit half so they will stand flat. Place grapefruit, cut sides up, in jelly roll pan, 15½×10½×1 inch. Mix honey and sour cream; brush over grapefruit. Broil 4 inches from heat 5 to 7 minutes or until light brown. Cut each grapefruit half into fourths. *6 servings*

NUTRITION INFORMATION PER SERVING

1 serving		Percent of U.S. RDA	
Calories	75	Protein	2%
Protein, g	1	Vitamin A	2%
Carbohydrate, g	18	Vitamin C	42%
Fat, g	0	Thiamin	4%
Unsaturated	0	Riboflavin	2%
Saturated	0	Niacin	2%
Dietary Fiber, g	2	Calcium	2%
Cholesterol, mg	0	Iron	*
Sodium, mg	5		
Potassium, mg	220		

Papaya Dessert

3 papayas
½ lime
2 tablespoons orange juice or orange-flavored liqueur
1 cup frozen (thawed) "lite" whipped topping
1 kiwifruit, peeled and sliced

Cut papayas lengthwise into halves; remove seeds. Peel papaya halves. Cut 4 papaya halves lengthwise into slices. Arrange papaya slices on 4 dessert plates. Squeeze juice from lime over papaya slices.

Cut remaining papaya into 1-inch pieces. Place papaya pieces and orange juice in blender or food processor. Cover and blend, stopping occasionally to scrape sides, until smooth. Fold blended mixture into whipped topping. Spoon whipped topping mixture over papaya slices. Top with kiwifruit. *4 servings*

NUTRITION INFORMATION PER SERVING

1 serving		Percent of U.S. RDA	
Calories	150	Protein	2%
Protein, g	2	Vitamin A	6%
Carbohydrate, g	29	Vitamin C	100%
Fat, g	3	Thiamin	4%
Unsaturated	1	Riboflavin	4%
Saturated	2	Niacin	4%
Dietary Fiber, g	5	Calcium	6%
Cholesterol, mg	0	Iron	2%
Sodium, mg	20		
Potassium, mg	660		

Minty Mixed Melon

Mix all ingredients in glass or plastic bowl. Cover and refrigerate at least 2 hours or until chilled. *6 servings*

2 cups chopped cantaloupe (about 1 large)

2 cups chopped honeydew melon (about 1 medium)

2 cups chopped watermelon (about ½ small)

1 teaspoon grated lime peel

¼ cup lime juice

2 tablespoons chopped fresh or 2 teaspoons dried mint leaves

2 tablespoons honey

NUTRITION INFORMATION PER SERVING			
I serving		**Percent of U.S. RDA**	
Calories	85	Protein	2%
Protein, g	I	Vitamin A	16%
Carbohydrate, g	20	Vitamin C	74%
Fat, g	0	Thiamin	8%
Unsaturated	0	Riboflavin	2%
Saturated	0	Niacin	4%
Dietary Fiber, g	I	Calcium	2%
Cholesterol, mg	0	Iron	2%
Sodium, mg	15		
Potassium, mg	400		

Minty Mixed Melon, Watermelon with Blackberries and Pear Puree

Watermelon with Blackberries and Pear Puree

3 slices watermelon, ³/₄ inch thick
1¹/₂ cups blackberries
2 medium pears
¹/₄ cup light rum or apple juice

Cut each watermelon slice into 10 wedges. Cut rind from wedges; remove seeds. Arrange wedges on 6 dessert plates. Top with blackberries. Refrigerate at least 1 hour.

Peel pears; cut into fourths and remove cores and stems. Place pears and rum in blender or food processor. Cover and blend, stopping occasionally to scrape sides, until smooth. Spoon over watermelon and blackberries. *6 servings*

NUTRITION INFORMATION PER SERVING

1 serving		Percent of U.S. RDA	
Calories	150	Protein	2%
Protein, g	2	Vitamin A	10%
Carbohydrate, g	30	Vitamin C	54%
Fat, g	1	Thiamin	14%
Unsaturated	1	Riboflavin	4%
Saturated	0	Niacin	2%
Dietary Fiber, g	4	Calcium	4%
Cholesterol, mg	0	Iron	4%
Sodium, mg	5		
Potassium, mg	420		

Gingered Pineapple

1 medium pineapple (with green leaves)
¹/₄ cup dark rum or apple juice
2 teaspoons finely chopped gingerroot or 1 teaspoon ground ginger
¹/₄ cup shredded coconut, toasted if desired

Cut pineapple lengthwise into fourths; remove core. Cut along curved edges to loosen pineapple from rind without cutting rind. Cut fruit in rind crosswise into ³/₄-inch slices; then cut lengthwise down center of slices, leaving the cut fruit in the rind shell. Mix rum and gingerroot; spoon over pineapple. Cover and refrigerate at least 4 hours. Sprinkle with coconut. Garnish with strawberries and mint leaves if desired. *4 servings*

NUTRITION INFORMATION PER SERVING

1 serving		Percent of U.S. RDA	
Calories	90	Protein	*
Protein, g	0	Vitamin A	*
Carbohydrate, g	15	Vitamin C	30%
Fat, g	1	Thiamin	6%
Unsaturated	1	Riboflavin	2%
Saturated	0	Niacin	2%
Dietary Fiber, g	1	Calcium	*
Cholesterol, mg	0	Iron	2%
Sodium, mg	0		
Potassium, mg	140		

Brandied Peach Sundaes

Served warm or cold over frozen yogurt, the pretty red color of this brandy and peach sauce comes from grenadine syrup. Grenadine is a sweet syrup made from pomegranate and other fruit juices.

1½ teaspoons cornstarch
1½ teaspoons cold water
Dash of salt
½ cup grenadine syrup
¼ cup brandy or apple juice
2 cups sliced peeled peaches (about 2
     medium)*
1 pint vanilla nonfat frozen yogurt

Mix cornstarch, cold water and salt in 1-quart saucepan. Stir in grenadine syrup. Heat to boiling; reduce heat. Cook over low heat about 3 minutes, stirring constantly, until thickened. Stir in brandy and peaches. Cool slightly and serve warm, or cover and refrigerate until chilled. Serve peach mixture over frozen yogurt. *4 servings*

* Frozen (thawed) or canned sliced peaches in juice, drained, can be substituted for the fresh peaches.

NUTRITION INFORMATION PER SERVING

I serving		Percent of U.S. RDA	
Calories	250	Protein	8%
Protein, g	4	Vitamin A	12%
Carbohydrate, g	58	Vitamin C	4%
Fat, g	0	Thiamin	6%
Unsaturated	0	Riboflavin	12%
Saturated	0	Niacin	8%
Dietary Fiber, g	I	Calcium	12%
Cholesterol, mg	2	Iron	4%
Sodium, mg	170		
Potassium, mg	350		

Double Orange Delight

Arranging the fruit over the yogurt sauce gives this dessert a very elegant look. The oranges can be peeled easily by hand, while peeling with a knife will give a more finished look.

½ cup plain nonfat yogurt
1 tablespoon frozen (partially thawed)
     orange juice concentrate
2 large oranges, peeled and sectioned
2 tablespoons semisweet chocolate chips
1 teaspoon shortening

Mix yogurt and orange juice concentrate. Spoon 2 tablespoons yogurt mixture onto each of 4 dessert plates. Arrange orange sections on yogurt mixture. Heat chocolate chips and shortening over low heat, stirring constantly, until chocolate is melted. Carefully drizzle chocolate in thin lines over oranges. *4 servings*

NUTRITION INFORMATION PER SERVING

I serving		Percent of U.S. RDA	
Calories	110	Protein	4%
Protein, g	3	Vitamin A	2%
Carbohydrate, g	18	Vitamin C	92%
Fat, g	3	Thiamin	8%
Unsaturated	I	Riboflavin	6%
Saturated	2	Niacin	2%
Dietary Fiber, g	3	Calcium	10%
Cholesterol, mg	0	Iron	2%
Sodium, mg	25		
Potassium, mg	290		

Topped Fruit Trio (page 376), Double Orange Delight

Citrus-Kiwi Ambrosia

1 medium grapefruit, peeled and sectioned
1 kiwifruit, peeled and sliced
1 can (11 ounces) mandarin orange
    segments, drained
¼ cup orange marmalade spreadable fruit
¼ cup flaked coconut, toasted
¼ cup pomegranate seeds

Divide grapefruit, kiwifruit and orange segments among 4 dessert plates. Heat orange marmalade spreadable fruit until warm; drizzle over fruit. Sprinkle with coconut and pomegranate seeds. *4 servings*

NUTRITION INFORMATION PER SERVING			
1 serving		Percent of U.S. RDA	
Calories	150	Protein	2%
Protein, g	1	Vitamin A	*
Carbohydrate, g	32	Vitamin C	100%
Fat, g	2	Thiamin	4%
Unsaturated	0	Riboflavin	2%
Saturated	2	Niacin	2%
Dietary Fiber, g	3	Calcium	2%
Cholesterol, mg	0	Iron	2%
Sodium, mg	15		
Potassium, mg	320		

Topped Fruit Trio

Whipped Ricotta Topping (page 418)
2 cups blueberries (about 1 pint)
2 cups chopped kiwifruit (about 4)
2 cups chopped papaya (about 1 large)

Prepare Whipped Ricotta Topping. Mix remaining ingredients. Serve topping over fruit. Sprinkle individual servings with ground nutmeg if desired. *6 servings*

NUTRITION INFORMATION PER SERVING			
1 serving		Percent of U.S. RDA	
Calories	190	Protein	12%
Protein, g	8	Vitamin A	6%
Carbohydrate, g	35	Vitamin C	100%
Fat, g	2	Thiamin	4%
Unsaturated	2	Riboflavin	12%
Saturated	0	Niacin	4%
Dietary Fiber, g	3	Calcium	18%
Cholesterol, mg	5	Iron	4%
Sodium, mg	85		
Potassium, mg	510		

Saucy Raspberry Rhubarb

3 cups chopped fresh or 1 package (16
    ounces) cut frozen rhubarb, thawed
½ cup apple juice
3 tablespoons packed brown sugar
2¼ cups raspberries (about 1 pint)
2 tablespoons low-fat sour cream

Heat all ingredients except 1 cup of the raspberries and the sour cream to boiling in 1-quart saucepan; reduce heat to medium-low. Simmer uncovered about 10 minutes or until rhubarb is soft; cool. Stir in remaining raspberries. Serve topped with sour cream. *6 servings*

NUTRITION INFORMATION PER SERVING			
1 serving		Percent of U.S. RDA	
Calories	80	Protein	2%
Protein, g	1	Vitamin A	2%
Carbohydrate, g	17	Vitamin C	12%
Fat, g	1	Thiamin	2%
Unsaturated	1	Riboflavin	2%
Saturated	0	Niacin	2%
Dietary Fiber, g	3	Calcium	6%
Cholesterol, mg	2	Iron	4%
Sodium, mg	10		
Potassium, mg	330		

Poached Raspberry Pears

Poached Raspberry Pears

Bosc pears are perfect here as they hold up well to cooking; firm Anjous can also be used. Apricot spreadable fruit would make a nice flavor and color variation in place of the raspberry.

½ **cup seedless raspberry spreadable fruit**
1 **cup apple juice**
2 **teaspoons grated lemon peel**
2 **tablespoons lemon juice**
3 **firm Bosc pears, peeled and cut into fourths**

Mix all ingredients except pears in 10-inch skillet. Add pears. Heat to boiling; reduce heat to medium-low. Simmer uncovered 30 minutes, spooning juice mixture over pears and turning every 10 minutes, until pears are tender. Serve warm or chilled. *6 servings*

NUTRITION INFORMATION PER SERVING

1 serving		Percent of U.S. RDA	
Calories	110	Protein	*
Protein, g	0	Vitamin A	*
Carbohydrate, g	28	Vitamin C	8%
Fat, g	0	Thiamin	2%
Unsaturated	0	Riboflavin	2%
Saturated	0	Niacin	*
Dietary Fiber, g	3	Calcium	*
Cholesterol, mg	0	Iron	2%
Sodium, mg	5		
Potassium, mg	190		

Mixed Summer Fruit Compote

3 cups fresh or frozen (thawed) unsweetened, pitted dark sweet cherries (about 1 pound)

2 cups chopped nectarines (about 4 medium)

2 cups chopped peaches (about 3 medium)

2 cups chopped pineapple (about ½ medium)

2 cups strawberries, cut in half (about 1 pint)

½ cup apple juice

2 teaspoons finely shredded lemon peel

1 teaspoon vanilla

1 teaspoon honey

2½ cups raspberries (about 1½ pints)

Heat all ingredients except raspberries to boiling in 3-quart saucepan over medium heat; reduce heat to medium-low. Cover and cook 3 minutes; remove from heat. Stir in raspberries; cool 30 minutes. Cover and refrigerate about 4 hours or until chilled. *9 servings*

NUTRITION INFORMATION PER SERVING

1 serving		Percent of U.S. RDA	
Calories	135	Protein	2%
Protein, g	2	Vitamin A	4%
Carbohydrate, g	29	Vitamin C	34%
Fat, g	1	Thiamin	6%
Unsaturated	1	Riboflavin	8%
Saturated	0	Niacin	6%
Dietary Fiber, g	4	Calcium	2%
Cholesterol, mg	0	Iron	4%
Sodium, mg	0		
Potassium, mg	420		

Meringue-topped Apples

6 cups thinly sliced peeled tart cooking apples (about 4 large)

2 tablespoons margarine, melted

2 tablespoons sugar

¼ cup raisins or currants

2 tablespoons apple juice or brandy

3 egg whites

¼ teaspoon cream of tartar

¼ cup sugar

Heat oven to 350°. Spray square baking dish, 8 ×8×2 inches, with nonstick cooking spray. Arrange apples in baking dish. Drizzle margarine over apples. Sprinkle with 2 tablespoons sugar, the raisins and apple juice. Cover with aluminum foil and bake about 30 minutes or until apples are tender.

Beat egg whites and cream of tartar in medium bowl until foamy. Beat in ¼ cup sugar, 1 tablespoon at a time; continue beating until stiff and glossy. Do not underbeat. Spread meringue over apples. Bake uncovered 12 to 15 minutes or until meringue is golden brown. *6 servings*

NUTRITION INFORMATION PER SERVING

1 serving		Percent of U.S. RDA	
Calories	205	Protein	2%
Protein, g	2	Vitamin A	6%
Carbohydrate, g	40	Vitamin C	6%
Fat, g	4	Thiamin	2%
Unsaturated	3	Riboflavin	6%
Saturated	1	Niacin	*
Dietary Fiber, g	3	Calcium	*
Cholesterol, mg	0	Iron	2%
Sodium, mg	80		
Potassium, mg	250		

Praline-Apple Crisp

1 tablespoon water

1 teaspoon almond extract

6 cups sliced unpeeled tart eating apples
   (about 6 medium)

2 tablespoons firm margarine

2 tablespoons all-purpose flour

2 tablespoons packed brown sugar

½ teaspoon ground cinnamon

½ cup coarsely crushed zwieback crackers

2 tablespoons chopped pecans

Yogurt Topping (page 418)

Heat oven to 375°. Spray 1½-quart casserole with nonstick cooking spray. Mix water and almond extract; toss with apples in casserole.

Cut margarine into flour, brown sugar and cinnamon with pastry blender in small bowl until crumbly. Stir in zwieback and pecans. Sprinkle over apples. Bake uncovered about 30 minutes or until top is golden brown and apples are tender. Serve warm with the Yogurt Topping. *6 servings*

NUTRITION INFORMATION PER SERVING			
1 serving		**Percent of U.S. RDA**	
Calories	185	Protein	4%
Protein, g	2	Vitamin A	6%
Carbohydrate, g	31	Vitamin C	4%
Fat, g	6	Thiamin	6%
Unsaturated	5	Riboflavin	4%
Saturated	1	Niacin	2%
Dietary Fiber, g	3	Calcium	6%
Cholesterol, mg	2	Iron	2%
Sodium, mg	75		
Potassium, mg	230		

Praline-Apple Crisp

Apple-Cocoa Roll

A tart apple such as Granny Smith is the apple of choice in this recipe. The roll is best served warm, topped with nonfat plain, vanilla or cinnamon-apple yogurt, or frozen yogurt.

1 package regular active dry yeast
¹/₂ cup warm low-fat milk (105° to 115°)
¹/₄ cup cholesterol-free egg product or 2 egg whites
3 tablespoons frozen (thawed) apple juice concentrate
1 tablespoon vegetable oil
¹/₂ teaspoon ground cardamom
¹/₄ teaspoon salt
2¹/₄ to 2³/₄ cups all-purpose flour
Apple-Cocoa Filling (right)

Dissolve yeast in milk in large bowl. Stir in remaining ingredients except flour and Apple-Cocoa Filling. Gradually stir in enough flour to make a smooth dough. Turn dough onto lightly floured surface; gently roll in flour to coat. Knead 5 minutes, adding enough flour to keep dough from sticking. Spray large bowl with nonstick cooking spray. Place dough in bowl, and turn greased side up. Cover and let rise in warm place about 1 hour or until double. (Dough is ready if indentation remains when touched.)

Heat oven to 350°. Prepare Apple-Cocoa Filling. Spray cookie sheet with nonstick cooking spray. Punch down dough. Roll into rectangle, 13×9 inches, on lightly floured surface. Spread filling over dough to within 1 inch of edges. Roll up rectangle, beginning at 9-inch side. Pinch edge of dough into roll to seal. Place seam side down on cookie sheet. Bake about 45 minutes or until roll sounds hollow when tapped and is brown. Cool completely. Cut into about ¹/₂-inch slices. Serve topped with apple nonfat yogurt if desired. *20 servings*

Apple-Cocoa Filling

2 cups shredded all-purpose apples (about 2 medium)
¹/₃ cup fresh bread crumbs
1 tablespoon cocoa
2 tablespoons frozen (thawed) apple juice concentrate
1 tablespoon bourbon or 1 teaspoon brandy flavoring
1 tablespoon honey
1 teaspoon ground cinnamon
¹/₄ teaspoon ground nutmeg

Mix all ingredients.

NUTRITION INFORMATION PER SERVING			
I serving		**Percent of U.S. RDA**	
Calories	90	Protein	4%
Protein, g	2	Vitamin A	*
Carbohydrate, g	18	Vitamin C	*
Fat, g	I	Thiamin	10%
Unsaturated	I	Riboflavin	8%
Saturated	0	Niacin	6%
Dietary Fiber, g	I	Calcium	2%
Cholesterol, mg	0	Iron	6%
Sodium, mg	50		
Potassium, mg	75		

Baked Maple Apples

Rome Beauty, Golden Delicious and Greening apples all work well in this recipe. We've replaced the usual brown sugar and cinnamon with reduced-calorie maple-flavored syrup to lower calories, but keep the taste.

4 medium cooking apples
2 teaspoons margarine
¼ cup reduced-calorie maple-flavored
**   syrup**

Heat oven to 375°. Core apples; peel 1-inch strip of skin from around middle of each apple, or peel upper half of each apple to prevent splitting. Place apples upright in ungreased square baking dish, 8×8×2 inches. place ½ teaspoon margarine and 1 tablespoon maple-flavored syrup in center of each apple. Pour water into baking dish until ¼ inch deep.

Bake uncovered 30 to 40 minutes or until apples are tender when pierced with fork. Spoon syrup in dish over apples several times during baking. *4 servings*

NUTRITION INFORMATION PER SERVING

1 serving		Percent of U.S. RDA	
Calories	135	Protein	*
Protein, g	0	Vitamin A	2%
Carbohydrate, g	29	Vitamin C	6%
Fat, g	2	Thiamin	2%
Unsaturated	2	Riboflavin	*
Saturated	0	Niacin	*
Dietary Fiber, g	3	Calcium	*
Cholesterol, mg	0	Iron	*
Sodium, mg	55		
Potassium, mg	160		

Caribbean Bananas

4 medium bananas
2 tablespoons margarine, melted
1 tablespoon lemon juice
½ teaspoon ground allspice
⅓ cup packed brown sugar

Heat oven to 350°. Cut bananas crosswise into halves; cut each half lengthwise into halves. Place cut sides up in square baking dish, 9×9×2 inches. Mix margarine, lemon juice and allspice; brush over bananas. Sprinkle with brown sugar. Bake uncovered about 15 minutes or until bananas are hot. *4 servings*

NUTRITION INFORMATION PER SERVING

1 serving		Percent of U.S. RDA	
Calories	240	Protein	2%
Protein, g	1	Vitamin A	8%
Carbohydrate, g	45	Vitamin C	8%
Fat, g	6	Thiamin	2%
Unsaturated	5	Riboflavin	6%
Saturated	1	Niacin	2%
Dietary Fiber, g	2	Calcium	2%
Cholesterol, mg	0	Iron	4%
Sodium, mg	75		
Potassium, mg	520		

Chocolate-Cherry Cobbler

2 tablespoons packed brown sugar

2 tablespoons cornstarch

1 can (16 ounces) pitted red tart cherries
     packed in water, undrained

¼ teaspoon almond extract

6 drops red food color, if desired

2 tablespoons margarine

½ cup all-purpose flour

1 tablespoon plus 1 teaspoon cocoa

1 tablespoon packed brown sugar

¾ teaspoon baking powder

⅛ teaspoon salt

⅓ cup low-fat milk

1 teaspoon vanilla

Heat oven to 375°. Mix 2 tablespoons brown
sugar and the cornstarch in 2-quart saucepan.
Stir in cherries. Cook over medium heat 4 to 5
minutes, stirring occasionally, until slightly
thickened. Stir in almond extract and food
color. Pour into ungreased 1-quart casserole.

Cut margarine into flour, cocoa, brown sugar,
baking powder and salt until mixture resembles
fine crumbs. Stir in milk and vanilla.

Drop dough by 6 spoonfuls onto hot cherry
mixture. Bake 20 to 25 minutes or until topping
is no longer doughy. Serve warm. *6 servings*

NUTRITION INFORMATION PER SERVING

I serving		Percent of U.S. RDA	
Calories	160	Protein	4%
Protein, g	2	Vitamin A	6%
Carbohydrate, g	27	Vitamin C	2%
Fat, g	5	Thiamin	8%
Unsaturated	4	Riboflavin	6%
Saturated	1	Niacin	4%
Dietary Fiber, g	1	Calcium	6%
Cholesterol, mg	0	Iron	6%
Sodium, mg	150		
Potassium, mg	180		

Dessert Pizza

*Pizza isn't all pepperoni and mushrooms! This
free-form fruit version tops nectarines with an
oat struesel, then is brushed with spreadable
fruit and broiled, for a fun dessert everyone will
love.*

½ cup warm low-fat milk (105° to 115°)

¼ cup cholesterol-free egg product

3 tablespoons frozen (thawed) apple juice
     concentrate

2 tablespoons margarine

1½ teaspoons regular active dry yeast

½ teaspoon ground ginger

¼ teaspoon salt

¼ teaspoon ground nutmeg

¼ teaspoon ground allspice

2 cups all-purpose flour

2 tablespoons frozen (thawed) apple juice
     concentrate

3 cups chopped nectarines (about 6
     medium)

½ cup all-purpose flour

¼ cup quick-cooking oats

2 tablespoons packed brown sugar

2 tablespoons low-fat sour cream

1 teaspoon ground cinnamon

3 tablespoons apricot spreadable fruit,
     melted

Mix milk, egg product, 3 tablespoons apple
juice concentrate, the margarine, yeast, ginger,
salt, nutmeg and allspice in large bowl. Gradually stir in 2 cups flour until a smooth dough
forms. Turn dough onto lightly floured surface;
gently roll in flour to coat. Knead about 5 minutes or until smooth and elastic. Spray large
bowl with nonstick cooking spray. Place dough
in bowl, and turn greased side up. Cover and let
rise in warm place about 1 hour or until double.
(Dough is ready if indentation remains when
touched.)

Dessert Pizza

Heat oven to 350°. Spray cookie sheet with nonstick cooking spray. Punch down dough. Roll into 12-inch circle on floured surface. Place dough on prepared cookie sheet. Brush 2 tablespoons apple juice concentrate over dough. Sprinkle nectarines over dough. Mix remaining ingredients except spreadable fruit; sprinkle over nectarines. Bake 40 to 45 minutes or until topping is brown. Set oven control to broil. Brush spreadable fruit over hot pizza. Broil with top of pizza 5 inches from heat about 3 minutes or until glaze is bubbly. Serve warm.
8 servings

PEAR DESSERT PIZZA: Substitute 3 cups chopped pears for the nectarines and 2 tablespoons granulated sugar for the packed brown sugar.

NUTRITION INFORMATION PER SERVING			
I serving		**Percent of U.S. RDA**	
Calories	260	Protein	10%
Protein, g	6	Vitamin A	6%
Carbohydrate, g	50	Vitamin C	4%
Fat, g	4	Thiamin	24%
Unsaturated	3	Riboflavin	18%
Saturated	I	Niacin	14%
Dietary Fiber, g	3	Calcium	4%
Cholesterol, mg	2	Iron	14%
Sodium, mg	130		
Potassium, mg	280		

Cherry-Apple Crumble

Mix ½ cup each unsweetened applesauce and nonfat vanilla yogurt for a delicious topping to this down-home dessert.

3 cups fresh or frozen (thawed)
 unsweetened pitted dark sweet cherries
 (about 1 pound)
3 cups chopped all-purpose apples (about 3
 medium)
¼ cup golden raisins
1 cup all-purpose flour
2 tablespoons margarine
2 tablespoons honey
1 tablespoon packed brown sugar
1 teaspoon ground cinnamon

Heat oven to 375°. Spray square pan, 8×8×2 inches, with nonstick cooking spray. Mix cherries, apples, raisins and 1 tablespoon of the flour. Spread in pan. Cut margarine into remaining flour, the honey, brown sugar and cinnamon until crumbly; sprinkle over fruit. Bake about 30 minutes or until brown. Serve warm or chilled. *6 servings*

NUTRITION INFORMATION PER SERVING

1 serving		Percent of U.S. RDA	
Calories	260	Protein	4%
Protein, g	3	Vitamin A	6%
Carbohydrate, g	51	Vitamin C	6%
Fat, g	5	Thiamin	14%
Unsaturated	4	Riboflavin	10%
Saturated	1	Niacin	8%
Dietary Fiber, g	3	Calcium	2%
Cholesterol, mg	0	Iron	10%
Sodium, mg	50		
Potassium, mg	330		

Rice Pudding

1 cup uncooked regular long grain rice
3 cups low-fat milk
2 tablespoons packed brown sugar
2 tablespoons chopped raisins
1 teaspoon vanilla
½ teaspoon ground cinnamon
½ teaspoon ground cardamom
½ cup low-fat milk

Heat all ingredients except ½ cup milk to boiling in 2-quart saucepan, stirring occasionally; reduce heat to medium. Cook 18 to 20 minutes, stirring occasionally, until rice is tender and all milk is absorbed; remove from heat. Cover and let stand 5 minutes. Stir in ½ cup milk. Serve warm or chilled. *6 servings*

NUTRITION INFORMATION PER SERVING

1 serving		Percent of U.S. RDA	
Calories	210	Protein	10%
Protein, g	7	Vitamin A	8%
Carbohydrate, g	39	Vitamin C	*
Fat, g	3	Thiamin	12%
Unsaturated	1	Riboflavin	14%
Saturated	2	Niacin	6%
Dietary Fiber, g	1	Calcium	18%
Cholesterol, mg	10	Iron	8%
Sodium, mg	75		
Potassium, mg	300		

Ricotta Cream

This creamy mixture can be whipped up in a snap. It's also good topped with fresh berries.

Tangy Fruit Salsa (page 416)
2 cups nonfat ricotta cheese (about 15 ounces)
⅓ cup sugar
¼ teaspoon vanilla
½ package (8-ounce size) light cream cheese (Neufchâtel)

Prepare Tangy Fruit Salsa. Place remaining ingredients in blender or food processor. Cover and blend, stopping occasionally to scrape sides, until smooth. Spoon into 6 dessert dishes. Serve with salsa. *6 servings*

NUTRITION INFORMATION PER SERVING			
I serving		**Percent of U.S. RDA**	
Calories	225	Protein	16%
Protein, g	10	Vitamin A	12%
Carbohydrate, g	24	Vitamin C	70%
Fat, g	10	Thiamin	2%
Unsaturated	4	Riboflavin	12%
Saturated	6	Niacin	*
Dietary Fiber, g	0	Calcium	22%
Cholesterol, mg	35	Iron	2%
Sodium, mg	170		
Potassium, mg	250		

Ricotta Cream

Apple-Noodle Pudding

1½ cups nonfat ricotta cheese
½ cup plain nonfat yogurt
½ cup cholesterol-free egg product
1 teaspoon ground cinnamon
1 teaspoon vanilla
¼ teaspoon ground nutmeg
1 egg white
3 cups cooked cholesterol-free noodles
   (about 6 ounces)
1 cup finely chopped all-purpose apple
   (about 1 medium)
½ cup golden raisins

Heat oven to 350°. Spray square pan, 8×8×2 inches, with nonstick cooking spray. Place all ingredients except noodles, apple and raisins in blender or food processor. Cover and blend until smooth. Pour into large bowl. Stir in remaining ingredients. Spread mixture into pan. Bake 25 to 30 minutes or until light brown. Serve warm or chilled. *6 servings*

NUTRITION INFORMATION PER SERVING

I serving		Percent of U.S. RDA	
Calories	265	Protein	22%
Protein, g	14	Vitamin A	8%
Carbohydrate, g	39	Vitamin C	*
Fat, g	6	Thiamin	14%
Unsaturated	3	Riboflavin	20%
Saturated	3	Niacin	6%
Dietary Fiber, g	2	Calcium	24%
Cholesterol, mg	5	Iron	12%
Sodium, mg	150		
Potassium, mg	320		

Pumpkin Custard

1¾ cups low-fat milk
½ cup canned pumpkin
⅓ cup packed brown sugar
2 tablespoons reduced-calorie maple-
   flavored syrup
1 teaspoon ground cinnamon
¼ teaspoon ground ginger
2 eggs
4 egg whites
⅓ cup raisins
½ cup water
2 tablespoons reduced-calorie maple-
   flavored syrup

Heat oven to 350°. Heat milk in heavy 1-quart saucepan until hot but not boiling. Mix pumpkin, brown sugar, 2 tablespoons syrup, the cinnamon, ginger, eggs and egg whites in large bowl until smooth. Beat in hot milk. Divide evenly among 6 ungreased 10-ounce custard cups. Place cups in rectangular pan, 13×9×2 inches, on oven rack. Pour very hot water into pan to within 1 inch of tops of cups.

Bake 30 to 35 minutes or until knife inserted halfway between center and edge comes out clean; cool. Cook remaining ingredients over medium heat until raisins are soft. Serve over custard. *6 servings*

NUTRITION INFORMATION PER SERVING

I serving		Percent of U.S. RDA	
Calories	170	Protein	10%
Protein, g	7	Vitamin A	50%
Carbohydrate, g	29	Vitamin C	2%
Fat, g	3	Thiamin	4%
Unsaturated	1	Riboflavin	20%
Saturated	2	Niacin	*
Dietary Fiber, g	1	Calcium	12%
Cholesterol, mg	75	Iron	6%
Sodium, mg	125		
Potassium, mg	320		

Raspberry-Bread Pudding

Raspberry-Bread Pudding

Stale bread that is not quite totally dried out is best for this bread pudding. White, whole wheat or cinnamon-raisin bread all work equally well. If using cinnamon-raisin bread, omit raisins and cinnamon from recipe. Blueberries also make a nice substitution for the raspberries.

4 cups 2-inch cubes day-old bread (5 to 7 slices bread)

1 cup fresh raspberries

1/2 cup raisins

2 1/2 cups low-fat milk

1/2 cup cholesterol-free egg product or Egg Substitute (page 28)

2 tablespoons packed brown sugar

1 teaspoon vanilla

1/2 teaspoon ground cinnamon

1/4 teaspoon ground nutmeg

Heat oven to 350°. Spray square baking dish, 8×8×2 inches, with nonstick cooking spray. Mix all ingredients; let stand 15 minutes. Spread mixture in baking dish. Place baking dish in rectangular pan, 13×9×2 inches, on oven rack. Pour boiling water into pan until 1 inch deep. Bake 25 to 30 minutes or until brown. *6 servings*

NUTRITION INFORMATION PER SERVING

1 serving		Percent of U.S. RDA	
Calories	185	Protein	12%
Protein, g	7	Vitamin A	6%
Carbohydrate, g	33	Vitamin C	4%
Fat, g	3	Thiamin	10%
Unsaturated	1	Riboflavin	18%
Saturated	2	Niacin	4%
Dietary Fiber, g	1	Calcium	16%
Cholesterol, mg	10	Iron	8%
Sodium, mg	200		
Potassium, mg	360		

Cantaloupe Sorbet

Cantaloupe makes a light-colored and refreshing sorbet. Honeydew melon can easily be substituted and has its own lovely, subtle color.

1 cantaloupe (about 2½ pounds) peeled and cut into 1-inch pieces
2 tablespoons sugar
2 tablespoons lemon juice
Fresh mint leaves

Place cantaloupe, sugar and lemon juice in blender or food processor. Cover and blend, stopping occasionally to scrape sides, until uniform consistency. Pour into square pan, 9×9×2 inches. Cover and freeze 1 to 1½ hours or until partially frozen.

Spoon partially frozen mixture into blender or food processor. Cover and blend until smooth. Pour into pan. Cover and freeze about 2 hours or until firm. Let stand 10 minutes at room temperature before spooning into dessert dishes. Or, pour into 1-quart ice-cream freezer. Freeze according to manufacturer's directions. Garnish with mint leaves. *6 servings*

NUTRITION INFORMATION PER SERVING

1 serving		Percent of U.S. RDA	
Calories	70	Protein	2%
Protein, g	1	Vitamin A	42%
Carbohydrate, g	17	Vitamin C	100%
Fat, g	0	Thiamin	4%
Unsaturated	0	Riboflavin	2%
Saturated	0	Niacin	4%
Dietary Fiber, g	1	Calcium	2%
Cholesterol, mg	0	Iron	2%
Sodium, mg	15		
Potassium, mg	480		

Strawberry-Honey Sorbet

2 cups chopped strawberries (about 1 pint)
2 cups red wine or apple juice
¼ cup chopped fresh or 1 tablespoon dried mint leaves
3 tablespoons honey
1 teaspoon grated lemon peel

Heat strawberries, wine, mint and honey in 1½-quart saucepan over medium heat 5 minutes, stirring occasionally; remove from heat. Cover and refrigerate at least 4 hours.

Place strawberry mixture in blender or food processor. Cover and blend until smooth; strain.

Stir in lemon peel. Pour into 1-quart ice-cream freezer. Freeze according to manufacturer's directions. *8 servings*

NUTRITION INFORMATION PER SERVING

1 serving		Percent of U.S. RDA	
Calories	70	Protein	*
Protein, g	0	Vitamin A	*
Carbohydrate, g	10	Vitamin C	20%
Fat, g	0	Thiamin	*
Unsaturated	0	Riboflavin	2%
Saturated	0	Niacin	*
Dietary Fiber, g	1	Calcium	*
Cholesterol, mg	0	Iron	2%
Sodium, mg	5		
Potassium, mg	130		

Pineapple Ice

4 cups 1-inch pieces pineapple (about 1
  medium)
½ cup light corn syrup
2 tablespoons lemon juice

Place all ingredients in blender or food processor. Cover and blend, stopping occasionally
to scrape sides, until smooth. Pour into loaf
pan, 9×5×3 inches. Cover and freeze about 2
hours or until firm around edges but soft in
center.

Spoon partially frozen mixture into blender or
food processor. Cover and blend until smooth.
Pour into pan. Cover and freeze about 3 hours
or until firm. Let stand 10 minutes at room
temperature before spooning into dessert
dishes. Or, pour into 1-quart ice-cream freezer.
Freeze according to manufacturer's directions.
8 servings

NUTRITION INFORMATION PER SERVING			
1 serving		**Percent of U.S. RDA**	
Calories	105	Protein	*
Protein, g	0	Vitamin A	*
Carbohydrate, g	26	Vitamin C	20%
Fat, g	0	Thiamin	4%
Unsaturated	0	Riboflavin	2%
Saturated	0	Niacin	2%
Dietary Fiber, g	1	Calcium	*
Cholesterol, mg	0	Iron	2%
Sodium, mg	25		
Potassium, mg	90		

Maple-Vanilla Ice

½ cup sugar
2 cups evaporated skimmed milk
2 cups low-fat milk
2 tablespoons reduced-calorie maple-
  flavored syrup
2 tablespoons light corn syrup
1 tablespoon vanilla

Mix all ingredients until sugar is dissolved.
Pour into 1-quart ice-cream freezer. Freeze
according to the manufacturer's directions.
8 servings

HONEY-VANILLA ICE: Substitute 2 tablespoons
honey for the maple-flavored syrup.

NUTRITION INFORMATION PER SERVING			
1 serving		**Percent of U.S. RDA**	
Calories	155	Protein	10%
Protein, g	7	Vitamin A	10%
Carbohydrate, g	29	Vitamin C	2%
Fat, g	1	Thiamin	2%
Unsaturated	0	Riboflavin	18%
Saturated	1	Niacin	*
Dietary Fiber, g	0	Calcium	26%
Cholesterol, mg	5	Iron	*
Sodium, mg	120		
Potassium, mg	310		

Cheesecake with Strawberry Topping

4 cups plain nonfat yogurt

4 chocolate wafers, crushed (about ¼ cup)

1 package (8 ounces) light cream cheese (Neufchâtel), softened

⅔ cup sugar

¼ cup low-fat milk

2 tablespoons all-purpose flour

2 teaspoons vanilla

3 egg whites or ½ cup cholesterol-free egg product

Strawberry Topping (below)

Line 6-inch strainer with basket-style paper coffee filter or double-thickness cheesecloth. Place strainer over bowl. Spoon yogurt into strainer. Cover and refrigerate 12 hours, draining liquid from bowl occasionally.

Heat oven to 300°. Spray springform pan, 9×3 inches, with nonstick cooking spray. Sprinkle chocolate wafer crumbs on bottom of pan. Beat yogurt and cream cheese in medium bowl on medium speed until smooth. Add sugar, milk, flour, vanilla and egg whites. Beat on medium speed about 2 minutes or until smooth. Carefully spread batter over crumbs in pan.

Bake 1 hour. Turn off oven; leave cheesecake in oven 30 minutes. Remove from oven. Cool 15 minutes. Prepare Strawberry Topping; spread over cheesecake. Cover and refrigerate at least 3 hours. Run metal spatula along side of cake to loosen; remove side of pan. Refrigerate any remaining cheesecake. *12 servings*

Strawberry Topping

1 package (10 ounces) frozen strawberries in "lite" syrup, thawed, drained and syrup reserved

¼ cup sugar

2 tablespoons cornstarch

Add enough water to reserved syrup to measure 1¼ cups. Mix sugar and cornstarch in 1½-quart saucepan. Stir in juice mixture and strawberries. Heat to boiling over medium heat, stirring frequently. Boil and stir 1 minute; cool.

NUTRITION INFORMATION PER SERVING			
1 serving		Percent of U.S. RDA	
Calories	190	Protein	12%
Protein, g	8	Vitamin A	4%
Carbohydrate, g	28	Vitamin C	24%
Fat, g	5	Thiamin	4%
Unsaturated	2	Riboflavin	18%
Saturated	3	Niacin	2%
Dietary Fiber, g	1	Calcium	18%
Cholesterol, mg	15	Iron	2%
Sodium, mg	170		
Potassium, mg	300		

Lime-Ricotta Cheesecake

A cheesecake for only 135 calories per serving! The hint of lime is refreshing and is even tastier served with seasonal berries.

2 cups nonfat ricotta cheese (about 15 ounces)

1 package (8 ounces) light cream cheese (Neufchâtel), softened

½ cup sugar

½ cup cholesterol-free egg product or 3 egg whites

¼ cup low-fat milk

2 tablespoons all-purpose flour

1 teaspoon grated lime peel

2 tablespoons lime juice

1 teaspoon vanilla

Whipped Ricotta Topping (page 418)

Move oven rack to middle position. Heat oven to 300°. Spray springform pan, 9×3 inches, with nonstick cooking spray. Beat ricotta cheese and cream cheese in large bowl on medium speed until smooth. Add remaining ingredients except Whipped Ricotta Topping. Beat on medium speed about 2 minutes or until smooth. Pour into pan.

Bake about 1 hour or until center is almost set. Turn off oven; leave cheesecake in oven 30 minutes. Remove from oven; cool 15 minutes. Refrigerate uncovered about 2½ hours or until chilled. Prepare Whipped Ricotta Topping—except reduce buttermilk to ⅔ cup. When topping is almost set, spread over cheesecake. Cover and refrigerate about 2 hours or until topping is very firm. Run metal spatula along side of cheesecake to loosen; remove side of pan. Refrigerate any remaining cheesecake.

16 servings

NUTRITION INFORMATION PER SERVING

1 serving		Percent of U.S. RDA	
Calories	135	Protein	12%
Protein, g	8	Vitamin A	8%
Carbohydrate, g	14	Vitamin C	*
Fat, g	5	Thiamin	2%
Unsaturated	4	Riboflavin	10%
Saturated	1	Niacin	*
Dietary Fiber, g	0	Calcium	14%
Cholesterol, mg	20	Iron	2%
Sodium, mg	125		
Potassium, mg	110		

Orange-Cinnamon Cheesecake Squares

1 cup graham cracker crumbs (about 14 squares)
2 tablespoons margarine, melted
1 teaspoon grated orange peel
1⅓ cups nonfat cottage cheese
⅓ cup orange marmalade spreadable fruit

¼ cup cholesterol-free egg product or 2 egg whites
2 tablespoons lemon juice
1 teaspoon vanilla
¼ teaspoon ground cinnamon
½ package (8-ounce size) light cream cheese (Neufchâtel)
2 egg whites
2 tablespoons orange marmalade spreadable fruit

Heat oven to 350°. Spray square pan, 8×8×2 inches, with nonstick cooking spray. Mix cracker crumbs, margarine and orange peel; press firmly in bottom of pan. Bake 10 minutes. Cool 5 minutes.

Place remaining ingredients except 2 tablespoons spreadable fruit in blender or food processor. Cover and blend until creamy. Pour over baked layer. Bake about 35 minutes or until slightly cracked and brown around edges. Spread 2 tablespoons spreadable fruit over warm cheesecake. Refrigerate about 2 hours or until chilled. Cut into 2-inch squares. Refrigerate any remaining squares. *16 squares*

NUTRITION INFORMATION PER SERVING

1 square		Percent of U.S. RDA	
Calories	85	Protein	6%
Protein, g	4	Vitamin A	4%
Carbohydrate, g	8	Vitamin C	*
Fat, g	4	Thiamin	*
Unsaturated	2	Riboflavin	4%
Saturated	2	Niacin	*
Dietary Fiber, g	0	Calcium	2%
Cholesterol, mg	5	Iron	2%
Sodium, mg	95		
Potassium, mg	45		

Italian Rice Cake

Italian Rice Cake

¹/₃ cup uncooked regular long grain rice

1 quart low-fat milk

1 teaspoon grated lemon peel

1 teaspoon grated orange peel

¹/₂ cup apricot spreadable fruit

¹/₄ cup chopped hazelnuts (filberts)

¹/₄ cup chopped dried apricots

1 cup cholesterol-free egg product

1 tablespoon rum or 1 teaspoon rum
   flavoring

2 tablespoons apricot spreadable fruit

Heat rice, milk, lemon peel and orange peel just to boiling in 2-quart saucepan over medium heat; reduce heat to medium-low. Simmer uncovered 1¹/₂ hours, stirring occasionally, until liquid has been absorbed and mixture is consistency of pudding; remove from heat. Cool 10 minutes.

Heat oven to 350°. Spray springform pan, 9×3 inches, with nonstick cooking spray. Stir re-

maining ingredients except 2 tablespoons spreadable fruit into rice mixture. Pour into pan. Bake about 1 hour or until toothpick inserted in center comes out clean. Spread 2 tablespoons spreadable fruit over hot cake. Cool cake in pan on wire rack 1 hour (cake will fall as it cools). Cover and refrigerate at least 12 hours.

Run metal spatula along side of cake to loosen; remove side of pan. Cover and refrigerate any remaining cake up to 3 days. *16 servings*

NUTRITION INFORMATION PER SERVING			
1 serving		Percent of U.S. RDA	
Calories	95	Protein	6%
Protein, g	4	Vitamin A	6%
Carbohydrate, g	13	Vitamin C	2%
Fat, g	3	Thiamin	4%
Unsaturated	2	Riboflavin	10%
Saturated	1	Niacin	2%
Dietary Fiber, g	0	Calcium	8%
Cholesterol, mg	5	Iron	2%
Sodium, mg	60		
Potassium, mg	170		

Tropical Trifle

1 loaf-shaped angel food cake
1 package (4-serving size) sugar-free vanilla
   instant pudding and pie filling
Low-fat milk
1 tablespoon grated orange peel
1 container (4 ounces) frozen "lite"
   whipped topping, thawed
1 can (20 ounces) pineapple chunks in
   juice, drained and 6 tablespoons juice
   reserved
1 cup strawberries, sliced
2 kiwifruit, peeled and sliced

Cut cake into 1-inch cubes. Prepare pudding
and pie filling as directed on package for pudding, using low-fat milk. Fold orange peel and
half of the whipped topping into pudding.

Place one-third of the cake cubes in large clear
glass bowl. Sprinkle with 2 tablespoons of the
reserved pineapple juice. Spread one-third of
the pudding mixture over cake cubes. Top with
one-third of the pineapple, strawberries and
kiwifruit. Repeat twice. Spread remaining
whipped topping over top. Cover and refrigerate at least 3 hours. Refrigerate any remaining
trifle. *12 servings*

NUTRITION INFORMATION PER SERVING

1 serving		Percent of U.S. RDA	
Calories	160	Protein	6%
Protein, g	4	Vitamin A	2%
Carbohydrate, g	32	Vitamin C	40%
Fat, g	2	Thiamin	6%
Unsaturated	0	Riboflavin	10%
Saturated	2	Niacin	2%
Dietary Fiber, g	1	Calcium	6%
Cholesterol, mg	2	Iron	2%
Sodium, mg	200		
Potassium, mg	220		

Creamy Raspberry-filled Angel Cake

1 cup boiling water
1 package (4-serving size) sugar-free
   raspberry-flavored gelatin
½ cup cold water
1 pint raspberries
1 container (8 ounces) frozen "lite"
   whipped topping, thawed
1 ten-inch angel food cake

Pour boiling water on gelatin in large bowl; stir
until gelatin is dissolved. Stir in cold water.
Refrigerate about 1 hour or until thickened but
not set. Fold in raspberries and half of the
whipped topping. Refrigerate about 15 minutes
or until thickened but not set.

Split cake horizontally to make 3 layers. (To
split, mark side of cake with toothpicks and cut
with long, thin serrated knife.) Fill layers with
gelatin mixture. Spread remaining whipped
topping over top. Garnish with raspberries if
desired. Refrigerate any remaining cake.
12 servings

NUTRITION INFORMATION PER SERVING

1 serving		Percent of U.S. RDA	
Calories	175	Protein	10%
Protein, g	5	Vitamin A	*
Carbohydrate, g	36	Vitamin C	8%
Fat, g	1	Thiamin	6%
Unsaturated	0	Riboflavin	12%
Saturated	1	Niacin	4%
Dietary Fiber, g	1	Calcium	*
Cholesterol, mg	0	Iron	4%
Sodium, mg	190		
Potassium, mg	110		

Pounder Bars, Apple-Oatmeal Crumbles (page 409)

Pounder Bars

No, these are not called pounder bars because they add pounds! Made with pound cake, they have only 88 calories per bar. Dip a knife in cold water for ease in cutting the meringue.

1 package (12 ounces) fat-free golden loaf
   cake
¹⁄₃ cup finely chopped semisweet chocolate
¹⁄₃ cup raspberry or apricot spreadable
   fruit
2 egg whites
¹⁄₄ teaspoon cream of tartar
3 tablespoons packed brown sugar
¹⁄₂ teaspoon vanilla

Heat oven to 400°. Cut cake horizontally into 3 layers. (To split, mark side of cake with toothpicks and cut with long, thin serrated knife.) Place layers on ungreased cookie sheet. Mix chocolate and spreadable fruit. Spread one-third of fruit mixture over each layer.

Beat egg whites and cream of tartar in medium bowl until foamy. Beat in brown sugar, 1 tablespoon at a time; continue beating until stiff and glossy. Do not underbeat. Beat in vanilla. Carefully spread one-third of meringue over each layer. Bake 6 to 10 minutes or until meringue is light brown. Remove from cookie sheet. Cool completely on wire rack. Cut each layer crosswise into about 1-inch bars. *18 bars*

NUTRITION INFORMATION PER SERVING

1 bar		Percent of U.S. RDA	
Calories	88	Protein	2%
Protein, g	2	Vitamin A	*
Carbohydrate, g	18	Vitamin C	*
Fat, g	1	Thiamin	*
Unsaturated	1	Riboflavin	*
Saturated	0	Niacin	*
Dietary Fiber, g	0	Calcium	*
Cholesterol, mg	0	Iron	*
Sodium, mg	75		
Potassium, mg	35		

Mocha Soufflé

Impress family and friends with this show-stopping, but easy, soufflé. Although wonderful served as is, flaked coconut or chopped nuts add extra excitement.

½ cup cocoa

⅓ cup sugar

4 teaspoons cornstarch

1 cup low-fat milk

2 teaspoons freeze-dried instant coffee

2 teaspoons vanilla

2 tablespoons sugar

7 egg whites

¼ teaspoon cream of tartar

⅓ cup sugar

¼ cup flaked coconut or chopped nuts, if desired

Mix cocoa, ⅓ cup sugar and the cornstarch in heavy 1-quart saucepan. Stir in milk. Heat to boiling over medium heat, stirring constantly. Cook and stir 1 minute; remove from heat. Stir in coffee and vanilla. Cool slightly.

Move oven rack to lowest position. Heat oven to 350°. Spray 2½-quart soufflé dish with non-stick cooking spray. Sprinkle with 2 tablespoons sugar; tap out excess. Beat egg whites and cream of tartar in large bowl until foamy. Beat in ⅓ cup sugar, 1 tablespoon at a time; continue beating until stiff and glossy. Do not underbeat. Stir cocoa mixture. Stir about one-fourth of the egg white mixture into cocoa mixture. Fold cocoa mixture into remaining egg whites. Carefully pour into soufflé dish; smooth top.

Place soufflé dish in rectangular pan, $13 \times 9 \times 2$ inches, on oven rack. Pour very hot water into pan until 1 inch deep. Bake about 40 minutes or until puffed and top feels firm. Sprinkle each serving with 1 teaspoon coconut. Serve immediately. *12 servings*

NUTRITION INFORMATION PER SERVING			
1 serving		**Percent of U.S. RDA**	
Calories	90	Protein	4%
Protein, g	3	Vitamin A	*
Carbohydrate, g	17	Vitamin C	*
Fat, g	1	Thiamin	*
Unsaturated	0	Riboflavin	8%
Saturated	1	Niacin	*
Dietary Fiber, g	1	Calcium	2%
Cholesterol, mg	2	Iron	2%
Sodium, mg	45		
Potassium, mg	120		

Whole Wheat–Strawberry Crepes

These crepes may be made, covered and refrigerated up to 3 days in advance. Or you can also freeze them up to 1 month; let them thaw in the refrigerator 24 hours before separating them. Nectarines are tasty substitutions for the strawberries; or the crepes can also be filled with Apple-Cocoa Filling (page 380).

2 cups strawberry halves (about 1½ pints)
¼ cup apple juice
1 tablespoon reduced-calorie maple-flavored syrup
1 teaspoon vanilla
Whole Wheat Crepes (right)
1½ cups nonfat ricotta cheese
¾ cup finely chopped strawberries (about ½ pint)

Place strawberry halves, apple juice, maple syrup and vanilla in blender or food processor. Cover and blend until smooth. Cover and refrigerate. Prepare Whole Wheat Crepes. Spread 2 tablespoons cheese over each crepe. Sprinkle 1 tablespoon chopped strawberries over cheese. Fold each crepe in half, then into thirds to form triangle. Spoon strawberry sauce over crepes. Sprinkle with powdered sugar if desired.
6 servings

Whole Wheat Crepes

⅓ cup whole wheat flour
⅓ cup all-purpose flour
⅔ cup low-fat milk
1 tablespoon reduced-calorie maple-flavored syrup
2 teaspoons margarine, melted
1 teaspoon vanilla
⅛ teaspoon ground nutmeg
⅛ teaspoon ground ginger
3 egg whites

Place all ingredients in blender or food processor. Cover and blend until smooth. Spray 6-inch nonstick skillet with nonstick cooking spray. Heat skillet over medium heat. For each crepe, pour 2 tablespoons batter into skillet. *Immediately* rotate skillet until thin film covers bottom. Cook 45 seconds to 1 minute or until batter is set. Run wide spatula around edge to loosen; turn and cook other side about 30 seconds or until light brown. Stack crepes, placing waxed paper between each; keep covered. Repeat with remaining batter to make 12 crepes.

NUTRITION INFORMATION PER SERVING			
1 serving		Percent of U.S. RDA	
Calories	225	Protein	18%
Protein, g	12	Vitamin A	10%
Carbohydrate, g	29	Vitamin C	100%
Fat, g	7	Thiamin	8%
Unsaturated	3	Riboflavin	22%
Saturated	4	Niacin	6%
Dietary Fiber, g	3	Calcium	22%
Cholesterol, mg	20	Iron	8%
Sodium, mg	150		
Potassium, mg	430		

Whole Wheat–Strawberry Crepes

Peach-Yogurt Pie

Very light and perfect for summer, this pie mixture can also be poured into a baked and cooled graham cracker crust.

¹/₂ **cup apple juice**
2 **envelopes unflavored gelatin**
2 **cups vanilla nonfat yogurt**
1 **cup peach nectar**
¹/₂ **teaspoon almond extract**

Spray springform pan, 9×3 inches, with non-stick cooking spray. Cook apple juice and gelatin over medium heat about 2 minutes, stirring occasionally, until gelatin is dissolved. Place gelatin mixture and remaining ingredients in blender or food processor. Cover and blend until smooth. Pour into pan. Refrigerate about 3 hours or until firm. Run metal spatula along side of pan to loosen; remove side of pan. Refrigerate any remaining pie. *8 servings*

NUTRITION INFORMATION PER SERVING			
1 serving		**Percent of U.S. RDA**	
Calories	75	Protein	6%
Protein, g	4	Vitamin A	6%
Carbohydrate, g	14	Vitamin C	2%
Fat, g	0	Thiamin	2%
Unsaturated	0	Riboflavin	8%
Saturated	0	Niacin	2%
Dietary Fiber, g	0	Calcium	8%
Cholesterol, mg	0	Iron	2%
Sodium, mg	35		
Potassium, mg	160		

Luscious Frozen Yogurt Pie

Carob adds a fresh new taste to this easy pie. It's also delicious served with Chocolate Sauce (page 417), or Chocolate-Almond Sauce (page 417.)

1¼ cups graham cracker crumbs (about 17 squares)
1 teaspoon carob powder or cocoa
2 tablespoons margarine, melted
1 quart vanilla or other flavor frozen yogurt, softened slightly
Carob-Peanut Sauce (page 417)

Mix cracker crumbs, carob powder and margarine. Press firmly against bottom and side of pie plate, 9×1¼ inches. Spoon frozen yogurt onto crust; spread carefully. Cover and freeze at least 1½ hours or until firm. (If frozen longer than 8 hours, let stand at room temperature 5 to 10 minutes before cutting.) Serve with Carob-Peanut Sauce. Freeze any remaining pie.
8 servings

NUTRITION INFORMATION PER SERVING			
I serving		**Percent of U.S. RDA**	
Calories	250	Protein	12%
Protein, g	8	Vitamin A	14%
Carbohydrate, g	34	Vitamin C	*
Fat, g	9	Thiamin	6%
Unsaturated	7	Riboflavin	18%
Saturated	2	Niacin	10%
Dietary Fiber, g	I	Calcium	22%
Cholesterol, mg	2	Iron	8%
Sodium, mg	180		
Potassium, mg	390		

Caramel Phyllo Triangles

⅔ cup fine soft white bread crumbs
⅔ cup finely chopped peeled apple
¼ cup packed brown sugar
2 tablespoons apple juice
½ teaspoon vanilla
6 frozen phyllo sheets, thawed
¼ cup (½ stick) margarine, melted

Heat oven to 400°. Spray cookie sheet with nonstick cooking spray. Mix bread crumbs, apple, brown sugar, apple juice and vanilla.

Place 1 phyllo sheet on flat surface. (Keep remaining phyllo sheets covered with a dampened towel to prevent them from drying out.) Brush phyllo lightly with margarine. Top with a second phyllo sheet; brush lightly with margarine. Top with a third phyllo sheet; brush lightly with margarine. Cut sheets lengthwise into halves, then cut each half crosswise into 8 strips. Place heaping ½ teaspoon bread crumb mixture on end of 1 strip. Fold a corner of strip over filling to form triangle, as one would fold a flag. Continue folding strip, keeping triangle shape. Place seam side down on cookie sheet.

Repeat with remaining phyllo and bread crumb mixture. Bake 10 to 12 minutes or until golden brown. Sprinkle lightly with powdered sugar if desired. *32 triangles*

NUTRITION INFORMATION PER SERVING			
I triangle		**Percent of U.S. RDA**	
Calories	45	Protein	*
Protein, g	I	Vitamin A	2%
Carbohydrate, g	6	Vitamin C	*
Fat, g	2	Thiamin	2%
Unsaturated	2	Riboflavin	*
Saturated	0	Niacin	*
Dietary Fiber, g	0	Calcium	*
Cholesterol, mg	0	Iron	*
Sodium, mg	45		
Potassium, mg	15		

Pumpkin Pie

Brown Sugar Topping (right)
1 can (16 ounces) pumpkin
1 can (12 ounces) evaporated skimmed milk
3 egg whites or ½ cup cholesterol-free egg
   product
½ cup sugar
½ cup all-purpose flour
1½ teaspoons pumpkin pie spice
¾ teaspoon baking powder
⅛ teaspoon salt
2 teaspoons grated orange peel

Heat oven to 350°. Prepare Brown Sugar Topping. Spray pie plate, 10×1½ inches, with nonstick cooking spray. Place remaining ingredients in blender or food processor in order listed. Cover and blend until smooth. Pour into pie plate. Sprinkle with topping. Bake 50 to 55 minutes or until knife inserted in center comes out clean. Cool 15 minutes. Refrigerate about 4 hours or until chilled. *8 servings*

Brown Sugar Topping

¼ cup packed brown sugar
¼ cup quick-cooking oats
1 tablespoon margarine, softened

Mix all ingredients.

NUTRITION INFORMATION PER SERVING			
1 serving		Percent of U.S. RDA	
Calories	185	Protein	10%
Protein, g	6	Vitamin A	100%
Carbohydrate, g	36	Vitamin C	2%
Fat, g	2	Thiamin	6%
Unsaturated	1	Riboflavin	14%
Saturated	1	Niacin	4%
Dietary Fiber, g	1	Calcium	16%
Cholesterol, mg	2	Iron	8%
Sodium, mg	160		
Potassium, mg	320		

Pumpkin Pie, Lucious Frozen Yogurt Pie

Apple-Raisin Pastry

This free-formed apple pie is made with a yeast-dough crust but doesn't require a rising time. It's handmade appearance makes this pastry just right for a casual brunch or weekend family breakfast.

½ cup granulated sugar
⅓ cup all-purpose flour
½ teaspoon ground cinnamon
5 cups thinly sliced unpeeled tart all-purpose apples (about 5 medium)
½ cup raisins
Pastry Dough (right)
Powdered sugar

Heat oven to 350°. Spray cookie sheet with nonstick cooking spray. Mix granulated sugar, flour and cinnamon; toss with apples and raisins.

Prepare Pastry Dough. Roll dough into 15-inch circle on lightly floured surface. Fold dough into fourths; carefully place on cookie sheet and unfold. Spoon apple mixture onto center of dough to within 3 inches of edge. Bring edge of dough up and over apple mixture, stretching slightly to make 4-inch opening in center.

Bake about 45 minutes or until crust is golden brown and apples are tender. Serve warm or cool. Sprinkle with powdered sugar immediately before serving. *12 servings*

Pastry Dough

1 package regular active dry yeast
½ cup warm water (105° to 115°)
1 cup whole wheat flour
⅓ cup sugar
¼ cup (½ stick) margarine, softened
¼ teaspoon salt
1 to 1¼ cups whole wheat or all-purpose flour

Dissolve yeast in warm water in large bowl. Add 1 cup flour, the sugar, margarine and salt. Beat until smooth. Stir in enough of the 1 to 1¼ cups flour to make dough easy to handle. Turn dough onto lightly floured surface; gently roll in flour to coat. Knead about 1 minute or until smooth.

NUTRITION INFORMATION PER SERVING

1 serving		Percent of U.S. RDA	
Calories	230	Protein	6%
Protein, g	3	Vitamin A	4%
Carbohydrate, g	46	Vitamin C	2%
Fat, g	4	Thiamin	10%
Unsaturated	3	Riboflavin	6%
Saturated	1	Niacin	8%
Dietary Fiber, g	4	Calcium	*
Cholesterol, mg	0	Iron	6%
Sodium, mg	90		
Potassium, mg	200		

Phyllo Tartlets with Winter Apples

Granny Smith apples are the apple of choice for these delicate, bite-size minitarts. The tartlets can be made, covered and frozen up to one month. Handle them carefully—they are fragile.

1 cup chopped dried apples
1 cup chopped peeled green apple (about 1 medium)
2 tablespoons frozen (thawed) apple juice concentrate
1 cup water
½ cup golden raisins
Phyllo Tartlets (right)

Heat dried apples, green apple, apple juice concentrate and water to boiling in 2-quart saucepan; reduce heat to medium-low. Cover and cook about 20 minutes or until all liquid is absorbed. Cool slightly. Place apple mixture in blender or food processor. Cover and blend until smooth. Stir in raisins. Cover and refrigerate about 2 hours or until chilled. Prepare Phyllo Tartlets. Fill each tartlet with 2 teaspoons filling. Sprinkle with ground nutmeg if desired. *About 36 tartlets*

Phyllo Tartlets

¼ cup apple juice
2 tablespoons margarine, melted
4 frozen phyllo sheets (13×9 inches), thawed

Heat oven to 400°. Heat apple juice and margarine over low heat until margarine is melted. Brush one phyllo sheet at a time with apple juice mixture. (Keep remaining phyllo sheets covered with a dampened towel to prevent them from drying out.) Fold sheets crosswise into thirds, overlapping the sides; cut into 10 pieces. Place pieces in ungreased small muffin cups, 1¾×1 inch, making pleats as necessary to fit into cups. Bake 5 to 7 minutes until brown. Remove from pan. Cool on wire rack.

NUTRITION INFORMATION PER SERVING			
1 tartlet		**Percent of U.S. RDA**	
Calories	35	Protein	*
Protein, g	0	Vitamin A	*
Carbohydrate, g	6	Vitamin C	*
Fat, g	1	Thiamin	*
Unsaturated	1	Riboflavin	*
Saturated	0	Niacin	*
Dietary Fiber, g	0	Calcium	*
Cholesterol, mg	0	Iron	*
Sodium, mg	15		
Potassium, mg	40		

Fruity Carrot Cake

This cake has a moist, pudding-like texture that is great as is or it can be split and filled with Whipped Ricotta Topping (page 418). The cake can be covered and refrigerated for up to five days or frozen for up to one month.

2 cups whole wheat flour

1½ teaspoons baking soda

1 teaspoon ground cinnamon

½ teaspoon salt

¼ teaspoon ground nutmeg

¼ teaspoon ground cloves

1¼ cups finely shredded carrots (about 2 medium)

1 cup unsweetened applesauce

1 cup vanilla nonfat yogurt

½ cup diced dried fruit and raisin mixture

¼ cup packed brown sugar

¼ cup apricot spreadable fruit

½ cup cholesterol-free egg product or 3 egg whites

¼ cup water

2 tablespoons vegetable oil

1 teaspoon vanilla

Heat oven to 350°. Spray springform pan, 9×3 inches, with nonstick cooking spray. Mix flour, baking soda, cinnamon, salt, nutmeg and cloves in large bowl. Add remaining ingredients. Beat on low speed about 1 minute or until blended. Pour into pan. Bake 45 to 50 minutes or until toothpick inserted in center comes out clean. Cool cake in pan on wire rack 10 minutes. Run metal spatula along side of cake to loosen; remove side of pan. Cool completely. *12 servings*

NUTRITION INFORMATION PER SERVING

1 serving		Percent of U.S. RDA	
Calories	180	Protein	6%
Protein, g	5	Vitamin A	20%
Carbohydrate, g	33	Vitamin C	2%
Fat, g	3	Thiamin	8%
Unsaturated	2	Riboflavin	8%
Saturated	1	Niacin	8%
Dietary Fiber, g	3	Calcium	4%
Cholesterol, mg	0	Iron	8%
Sodium, mg	230		
Potassium, mg	260		

Opposite: Apple-Raisin Pastry (page 402), Apple Cake

Apple Cake

¹⁄₃ cup boiling water

2 cups chopped unpeeled all-purpose apples

1¹⁄₄ cups packed brown sugar

1 cup all-purpose flour

1 cup whole wheat flour

³⁄₄ cup cholesterol-free egg product or
    5 egg whites

¹⁄₃ cup vegetable oil

1¹⁄₄ teaspoons baking soda

1 teaspoon ground cinnamon

1 teaspoon vanilla

¹⁄₂ teaspoon ground cloves

¹⁄₄ teaspoon salt

Nut Topping (right)

Heat oven to 350°. Spray rectangular pan, 13×9×2 inches, with nonstick cooking spray; dust with flour. Pour boiling water over apples in large bowl. Add remaining ingredients except Nut Topping. Beat on low speed 1 minute, scraping bowl constantly. Beat on medium speed 2 minutes, scraping bowl occasionally. Pour into pan. Sprinkle with Nut Topping. Bake 40 to 45 minute or until toothpick inserted in center comes out clean. *15 servings*

Nut Topping

¹⁄₃ cup finely chopped nuts

2 tablespoons packed brown sugar

Mix ingredients.

NUTRITION INFORMATION PER SERVING			
1 serving		**Percent of U.S. RDA**	
Calories	215	Protein	4%
Protein, g	3	Vitamin A	*
Carbohydrate, g	35	Vitamin C	*
Fat, g	7	Thiamin	8%
Unsaturated	6	Riboflavin	6%
Saturated	1	Niacin	4%
Dietary Fiber, g	2	Calcium	2%
Cholesterol, mg	0	Iron	8%
Sodium, mg	140		
Potassium, mg	150		

Blueberry-Cornmeal Cake

¾ cup vanilla nonfat yogurt

½ cup mashed ripe banana (about 1 medium)

2 tablespoons margarine, melted

2 tablespoons lemon juice

2 tablespoons honey

1½ cups all-purpose flour

½ cup stone-ground or degerminated cornmeal

1½ teaspoons baking powder

¼ teaspoon ground nutmeg

1 cup blueberries

3 egg whites

¼ teaspoon salt

Heat oven to 350°. Spray round pan, 9×1½ inches, with nonstick cooking spray. Mix yogurt, banana, margarine, lemon juice and honey in large bowl. Stir in flour, cornmeal, baking powder and nutmeg. Fold in blueberries. Beat egg whites and salt until stiff. Fold egg whites into batter. Pour into pan. Bake 50 to 55 minutes or until toothpick inserted in center comes out clean. Cool in pan on wire rack. Serve warm or cool. *8 servings*

NUTRITION INFORMATION PER SERVING

1 serving		Percent of U.S. RDA	
Calories	200	Protein	8%
Protein, g	5	Vitamin A	6%
Carbohydrate, g	38	Vitamin C	4%
Fat, g	3	Thiamin	18%
Unsaturated	2	Riboflavin	16%
Saturated	1	Niacin	10%
Dietary Fiber, g	2	Calcium	8%
Cholesterol, mg	0	Iron	10%
Sodium, mg	200		
Potassium, mg	180		

Lemon-topped Gingerbread

½ cup all-purpose flour

½ cup whole wheat flour

¼ cup molasses

¼ cup hot water

2 tablespoons packed brown sugar

2 tablespoons shortening

½ teaspoon baking soda

½ teaspoon ground ginger

½ teaspoon ground cinnamon

⅛ teaspoon salt

1 egg white or 2 tablespoons cholesterol-free egg product

Lemon Sauce (page 416)

Heat oven to 325°. Spray loaf pan, 8½×4½×2½ inches, with nonstick cooking spray. Beat all ingredients except Lemon Sauce in medium bowl on low speed 30 seconds, scraping bowl constantly. Beat on medium speed 3 minutes, scraping bowl occasionally. Pour into pan. Bake 30 to 35 minutes or until toothpick inserted in center comes out clean. Cool 10 minutes; remove from pan. Serve warm or cool with Lemon Sauce. *8 servings*

NUTRITION INFORMATION PER SERVING

1 serving		Percent of U.S. RDA	
Calories	145	Protein	4%
Protein, g	2	Vitamin A	*
Carbohydrate, g	28	Vitamin C	*
Fat, g	3	Thiamin	6%
Unsaturated	2	Riboflavin	4%
Saturated	1	Niacin	4%
Dietary Fiber, g	1	Calcium	2%
Cholesterol, mg	0	Iron	6%
Sodium, mg	100		
Potassium, mg	210		

Spice Islands Cake

½ cup golden raisins

¼ cup orange juice

2 tablespoons shredded coconut

2¼ cups all-purpose flour

⅓ cup packed brown sugar

2 teaspoons poppy seed

1 teaspoon baking powder

½ teaspoon baking soda

½ teaspoon ground cinnamon

¼ teaspoon ground ginger

¼ teaspoon ground cardamom

¼ teaspoon salt

1¼ cups nonfat buttermilk

½ cup cholesterol-free egg product or 3 egg whites

2 tablespoons vegetable oil

1 teaspoon vanilla

Orange Glaze (right)

Heat oven to 350°. Spray round pan, 9×1½ inches, with nonstick cooking spray. Mix raisins, orange juice and coconut; let stand 15 minutes. Mix flour, brown sugar, poppy seed, baking powder, baking soda, cinnamon, ginger, cardamom and salt in large bowl. Stir in raisin mixture and remaining ingredients except Orange Glaze. Pour into pan. Bake about 40 minutes or until toothpick inserted in center comes out clean. Meanwhile, prepare Orange Glaze; pour over hot cake. Cool cake completely in pan on wire rack. *12 servings*

Orange Glaze

¼ cup orange marmalade spreadable fruit

½ cup orange juice

1 tablespoon orange-flavored liqueur, if desired

Heat all ingredients in 1-quart saucepan until spreadable fruit is melted.

NUTRITION INFORMATION PER SERVING			
1 serving		**Percent of U.S. RDA**	
Calories	185	Protein	6%
Protein, g	4	Vitamin A	*
Carbohydrate, g	35	Vitamin C	6%
Fat, g	3	Thiamin	14%
Unsaturated	2	Riboflavin	12%
Saturated	1	Niacin	8%
Dietary Fiber, g	1	Calcium	8%
Cholesterol, mg	0	Iron	10%
Sodium, mg	160		
Potassium, mg	190		

Carob Chip Pound Cake

This thick batter that makes a dense, moist loaf cake. Serve slices drizzled with Carob-Peanut Sauce (page 417) or, if using chocolate chips, with Chocolate Sauce (page 417).

1¼ cups unsweetened applesauce
¾ cup packed brown sugar
½ cup vegetable oil
2 cups all-purpose flour
½ cup whole wheat flour
1 teaspoon baking powder
1 teaspoon baking soda
1 teaspoon ground cinnamon
1 teaspoon ground nutmeg
⅛ teaspoon salt
¾ cup carob or semisweet chocolate chips

Heat oven to 350°. Spray loaf pan, 9×5×3 inches, with nonstick cooking spray. Mix applesauce, brown sugar and oil in large bowl until well blended. Mix remaining ingredients except carob chips; stir into applesauce mixture until blended. Stir in carob chips. Pour into pan. Bake about 1 hour or until toothpick inserted in center comes out clean. Let stand 10 minutes before removing from pan. Cool on wire rack. *16 servings*

NUTRITION INFORMATION PER SERVING			
1 serving		Percent of U.S. RDA	
Calories	215	Protein	4%
Protein, g	3	Vitamin A	*
Carbohydrate, g	30	Vitamin C	*
Fat, g	9	Thiamin	10%
Unsaturated	7	Riboflavin	6%
Saturated	2	Niacin	6%
Dietary Fiber, g	2	Calcium	6%
Cholesterol, mg	0	Iron	6%
Sodium, mg	95		
Potassium, mg	140		

Pineapple Upside-down Cake

½ cup pineapple spreadable fruit
2 teaspoons grated lemon peel
2 tablespoons lemon juice
½ teaspoon ground cinnamon
1 can (8 ounces) crushed pineapple in juice, undrained
1 cup plus 1 tablespoon all-purpose flour
1½ teaspoons baking powder
¼ teaspoon salt
⅛ teaspoon ground nutmeg
½ cup cholesterol-free egg product
⅓ cup low-fat milk
1 tablespoon low-fat sour cream
1 teaspoon vanilla

Heat oven to 375°. Spray springform pan, 9×3 inches, with nonstick cooking spray. Mix spreadable fruit, lemon peel, lemon juice, cinnamon, pineapple and 1 tablespoon of the flour. Spread in pan. Mix remaining flour, the baking powder, salt and nutmeg in medium bowl. Stir in remaining ingredients; pour over fruit. Bake 25 to 30 minutes or until brown. Cool 10 minutes. Loosen and remove side of pan. Invert cake onto plate. Let pan remain over cake a few minutes; remove bottom of pan. *8 servings*

NUTRITION INFORMATION PER SERVING			
1 serving		Percent of U.S. RDA	
Calories	120	Protein	6%
Protein, g	3	Vitamin A	2%
Carbohydrate, g	25	Vitamin C	4%
Fat, g	1	Thiamin	10%
Unsaturated	1	Riboflavin	8%
Saturated	0	Niacin	4%
Dietary Fiber, g	1	Calcium	8%
Cholesterol, mg	1	Iron	6%
Sodium, mg	180		
Potassium, mg	110		

Chocolate-glazed Brownies

1 cup sugar
1/3 cup margarine, softened
1 teaspoon vanilla
3 egg whites
2/3 cup all-purpose flour
1/2 cup cocoa
1/2 teaspoon baking powder
1/4 teaspoon salt
Chocolate Glaze (below)

Heat oven to 350°. Spray square pan, 8×8×2 inches, with nonstick cooking spray. Mix sugar, margarine, vanilla and egg whites in medium bowl. Stir in remaining ingredients except Chocolate Glaze. Spread in pan.

Bake 20 to 25 minutes or until toothpick inserted in center comes out clean; cool. Spread Chocolate Glaze evenly over brownies. Cut into about 2-inch squares. *16 brownies*

Chocolate Glaze

2/3 cups powdered sugar
2 tablespoons cocoa
1/4 teaspoon vanilla
3 to 4 teaspoons hot water

Mix all ingredients.

NUTRITION INFORMATION PER SERVING			
1 brownie		Percent of U.S. RDA	
Calories	135	Protein	2%
Protein, g	2	Vitamin A	4%
Carbohydrate, g	23	Vitamin C	*
Fat, g	4	Thiamin	2%
Unsaturated	3	Riboflavin	4%
Saturated	1	Niacin	2%
Dietary Fiber, g	1	Calcium	*
Cholesterol, mg	0	Iron	4%
Sodium, mg	100		
Potassium, mg	70		

Apple-Oatmeal Crumbles

1 cup quick-cooking oats
1 cup whole wheat flour
1/3 cup packed brown sugar
1 teaspoon ground cinnamon
1/2 teaspoon ground allspice
1/2 teaspoon baking soda
3 tablespoons vegetable oil
3 tablespoons reduced-calorie maple-
    flavored syrup
1 cup unsweetened applesauce
1/2 cup finely chopped peeled all-purpose
    apple
1/4 cup chopped walnuts

Heat oven to 350°. Spray square nonstick pan, 8×8×2 inches, with nonstick cooking spray. Mix oats, flour, brown sugar, cinnamon, allspice and baking soda in large bowl. Stir in oil and syrup until mixture is crumbly; reserve 1/2 cup for topping. Press remaining mixture firmly in bottom of pan. Bake about 10 minutes or until set. Cool 10 minutes.

Spread applesauce over baked layer. Sprinkle chopped apple over applesauce. Sprinkle 1/2 cup oat mixture and the walnuts over apple. Bake about 15 minutes or until top is light brown; cool. Cut into 2-inch squares. *16 squares*

NUTRITION INFORMATION PER SERVING			
1 square		Percent of U.S. RDA	
Calories	110	Protein	2%
Protein, g	2	Vitamin A	*
Carbohydrate, g	17	Vitamin C	*
Fat, g	4	Thiamin	4%
Unsaturated	3	Riboflavin	2%
Saturated	1	Niacin	2%
Dietary Fiber, g	2	Calcium	*
Cholesterol, mg	0	Iron	4%
Sodium, mg	35		
Potassium, mg	90		

Chocolaty Meringue Stars

A star tip gives these morsels a pretty shape, but they can be made without one. Drop the meringue mixture by rounded tablespoonfuls onto parchment paper and continue as directed.

3 egg whites
¹/₂ teaspoon cream of tartar
²/₃ cup sugar
2 tablespoons plus 1 teaspoon cocoa
About ¹/₃ cup ground walnuts

Heat oven to 275°. Cover cookie sheets with cooking parchment paper or heavy brown paper. Beat egg whites and cream of tartar in medium bowl until foamy. Beat in sugar, 1 tablespoon at a time; continue beating until stiff and glossy. Do not underbeat. Fold in cocoa. (Batter will not be mixed completely; there will be some streaks of cocoa.)

Place meringue in decorating bag fitted with large star tip. Pipe 1¹/₄-inch stars onto cookie sheets. Sprinkle lightly with walnuts; brush excess nuts from cookie sheets. Bake 25 to 30 minutes or until outside is crisp and dry. (Meringues will be soft inside.) Cool 5 minutes before removing from cookie sheets. Cool on wire rack. Store in airtight container. *About 4 dozen meringues*

NUTRITION INFORMATION PER SERVING

I meringue		Percent of U.S. RDA	
Calories	15	Protein	*
Protein, g	0	Vitamin A	*
Carbohydrate, g	3	Vitamin C	*
Fat, g	0	Thiamin	*
Unsaturated	0	Riboflavin	*
Saturated	0	Niacin	*
Dietary Fiber, g	0	Calcium	*
Cholesterol, mg	0	Iron	*
Sodium, mg	5		
Potassium, mg	10		

Oaties

1¹/₄ cups all-purpose flour
1 cup quick-cooking oats
1 teaspoon ground cinnamon
¹/₂ teaspoon baking soda
¹/₈ teaspoon salt
3 egg whites or ¹/₂ cup cholesterol-free egg product
¹/₂ cup packed brown sugar
¹/₄ cup granulated sugar
¹/₃ cup unsweetened applesauce
¹/₄ cup (¹/₂ stick) margarine, softened
1 teaspoon vanilla
1 cup raisins or chopped dried fruit

Heat oven to 325°. Spray cookie sheet with nonstick cooking spray. Mix flour, oats, cinnamon, baking soda and salt; reserve. Beat egg whites in large bowl on medium speed until foamy. Add sugars, applesauce, margarine and vanilla. Beat on medium speed until smooth. Add flour mixture; beat on low speed just until mixed. Stir in raisins.

Drop dough by tablespoonfuls 2 inches apart onto cookie sheet; flatten slightly. Bake 12 to 15 minutes or until light brown. Cool slightly; remove from cookie sheet. Cool on wire rack. *About 3 dozen cookies*

NUTRITION INFORMATION PER SERVING

I cookie		Percent of U.S. RDA	
Calories	65	Protein	2%
Protein, g	I	Vitamin A	2%
Carbohydrate, g	13	Vitamin C	*
Fat, g	I	Thiamin	4%
Unsaturated	I	Riboflavin	2%
Saturated	0	Niacin	2%
Dietary Fiber, g	I	Calcium	*
Cholesterol, mg	0	Iron	2%
Sodium, mg	40		
Potassium, mg	65		

Chocolate Chip Cookies

½ cup granulated sugar

¼ cup packed brown sugar

¼ cup (½ stick) margarine, softened

1 teaspoon vanilla

1 egg white or 2 tablespoons cholesterol-
   free egg product

½ cup all-purpose flour

½ cup whole wheat flour

½ teaspoon baking soda

¼ teaspoon salt

½ cup miniature semisweet chocolate chips

Heat oven to 375°. Mix sugars, margarine, vanilla and egg white in large bowl. Stir in flours, baking soda and salt. Stir in chocolate chips. Drop dough by rounded teaspoonfuls about 2 inches apart onto ungreased cookie sheet. Bake 8 to 10 minutes or until golden brown. Cool slightly; remove from cookie sheet. Cool on wire rack. *About 2½ dozen cookies*

NUTRITION INFORMATION PER SERVING

1 cookie		Percent of U.S. RDA	
Calories	60	Protein	*
Protein, g	1	Vitamin A	2%
Carbohydrate, g	10	Vitamin C	*
Fat, g	2	Thiamin	2%
Unsaturated	1	Riboflavin	*
Saturated	1	Niacin	*
Dietary Fiber, g	0	Calcium	*
Cholesterol, mg	0	Iron	2%
Sodium, mg	50		
Potassium, mg	30		

Dried-Fruit Truffles

Naturally sweet dried fruits combine with honey for treats that are almost like candy. The balls can be rolled in powdered sugar or finely chopped nuts.

½ cup chopped dried apples

½ cup chopped pitted prunes

¼ cup golden raisins

¼ cup raisins

¼ cup flaked coconut

¼ cup chopped dried figs

1 tablespoon honey

1 tablespoon cocoa

Place all ingredients except cocoa in blender or food processor. Cover and blend, stopping occasionally to scrape sides, until a paste forms. Shape into 1-inch balls. Cover and refrigerate 1 hour. Roll balls in cocoa. Store tightly covered. *About 20 truffles*

NUTRITION INFORMATION PER SERVING

1 truffle		Percent of U.S. RDA	
Calories	40	Protein	*
Protein, g	0	Vitamin A	*
Carbohydrate, g	10	Vitamin C	*
Fat, g	0	Thiamin	*
Unsaturated	0	Riboflavin	*
Saturated	0	Niacin	*
Dietary Fiber, g	1	Calcium	*
Cholesterol, mg	0	Iron	2%
Sodium, mg	5		
Potassium, mg	95		

Lemony Cornmeal Cookies

1 cup packed brown sugar
³/₄ cup unsweetened applesauce
1 tablespoon grated lemon peel
2 tablespoons vegetable oil
1 tablespoon lemon juice
1 egg white
2³/₄ cups cake flour
¹/₂ cup yellow cornmeal
1 teaspoon baking soda
¹/₈ teaspoon salt
Poppy Seed Glaze (below)

Heat oven to 350°. Spray nonstick cookie sheet with nonstick cooking spray, or line with cooking parchment paper. Mix brown sugar, applesauce, lemon peel, oil, lemon juice and egg white in large bowl. Mix flour, cornmeal, baking soda and salt; stir into applesauce mixture just until blended. Cover and let stand 20 minutes.

Drop dough by tablespoonfuls about 2 inches apart onto cookie sheet. Bake 8 to 10 minutes or until set but not brown. Cool slightly; remove from cookie sheet. Cool on wire rack. Frost lightly with Poppy Seed Glaze. *About 3¹/₂ dozen cookies*

Poppy Seed Glaze

³/₄ cup low-fat sour cream
1 tablespoon honey
1 teaspoon poppy seed

Mix all ingredients.

NUTRITION INFORMATION PER SERVING

1 cookie		Percent of U.S. RDA	
Calories	65	Protein	2%
Protein, g	1	Vitamin A	*
Carbohydrate, g	13	Vitamin C	*
Fat, g	1	Thiamin	4%
Unsaturated	1	Riboflavin	2%
Saturated	0	Niacin	2%
Dietary Fiber, g	0	Calcium	*
Cholesterol, mg	0	Iron	4%
Sodium, mg	35		
Potassium, mg	45		

Raspberry Sauce

1 pint fresh raspberries
2 teaspoons honey
2 teaspoons lemon juice
2 teaspoons orange-flavored liqueur, if desired

Place all ingredients in blender or food processor. Cover and blend until smooth. Strain in fine-mesh strainer to remove seeds. Cover and refrigerate until serving time. *About ³/₄ cup sauce*

NUTRITION INFORMATION PER SERVING

1 tablespoon		Percent of U.S. RDA	
Calories	15	Protein	*
Protein, g	0	Vitamin A	*
Carbohydrate, g	3	Vitamin C	8%
Fat, g	0	Thiamin	*
Unsaturated	0	Riboflavin	*
Saturated	0	Niacin	*
Dietary Fiber, g	0	Calcium	*
Cholesterol, mg	0	Iron	*
Sodium, mg	0		
Potassium, mg	35		

Chocolate Sauce (page 417), Raspberry Sauce, Maple-Vanilla Ice (page 389)

Pear Sauce

This sauce can be used with sweet or savory dishes. Use it as you would applesauce. It makes a nice topping for cake and ice milk, and an unusual condiment for pork and poultry dishes.

2 cups chopped peeled Bosc pears (about 1 pound)

¼ cup water

2 tablespoons frozen (thawed) apple juice concentrate

½ teaspoon ground cinnamon

¼ teaspoon ground nutmeg

1 teaspoon vanilla

Cover and cook all ingredients in 1-quart saucepan over medium heat 10 minutes, stirring occasionally; reduce heat to medium-low. Cook about 30 minutes longer, stirring occasionally, until pears are very tender. Place mixture in blender or food processor. Cover and blend until chunky. *About 1 cup sauce*

NUTRITION INFORMATION PER SERVING

1 tablespoon		Percent of U.S. RDA	
Calories	15	Protein	*
Protein, g	0	Vitamin A	*
Carbohydrate, g	4	Vitamin C	*
Fat, g	0	Thiamin	*
Unsaturated	0	Riboflavin	*
Saturated	0	Niacin	*
Dietary Fiber, g	1	Calcium	*
Cholesterol, mg	0	Iron	*
Sodium, mg	0		
Potassium, mg	35		

Tangy Fruit Salsa

Fruits are sparked by lime and ginger for a tantalizing taste. Although the recipe says to chill the salsa, it would be wonderful served slightly warm over vanilla ice milk.

1 cup sliced strawberries

²/₃ cup chopped kiwifruit (about 1 medium)

¹/₂ cup chopped orange sections (about 1 medium orange)

1 tablespoon lime juice

2 teaspoons sugar

¹/₂ teaspoon finely chopped gingerroot or ¹/₄ teaspoon ground ginger

Mix all ingredients. Cover and refrigerate about 1 hour or until chilled. *About 1²/₃ cups salsa*

NUTRITION INFORMATION PER SERVING

1 tablespoon		Percent of U.S. RDA	
Calories	10	Protein	*
Protein, g	0	Vitamin A	*
Carbohydrate, g	2	Vitamin C	16%
Fat, g	0	Thiamin	*
Unsaturated	0	Riboflavin	*
Saturated	0	Niacin	*
Dietary Fiber, g	0	Calcium	*
Cholesterol, mg	0	Iron	*
Sodium, mg	0		
Potassium, mg	30		

Lemon Sauce

3 tablespoons sugar

1 tablespoon cornstarch

1 cup water

1 tablespoon grated lemon peel

1 tablespoon lemon juice

Mix sugar and cornstarch in 1-quart saucepan. Gradually stir in water. Cook over medium heat, stirring constantly, until mixture thickens and boils. Boil and stir 1 minute; remove from heat. Stir in remaining ingredients. Serve warm or cool. *About ³/₄ cup sauce*

NUTRITION INFORMATION PER SERVING

1 tablespoon		Percent of U.S. RDA	
Calories	15	Protein	*
Protein, g	0	Vitamin A	*
Carbohydrate, g	4	Vitamin C	*
Fat, g	0	Thiamin	*
Unsaturated	0	Riboflavin	*
Saturated	0	Niacin	*
Dietary Fiber, g	0	Calcium	*
Cholesterol, mg	0	Iron	*
Sodium, mg	0		
Potassium, mg	5		

Carob-Peanut Sauce

¹/₂ cup evaporated skimmed milk
¹/₂ cup carob or semisweet chocolate chips
¹/₄ cup chopped unsalted dry-roasted
   peanuts

Heat milk and carob chips to boiling over medium heat, stirring constantly. Boil and stir 1 minute; remove from heat. Stir in peanuts; cool. *About ³/₄ cup sauce*

NUTRITION INFORMATION PER SERVING			
I tablespoon		**Percent of U.S. RDA**	
Calories	50	Protein	*
Protein, g	I	Vitamin A	*
Carbohydrate, g	7	Vitamin C	*
Fat, g	2	Thiamin	*
Unsaturated	I	Riboflavin	*
Saturated	I	Niacin	*
Dietary Fiber, g	I	Calcium	2%
Cholesterol, mg	0	Iron	*
Sodium, mg	10		
Potassium, mg	35		

NUTRITION INFORMATION PER SERVING			
I tablespoon		**Percent of U.S. RDA**	
Calories	54	Protein	2%
Protein, g	2	Vitamin A	*
Carbohydrate, g	5	Vitamin C	*
Fat, g	3	Thiamin	*
Unsaturated	2	Riboflavin	2%
Saturated	I	Niacin	2%
Dietary Fiber, g	0	Calcium	6%
Cholesterol, mg	0	Iron	*
Sodium, mg	10		
Potassium, mg	105		

Chocolate Sauce

²/₃ cup semisweet chocolate chips
¹/₃ cup sugar
¹/₂ cup evaporated skimmed milk
1 teaspoon margarine

Heat chocolate chips, sugar and milk over medium heat, stirring constantly, until chocolate is melted and mixture boils; remove from heat. Stir in margarine. *About 1¹/₄ cups sauce*

Chocolate-Almond Sauce

¹/₂ cup sugar
¹/₄ cup cocoa
1 tablespoon cornstarch
1 can (12 ounces) evaporated skimmed milk
¹/₄ teaspoon almond extract

Mix sugar, cocoa and cornstarch in 1¹/₂-quart saucepan. Gradually stir in milk. Heat over medium heat, stirring constantly, until mixture thickens and boils; remove from heat. Stir in almond extract. (Beat with wire whisk if sauce becomes lumpy.) Serve warm, or press plastic wrap or waxed paper onto surface and refrigerate until chilled. *About 1³/₄ cups sauce*

NUTRITION INFORMATION PER SERVING			
I tablespoon		**Percent of U.S. RDA**	
Calories	30	Protein	2%
Protein, g	I	Vitamin A	*
Carbohydrate, g	6	Vitamin C	*
Fat, g	0	Thiamin	*
Unsaturated	0	Riboflavin	2%
Saturated	0	Niacin	*
Dietary Fiber, g	0	Calcium	4%
Cholesterol, mg	0	Iron	*
Sodium, mg	15		
Potassium, mg	50		

10

Eating for Good Health

Taking responsibility for your health by choosing nutritious food is the basis of healthy eating. It's a wise step to take whether you're trying to reduce your risk of diseases affected by diet, or working to manage a chronic condition that you or a member of your family already have. In this chapter, we give you the information you need to eat healthfully, to learn to manage or reduce your risk for developing some of the major illnesses common today. And, you won't have to give up great taste!

Just a reminder to our readers: This cookbook provides some general eating principles and food preparation guidelines that may help some individuals manage or reduce the risk of certain diseases. It is not designed to replace the individualized care or advice of your physician but rather to supplement it. For more information about these diseases or others that are not included in this book, please consult your physician.

CORONARY HEART DISEASE

Coronary heart disease (CHD) is characterized by a buildup of fatty, cholesterol-filled deposits in the arteries, which can eventually clog them, block the flow of blood and cause a heart attack. Although we've seen a drop in deaths from CHD of more than 40 percent since 1970, it still affects about 7 million Americans and remains the number one killer in the United States today.

The condition is caused by a variety of factors, some beyond our control. For example,

Preceding page: A sampling of delicious and nutritious low-fat foods.

your chances of developing CHD are greater if you have a family history of the disease, are male or are older. The risks also have an additive effect. If you're male *and* over age 50 *and* one of your parents or a sibling suffers from the disease, your chances for developing CHD become even greater.

Fortunately, several risk factors for the disease remain within our control. Cigarette smoking is considered the most significant modifiable risk; smokers can greatly decrease their chances of developing CHD by quitting. Other modifiable risk factors include high blood pressure, high blood cholesterol, obesity and physical inactivity.

Eating strategies to reduce or manage risks for CHD focus on a low-fat, low-cholesterol diet. Your daily diet should not consist of more than 30 percent of its calories from fat (see page 7 for recommended grams of fat per calorie level) with no more than 10 percent of those calories coming from saturated fat. These levels may be more strict for people who are already managing CHD. It's also advised that you limit cholesterol intake to no more than 300 milligrams per day. If you're eating to reduce CHD risk, make sure you don't eat more calories than you need to avoid weight gain and obesity. The introduction, Eating Right, discusses these recommendations in more detail.

If you already have CHD or your blood cholesterol levels remain too high even when you follow the above recommendations, your physician may advise you to cut back even more on the amount of fat and cholesterol you eat—to no more than 7 percent of calories from saturated fat and less than 200 milligrams of cholesterol daily.

The Food Guide Pyramid (page 14) provides the framework for a healthful diet to reduce risk for or manage heart disease. The recommended number of servings from each food group is based on individual differences, such as height and activity level. Taller, more active people need more calories than shorter, sedentary individuals and therefore should eat more servings from each group to maintain weight.

Meals planned on the basis of these recommendations feature plenty of whole-grain cereals and breads, fruits and vegetables with smaller amounts of lean meats, fish and poultry (without skin) and reduced-fat dairy products such as skim or 1% milk. Added fats and oils are used sparingly. And it's crucial to recognize that no one food group is more important than another. We must eat a balanced diet containing a variety of foods for good health.

TIPS FOR REDUCING RISK AND MANAGING HEART DISEASE

◆ If you smoke, stop.

◆ Follow your doctor's advice for controlling high blood pressure.

◆ Eat a diet low in fat and cholesterol that contains plenty of whole-grain cereals and breads, fruits and vegetables. Select lean meats, poultry (without skin) and fish and low-fat dairy products as well.

◆ Maintain a healthy weight. (See page 16 for a discussion of healthy weights.)

◆ Exercise regularly. If you have heart disease or haven't exercised lately, check with your doctor first. Start with light to moderate activity at less than 60 percent of maximum heart rate* for at least 30 minutes daily. Sug-

* Determine maximum heart rate by subtracting your age from 220. For example, if you're age 40, your maximum heart rate is 180. Sixty percent of 180 is 108. When trying to achieve the first activity goal of light to moderate exercise, aim to exercise at an intensity level that gets your heart beating faster but not exceeding 108 beats per minute.

gested activities include walking, swimming, cycling, dancing or gardening. Progress by aiming for vigorous physical activity at 60 percent of maximum heart rate 3 or more days per week for 20 or more minutes per occasion. Vigorous activities include brisk walking, jogging/running, lap swimming, cycling, skating, rowing and jumping rope.

◆ Have your blood cholesterol checked if you're over age 20. If it's in the desirable range, have it rechecked every five years (see Eating Right, page 7). If it's too high, work closely with your doctor and registered dietitian to bring it down and keep it down.

CANCER

One of every five Americans dies from cancer. Cancer encompasses more than 100 different diseases, but each is characterized by the uncontrolled growth and spreading of abnormal cells. While you can develop cancer at any age, you're more likely to do so as you age.

Studies show that about 35 percent of cancers may be related to diet. Too much fat in the diet has been associated with cancers of the breast, colon, rectum and prostate, and possibly pancreas, uterus and ovary. A high intake of alcohol has been associated with cancers of the mouth and throat, esophagus, liver, colon, breast, head and neck. Conversely, a diet high in fiber may help reduce risk for cancers of the colon and rectum.

Dietary recommendations to prevent cancer focus on reducing dietary fat and increasing fiber. Guidelines for total fat intake follow those for CHD: No more than 30 percent of calories from fat. Recommendations for fiber intake range from 20 to 30 grams daily, about twice the average consumption of Americans today.

Dietary recommendations emphasize increased consumption of fruits and vegetables, especially citrus fruits and green and yellow vegetables. There appears to be a link between low incidences of certain cancers and high intakes of vitamins C and A, and beta-carotene, a form of vitamin A. It's also recommended that we eat more of cruciferous vegetables, such as cabbage, broccoli and cauliflower. Studies suggest these vegetables may protect against colorectal, stomach and respiratory cancers. To be sure you consume the daily recommendation for fiber, include whole-grain breads and cereals with bran as part of each meal.

In addition, it's also advised to avoid obesity and be moderate about alcohol consumption. The U.S. government's *Dietary Guidelines for Americans* recommend no more than two drinks a day for men and one for women. One drink is measured as 12 ounces of regular beer, 5 ounces of wine or 1½ ounces of 80 proof distilled spirits such as gin, vodka and rum.

Finally, the American Cancer Society recommends we limit consumption of smoked, salt-cured and nitrite-cured foods, such as bacon, ham and sausage. Cancers of the esophagus and stomach are common in countries where these foods are eaten in large quantities.

Proactive eating to manage existing cancers can be quite different from the guidelines here. The dietary concerns of people who have cancer are so highly individual that it is unwise to make general recommendations. If you or a member of your family have cancer, your registered dietitian or physician can provide advice about your diet.

TIPS FOR REDUCING RISK OF CANCER

◆ If you smoke, stop.

◆ Get regular check-ups—once every 3 years if you're over 20, and every year if you're over 40. Follow your doctor's advice about how often you should be screened for specific cancers.

◆ Eat a low-fat diet featuring plenty of fiber such as whole-grain cereals and breads, fruits and vegetables rich in vitamins C and A, and beta-carotene, such as citrus fruits, red and green peppers, spinach, cantaloupe, peaches,

carrots and other dark green or yellow-orange items. Also, eat plenty of cruciferous vegetables such as broccoli, cabbage, cauliflower and Brussels sprouts.

◆ Limit consumption of salt-cured, smoked and nitrite-cured foods, such as bacon, sausage, ham and frankfurters.

◆ If you drink alcohol, be moderate—no more than two drinks a day for men and one drink a day for women.

◆ Maintain a healthy weight. (See page 16 for a discussion of healthy weights.)

◆ Limit your exposure to the sun or artificial sources of ultraviolet light.

OSTEOPOROSIS

Osteoporosis is a complex disorder characterized by a progressive loss of bone. While we all lose bone mass as we grow older, a person with osteoporosis loses it at such a rapid rate the bones become fragile and prone to fracture. As the disease progresses, its victims frequently become shorter and develop a "dowager's hump" (humped back).

Of the many risks that multiply the chances of developing osteoporosis, one of the greatest is being female. In general, women have smaller and less dense bones to begin with. In addition, women tend to live longer than men, and osteoporosis is a disease that comes with aging. Approximately one-half of American women over the age of 45 and 90 percent over age 75 have osteoporosis. Osteoporosis is not common among men until after age 60. Caucasian women are about twice as likely as African-American women to suffer hip fractures due to osteoporosis.

Menopause seems to be one of the greatest factors that puts women at risk. During menopause, women stop producing the hormone estrogen, which may cause compromised calcium status and result in rapidly accelerated bone loss. Calcium is one of the primary minerals involved in building and calcifying (hardening) bones. Increased calcium in the diet as the single treatment, however, does not seem to be as effective as estrogen replacement therapy in slowing bone loss after menopause.

The risk of developing osteoporosis is greater if you smoke, are sedentary and in general do not get enough calcium in your diet. Smoking may negatively affect estrogen levels, and exercise is important to build bone density. In particular, weight-bearing activities, such as walking or running, are beneficial to bone health.

A diet to prevent osteoporosis is built on ensuring an adequate supply of calcium throughout a lifetime. The process of building bone goes on until about age 25, when maximum bone mass is achieved. That bone mass is maintained without much change until about age 35 to 45, when we begin to lose bone (and calcium) as an unavoidable consequence of aging.

To ensure as much bone as possible is built during the crucial growing years, the Recommended Dietary Allowance (RDA) for calcium starts at 800 milligrams per day for children between age 1 and 11. It is then recommended that through age 24 we consume at least 1,200 milligrams of calcium each day. After that, the RDA returns to 800 milligrams daily for adults, except for pregnant and breast-feeding women. In order to meet the calcium needs of the fetus and the breast-fed child, these women also should consume at least 1,200 milligrams of calcium each day. Menopausal or post-menopausal women considered to be at risk for osteoporosis, and who are not undergoing estrogen replacement therapy, may also benefit from a calcium intake of about 1,200 milligrams per day.

Two to three servings from the milk, yogurt and cheese group of the Food Guide Pyramid (page 14), plus the other foods eaten daily in the average American diet, provide about 800 milligrams of calcium. To meet the 1,200-milligram requirement, increase milk, yogurt and cheese servings to four per day. Other good sources of calcium include fish with edible bones such as canned salmon or sardines, dried beans and peas, tofu processed with calcium sulfate, some green vegetables such as broccoli, kale and collards and grain products that contain calcium, such as lime-processed tortillas.

Even though you may get enough calcium in your diet, you may not absorb it all. Too little vitamin D (from lack of sunlight or vitamin D-fortified milk products), too much fiber (over 35 grams a day) and too much alcohol can cause calcium absorption problems. To effectively combat these risks, regularly choose vitamin D-fortified milk, avoid fiber supplements (get your fiber from food instead) and be moderate in your consumption of alcohol.

TIPS FOR REDUCING RISK AND MANAGING OSTEOPOROSIS

♦   Eat a calcium-rich diet, especially during adolescence. Aim for two to three servings daily from the milk, yogurt and cheese group throughout your lifetime.

♦   Engage regularly in weight-bearing exercises, such as walking or jogging.

♦   If you smoke, stop.

♦   If you're menopausal, discuss estrogen replacement therapy with your doctor.

♦   Be moderate in your consumption of alcohol.

OBESITY

Although many people associate obesity with excess weight, the term actually refers to an excessive amount of body fat. You can weigh more than is specified on standard height/weight charts and still have an acceptable amount of body fat. An example of such a person is a heavily-muscled football player or weight lifter. While these people commonly weigh much more than is generally recommended for their height, very little of that weight actually comes from body fat. Nevertheless, most people in the United States who weigh more than is recommended do so because of excess body fat, not muscle. As a result, when a person weighs 20 percent more than is recommended (one of the simplest measures of obesity), he or she is considered to be obese. And obese people run the risk of developing the chronic diseases associated with obesity.

Therein lies the real concern about obesity. Although the general public tends to be more concerned about the aesthetic impact of excess body weight or fat, most health professionals worry more about the impact on health. According to the U.S. Surgeon General, obesity increases risk for diabetes mellitus, high blood pressure and stroke, coronary heart disease, some types of cancer and gallbladder disease.

More than one-fourth of American adults are overweight. Although there seems to be a definite genetic component to the tendency for some people to become overweight, lifestyle plays a key role in the development of the condition. In general, Americans tend to eat too much and, very important, exercise too little. Regular exercise aids in losing weight and maintaining it. Effective weight management also depends on realistic goals. In other words, is the weight you consider desirable really possible for you to achieve and maintain (page 16)? Unrealistic weight goals may lead to eating disorders or "yo-yo-ing" weight (repeated weight loss and regain), which may be more harmful than if you had maintained your original weight (particularly if you were not significantly overweight to begin with).

In order to tackle obesity successfully you must change behavior that leads to overeating and weight gain. For example, many people regularly skip breakfast or other meals, thinking they can "save" calories. Instead, the practice can lead to excessive hunger and overeating at subsequent meals. For effective weight management, it's generally recommended that you eat at least three meals spaced throughout the day.

Eating to treat or prevent obesity takes a similar approach to weight management. The primary difference lies in the number of calories consumed. For weight loss to occur, fewer calories must be consumed than are used in daily activity. Generally, it takes a deficit of 3,500 calories to lose one pound. To meet the current recommendations for healthy weight loss, no more than 1/2 to 1 pound a week, it would be necessary to eat 250 to 500 calories less than you need each day. With too few calories, however, it's difficult to get enough of some of the necessary nutrients, so it's generally advised not to drop below 1,200 calories a day.

Perhaps the easiest way to approach weight loss, is to focus on healthful eating as outlined by the Food Guide Pyramid (page 14). Eat the minimum number of recommended servings from each group; if you're tall, have a large frame or are highly active, you may be able to eat even more servings and still lose weight. Check with a registered dietitian if you're unsure. With this approach, you get all the essential nutrients and calories you need to feel healthy, energetic and motivated to stay with your eating and exercising program. When eating to prevent obesity, and if you do not need to lose weight, you can have additional servings from the food groups.

Finally, weight-loss diets are not generally recommended for children. Instead, children should increase physical activity and eat healthfully to assure they get all the nutrients needed to grow and develop normally.

TIPS FOR REDUCING RISK AND MANAGING OBESITY

◆ Aim for a healthy weight rather than trying to achieve unrealistic goals based on societal standards.

◆ Eat a balanced, low-fat diet that does not exceed daily caloric requirements, and that features plenty of whole-grain cereals and breads, fruits and vegetables. Choose low-fat dairy products and lean meat, poultry and fish.

◆ Eat at least three meals a day to avoid out-of-control hunger.

◆ Allow yourself to enjoy moderate amounts of high-fat, high-calorie foods, if you want them, to avoid feelings of deprivation that can lead to overeating.

◆ Exercise regularly, focusing on moderate exercise of greater duration rather than short, intense workouts. Try walking, swimming, or cycling.

◆ Make changes gradually. To avoid overwhelming yourself, first work on improving one or two key habits. When you reach your goals, move on to others that you think are important.

DIABETES

People with diabetes have abnormally high levels of blood glucose, the blood sugar that serves as the primary source of energy for the body. Abnormal levels of blood fats, including cholesterol and triglycerides, also commonly accompany the disorder. Indeed, cardiovascular disease—in which high levels of blood fats play a definite role—accounts for more than half of all deaths among diabetics. In addition, people with diabetes commonly suffer vision and kidney difficulties and are at greater risk for blood circulation insufficiencies that can lead to foot problems and, in extreme cases, amputation.

Diabetes is caused either by a lack of insulin, which is necessary to metabolize the carbohydrate sugar called glucose, by improper functioning of the systems necessary to use insulin properly, or by a combination of the two. About seven million people in the United States suffer one of two major types of diabetes—Type I or Type II diabetes mellitus. Another five million Americans may have diabetes, yet not know it.

The onset of Type I diabetes tends to be abrupt and generally occurs before age 30. There is no known means of preventing the disease and we cannot predict who will develop it. While dietary strategies to manage Type I are similar to those for Type II, people with Type I diabetes generally require daily injections of insulin to survive.

Type II diabetes most commonly develops after age 40 and is often preceded by obesity. Proper diet and exercise help manage Type II, and may help prevent it to the extent that overweight and obesity are avoided. It has long been known that with weight reduction alone, normal blood glucose levels can be re-established in people with Type II diabetes. In addition, people with Type II diabetes sometimes require insulin to manage the disease, but weight reduction often alleviates that need.

Eating healthfully to prevent Type II diabetes follows the guidelines recommended for reducing the risks of obesity (left). In addition, dietary guidelines for managing the disease are quite similar: A low-fat diet featuring plenty of whole-grain cereals and breads, fruits and vegetables and one that does not exceed the calorie levels needed to lose or maintain weight (whichever is necessary for the individual). Concentrated sweets, such as table sugar, candies and honey, should be used sparingly.

Some research shows that people with diabetes fare better in the management of all the complications of the disease when they consume slightly more dietary fat than is recommended for the general population—35 to 40 percent of calories versus the 30 percent usually recommended. However, it is still important to reduce saturated fat and cholesterol intake to the levels advised for the general population.

TIPS FOR REDUCING RISK AND MANAGING TYPE II DIABETES MELLITUS

◆ Eat a low-fat diet featuring plenty of whole-grain cereals and breads, fruits and vegetables. Enjoy low-fat dairy foods and lean meat, poultry (without skin) and fish. Limit concentrated sweets such as table sugar, candies and honey.

◆ Maintain a healthy weight (see page 16, for a discussion of healthy weights). If you already have diabetes, check with your doctor to determine what a healthy weight is for you.

◆ Exercise regularly. If you're sedentary, start with light to moderate physical activity at less than 60 percent of maximum heart rate* for at least 30 minutes a day. Try walking, swimming, cycling, dancing or gardening.

◆ If you have diabetes, develop a management plan with your doctor that includes proper foot care and regular monitoring of your blood glucose and blood fat levels.

HIGH BLOOD PRESSURE

High blood pressure (hypertension) affects approximately fifty-eight million people in the United States today. Although it is a disease that develops more frequently as we grow older, well over one-half of the Americans who suffer from it are under the age of 65.

High blood pressure is defined as blood pressure equal to or greater than 140/90 millimeters of mercury. High blood pressure triples the risk for developing CHD and increases the risk of stroke by as much as seven times. Unfortunately, many people do not realize they have this potentially crippling disease: One-third of Americans afflicted may be unaware of their hypertension.

There are no general symptoms associated with high blood pressure. That's why it's often called a "silent killer." Many people think they can tell when their blood pressure is high, but the only way really to know is by having blood pressure measured. Because blood pressure can vary on any given day, an elevated blood pressure should be measured on at least two separate occasions before a diagnosis of high blood pressure is made.

While the exact cause of the condition is generally unknown, whether you will develop high blood pressure or not seems to depend on a combination of factors. Your chances for developing hypertension are greater if others in your family are affected by the disease, but environmental influences are usually present as well. These influences include obesity, a habitually high alcohol intake (more than two drinks per day), a sedentary life-style and various dietary factors.

Although there is some evidence that increased intakes of potassium, calcium, magnesium and fiber may help control blood pressure, the research is too preliminary to make any definite recommendations regarding these nutrients. There has been a great deal of investigation into the impact of sodium on high blood pressure and people with high blood pressure are generally advised to limit their intake of sodium.

It's controversial whether people who do not have high blood pressure need to limit sodium. The controversy centers on the concept of sodium sensitivity, which means that some people are able to maintain normal blood pressures while consuming a wide range in amounts of sodium, while others are more sensitive to it— they develop elevated blood pressure when eating a great deal of high-sodium foods. It's impossible to tell if you will develop high blood pressure and if you do, whether or not you will be among the sodium sensitive. As a result, many experts suggest most people limit sodium consumption.

The National Heart, Lung and Blood Institute advises healthy adults to restrict sodium intake to no more than 3,300 milligrams each day. Americans currently consume an average of 4,000 to 5,800 milligrams daily. About one-third of this consumed sodium is estimated to

---

* Determine maximum heart rate by subtracting your age from 220. For example, if you're age 40, your maximum heart rate is 180. Sixty percent of 180 is 108. So when aiming for light to moderate activity, exercise at an intensity level that gets your heart beating faster but not to exceed 108 beats per minute.

occur naturally in foods, one-third comes from processed foods and one-third is added during cooking or at the table. A teaspoon of regular table salt contains about 2,400 milligrams of sodium.

A well-balanced, low-fat diet that promotes healthy weights (page 16) and is moderate in sodium and alcohol is the best approach to a proactive eating plan to help prevent or manage high blood pressure. If you currently have high blood pressure, it is recommended that you limit sodium even if your blood pressure is not sodium sensitive. Low sodium intake may enhance the effectiveness of medications used to treat high blood pressure. Your doctor can advise you about how much sodium you should consume.

TIPS FOR REDUCING RISK OR MANAGING HIGH BLOOD PRESSURE

◆ Maintain a healthy weight. (See page 16 for a discussion of healthy weights.)

◆ If you drink alcohol, be moderate—no more than two drinks a day for men and one drink a day for women.

◆ Exercise regularly.

◆ Use salt and sodium in moderation. Use salt sparingly in cooking and at the table. Limit consumption of highly-salted foods such as chips, pickles and salted nuts. Check package labels for the amount of sodium in foods, and choose those lower in sodium whenever possible.

◆ Eat a well-balanced, low-fat diet that does not exceed daily caloric requirements and features plenty of whole-grain breads and cereals, fruits and vegetables. Select low-fat dairy products as well as lean meats, poultry (without skin) and fish.

◆ Have your blood pressure checked regularly. If you have high blood pressure, follow your doctor's advice for managing it and discuss stress management techniques such as relaxation.

MANAGING FOOD SENSITIVITIES

If you're sensitive to certain foods, you'll probably know it or at least suspect it. You may experience a wide variety of symptoms ranging from skin rashes, hives or asthma to stomach cramps and diarrhea after eating a particular food. Allergies to other substances, such as pollens, animal dander and medications, also may produce some of these symptoms.

Food sensitivities can be divided into several types: true allergies, intolerances to food, gluten sensitivities and idiosyncratic reactions. True allergies trigger the body's immune system, causing it to produce antibodies the first time the food is eaten. When the food is eaten again, negative reactions occur. The most serious of these is anaphylactic shock, a sometimes fatal response that can involve hives, wheezing and fainting. It is generally advised that people with true allergies to specific foods totally avoid those foods.

Although as many as 17 percent of American households believe at least one member has a food allergy, only about 1 percent of adults and 7 percent of children probably suffer from true food allergies. Common foods to which people are allergic include peanuts, eggs, shellfish and cow's milk.

Difficulty with digesting a particular food is called malabsorption or food intolerance and the most common example may be lactose intolerance. In the United States, it's estimated that as many as 79 percent of Native Americans, 75 percent of African Americans, 51 percent of Hispanics and 21 percent of Caucasians have difficulty digesting lactose.

If you're lactose intolerant, it is because you

lack lactase, the enzyme necessary to digest lactose, the major carbohydrate in milk. Therefore, when you drink milk, you may develop stomach cramps, pain, diarrhea and/or nausea. But there are several remedies for those who are lactose-intolerant. Many individuals can consume a small amount of milk (8 ounces or less) without symptoms. Some tolerate milk better if it is consumed with solid foods, such as at mealtime. Some dairy products, such as yogurt with active cultures and aged cheese, contain less lactose than milk and are therefore better tolerated. Some supermarkets now regularly stock lactose-reduced milks for lactose-intolerant people.

Some people are sensitive to gluten, the protein in many grains including wheat, oats, rye and barley. Gluten sensitivity can result in diarrhea, weight loss and malnutrition, making it a serious condition indeed. If you suspect you are gluten sensitive, work with your physician or registered dietitian to devise a gluten-free diet. This can be tricky because many foods contain gluten either as an integral part of the food (such as the wheat in bread) or as part of an additive used in the food.

Idiosyncratic reactions to specific foods or substances occur in some people and can be fatal. One example is asthmatic attacks after ingesting sulfites, preservatives used to keep foods from discoloring. Wines often contain sulfites, as do many dried fruits. Because of such negative reactions, foods that contain sulfites must be so labeled.

TIPS FOR MANAGING FOOD SENSITIVITIES

◆   See your physician to determine whether you're allergic to a specific food. If you find you're truly allergic, avoid the food completely.

◆   Try drinking milk in small amounts (less than 8 ounces) with solid foods if you're lactose

intolerant. You may also be able to eat yogurt and aged cheeses.

◆   Work with your physician or registered dietitian to ensure an adequate diet for your child if he or she is intolerant to milk. Infants who are diagnosed as allergic to cow's milk usually outgrow the condition by the third or fourth year of life.

◆   Read labels carefully if you're sensitive to substances such as gluten or sulfites. If you're not sure if a specific product contains an offending substance, contact the manufacturer.

GASTROINTESTINAL DISORDERS

When we speak of gastrointestinal difficulties, constipation is often the first subject that comes to mind. But there is some confusion about just what is constipation. While daily elimination is deemed desirable by many, less than daily bowel movements are not necessarily abnormal.

Chronic constipation, however, is a real disorder characterized by small, hard stools that require significant straining to eliminate. The number of people who suffer from chronic constipation is not known, but it is believed that the condition may lead to the development of varicose veins, hemorrhoids and diverticular disease. In diverticular disease, small herniations (protrusions) form in the colon possibly as a result of increased colonic pressure that arises from constipation. People with diverticular disease often show no symptoms, so the prevalence of this condition is unknown. It occurs more frequently with age and up to 70 percent of people between the ages of 40 and 70 may be affected. Some people suffer lower abdominal pain and distention as a result of diverticular disease. Furthermore, the herniations may become inflamed, resulting in diverticulitis and bleeding.

Eating to help prevent and treat both constipation and diverticular disease focuses on achieving an adequate intake of fiber. Fiber, particularly insoluble fiber such as that found in wheat (page 10), increases intestinal bulk and draws water into the intestines. The result is faster stool movement through the intestinal tract, thereby preventing constipation. When diverticulitis develops, however, many physicians recommend a reduced-fiber intake until symptoms subside.

In addition, stress, fluid intake and exercise levels influence elimination patterns. Some people become constipated as a reaction to high stress levels. An insufficient intake of fluid may also contribute to development of the disorder. Regular exercise may help establish regular elimination patterns.

TIPS FOR REDUCING AND MANAGING CONSTIPATION AND DIVERTICULAR DISEASE

◆ Eat a high-fiber diet daily containing at least six servings of breads and cereals, with several of those servings as whole-grains and five servings of fruits and vegetables.

◆ Drink plenty of fluids.

◆ Exercise regularly.

◆ Manage stress levels. Discuss relaxation techniques with your doctor.

REFERENCES

American Council on Science and Health, "High Blood Pressure: A Silent Killer, Hypertension." New York, 1989.

American Cancer Society, "Taking Control, 10 Steps to a Healthier Life and Reduced Cancer Risk." Atlanta, 1985.

Best, D., "Allergy Activism," *Prepared Foods.* Delta Communications, Chicago, February, 1992.

International Life Sciences Institute, *Present Knowledge in Nutrition.* Edited by M.L. Brown. Nutrition Foundation, Washington, D.C., 1990.

Journal of the American Dietetic Association, "Position of The American Dietetic Association: Health Implications of Dietary Fiber." Chicago, February, 1988.

Mayo Foundation for Medical Education and Research, "Food Allergies," *Mayo Clinic Nutrition Letter.* Rochester, July, 1990.

U.S. Department of Health and Human Services, *The Surgeon General's Report on Nutrition and Health.* U.S. Government Printing Office, Washington, D.C., 1988.

National Dairy Council, "Are You At Risk for Bone Disease?," Rosemont, 1987.

————, *Calcium, A Summary of Current Research for the Health Professional.* Rosemont, 1987.

————, "Diet and Cancer Prevention," *Dairy Council Digest.* Rosemont, January–February, 1991.

————, "Food Sensitivity and Dairy Products," *Dairy Council Digest.* Rosemont, September–October, 1989.

National Research Council, *Diet and Health, Implications for Reducing Chronic Disease Risk.* National Academy Press, Washington, D.C., 1989.

————, *Recommended Dietary Allowances*, 10th Ed. National Academy Press, Washington, D.C., 1989.

National Heart, Lung and Blood Institute, *Report of the Expert Panel on Detection, Evaluation and Treatment High Blood Cholesterol in Adults.* NIH Publication No. 88-2925, U.S. Government Printing Office, Washington, D.C., 1988.

U.S. Department of Agriculture, U.S. Department of Health and Human Services, "Nutrition and Your Health: Dietary Guidelines for Americans." Home and Garden Bulletin No. 232, U.S. Government Printing Office, Washington, D.C., 1990.

U.S. Department of Health and Human Services, *Healthy People 2000, National Health Promotion and Disease Prevention Objectives.* DHHS Publication, No. (PHS) 91-50212, U.S. Government Printing Office, Washington, D.C., 1990.

————, *The Right Moves.* National Heart, Lung and Blood Institute, National Institutes of Health, Bethesda, MD, 1990.

METRIC CONVERSION GUIDE

U.S. UNITS	CANADIAN METRIC	AUSTRALIAN METRIC
Volume		
1/4 teaspoon	1 mL	1 ml
1/2 teaspoon	2 mL	2 ml
1 teaspoon	5 mL	5 ml
1 tablespoon	15 mL	20 ml
1/4 cup	50 mL	60 ml
1/3 cup	75 mL	80 ml
1/2 cup	125 mL	125 ml
2/3 cup	150 mL	170 ml
3/4 cup	175 mL	190 ml
1 cup	250 mL	250 ml
1 quart	1 liter	1 liter
1 1/2 quarts	1.5 liter	1.5 liter
2 quarts	2 liters	2 liters
2 1/2 quarts	2.5 liters	2.5 liters
3 quarts	3 liters	3 liters
4 quarts	4 liters	4 liters
Weight		
1 ounce	30 grams	30 grams
2 ounces	55 grams	60 grams
3 ounces	85 grams	90 grams
4 ounces (1/4 pound)	115 grams	125 grams
8 ounces (1/2 pound)	225 grams	225 grams
16 ounces (1 pound)	455 grams	500 grams
1 pound	455 grams	1/2 kilogram

Measurements

Inches	Centimeters
1	2.5
2	5.0
3	7.5
4	10.0
5	12.5
6	15.0
7	17.5
8	20.5
9	23.0
10	25.5
11	28.0
12	30.5
13	33.0
14	35.5
15	38.0

Temperatures

Fahrenheit	Celsius
32°	0°
212°	100°
250°	120°
275°	140°
300°	150°
325°	160°
350°	180°
375°	190°
400°	200°
425°	220°
450°	230°
475°	240°
500°	260°

NOTE

The recipes in this cookbook have not been developed or tested using metric measures. When converting recipes to metric, some variations in quality may be noted.

Index